Certificate Chemistry

Fourth Edition

Arthur Atkinson

BSc, ARIC, BSc(ECON), DipEd

**Education Services of Malaya, Uganda and Hong Kong.
Formerly Senior Chemistry Master, Municipal Grammar
Schools, Wolverhampton and Stockton-on-Tees**

Longman

Acknowledgements

We are indebted to the Joint Matriculation Board of the Universities of Manchester, Liverpool, Leeds, Sheffield and Birmingham, the Oxford Delegacy of Local Examinations, the Senate of the University of London, and the University of Cambridge Local Examinations Syndicate for permission to reproduce questions from various past examination papers.

LONGMAN GROUP LIMITED
Longman House
Burnt Mill, Harlow, Essex CM20 2JE, England
and Associated Companies throughout the World

First published 1964
Fourth edition 1983
ISBN 0 582 33135 8

Printed in Hong Kong by
Yu Luen Offset Printing Factory Ltd

By the same author:
Elementary Qualitative Analysis
Elementary Volumetric Analysis
General Science for Hong Kong
Health Science Workbook
Certificate Chemistry Workbook
Certificate Physics Workbook
Complete Junior Chemistry
Complete Junior Physics
Certificate Biology Workbook
Elementary Chemical Arithmetic
General Science Workbooks for Hong Kong
Objective Tests in Chemistry
Objective Tests in Physics
Objective Tests in Biology

Contents

Preface

This book is intended for use during the final two or three years of an Ordinary level course in Chemistry. It covers most Chemistry syllabuses, particularly those of London, Oxford, Northern Universities, and the Cambridge G.C.E. and overseas syllabus.

The theoretical work is based on the metal activity series, the electrochemical series, and the electronic theory. This is in accordance with modern teaching ideas, the recommendations of the Science Masters' Association, and the requirements in the latest syllabuses. Definitions of acids, bases, salts and oxidation, etc., are based on the existence of ions and electrons; the older meanings have also been given for those teachers who prefer them. Ionic equations are given in addition to molecular equations in many places.

A wide selection of questions taken from recent examination papers of the major examining bodies should prove invaluable both for learning and revision purposes. The many labelled diagrams ensure that the descriptive parts of the text are readily understood and will provide students with a model for their own diagrams.

A Atkinson

Preface to Fourth Edition

Several outdated topics have been removed, the treatment of topics now considered of lesser importance has been reduced, and many experimental procedures have been simplified in this edition. Extra material is included on the Periodic Table, electrolysis (including cells, conductivity, and migration of ions), dynamic equilibria and the factors affecting them, rates of reaction, experimental determination of equations, and organic chemistry. These are all included in current syllabuses. SI units and chemical names are those recommended by examining bodies.

1
Solutions and Crystals

Solutions

When we shake a little sugar with water, the sugar mixes uniformly with the water and all parts of the liquid are exactly the same, i.e. the liquid is homogeneous. We say that sugar is *soluble* in water and *dissolves* in it. The sugar is a solute, the water is a solvent, and the mixture is a solution.

A solution is a uniform mixture of two or more substances.
A solute is a dissolved substance (solid, liquid, or gas).
A solvent is a substance which dissolves a solute.

Any liquid can be a solvent. Solids and gases can also be solvents; for example, brass is a solution of zinc in copper, and air is a solution of oxygen in nitrogen. A solute can be either a solid, liquid, or gas; e.g. water can dissolve sodium chloride, ethanol and air. A solution in water is an *aqueous* solution.

To find if various substances are soluble in cold water

Half-fill a test-tube with cold water. Add a little sodium chloride and shake. The sodium chloride dissolves. Add more, a little at a time, and shake after each addition. The first amounts dissolve, but later amounts settle to the bottom of the solution on standing. Filter and collect the clear solution (*filtrate*) in an evaporating basin. The solid on the filter paper is the *residue*.

Evaporating to dryness

a *Using an evaporating basin.* Heat the basin on a gauze until all the water has evaporated. Warm gently when almost all the water has gone because the mixture begins to 'spit', i.e. pieces of hot solid or solution jump out of the basin.
b *Using a sand bath.* Heat the basin on a sand bath (see Fig. 1.1). Remove the flame before evaporation is complete. The hot sand evaporates the last water and avoids 'spitting'.
c *Using a water bath.* See Fig. 1.2. Solvents that catch fire easily, e.g. ethanol and petrol, must always be evaporated on a water bath.
d *Using a simple water bath.* See Fig. 1.3. White, solid sodium chloride remains when evaporation is complete. This proves that it is soluble in cold water.

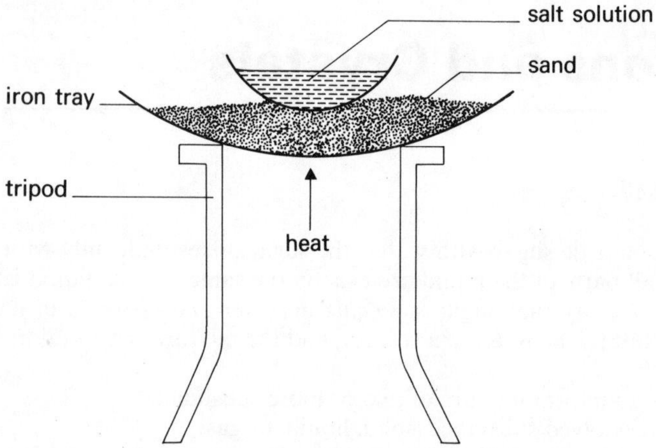

Fig. 1.1 Evaporating to dryness on a sand bath

Repeat the test with other substances, e.g. potassium nitrate, calcium hydroxide, calcium carbonate and blackboard chalk. Some of these leave only a little solid after evaporation. This proves that they are slightly soluble or 'insoluble' in cold water. Probably no substance is completely insoluble in water, which even dissolves tiny amounts of glass and sand, which we sometimes regard as completely insoluble. If a litre of water dissolves less than 10 grams of a substance we say that it is 'insoluble'.

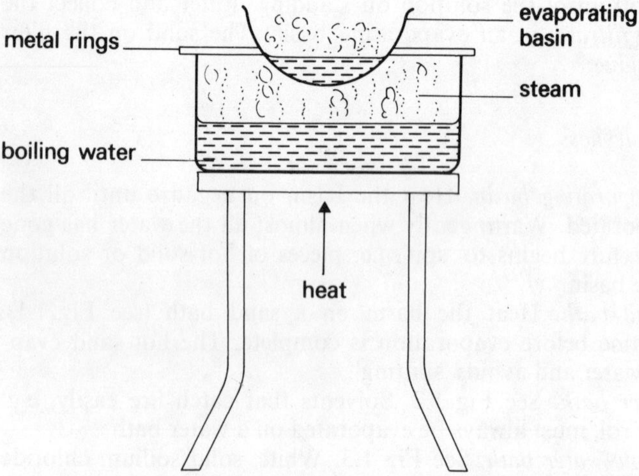

Fig. 1.2 Water bath

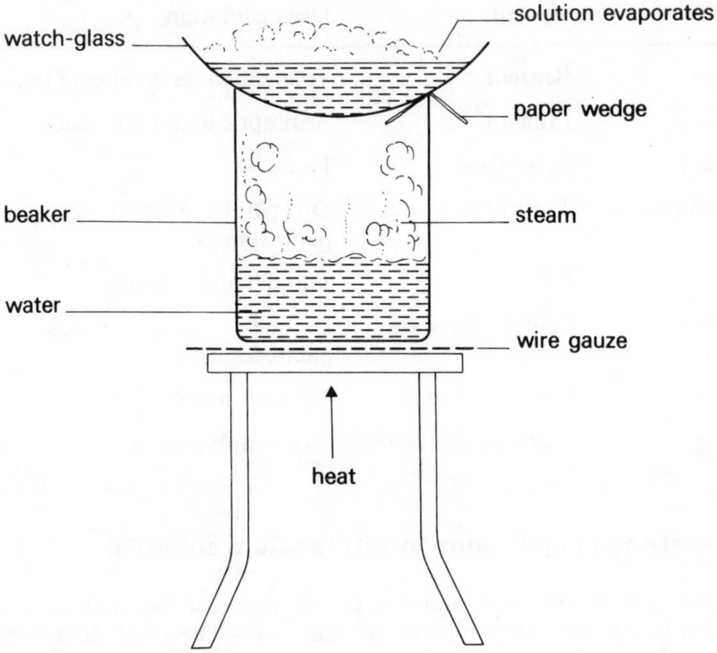

Fig. 1.3 A simple water bath

Suspensions

Shake powdered blackboard chalk with water; a milky liquid is formed. Particles of chalk settle on standing. Chalk is almost insoluble. The milky mixture of chalk and water is a suspension. Muddy water, paints, and many medicines are suspensions.

> A suspension is a liquid containing small particles of solid spread throughout it and which settle on standing.

A suspension differs from a solution in three ways:
1 it contains solid particles which can be seen;
2 its solid particles settle on standing;
3 filtration separates it into a filtrate and a residue.

Solvents

Substances that are insoluble in water may be soluble in other solvents. Some examples and their uses are shown in the following table.

Solute	Solvent	Use of solution
Rubber	Benzene	To mend holes in tubes of tyres
Iodine	Ethanol	Antiseptic used on wounds
Pigments	Linseed oil	Paints
Oil and paint	Turpentine	Oil paints. Solvent removes paint stains
Shellac	Ethanol	Varnish and lacquers
Cellulose	Pentyl ethanoate	Lacquers and nail varnishes; paints for cars
Grease	Trichloroethene	To clean metals
Grease	Tetrachloroethene	Dry-cleaning clothes

To separate sand and common salt (sodium chloride)

Place a mixture of sand and common salt in a beaker and add water. Warm gently and stir until all the salt dissolves. The sand does not dissolve. Filter and collect the filtrate in an evaporating basin. The sand remains as a residue on the filter paper or in the beaker. Evaporate the filtrate to dryness; the white solid is common salt. Pour water on the sand to remove the salt solution. Dry the sand in an oven or in sunshine.

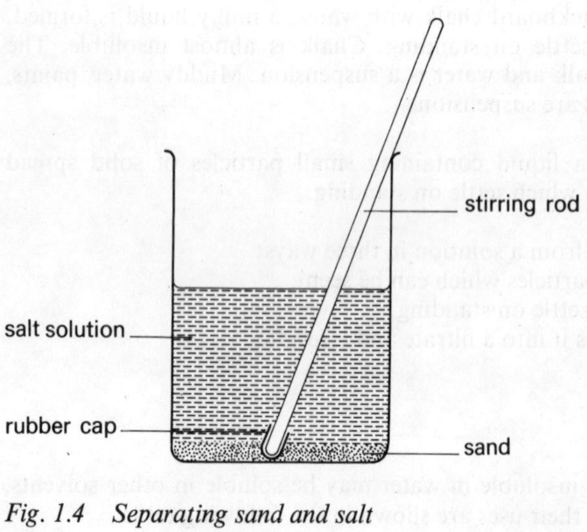

Fig. 1.4 Separating sand and salt

Crystals

A crystal is a solid that consists of particles (atoms, molecules or ions) arranged in an orderly and repetitive manner.

A crystal has a definite geometrical shape, with flat sides and sharp edges. Some solids, e.g. charcoal, glass and pitch, do not form crystals, and are *non-crystalline* or *amorphous* ('of no definite shape'). Their particles are arranged in a random manner.

To obtain crystals of various substances

Crystals can form from both hot and cold solutions. Solids are usually more soluble in hot solvents than in cold. When a hot saturated solution cools, some solute is deposited. Crystals also form when a cold saturated solution is left in the air for some time; part of the solvent evaporates and excess solid forms crystals. The solution left after crystals form is saturated and is called the *mother liquor*. Crystals can also form when a molten substance solidifies.

From a hot solution. Make a cold saturated solution of potassium nitrate. Now add more nitrate—the amount you want as crystals. Warm the mixture until all the nitrate dissolves. Allow the solution to cool slowly. The extra nitrate added forms crystals.

Repeat the experiment using other substances, e.g. potassium chlorate(V), copper(II) sulphate, sodium carbonate, sodium sulphate and chromium potassium sulphate-12-water.

From a cold solution. Make a cold saturated solution of potassium nitrate or another solute. Leave it so that evaporation can occur. Some solvent evaporates. Crystals of solute form slowly, and their shapes are good.

Rate of crystallization and crystal size

Add potassium nitrate (about 5 g) and water (about 10 cm^3) to each of two test-tubes. Place them in water in a beaker. Warm the water to about 35 °C. Shake the tubes until the potassium nitrate dissolves and the solutions are warm. Cool one test-tube quickly by placing it in a beaker of cold water, and observe what happens. Allow the other tube to cool slowly and do not touch it while it is cooling. Pour off the liquid, remove the crystals, and compare their sizes.

If a hot solution cools rapidly, the crystals are small; if it cools slowly, they are larger and a better shape.

To grow large crystals

Add a cold saturated solution of copper(II) sulphate to a beaker. Choose one good crystal of copper(II) sulphate, and tie a thin thread around it.

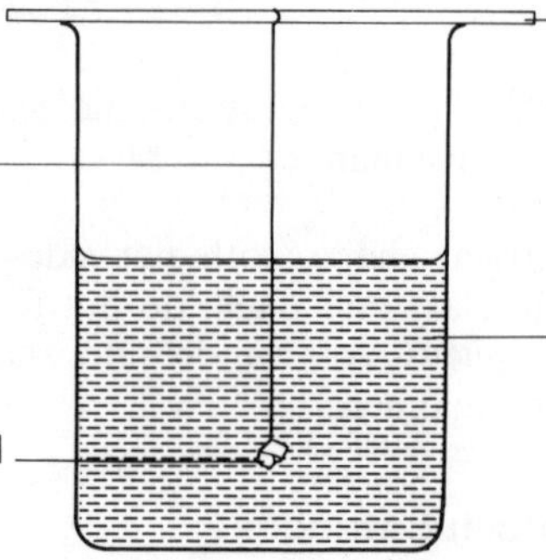

Fig. 1.5 Growing large crystals

Hang it as shown in Fig. 1.5. Cover the beaker with paper to keep out dust and leave it for several weeks. The temperature must remain nearly constant for best results. As the water slowly evaporates, copper(II) sulphate forms on all sides of the crystal, which slowly grows large.

Repeat with chromium potassium sulphate-12-water.

Water of crystallization

Some substances form crystals that contain water chemically combined with them. The water is *water of hydration* or *crystallization*, and the products are *hydrates*. The crystals cannot form without water, which is necessary for their regular shape. The water comes off on heating, and the crystals lose their shape and their colour. Crystals with no water of crystallization are *anhydrous* ('without water').

> Water of crystallization is the definite amount of water with which some substances chemically combine when they form crystals from their solutions in water. A hydrate is a compound which contains water of crystallization.

To find if some crystals contain water of crystallization

Half-fill a test-tube with powdered copper(II) sulphate crystals, then arrange the apparatus as in Fig. 1.6. The test-tube must slope downwards so that any water formed inside it cannot drop on to the hot glass and crack it. Heat the crystals gently. The blue crystals change to a white powder [anhydrous copper(II) sulphate]; water vapour comes off and condenses in the cooled test-tube. (Add a few drops of water to the

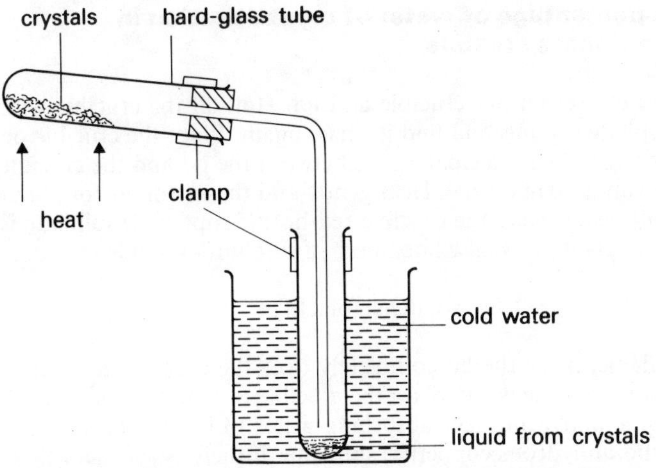

Fig. 1.6 Finding out if crystals contain water of crystallization

powder; the solid becomes blue and warm.)

$$\text{(blue) } CuSO_4 \cdot 5H_2O(s) \rightarrow 5H_2O(g) + CuSO_4(s) \text{ (white)}$$

Repeat the test with crystals of sodium carbonate, sodium sulphate, iron(II) sulphate, magnesium sulphate, sodium chloride and potassium chloride.

One-third of the mass of copper(II) sulphate crystals and almost two-thirds of sodium carbonate crystals are water.

Hydrated crystals	Anhydrous crystals
Sodium carbonate-10-water, $Na_2CO_3 \cdot 10H_2O$	Sodium chloride (common salt), NaCl
Sodium sulphate-10-water, $Na_2SO_4 \cdot 10H_2O$	All common potassium and ammonium salts, e.g. potassium nitrate, potassium chlorate(V), ammonium chloride and ammonium nitrate
Copper(II) sulphate-5-water, $CuSO_4 \cdot 5H_2O$	
Iron(II) sulphate-7-water, $FeSO_4 \cdot 7H_2O$	
Magnesium sulphate-7-water, $MgSO_4 \cdot 7H_2O$	Sugar
Calcium chloride-6-water, $CaCl_2 \cdot 6H_2O$	

To find the percentage of water of crystallization in copper(II) sulphate crystals

Find the mass of a clean dry crucible and lid. Half-fill the crucible with copper(II) sulphate crystals and find its mass again. Place the crucible on a pipe-clay triangle. Leave a small space between the lid and the crucible so that water vapour can escape. Heat gently and then strongly for about 15 minutes but never make the crucible red-hot. If copper(II) sulphate is heated too strongly it gives off white fumes of sulphur(VI) oxide.

$$\text{(white) } CuSO_4(s) \rightarrow SO_3(g) + CuO(s) \text{ (black)}$$

Remove the flame, place the lid completely over the crucible, and allow to cool. (In very accurate work, place the crucible in a desiccator to cool; this prevents the anhydrous salt absorbing water.) Find the mass of the crucible, lid and anhydrous copper(II) sulphate. If there is sufficient time, repeat the heating (for 5 minutes) until a constant mass is reached. This *heating to constant mass* proves that all the water has been driven off.

$$CuSO_4 \cdot yH_2O(s) \rightarrow CuSO_4(s) + yH_2O(g)$$

1 Mass of crucible and lid	$= a$ g
2 Mass of crucible, lid and crystals	$= b$ g
3 Mass of crucible, lid and anhydrous copper sulphate	$= c$ g
2 – 1 Mass of copper(II) sulphate crystals	$= (b-a)$ g
2 – 3 Mass of water of crystallization	$= (b-c)$ g

Mass $(b-a)$ g of crystals contain a mass $(b-c)$ g of water of crystallization.

$$\therefore \text{ 100 g of crystals contain } \frac{(b-c)\times 100}{b-a} \text{ g of water.}$$

$$\text{Percentage of water of crystallization is } \frac{(b-c)\times 100}{b-a}.$$

Saturated solutions

If a solution can dissolve more solute at the same temperature it is *unsaturated*. If we shake much sugar or common salt with water, some solid dissolves but the rest settles on standing. The water cannot dissolve any more solid and the solution is *saturated*.

A saturated solution of a solute at a particular temperature is one which can dissolve no more solute at that temperature (in the presence of undissolved solute).

The last part of the definition is necessary because certain solutions can be *supersaturated* (more than saturated).

A supersaturated solution is one that contains more solute than it can hold at the same temperature in the presence of undissolved solute.

To demonstrate supersaturation

Fill a clean test-tube with sodium thiosulphate crystals, $Na_2S_2O_3 \cdot 5H_2O$. Heat gently. The crystals split up into water and sodium thiosulphate, which dissolves in the water. Add more water only if necessary. Cool the test-tube containing the clear solution in a beaker of cold water. Close the mouth of the tube with cotton wool to keep out dust, and do not shake or move it. No crystals form, and the solution is supersaturated.

Hold the test-tube in the palm of the hand and add a small crystal of thiosulphate. Crystals form at once and spread until the solution is all solid. The mixture becomes hot.

To prepare a supersaturated solution we must:

a cool a hot saturated solution slowly (sodium thiosulphate solution is an exception and can be cooled quickly);

b keep out crystals, dust, and other small particles;

c not shake or disturb the solution.

Sodium sulphate can form supersaturated solutions. Most substances do not form them.

To find the effect of temperature on solubilities

Add 100 cm^3 of water at room temperature to each of two beakers. To one add potassium nitrate (about 25 g) and to the other add calcium hydroxide (about 0.10 g). Stir or shake until clear solutions form, adding more water if necessary. Now warm the solutions separately until they are almost boiling, and look at them.

The potassium nitrate remains a clear solution; the calcium hydroxide becomes cloudy showing that some solid has formed. Calcium hydroxide is less soluble in warm water than in cold.

Solubility curves

The solubility of a solute in a solvent at a particular temperature is the number of grams of solute required to saturate 100 grams of solvent at that temperature.

The solubility curve of a substance is a graph showing how its solubility varies with temperature.

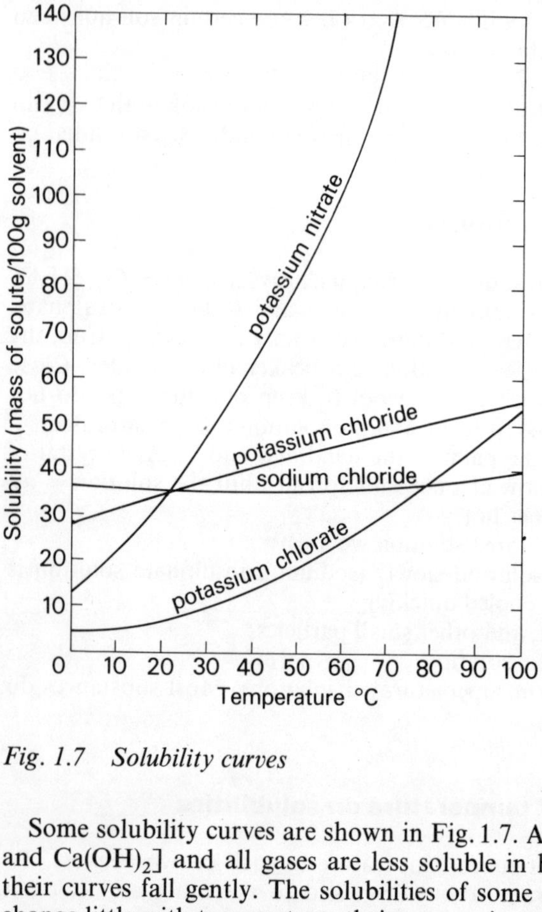

Fig. 1.7 Solubility curves

Some solubility curves are shown in Fig. 1.7. A few solids [e.g. $CaSO_4$ and $Ca(OH)_2$] and all gases are less soluble in hot water than in cold; their curves fall gently. The solubilities of some compounds (e.g. NaCl) change little with temperature; their curves rise gently. The solubilities of other compounds (e.g. KNO_3 and $KClO_3$) increase rapidly with temperature; their curves rise steeply.

Solubility of gases in liquids

Solutions of gases differ from solutions of solids in two ways:

1 all gases are less soluble in hot solvents than in cold; and
2 an increase of pressure causes a greater mass of gas to dissolve but has practically no effect on the solubility of solids.

The mass of gas dissolved by a given volume of solvent is directly proportional to the pressure (*Henry's Law*); e.g. if the pressure is doubled the mass is doubled.

Gases are insoluble in boiling solvents, e.g. by boiling water we can obtain all the dissolved oxygen, nitrogen and carbon dioxide (p. 45).

Aerated drinks contain carbon dioxide under pressure; on opening a bottle, the gas bubbles out of solution. When a diver goes deep into water, more nitrogen dissolves in his blood. As he rises to the surface, this gas forms bubbles in his veins and may kill him. For this reason, divers breathe oxygen and helium; helium passes (diffuses) easily through skin and forms no bubbles.

Questions

1 Describe experiments by which you would find (*a*) whether sodium chloride is soluble in ethanol at room temperature, (*b*) whether tap water contains dissolved solids. (N.)

2 How would you obtain all the sand and all the salt as solids from a mixture of the two substances? How would you prove that your sand was free from salt? (C.)

3 Name some solvents for iodine, shellac, and rubber, and state briefly any uses of solutions of these substances. What is meant by a supersaturated solution? The solubility of copper(II) sulphate at 85 °C is 60 g in 100 g of water, and at 15 °C is 18.8 g in 100 g of water. If 120 g of solution saturated at 85 °C were cooled to 15 °C, what mass of copper(II) sulphate crystals would be deposited? (L.)

4 You are given a solution of sodium thiosulphate. Describe how you would find if it is saturated or unsaturated or supersaturated. Describe two tests by which you would distinguish between calcium sulphate solution and distilled water. (C.)

5 The solubility of copper(II) sulphate is 75 g in 100 g of water at 100 °C and 25 g at 30 °C. What mass of the salt would crystallize if 50 g of a copper(II) sulphate solution saturated at 100 °C were cooled to 30 °C? How would you grow a large crystal of copper(II) sulphate? (C.)

6 Define 'solubility'. Describe how you would prove or disprove experimentally the statement: 'Calcium ethanedioate is insoluble in water'. Draw a solubility curve for calcium hydroxide.

2
States of Matter. Physical and Chemical Changes. Elements, Compounds and Mixtures

States of matter

Solids, liquids and gases

All physical objects in the universe are made of matter, which can exist in three states: solid, liquid and gas (or vapour). For example, water can exist as ice, liquid water, and steam or water vapour. A *vapour* is the gaseous form of a substance which usually is a solid or liquid, e.g. iodine vapour and petrol vapour.

A solid has a definite size (or volume) and shape.
A liquid has a definite size but no definite shape.
A gas or vapour has no definite size and no definite shape.

$$\text{Solid} \underset{\substack{\text{Freezing} \\ \text{Solidifying}}}{\overset{\substack{\text{Melting,} \\ \text{Fusing}}}{\rightleftarrows}} \text{Liquid} \underset{\substack{\text{Condensing,} \\ \text{Liquefying}}}{\overset{\substack{\text{Evaporating,} \\ \text{Boiling}}}{\rightleftarrows}} \text{Gas or Vapour}$$

The particles of solid and liquids, and, to a lesser extent, gases are held together by *intermolecular forces* or *electrical forces*. The particles attract each other when they are fairly close. When the particles are very close (less than one particle diameter apart) the outer electrons, p. 94, repel one another strongly. Clearly, if particles exerted only attractive forces matter would contract until all particles touched (this has happened in neutron stars and their densities are enormous).

Movement of molecules

The fundamental difference between solids, liquids and gases is the extent of movement of their molecules.
Solids. The molecules are held in regular patterns by strong forces. They can vibrate but cannot move from one position to another. Heat makes the vibrations stronger until, at the melting point, molecules break free of the forces holding them in fixed positions.

Liquids. The molecules can move about from place to place within the liquid, but forces of attraction still hold them together. At the surface of the liquid, these forces are weaker and some molecules leave the liquid, i.e. evaporation occurs. Heat makes the movements faster and stronger, and evaporation occurs more easily. At the boiling point, the molecules break free from the forces and the liquid becomes a gas.
Gases. The molecules move freely in all directions and forces between them are negligible. The pressure of a gas is due to bombardment by its molecules of the walls of the vessel which contains it. The free movement of molecules explains the diffusion of liquids and gases (p. 66). Later we shall learn that metals, p. 103, and ionic compounds, p. 97, consist of charged particles called ions and not of molecules. These ions move in exactly the same way as the molecules mentioned above. The theory that molecules and ions are in continuous movement and possess kinetic energy is the *kinetic theory of matter*.

To study the effect of heat on some substances

Wax. Heat some wax, e.g. candle wax, in a test-tube, until it melts. Allow it to cool. The substance left is still wax.
Platinum or nichrome wire. Heat the wire in a flame until it becomes white-hot. Allow it to cool. The wire has not changed.
Sulphur. Heat sulphur powder *gently* in a test-tube until it just melts. The powder forms an amber liquid which, on cooling, forms sulphur again (the solid is usually darker in colour than the original powder).
Iodine. Place solid iodine in a dry test-tube. Heat the iodine, but keep the top of the tube cold by holding it horizontally. The iodine does not melt. It changes directly to a violet vapour which condenses on the cold glass to form black shining crystals of iodine. This change is *sublimation*.

$$\text{Solid} \underset{}{\overset{\text{Sublimation}}{\rightleftarrows}} \text{Gas or Vapour}$$

No new substance is formed in any of the above changes.

Magnesium. Hold magnesium ribbon by tongs and heat in a flame. It burns with a brilliant light and forms a white powder:

$$2Mg(s) + O_2(g) \rightarrow 2MgO(s), \text{ magnesium oxide}$$

(*Mercury*: its vapour and compounds are poisonous. The following experiment must be demonstrated, in a fume cupboard or well-ventilated laboratory. It can be replaced by the silver oxide experiment.)
Mercury(II) oxide. Heat mercury(II) oxide *gently* in a dry test-tube, but keep the top of the tube cool. The colour becomes darker. Allow the oxide to cool. The dark colour changes back to the original red colour.

Now heat the oxide *strongly*. Silvery drops of mercury form on the cool glass, and a gas is evolved. The gas re-lights a glowing splint:

$$2HgO(s) \rightarrow 2Hg(l) + O_2(g)$$

Silver oxide. Add aqueous sodium hydroxide to silver nitrate solution; brown silver oxide is precipitated. Place the moist precipitate on porous pot or ceramic wool paper and heat it gently. A white powder forms. Wet the rounded end of a spatula and rub it on the powder; a layer of shiny silver appears:

$$2Ag_2O(s) \rightarrow 4Ag(s) + O_2(g)$$

New substances are formed in the above three changes.

Physical and chemical changes

A physical change is one in which the products have the same chemical properties as the reactants (no new substance is formed). A chemical change is one in which the products have chemical properties different from those of the reactants (one or more new substances are formed).

When wax, platinum, sulphur and iodine are heated, no new substances are formed and their masses do not alter. The changes are physical. Other physical changes include the melting or sublimation of solids, boiling of liquids, and the making of solutions.

Magnesium, mercury(II) oxide and silver oxide form new substances when heated. The changes are chemical. In many chemical changes, energy is given out as heat and perhaps as light and sound, e.g. in explosions. Chemical changes are not easily reversible, e.g. it is difficult or impossible to change the new substances back to the original magnesium or mercury oxide. The magnesium oxide weighs more than the magnesium and the mercury and silver weigh less than the mercury oxide and silver oxide.

Physical change	Chemical change
1 No new substance formed.	A new *substance* is formed.
2 Usually the change is easily reversible.	Usually the change is *irreversible*.
3 Usually no energy is given out or absorbed.	Usually *energy* is given out or absorbed.
4 The mass of the substance does not alter.	The *mass* of the substance does alter.

The word MISE (for Mass, Irreversible, Substance and Energy) may help to recall these differences. There are many exceptions to differences 2 and 3. For example, reversible reactions (p. 58) are easily reversible although they are chemical changes; heat is absorbed when ice melts and when water boils although the changes are physical.

To collect the gas formed by a heated solid

Collection over water. See Fig. 2.1. Add the solid, e.g. mercury(II) oxide, potassium manganate(VII) or red lead oxide, to the test-tube. If potassium manganate(VII) is used, cover it with a loose plug of glass wool to prevent specks of solid coming out with evolved gas. Heat the solid gently until bubbles of gas pass through the water in the trough. Let the first bubbles, mainly air, escape and then collect tubes of gas. Remove the end of the delivery tube from the water before you stop heating, otherwise water is sucked back into the hot test-tube as it cools and breaks it. (Red lead oxide spoils the tube by combining with the glass. Wrap it in heat resistant paper so that it does not touch the glass.)

Collection in a syringe. See Fig. 2.2. Push the piston right into the syringe. Heat the solid. Any gas evolved collects, mixed with air, in the syringe.

The syringe experiment can be quantitative. Weigh the solid put into the test-tube. Heat it until no more gas is evolved. Allow the gas in the syringe to cool to room temperature before reading the volume of gas evolved. [Use not more than 2 g of mercury(II) oxide, 5 g of red lead oxide or 1.5 g of potassium manganate(VII), as larger masses form too much gas for a 100 cm^3 syringe.]

Mass of solid $= m$ (g)
Volume of gas evolved $= V$ (cm^3)

m (g) of solid form V (cm^3) of gas, therefore 1 g of solid forms $\frac{V}{m}$ cm^3 of gas.

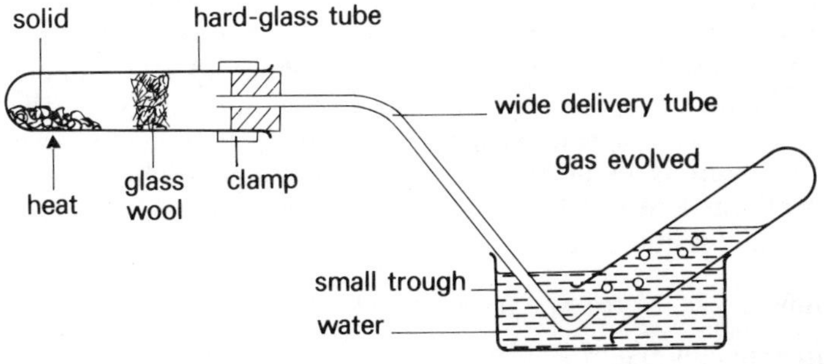

Fig. 2.1 To collect the gas from a heated solid (collection over water)

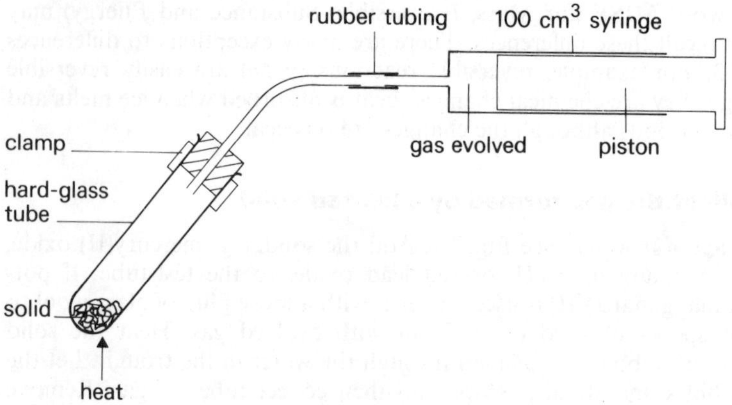

Fig. 2.2 To collect the gas from a heated solid (using a syringe)

Melting points and boiling points

The melting point (**m.p.**) of a solid is the temperature at which it melts to form a liquid under a total pressure (air and vapour) of 1 atmosphere (760 mm Hg or 101 325 pascal, Pa). The boiling point (**b.p.**) of a liquid is the temperature of the vapour from the liquid boiling at a pressure of 1 atmosphere.

Many substances can be recognized by their melting points or boiling points. Some substances (e.g. glass, glue, plastics) do not have definite melting points and gradually become softer on warming. Impure substances do not have definite melting points or boiling points; they melt or boil over a range of temperatures.

To find the melting point of a solid

Add a powdered solid, e.g. naphthalene, to a depth of about 2 cm in a test-tube. Clamp the tube in a beaker of water. The water level must be above the powder level in the tube. Place a thermometer with its bulb in the solid. Heat the water until its temperature is about 90 °C, i.e. about 10 °C above the melting point of naphthalene. Remove the flame. The hot water melts the naphthalene. Read the thermometer every half-minute until the temperature is about 5 °C below the freezing point. Now warm the water gently and record the temperature of the naphthalene every half-minute until it is about 85 °C.

Time in min	0	$\frac{1}{2}$	1	$1\frac{1}{2}$	2 etc.
Temperature (cooling) in °C					
Temperature (warming) in °C					

Draw two graphs of temperature (vertical axis) against time. The temperature of the horizontal parts of the graph indicates the freezing and melting points.

Repeat the experiment with a mixture, e.g. paraffin wax. Part of the curve is flattened but not horizontal because the wax has no definite melting point.

The *boiling point* of a liquid is measured on a thermometer with its bulb in the vapour of the boiling liquid. Heat the liquid with a flame if it does not burn readily. Inflammable liquids (e.g. ethanol, petrol) must be heated in a beaker of hot water with no flames near.

Physical properties

Physical properties are those which affect sight, hearing, taste, smell and touch. Those properties which can be measured exactly include melting point, boiling point, and density; these are *physical constants*. For example, a colourless, odourless liquid may be water. If it freezes at 0 °C, boils at 100 °C, and has a density of 1 g/cm^3 at 4 °C, it is definitely water.

Elements, compounds and mixtures

An element is a substance which cannot be split up into two or more simpler substances by chemical means.

Every substance that occurs naturally in the world consists of one or more of about 90 elements; another 13 elements have been made artificially.

A compound is a substance which consists of two or more elements chemically combined together.

A mixture is a substance which consists of two or more elements or compounds not chemically combined together.

Several million compounds are known. Common mixtures are ink, milk, paint, sea-water, air, solutions, brass, cast iron and steel.

Relative abundance of the elements

The earth's crust is the thin layer, a few kilometres deep, on the outside of the earth. The percentages of the common elements in this crust and in the waters on it are:

Oxygen	50%	Calcium	3%
Silicon	26%	Sodium	2.5%
Aluminium	7%	Potassium	2.5%
Iron	4%	Magnesium	2%

These elements make up about 97 per cent of the crust; the other elements make up only 3 per cent. Copper, lead and zinc are not in the above list, and neither are carbon and nitrogen, which are essential for living things.

The diameter of an oxygen atom is four times that of a silicon atom, and therefore its volume is about sixty-four times greater. Aluminium and iron atoms are also quite small. Therefore our solid earth is made up almost entirely of oxygen atoms with the other most common elements (silicon, aluminium and iron) merely holding them together.

To prepare sulphides of metals

Mix one spatula measure each of sulphur powder and zinc dust. Fold heat resistant paper so that its cross-section is V-shaped, hold it with tongs, and add the mixture. Heat until reaction occurs. (Iron filings or copper powder can replace the zinc; the reaction with zinc is most vigorous.) Zinc sulphide is white, iron(II) sulphide is black, and copper(II) sulphide is black.

$$Zn(s) + S(l) \rightarrow ZnS(s) + \text{heat}$$

Iron filings are greasy and do not react readily. Remove the grease before use by stirring with ethanol or methylated spirits for several minutes, filtering and drying. Once the reaction starts, Fig. 2.3(b), a red-hot glow spreads through the whole mixture.

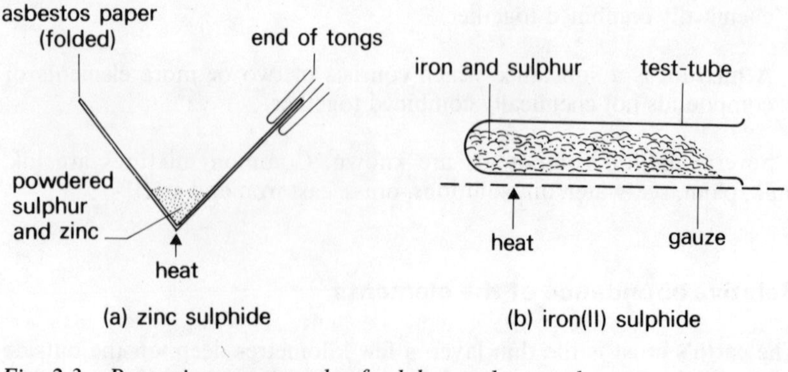

Fig. 2.3 Preparing compounds of sulphur and a metal

To study the differences between a metal sulphide and a mixture of metal and sulphur

1 *Appearance*. Look at the mixture and the compound through a magnifying glass. The elements can be seen separately in the mixture only; the compound is homogeneous.

2 *Water*. Add a little of the mixture to water in a test-tube, shake and allow to stand. Repeat with the compound. The metal of the mixture settles first, because it is denser, and sulphur settles on top of the metal (they do not separate completely); some sulphur powder floats. The compound settles as a single layer, and no partial separation occurs.

3 *Dilute acid*. Add dilute hydrochloric or sulphuric acid to the mixture in a test-tube and warm gently. Smell any gas evolved and test it with a burning splint. Repeat with the compound. The acid reacts with the zinc or iron in the mixture, forming hydrogen which burns with a slight 'pop'; the sulphur does not react:

$$Fe(s) + H_2SO_4(aq) \rightarrow H_2(g) + FeSO_4(aq)$$

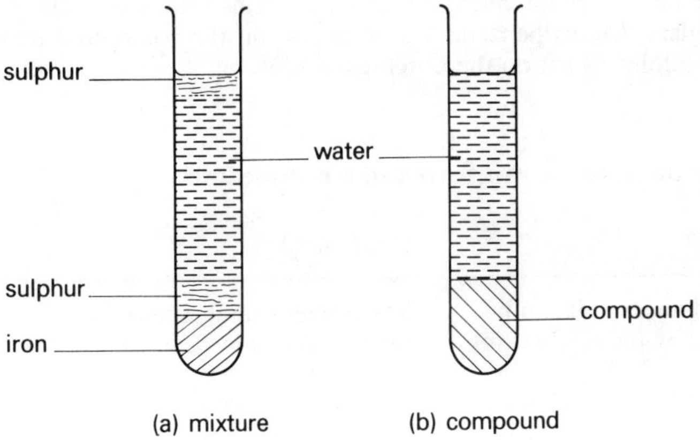

Fig. 2.4 Action of water

The compound reacts to form hydrogen sulphide, which smells of bad eggs and burns quietly with a blue flame:

$$FeS(s) + H_2SO_4(aq) \rightarrow H_2S(g) + FeSO_4(aq)$$
$$2H_2S(g) + 3O_2(g) \rightarrow 2H_2O(g) + 2SO_2(g)$$

4 *Methylbenzene*. (It is inflammable; do not use it until all flames are out. The vapour is poisonous so use a fume cupboard for this experiment.) Shake the mixture with methylbenzene in a test-tube.

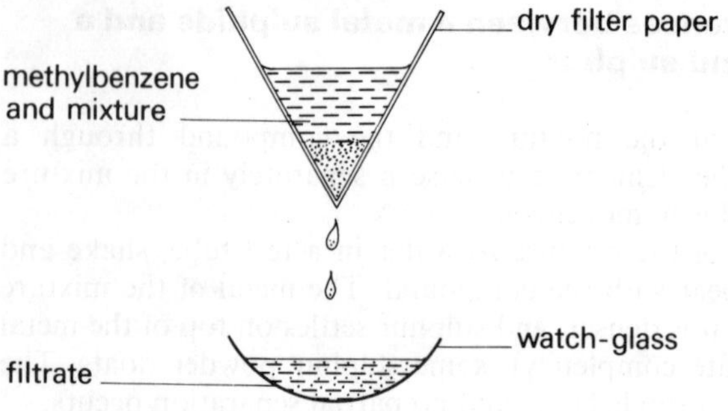

Fig. 2.5 Action of methylbenzene

Filter the product through a *dry* filter paper without a funnel (methylbenzene will not pass through wet paper, and sulphur crystallizes in the stem if a funnel is used). Collect the filtrate on a watch-glass, and let it evaporate to dryness in a fume cupboard or in the open air. Repeat with the compound. Methylbenzene dissolves the sulphur of the mixture but leaves the metal; the sulphur forms yellow crystals on the watch-glass. Methylbenzene has no action on the compound and little or no sulphur is left on the watch-glass.

Differences between a mixture and a compound

	Mixture	Compound
1	The substances in it can be *separated* by physical means.	The elements in it cannot be separated by physical means.
2	Its *properties* (e.g. colour, density) are the average of those of the substances in it.	Its properties are quite different from those of the elements in it.
3	*Energy* (heat, light or sound) is not usually given out or absorbed when a mixture is made.	Energy is usually given out or absorbed when a compound is made.
4	Its *composition* is variable; the substances can be present in any proportions by mass.	Its composition is not variable; the elements are combined in definite proportions by mass.

The word SPEC (for Separated, Properties, Energy and Composition) may help you to remember these differences.

Separating mixtures

Distillation

Distillation is the process of boiling a liquid to form vapour and then cooling the vapour to obtain the liquid.

To obtain pure water by distillation

Add water, sand and any coloured crystals, e.g. copper(II) sulphate or potassium manganate(VII) to a distilling flask. Pass water from a tap up the outer tube of the condenser until it flows out gently into a sink. Boil the water in the flask. The steam condenses in the condenser and collects as a *distillate* in the receiving flask. Dissolved or suspended solids are left behind; dissolved gases come off with the steam. Distilled water is

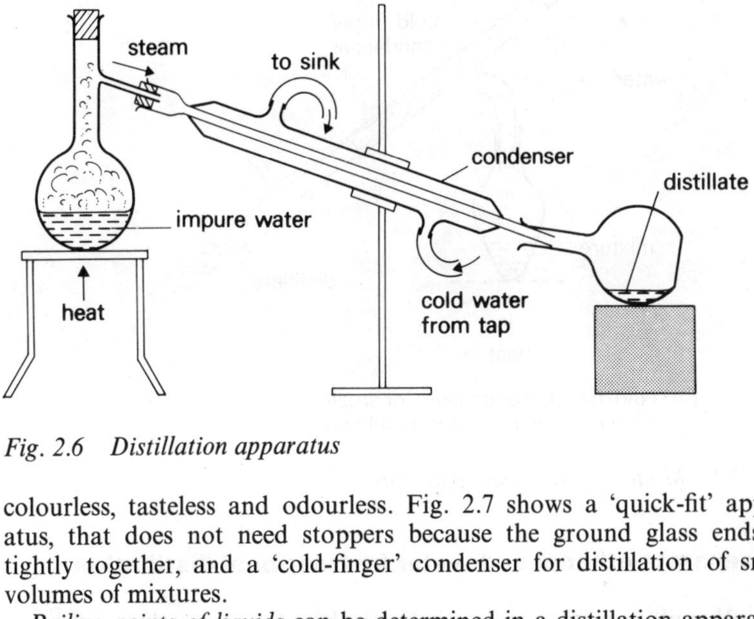

Fig. 2.6 Distillation apparatus

colourless, tasteless and odourless. Fig. 2.7 shows a 'quick-fit' apparatus, that does not need stoppers because the ground glass ends fit tightly together, and a 'cold-finger' condenser for distillation of small volumes of mixtures.

Boiling points of liquids can be determined in a distillation apparatus. Insert a thermometer through the one-holed stopper of the distilling flask so that its bulb is opposite the side tube of the flask. The thermometer measures the temperature of the vapour from the boiling liquid.

Fractional distillation is the process of separating two liquids by distillation, the distillate being collected as fractions which boil at different temperatures.

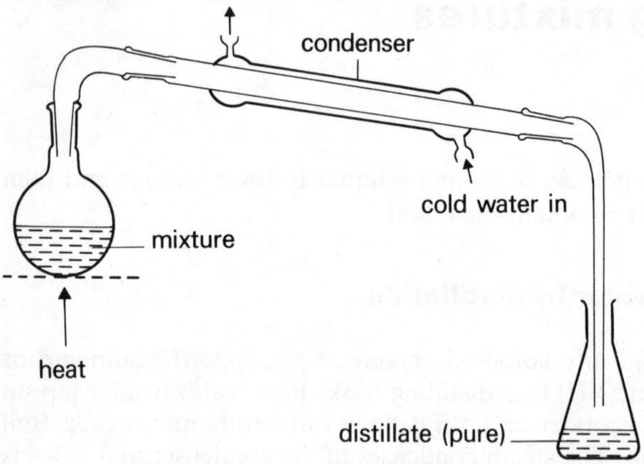

(a) quick-fit apparatus

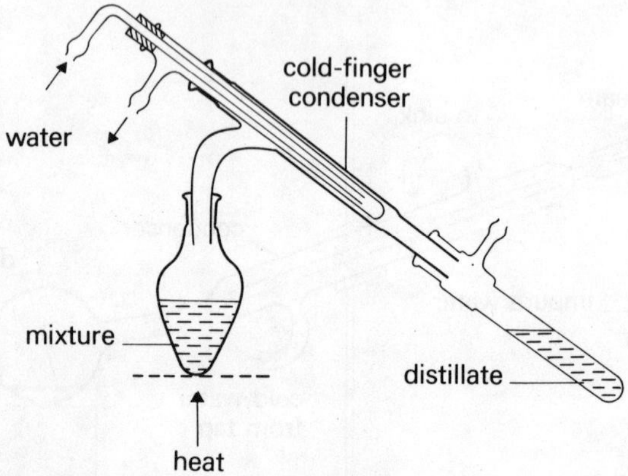

(b) 'cold-finger' condenser (for small volumes of mixture and distillate)

Fig. 2.7 Modern distillation apparatus

To separate ethanol and water by fractional distillation

Mix ethanol (or methylated spirits) with three times its volume of water. Pour the mixture into a distilling flask fitted with a fractionating column, of which there are several kinds. Heat the mixture. The temperature recorded by the thermometer rises to about 78 °C (the b.p. of ethanol), remains fairly constant for a time, and then rises slowly. Collect the distillate in a flask until the temperature is 82 °C. Test a little of the distillate with a flame; it burns readily, unlike the mixture in the distilling flask, because it is mainly ethanol.

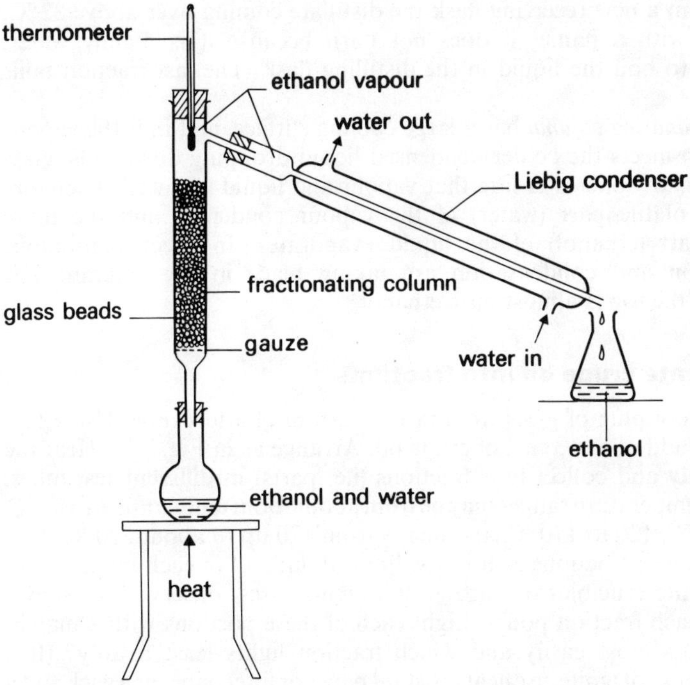

Fig. 2.8 Separating ethanol and water by fractional distillation

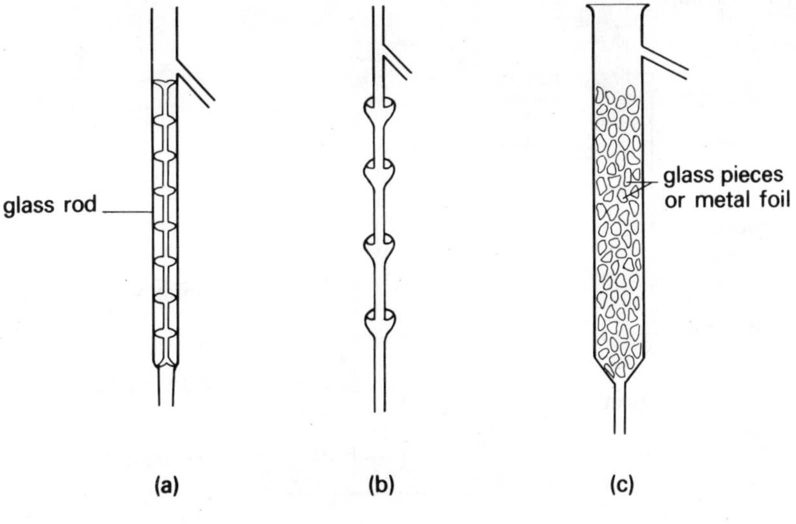

Fig. 2.9 Some fractionating columns

Collect in a new receiving flask the distillate coming over above 82 °C. Test this with a flame; it does not burn because it is mainly water. Continue to boil the liquid in the distilling flask. The last fraction boils at 100 °C.

A *fractionating column* has a large cooling surface, and in it the vapour passing up meets the colder condensed liquid dropping down. The glass beads, rods or spheres ensure that vapour and liquid mix well. Therefore the less volatile part (water) of the vapour condenses and the more volatile part (ethanol) of the liquid evaporates. In effect, continuous evaporation and condensation are taking place in the column. The vapour at the top is almost pure ethanol.

To separate crude oil into fractions

Place a loose plug of glass wool in the bottom of a test-tube. Use a teat pipette to add about 3 cm^3 of crude oil. Arrange as in Fig. 2.10. Heat the oil carefully and collect four fractions (i.e. parts) in different test-tubes. Suitable temperature ranges may be from about room temperature to 80 °C, 80 to 120 °C, 120 to 170 °C, and finally from 170 up to about 220 °C.

Test the four fractions as follows. Pour about half of each fraction into four separate crucibles or hard-glass watch-glasses; observe how slowly or easily each fraction pours. Light each of these portions with a match; which lights most easily and which fraction lights least readily? (If a fraction does not ignite, use heat resistant paper or filter paper as a wick and it should burn easily.)

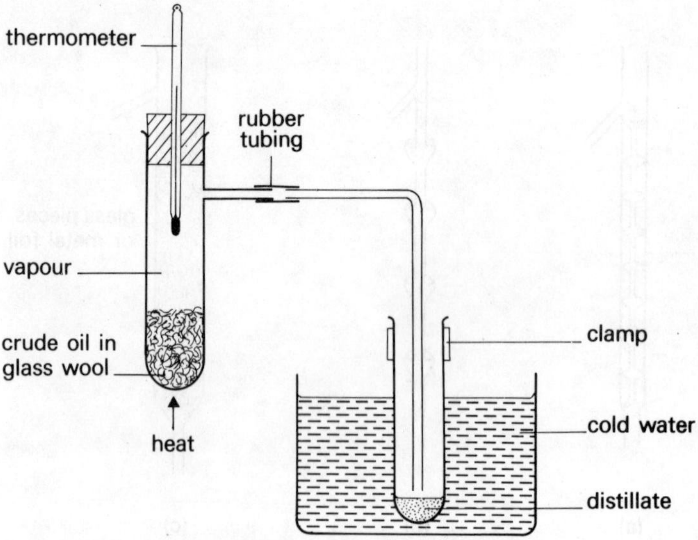

Fig. 2.10 Separating crude oil into fractions

Paper chromatography

Chromatography is a process for the separation of a mixture of solutes by using their different rates of movement over a porous medium, e.g. filter paper, caused by a moving solvent.

To separate various solutes by paper chromatography

Ink. Lay a filter paper horizontally on the rim of an evaporating basin or Petri dish. Add one drop of ink to the centre of the paper. When it has finished spreading, add a second drop, and then a third drop. Let the ink dry. Now add one drop of water (the moving solvent) to the dried ink. It spreads across the paper. Let it dry and then add a second drop of water, and so on. Continue until a disc of coloured substance almost reaches the edge of the paper.

Fig. 2.11 shows a slightly different method. The solvent moves up the 'wick' of paper dipping into it and separates the solutes into rings on the horizontal filter paper. Continue until the solvent reaches about 1 cm from the edge of the paper. Dry the paper at once in bright sunlight or on a radiator, etc., otherwise the separated dyes may merge again. The cover over the paper (see the diagram) is essential so that the moving solvent does not evaporate before it has time to spread. The dried paper with separated dyes is a *chromatogram.*

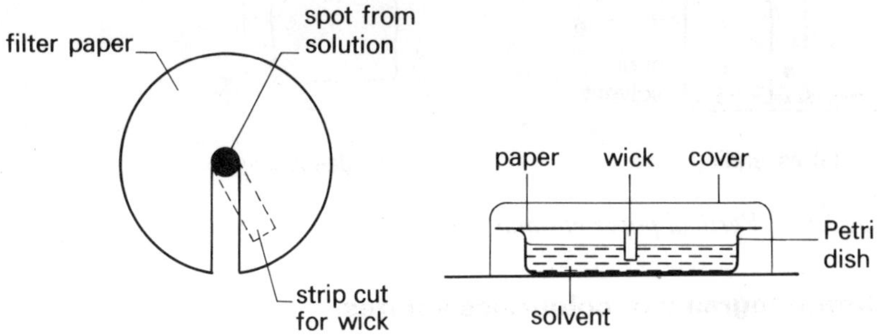

Fig. 2.11 Paper chromatography

Most inks split up into two or more bands of colour. The coloured solutes distribute themselves between the adsorbed water in the cellulose fibres of the filter paper and the moving water. The solute most soluble in the moving water migrates more rapidly than those which are less soluble. In this experiment the moving and stationary solvents are the same (i.e. water) but often they are different.

Screened methyl orange. This contains a blue and a yellow dye in 50 per cent ethanol–water mixture. Separate them as above. The yellow dye remains close to the centre of the paper and the blue dye moves farther towards the edge.

Pigments in grass. Cut grass or spinach into tiny pieces. Dry in an oven at 100 °C for about 15 minutes until they are brittle. Grind them in a mortar with propanone or ethanol and decant the green solution into a test-tube. Separate the different solutes as above, using propanone or ethanol as the moving solvent. Green and yellow bands form. The green substance is chlorophyll.

The filter paper may be vertical. Fig. 2.12(a) shows the *ascending* method in which the solvent moves up the paper. The glass bottle can be a gas jar, milk bottle, jam jar, or even a bucket. Fig. 2.12(b) shows the *descending* method. The cotton wool is soaked in solvent but must not be too wet. In these methods, the paper must not touch the sides of the bottle or plastic bag. The bottle and bag keep the air saturated with solvent vapour and stop the moving solvent evaporating.

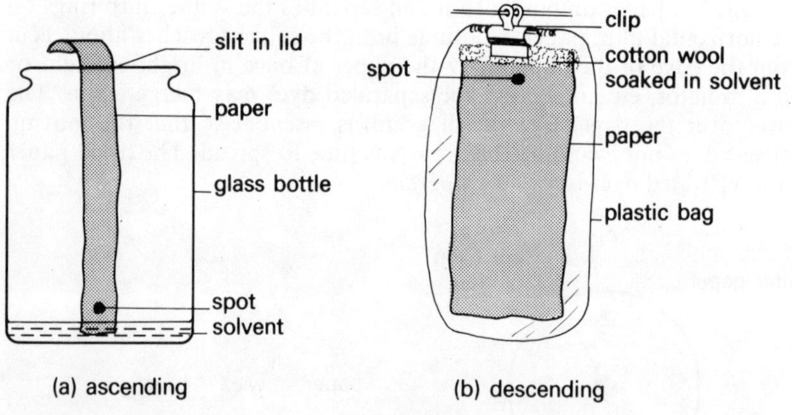

Fig. 2.12 Vertical paper chromatography

Chromatograms of colourless solutes

Chromatograms obtained in the experiments already described are of coloured solutes, which are easily visible. However, colourless compounds are invisible on chromatograms. Methods used to make them visible include the following:

1 Place the chromatogram under an ultraviolet lamp. Many compounds (especially those from plant tissues) become visible because they fluoresce, i.e. they absorb the ultraviolet radiation and emit coloured light. This method has the advantage that it does not chemically alter the solutes.

2 Add to the chromatogram a reagent which changes the colourless solute to a coloured compound. Reagents used include hydrogen sulphide and solutions of various chemicals in either water, an alcohol or propanone. Both the solute and its coloured reaction product must, of course, be insoluble in the solution used, otherwise the solute either spreads on the paper or dissolves completely. Some colourless sugars (e.g. glucose, maltose) are detected by silver nitrate solution, which is changed by the sugar to brown spots of finely divided silver. Aminoacids, p. 323, are made visible by a solution of ninhydrin in propanone, which converts them to blue-black products.

Questions

1 Classify each of the following naturally occurring substances as an element, compound, or mixture, in each case giving evidence in support of your answer: diamond, petroleum, sand, common salt, coal. (O.)

2 Explain the difference between the solution in water of sugar and the 'solution' in dilute acid of zinc. Explain carefully how you would convert zinc as completely as possible into zinc sulphide. How would you test your product to find if it contained zinc which had failed to combine?

3 Describe with practical details how you would obtain in a state of reasonable purity each of the constituents from the following mixtures: (*a*) common salt and sand; (*b*) ammonium chloride and sodium chloride; (*c*) iron filings and sulphur; (*d*) copper(II) sulphate and water. (N.)

4 Describe carefully how you would separate a reasonably pure specimen of one of the constituents from each of the following mixtures: (*a*) common salt and potassium nitrate; (*b*) chalk and ammonium chloride; (*c*) hydrogen sulphide and hydrogen chloride. In (*a*) and (*b*) state how you would show experimentally that the product obtained was free from the substance with which it was formerly mixed. (L.)

3
Burning and Rusting

To find what substances are formed when a candle or petrol burns

Fig. 3.1 shows an apparatus for passing the hot gases from a burning candle, petrol or oil through a cooled U-tube and calcium hydroxide solution.

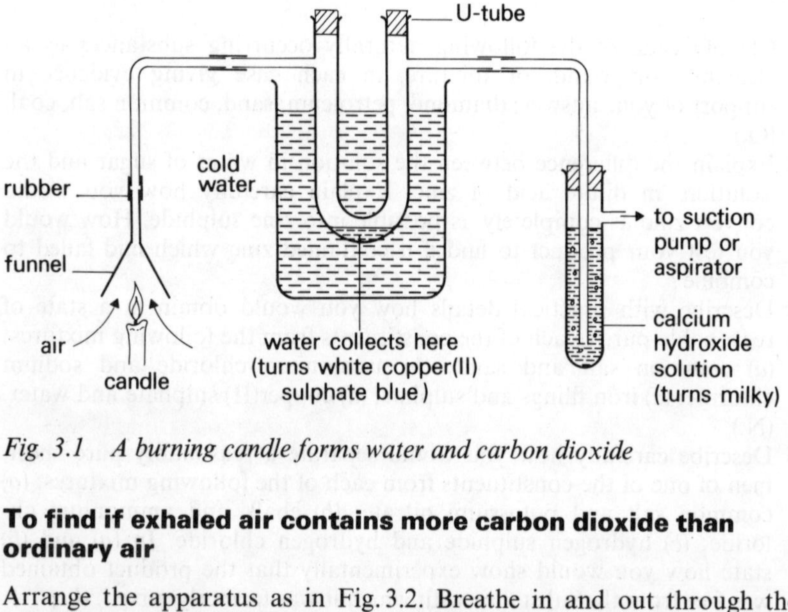

Fig. 3.1 A burning candle forms water and carbon dioxide

To find if exhaled air contains more carbon dioxide than ordinary air

Arrange the apparatus as in Fig. 3.2. Breathe in and out through the mouth. The inhaled air passes through calcium hydroxide solution, which removes carbon dioxide from it. The exhaled air passes through the calcium hydroxide solution in the right hand tube. The solution in the left hand tube remains clear for some time, but that in the right hand tube quickly turns milky. Therefore exhaled air contains more carbon dioxide than ordinary air. Exhaled air contains 3 per cent of carbon dioxide, 100 times more than ordinary air (0.03 per cent).

To study what happens when metals are heated in air

Hold copper foil in tongs and heat it. Heat a thicker piece of copper for a minute and allow it to cool. Rub it to find if it has changed completely or only on the surface. Heat in a crucible, or on heat resistant paper, pieces of

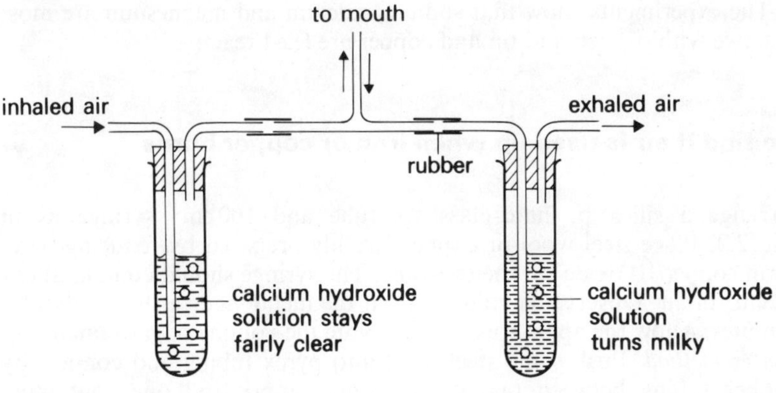

Fig. 3.2 Exhaled air contains more carbon dioxide than ordinary air

other metals, e.g. sodium, aluminium, zinc, iron, tin and lead, making them red-hot if necessary.

Metal bottle tops may be used as disposable crucibles. Heat the tops in a fume cupboard to remove the cork or plastic linings; scrape off any bits of lining that remain. Hold the cleaned tops in tongs. Since the metal is thin and a good conductor of heat, metals are made hot more quickly than in porcelain crucibles.

The effect of heating substances in air

Sodium burns with a bright yellow flame and *calcium* with a red flame. *Magnesium* burns with a brilliant light, forming a white smoke and powder. *Aluminium* burns when strongly heated. *Lead* melts and then forms a brown oxide. *Zinc* burns with a blue-green flame. *Iron* powder burns and forms white-hot sparks. *Tin* melts and then forms a white solid. *Copper* foil burns with a blue-green flame and turns black; thick copper changes only on the outside.

$4Na(s) + O_2(g) \rightarrow 2Na_2O(s)$ (white)
$2Na(s) + O_2(g) \rightarrow Na_2O_2(s)$ (yellowish)

$2Ca(s) + O_2(g) \rightarrow 2CaO$ (white)

$2Mg(s) + O_2(g) \rightarrow 2MgO(s)$ (white)

$4Al(s) + 3O_2(g) \rightarrow 2Al_2O_3$ (white)

$2Zn(s) + O_2(g) \rightarrow 2ZnO(s)$ (hot, yellow; cold, white)

$3Fe(s) + 2O_2(g) \rightarrow Fe_3O_4(s)$ (blueish-black)

$2Pb(s) + O_2(g) \rightarrow 2PbO(s)$ (hot, brown; cold, yellow)

$Sn(s) + O_2(g) \rightarrow SnO_2(s)$ (white)

$2Cu(s) + O_2(g) \rightarrow 2CuO(s)$ (black)

The experiments show that sodium, calcium and magnesium are most reactive with oxygen and tin and copper are least reactive.

To find if air is used up when iron or copper burns

Arrange a silica or hard-glass test-tube and 100 cm^3 syringe as in Fig. 2.2. Place steel wool or copper [freshly prepared by reducing wire-form copper(II) oxide] in the test-tube. The syringe should contain about 50 cm^3 of air. Observe its volume. Heat the metal vigorously for about 5 minutes. Allow the apparatus to cool. Note the volume of gas remaining. *Better method.* Push some steel wool into pyrex tubing and connect by rubber tubing between two syringes, one empty and one containing 100 cm^3 of air. Heat the steel and slowly push the air over it and then back again. The steel glows (copper does not and it reacts more slowly). When the visible reaction is complete allow the apparatus to cool. Note the volume of gas remaining. Observe the change in colour of the steel to blue-black. (The steel can be weighed before and after reaction. Its mass increases by about 0.027 g.)

To find if there is a change in mass when magnesium burns in air

Place clean magnesium in a crucible. Find the mass of the crucible, lid and magnesium. Heat the crucible on a pipe-clay triangle, keeping its lid on. The magnesium burns and uses up all the air in the crucible. Therefore lift the lid with tongs about every 10 seconds; air goes in but not much oxide escapes. When the burning seems to be finished, move the lid to one side and heat the crucible strongly. Allow to cool and find

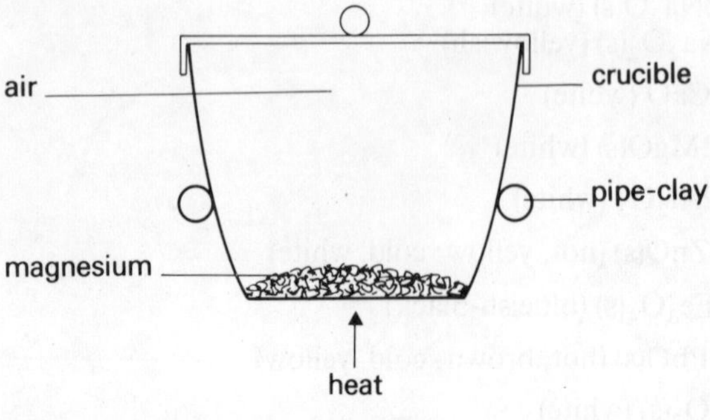

Fig. 3.3 Burning magnesium in a crucible

the mass again.

Mass of crucible, lid and magnesium = a g
Mass of crucible, lid and oxide = b g

When magnesium burns in air its mass increases.

To find if there is a change in mass when a candle burns

Find the mass of the whole apparatus shown in Fig. 3.4 (candle, funnel and U-tube). Sodalime is used to absorb carbon dioxide and water formed by a burning candle.

Light the candle, place it under the funnel, and use a pump to suck the hot gases through the sodalime. After about 5 minutes, put out the candle. Allow the apparatus to cool and find the mass again.

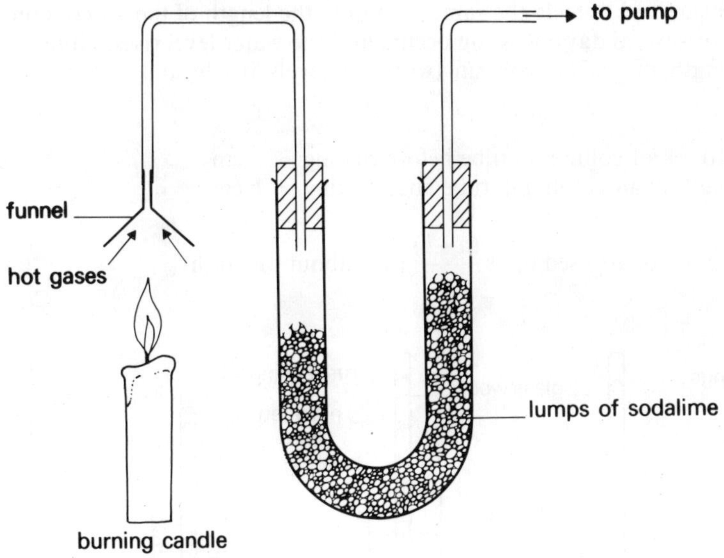

Fig. 3.4 Is there a change in mass when a candle burns?

There should be an increase in mass, showing that the carbon dioxide and water have greater mass than the wax used up. The increase in mass is equal to that of the oxygen of the air which has combined with the wax.

$$C_xH_y + \left(x + \frac{y}{4}\right)O_2 \rightarrow xCO_2 + \frac{y}{2}H_2O$$

To find if there is a change in mass when iron rusts

Place non-greasy iron filings on a watch-glass and find the mass. Cover the iron with water and leave for a few days. If the water evaporates, add more to keep the iron wet. Dry the iron rust in a desiccator or oven. Find the mass of the watch-glass and rust.

Mass of watch-glass and iron $= a$
Mass of watch-glass and rust $= b$

When iron rusts in air its mass increases.

To measure the fraction of air used up when iron rusts

Add non-greasy iron filings to a tube, cover with water, and keep them in position with glass wool. Invert in a tall jar of water. Make the water levels inside and outside the same, and note the length of the air column. Leave for several days. Rusting occurs and the water level rises. Note the final length of the air column (with the levels inside and outside the same).

Length of air column in tube before rusting $= a$ cm
Length of air column in tube after rusting $= b$ cm

The fraction of air used up is $\frac{(a-b)}{a}$ (it is about one-fifth).

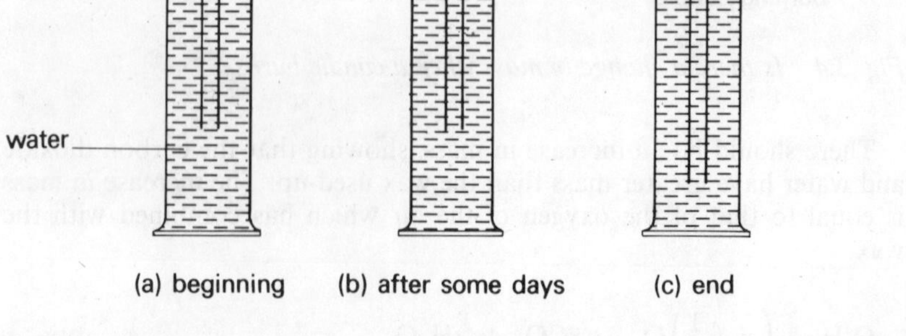

Fig. 3.5 Measuring the air used up when iron rusts

To measure the fraction of air used up when phosphorus burns

(*Caution*. White phosphorus is dangerous because it catches fire very easily. Always store it and cut it under water. Its vapour and that of its oxide are poisonous. Experiments with it should be done in a fume cupboard and demonstrated by the teacher.)

Cut, under water, a small piece of white phosphorus. Repeat the previous experiment, using phosphorus in place of iron filings. Leave the apparatus for one day, although slow changes begin at once. Dense white fumes form, fall towards the water and react with it. Measure the volume readings as before. (Refer to p. 39 for the reactions.)

Changes during burning and rusting

The experiments show that only part of the air is used up when a candle or phosphorus burns and when iron rusts. Air contains at least two gases. One is used up when a substance burns and the other is not. One-fifth of the air (oxygen) is used up when iron rusts and phosphorus burns. The other four-fifths (nitrogen) is not used up.

Combustion in air is a chemical change in which substances combine with oxygen to form oxides. Substances burn in other gases, e.g. phosphorus in chlorine, and magnesium in carbon dioxide and sulphur dioxide.

Combustion is a chemical change in which heat and perhaps light are given out and one or more of the reactants is a gas.

Rusting of iron

When iron is left in damp air for some time it becomes covered with red-brown rust [hydrated iron(III) oxide, $Fe_2O_3 \cdot xH_2O$]. Rust is soft and readily drops off, and then the metal below rusts. Iron which is left in air for long enough rusts completely.

To find if iron rusts in dry air and in air-free water

Dry air. Arrange the apparatus as in Fig. 3.6. Calcium chloride removes water vapour from the air. Leave for several weeks. The iron does not rust.

Dry air (*second method*). Leave clean iron nails or filings in a desiccator for a long time (even years). The iron does not rust.

Air-free water. Boil water in a test-tube to drive out dissolved air. Put several clean nails in the water. Add paraffin oil, coconut oil or Vaseline to form a layer on the surface of the water and keep out air (Fig. 3.7). Leave for a long time. The nails do not rust.

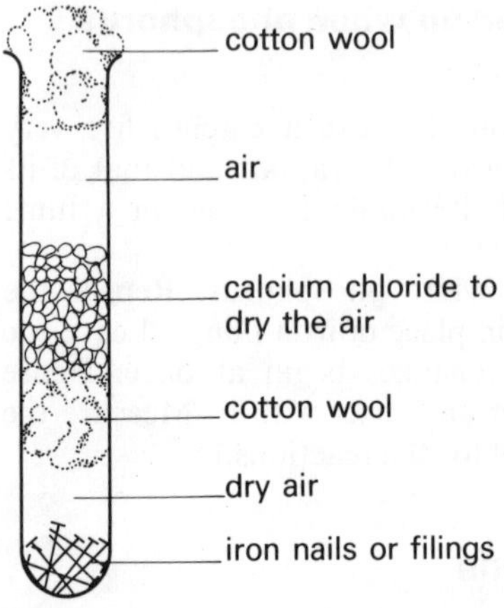

Fig. 3.6 Iron in dry air

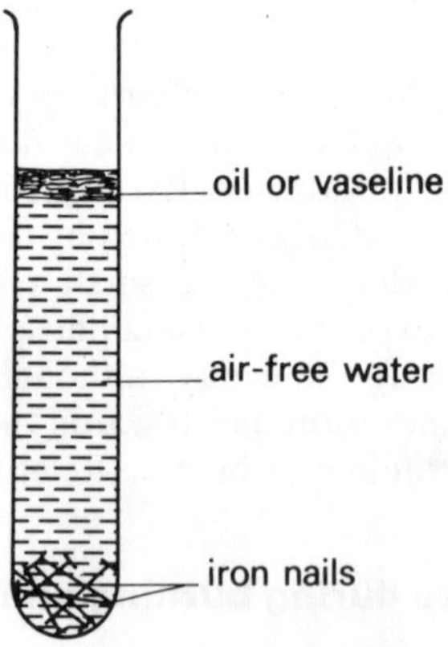

Fig. 3.7 Iron in air-free water

Methods of preventing rusting

The rusting of iron needs air (or oxygen) and water together.

Iron + Oxygen + Water → Iron rust, $Fe_2O_3 \cdot xH_2O$

The only way to stop iron and steel from rusting is to keep air and water away from them. This is done as follows:

1 *Oil or grease*. A layer of oil or grease is put on the metal. This is used to stop metal tools and parts of machines from rusting.

2 *Paint or tar*. Paint is usually put on the iron of windows, doors, bicycles, cars, bridges, and so on. Tar is used on iron that we do not see, e.g. the bottom parts of bridges or ships.

3 *Other metals*. A layer of another metal is put on the iron. Iron coated with tin is called *tinplate*, which is used for making 'tins' that contain food, paint, petrol, and so on. A tin can is about 99 per cent iron and only 1 per cent tin. Tinplate is made by dipping a sheet of iron into molten tin. It rusts very quickly if the coat of tin is broken.

Iron coated with zinc is *galvanized iron* made by dipping a sheet of iron in molten zinc. It is used for making roofs, baths, buckets, and so on. It is better than tinplate because it does not rust easily even if the zinc coat is broken. Iron coated with chromium (and nickel) is *chromium-plated* and it shines almost like silver. It is used on motor cars, bicycles, and other things where an attractive appearance is required.

4 *Stainless steel*. Stainless steel is iron that contains carbon, chromium, nickel, and other elements. It does not rust. Knives, scissors, and other tools are often made from stainless steel.

5 *Rust-proofing cars.* Some parts, such as the radiator grill and the bumpers, are plated with chromium. The car body is protected by paint. First the metal is cleaned with special solvents and sodium hydroxide solution. It is then coated with zinc phosphate, which retards rusting, and then with a special anti-rust paint. The body is immersed in the paint to ensure that it reaches otherwise inaccessible parts. This paint is dried in an oven to make it hard. Five or more coats of paint are then sprayed on the body.

Questions

1 How would you prove experimentally that air contains (*a*) water vapour, (*b*) carbon dioxide, (*c*) oxygen? Describe an accurate experiment (without using phosphorus) by which you could determine the percentage of oxygen by volume in the air. (L.)

2 Describe fully what you observe when two named metals and two named non-metals burn in air. Write equations for the reactions.

3 State conditions necessary for the rusting of iron. Draw and label a diagram of the apparatus you would use to remove oxygen, carbon dioxide and water from a sample of air. Name three gases that would still remain in the sample.

4
The Atmosphere and Oxygen

Gases of the atmosphere

The average percentage composition of dry air is:

	Volume	Mass
Nitrogen	78	75.5
Oxygen	21	23.2
Noble gases	1	1.3
Carbon dioxide	0.03	0.05

Nitrogen. This gas dilutes the oxygen and makes combustion, respiration and rusting slower.

Noble gases. These are argon, neon, helium, krypton, and xenon. Burning, respiration, and other processes do not need these gases. They do not react with any substances under ordinary conditions.

Some electric light bulbs contain about 95 per cent *argon* mixed with nitrogen, which stops the hot metal filament slowly darkening the glass. Argon, at a pressure of about 3 mm Hg, is in fluorescent lamps. *Krypton* is used in light bulbs when maximum efficiency is required, e.g. in bulbs used by miners. *Neon* is in red-coloured electric signs used for advertising. *Helium* is a very light gas (air is seven times denser than helium) and is therefore used in balloons instead of inflammable hydrogen.

Water vapour. There is always water vapour, usually between 1 and 4 per cent, in the atmosphere, even over deserts.

Dust and bacteria. Tiny solid particles float in the atmosphere. The wind carries dust, and soot comes from fires, motor cars and diesel engines. *Smoke* is solid particles of carbon, tarry matter and ash from fires. Town air contains more solids than country air. Bacteria and viruses are always in the air.

Pollutants. These include coarse particles, usually formed in steelworks and other heavy industries, fine particles and smoke particles, including asbestos fibres from building materials, insulating materials and brake drums. Gases and vapour pollutants include sulphur dioxide and sulphur(VI) oxide, sulphurous and sulphuric acids, and hydrogen sulphide. The burning of coal and fuel oils produce the sulphur compounds. Exhaust fumes of cars and other vehicles burning petrol or oil produce carbon monoxide, oxides of nitrogen, unburnt hydrocarbons and lead compounds.

The sulphur compounds affect the lungs, kill lichens and other plants, and attack fabrics, masonry and metals. Carbon monoxide is poisonous, and so are lead compounds, which cause depression, brain damage and even death.

To study the action of heat on some compounds

Heat potassium chlorate in a hard-glass tube. Test any gas evolved with a glowing splint. Note the colour of the residue when cold. Repeat with other compounds, e.g. potassium nitrate, sodium nitrate, lead(IV) oxide, PbO_2, and red lead oxide, Pb_3O_4 (trilead tetraoxide). Remember that hot lead compounds ruin test-tubes.
Potassium chlorate melts at 368 °C to a colourless liquid, which gives off oxygen when heated strongly. The residue is potassium chloride:

$$2KClO_3(l) \rightarrow 3O_2(g) + 2KCl(s), \text{ white}$$

Potassium nitrate and *sodium nitrate* melt at 337 °C and 310 °C respectively to form colourless liquids, which decompose slowly to form oxygen and potassium or sodium nitrite:

$$2NaNO_3(l) \rightarrow O_2(g) + 2NaNO_2(l), \text{ pale-yellow}$$

Both nitrites decompose at high temperatures:

$$4NaNO_2(l) \rightarrow 2Na_2O(s) + 4NO(g) + O_2(g)$$

In air, the nitrogen oxide forms brown nitrogen dioxide, NO_2.

To study the effect of copper(II) oxide on the decomposition of potassium chlorate

(The reaction between potassium chlorate and manganese oxide can be violent; it must be demonstrated by the teacher and safety screens must be used.) Add potassium chlorate(V) powder to a depth of about 1 cm to each of two hard-glass test-tubes. To one tube add a little dry copper(II) oxide or manganese(IV) oxide and mix well. Now heat both tubes equally in a non-roaring flame. Test for oxygen by holding a glowing splint at the mouths of the tubes. Oxygen forms more readily in the tube containing the mixture.

Catalysis

Copper(II) oxide and manganese(IV) oxide cause potassium chlorate to give off oxygen at a much lower temperature (about 200 °C) than usual.

The oxide itself does not change, and its mass remains the same. It is a catalyst, and the process is called *catalysis*.

A catalyst is a substance which changes the speed of a chemical reaction but remains unchanged chemically and unchanged in mass at the end of the reaction.

Oxygen, O_2

To prepare oxygen

From hydrogen peroxide. Drop hydrogen peroxide (10 or 20 volume) from a dropping funnel into a flask containing manganese(IV) oxide powder. Do not heat. Oxygen comes off readily. The oxide acts as a catalyst:

$$2H_2O_2(aq) \rightarrow O_2(g) + 2H_2O(l)$$

If the oxygen is required dry, pass it through concentrated sulphuric acid in a wash bottle or solid calcium chloride in a U-tube.

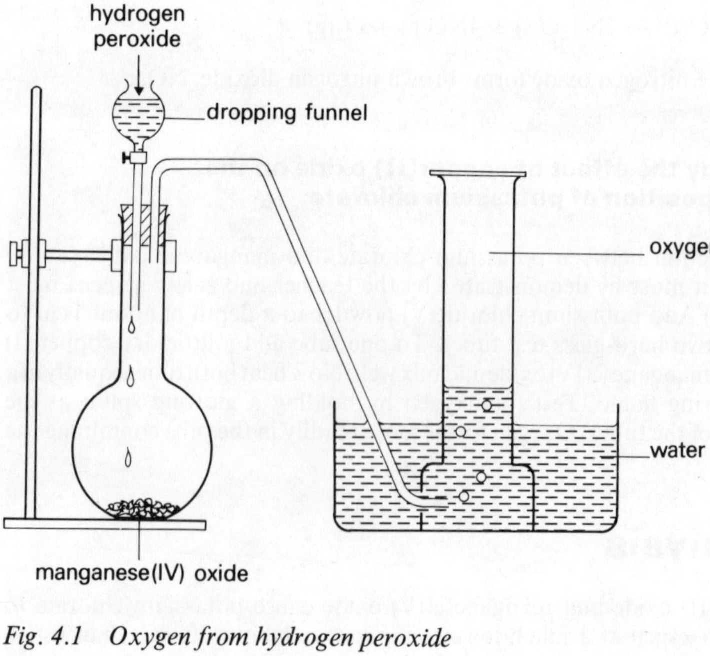

Fig. 4.1   Oxygen from hydrogen peroxide

Properties of oxygen

Oxygen is a colourless, odourless, tasteless gas. It is slightly soluble in cold water (100 cm^3 dissolve about 4 cm^3 of oxygen). Water plants, fish and other water animals 'breathe' the dissolved oxygen. It is neutral to litmus. It is 1.1 times denser than air. Oxygen does not burn. Many metals and non-metals burn in it.

Test for oxygen

Oxygen re-lights a glowing splint (dinitrogen oxide also does this).

Combustion of non-metals in oxygen

Non-metals burn in oxygen to form acidic oxides which react with water to form acids. An acid anhydride is an oxide of a non-metal which reacts with water to form an acid.

Sulphur burns with a bright blue flame and forms cloudy fumes with a choking smell

$$S(l) + O_2(g) \rightarrow SO_2(g);\ SO_2(g) + H_2O(l) \rightarrow H_2SO_3(aq)$$

Carbon burns with an orange flame and makes bright sparks.

$$C(s) + O_2(g) \rightarrow CO_2(g);\ CO_2(g) + H_2O(l) \rightarrow H_2CO_3(aq)$$

Phosphorus burns with a very bright, yellow flame and produces a dense white smoke,

$$4P(s) + 5O_2(g) \rightarrow 2P_2O_5(s) \text{ or } P_4O_{10}(s), \text{ phosphorus(V) oxide}$$

$$4P(s) + 3O_2(g) \rightarrow 2P_2O_3(s) \text{ or } P_4O_6(s), \text{ phosphorus(III) oxide}$$

$$P_2O_5(s) + 3H_2O(l) \rightarrow 2H_3PO_4(aq), \text{ phosphoric acid}$$
$$P_2O_3(s) + 3H_2O(l) \rightarrow 2H_3PO_3(aq), \text{ phosphorous acid}$$

Sulphur dioxide, sulphur(VI) oxide, carbon dioxide and phosphorus oxides are acidic oxides and acid anhydrides.

Combustion of metals in oxygen

Metals burn in oxygen to form basic oxides which, if they react with water, form alkalis.

Sodium burns with a bright yellow flame and forms a yellowish solid.

$2Na + O_2 \rightarrow Na_2O_2$ (sodium peroxide)

Calcium burns with a bright red flame and forms a white solid.

$2Ca + O_2 \rightarrow 2CaO; CaO(s) + H_2O \rightarrow Ca(OH)_2(aq)$

Magnesium burns in oxygen with a very bright light and forms a light, white ash.

$2Mg + O_2 \rightarrow 2MgO; MgO(s) + H_2O \rightarrow Mg(OH)_2(aq)$

Iron wire or filings burn with a shower of bright sparks and forms a blue-black solid insoluble in water.

$3Fe(s) + 2O_2(g) \rightarrow Fe_3O_4(s)$ (triiron tetraoxide)

Metal or non-metal	Oxide	Acid or alkali
Sulphur	Colourless gas; pungent or choking smell. (Sulphur dioxide.) Some white fumes. [Sulphur(VI) oxide.]	Sulphurous acid, H_2SO_3. (A little sulphuric acid.)
Carbon	Colourless, odourless gas (Carbon dioxide.)	Carbonic acid, H_2CO_3
Phosphorus	White smoke that forms a white solid. [Phosphorus(V) oxide and a little phosphorus(III) oxide.]	Phosphoric acid, H_3PO_4. (A little phosphorous acid, H_3PO_3)
Sodium	Yellow solid. (Sodium peroxide.)	Sodium hydroxide, NaOH
Calcium	White solid. (Calcium oxide.)	Calcium hydroxide, $Ca(OH)_2$
Magnesium	White solid. (Magnesium oxide.)	Magnesium hydroxide, $Mg(OH)_2$
Iron	Blueish-black solid [Triiron tetraoxide or iron(II) diiron(III) oxide.]	None; the oxide is insoluble

Commercial preparation of oxygen

The temperature of a gas falls as it expands when passing from a high pressure to low pressure. The air molecules move further apart, do work against their attractive forces, lose energy by doing internal work, and so the temperature falls (*Joule–Thomson effect*). In 1900 Claude obtained liquid air on a commercial scale for the first time. Air was compressed to about 200 atmospheres and was then allowed to expand and do external work (*Claude effect*). Both cooling effects are used in modern liquefaction plants. Carbon dioxide and water vapour are removed from air by sodium hydroxide solution and silicon(IV) oxide respectively. If left they would solidify and block the apparatus. The air is compressed to 200 atmospheres, cooled by liquid nitrogen and part passes through a small jet (*Joule–Thomson cooling*) and part drives the compression pump (*Claude effect*). The air cools when it expands rapidly. The cooling process is repeated and the air finally liquefies to a pale-blue liquid. It is a mixture of colourless nitrogen (b.p. −196 °C) and blue liquid oxygen (b.p. −183 °C). Nitrogen boils off first when the liquid air evaporates. The liquid left becomes richer in oxygen and bluer in colour. Fractional distillation is used in a very cold fractionating tower (similar to that of Fig. 2.9) to obtain a perfect separation of the gases. They are stored and sold under pressure in steel cylinders, or transported by pipe-line or special insulated rail and road tankers.

Noble gases. Helium (b.p. −269 °C) and neon (b.p. −246 °C) are in the liquid nitrogen fraction; argon (b.p. −189 °C), krypton and xenon are in the liquid oxygen fraction. The noble gases are obtained by further fractionation of the liquid nitrogen and oxygen fractions. The argon contains a little oxygen which is removed by burning in hydrogen or by passage over hot copper.

Natural gas is the most important source of helium. It is cooled to about −200 °C or lower and all gases present liquefy except helium. The almost pure helium is then pumped off. Millions of cubic metres of helium are obtained annually by this method.

By electrolysis. Oxygen (and hydrogen) is obtained by electrolysis of sodium hydroxide solution in countries where electricity is cheap.

Uses of oxygen

1 *Respiration.* Oxygen is given to some people who are ill or injured. Some diseases damage the lungs and stop them taking enough oxygen from the air, but they may be able to take enough from pure oxygen. Oxygen mixed with dinitrogen oxide is used by dentists. Oxygen is also given to people under anaesthetics and having operations. People who have almost drowned or have breathed poisonous gases are often given oxygen. Divers breathe oxygen mixed with helium. Mountain climbers and airmen who fly very high use oxygen as there is not enough in the atmosphere at great heights.

2 *Flames and metal cutting.* Acetylene (ethyne) burns in oxygen and forms the *oxyacetylene flame* with a temperature of about 3000 °C. This is used to ‘cut’ steel. The metal is heated in the flame and then extra oxygen is turned on. The hot metal changes to oxide, which drops off in small

pieces and leaves a clean 'cut'. Bottled gas which consists of hydrocarbons is often used instead of acetylene. The *oxyhydrogen flame* is not quite so hot but is also used. These flames melt iron easily, and can be used to join pieces of the metal together.

3 *Oxygen in steel production.* Oxygen is sometimes used instead of air in making steel from pig-iron. A blast of oxygen is blown through the molten pig-iron and oxidizes the impurities, e.g. carbon, sulphur, phosphorus. Since tons of oxygen are used the steelworks are called *tonnage oxygen plants*.

4 *Fuel.* Liquid oxygen is used to burn the fuel in some space rockets. Kerosine and liquid hydrogen are common fuels; an oxygen–hydrogen liquid mixture is the most powerful propellant known.

Nitrogen, N_2

Nitrogen, mixed with a small amount of noble gases, remains when oxygen is removed from air by heated steel wool or copper, p. 30, or by iron or phosphorus, pp. 32–3.

Properties of nitrogen

Nitrogen is a colourless, tasteless, odourless gas. It is slightly soluble in water (100 cm^3 dissolve 2 cm^3 of nitrogen), and is neutral to litmus. It is slightly less dense than air. Nitrogen is inert. It has no action on calcium hydroxide solution, does not burn, and extinguishes a burning splint. Most substances do not burn in the gas. However, magnesium and calcium burn to form nitrides:

$$3Mg(s) + N_2(g) \rightarrow Mg_3N_2(s)$$

Nitrogen can combine with hydrogen and oxygen to form ammonia, NH_3, and nitrogen oxide, NO, respectively.
Test for nitrogen. Nitrogen has no colour or smell, does not burn, does not support combustion, and does not turn calcium hydroxide solution milky (there are no simple positive tests).

Uses of nitrogen

Atmospheric nitrogen is converted to ammonia in the Haber process and then ammonium salts or nitrates, which are fertilizers. Gaseous nitrogen is used to fill petrol and oil storage tanks as the liquid is run out; it is inert and reduces the risk of explosion. Liquid nitrogen is the refrigerating agent used to freeze soft fruits, sea foods, pastry goods, meat products and other foods with a high moisture content. It freezes them so fast that the ice crystals are too tiny to break the cell walls of the food and therefore the taste and colour do not change. Some instant coffee is made by freezing coffee powder in liquid nitrogen. The outside parts of high-flying aircraft and spacecraft are tested by leaving them in liquid nitrogen, thus simulating the low temperatures of outer space.

Questions

1 Describe in detail an accurate method of finding the relative proportions by volume of nitrogen and oxygen in the air. Name two other very common constituents of air and describe how you would detect each of them. (C.)

2 What steps can be taken to prevent iron from rusting? Describe experiments by which you would prove that iron does not rust unless both air and water are present. State briefly three ways in which rust differs from a mixture of iron and oxygen. (O.)

3 How would you prepare jars of oxygen from (*a*) potassium chlorate, and (*b*) hydrogen peroxide? How would you use two of these jars to make (*a*) an acidic oxide, (*b*) a basic oxide? How would you show that such oxides had been formed? (N.)

4 Describe fully what you would observe when sulphur and iron burn in oxygen. How are nitrogen and oxygen prepared from air on the industrial scale? (O.)

5 What is meant by catalysis? Describe simple experiments to show that manganese(IV) oxide acts as a catalyst in the decomposition of potassium chlorate by heat. Describe how oxygen is manufactured. Indicate two important uses of this gas. (L.)

5
Water and Hydrogen

Natural waters

Natural water is never pure. It always contains dissolved solids and usually contains suspended solids. Four natural waters are rain-water, spring-water (or well-water), river-water and sea-water, which contains 3.6 per cent by mass of dissolved solids:

Common salt	2.8%	Calcium salts	0.1%
Magnesium salts	0.6%	Potassium salts	0.1%

Pollutants in rivers and seas include sewage, waste from industries, farmyard manure, nitrates washed by rain from fertilizers used in agriculture, insecticides, mercury and lead. Many towns discharge sewage and toxic industrial waste directly into rivers and seas. Nitrates promote the growth of green slimy algae, which then rot and use up dissolved oxygen, thus killing fish and other living organisms that need this oxygen. Insecticides do not decompose readily and accumulate in water. Mercury from industrial waste accumulates in fish and may cause brain damage to people who eat the fish. Lead compounds poured into the atmosphere from car exhausts is washed into rivers and seas and is sometimes found in drinking water. Lead is a dangerous poison because it accumulates in the body (Pb^{2+} replaces Ca^{2+} in bones).

To find if various kinds of water contain dissolved solids

Fill a clock-glass with tap-water and place it on a beaker or water bath (Fig. 1.3 or 1.2). When all the water on the clock-glass has evaporated, turn off the gas. Wipe any water from the bottom of the clock-glass. Look at the dry glass. The solids dissolved in the tap-water are left on it. Repeat the test with other waters.
Alternative method. A quicker method is to place the tap-water on a Pyrex clock-glass and evaporate it on an asbestos mat heated with a small flame.

To find if tap-water contains dissolved gases

Arrange the apparatus as in Fig. 5.1. The end of the delivery tube in the flask must not be below the bottom of the stopper, otherwise gas formed cannot pass up the tube. Use the dropping funnel to fill the flask and delivery tube completely with tap-water. Close the tap of the funnel. Fill the test-tube with water and clamp it over the end of the delivery tube. Heat the flask until the water is almost boiling, then turn down the flame

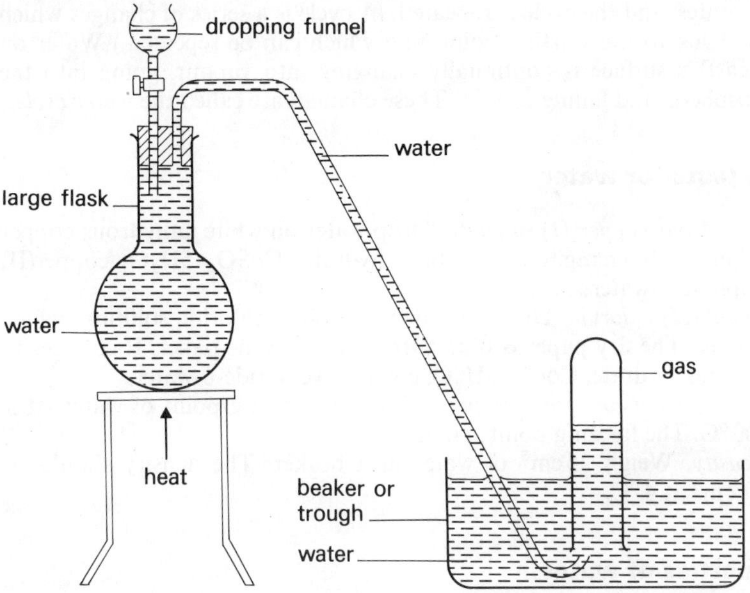

Fig. 5.1 Does water contain dissolved gases?

and warm *gently*. Bubbles of gas and then steam form at the bottom of the flask. The first steam bubbles condense before they reach the top of the flask.

Continue to boil gently while the steam pushes gas down the delivery tube and into the test-tube. The steam makes a noise as it condenses in the trough. Remove the flame and watch the apparatus. Water from the trough rises up the delivery tube as the steam condenses. The first drops of water 'sucked back' into the flask condense the steam in it and water rapidly takes its place. If any gas remains in the delivery tube or flask, boil the water once again and drive the gas into the test-tube.

The gas re-lights a glowing splint and therefore contains more oxygen than air does. (The percentage of oxygen in the gas is about 33 per cent, but is less if the water contains hydrogencarbonates.) The gas contains about 1 per cent of carbon dioxide (much more if the water contains hydrogencarbonates) and some chlorine.

The water cycle

Water-vapour forms in the air when the sun shines on, or winds blow across, water. It is less dense than air and therefore rises. As it rises, the vapour cools. Finally, it condenses to tiny drops of water which float in the sky and form a cloud. The drops may join together and fall as rain. The rain-water passes into springs, rivers and seas. Once again it evaporates, and the cycle is repeated. (A cycle is a series of changes which come back to the starting point, and which can be repeated.) Water on the earth's surface is continually changing into vapour, going into the atmosphere, and falling as rain. These changes are called the *water cycle.*

The tests for water

1 *Anhydrous copper(II) sulphate.* Drop water on white anhydrous copper sulphate. It changes to the blue hydrate, $CuSO_4 \cdot 5H_2O$, copper(II) sulphate-5-water.
2 *Cobalt(II) chloride.* Dip filter paper in cobalt chloride solution, which is pink. The dry paper is blue. Drop water on the paper. It changes to the pink hydrate, $CoCl_2 \cdot 6H_2O$, cobalt(II) chloride-6-water.
3 *Boiling point and freezing point.* Find the boiling point of water. It is 100 °C. The freezing point is 0 °C.
4 *Density.* Weigh 25 cm^3 of water in a beaker. The density should be 1 g/cm^3 at 4 °C.

Properties of water

Pure water is a clear, colourless, odourless liquid. Its taste is described as 'flat'. It is more pleasant to drink water which contains dissolved gases or solids, which give natural waters their taste. It freezes at 0 °C or 273 K and boils at 100 °C or 373 K. It boils away completely and does not leave any residue. 1 cm^3 of water at 4 °C has a mass of 1 g.

Water is neutral to litmus. It turns white anhydrous copper(II) sulphate blue. Any liquids that contain water, e.g. dilute acids, also do this:

$$\text{(white) } CuSO_4(s) + 5H_2O \rightleftharpoons CuSO_4 \cdot 5H_2O \text{ (blue)}$$

Water turns blue cobalt(II) chloride pink. Cobalt(II) chloride paper is often placed inside desiccators and fresh drying agent is needed when it turns pink. Water is an excellent solvent and dissolves practically everything. Ordinary distilled water is not perfectly pure because it dissolves small traces of glass. Oxygen is more soluble than nitrogen, and therefore the gas dissolved in water contains more oxygen (about 33 per cent) than air does. 1000 cm^3 of water contain about 20 cm^3 of dissolved gases. Fish and water plants 'breathe' the dissolved oxygen in water, which also causes rusting of iron. Water contains dissolved carbon dioxide as carbonic acid, and this can cause erosion of rocks and hardness of water.

To find what happens when certain compounds are left in air

On separate watch-glasses, place dry calcium chloride, clear crystals of sodium carbonate and sodium sulphate, solid iron(III) chloride, and hydroxides of sodium and potassium. Leave in air and observe any changes after a few minutes, one day, and one week or more.

Water in the atmosphere

A hygroscopic substance is one which absorbs water from the atmosphere.

Calcium chloride absorbs so much water from the atmosphere that it dissolves in it. It is *deliquescent* ('becoming a liquid') and the process is *deliquescence*. All deliquescent substances are hygroscopic, but hygroscopic substances are not necessarily deliquescent. Deliquescent compounds are very soluble in water.

Deliquescence is the absorbing of water from the atmosphere by a solid to form a solution.

When a clear crystal of hydrated sodium carbonate is left in the air, a white powder slowly forms on its surface and soon the crystal changes to powder. It loses water of crystallization (only 9 of its 10 molecules) which passes into the air:

$$\underset{\text{(10-water hydrate)}}{Na_2CO_3 \cdot 10H_2O(s)} \rightarrow \underset{\text{(1-water hydrate)}}{Na_2CO_3 \cdot H_2O(s)} + 9H_2O(g)$$

Such crystals *effloresce* and the process is *efflorescence*.Sodium sulphate crystals, $Na_2SO_4 \cdot 10H_2O$, lose all their water by efflorescence.

Efflorescence is the giving up of water of crystallization by a crystal to the atmosphere.

Deliquescent	Hygroscopic	Efflorescent
Calcium chloride	Copper(II) oxide	Sodium-carbonate-10-water
Sodium hydroxide	Anhydrous copper(II) sulphate	Sodium sulphate-10-water
Potassium hydroxide	Calcium oxide	
Sodium nitrate	Sulphuric acid (conc.)	
Phosphorus(V) oxide	Ethanol	
Iron(III) chloride	All deliquescent substances	

Drying agents. Hygroscopic and deliquescent substances are used to dry other compounds. The following dry gases:

Sulphuric acid (concentrated) Calcium chloride (fused)	All gases except ammonia and hydrogen sulphide
Phosphorus(V) oxide	All gases except ammonia
Silicon(IV) oxide (silica gel)	All gases
Calcium oxide	Ammonia

Silicon(IV) oxide is often used in desiccators. It can be dried by heating and therefore can be used repeatedly.

Hydrogen, H_2

To examine the reactions between dilute acids and metals

Add a metal to dilute hydrochloric acid in a test-tube. What happens? If no reaction occurs in the cold, warm gently *but do not boil* (otherwise acid fumes are given off). Test any gas formed with a burning splint. Repeat with the same metal and dilute sulphuric acid, and then with dilute nitric acid.

Repeat the whole test with various metals, e.g. magnesium, aluminium, zinc, iron, lead and copper.

Magnesium and nitric acid. Add magnesium to *very dilute* nitric acid made by mixing dilute nitric acid with twice its volume of water. Warm gently and test for hydrogen. The hydrogen can be collected more easily by using a test-tube and funnel, Fig. 5.8. The dilute nitric acid should just cover the stem of the inverted funnel.

Displacement of hydrogen from acids

Magnesium, zinc and iron react with dilute sulphuric acid and with hydrochloric acid to form hydrogen. Aluminium reacts with warm dilute hydrochloric acid to form hydrogen and the powder reacts slowly with warm dilute sulphuric acid. Ionic equations are:

$$Mg(s) + 2H^+(aq) \rightarrow Mg^{2+}(aq) + H_2(g)$$

$$Fe(s) + 2H^+(aq) \rightarrow Fe^{2+}(aq) + H_2(g)$$

$$2Al(s) + 6H^+(aq) \rightarrow 2Al^{3+}(aq) + 3H_2(g)$$

Dilute nitric acid does not react with metals (except magnesium) to form hydrogen and *copper and lead do not react* with dilute acids to form hydrogen.

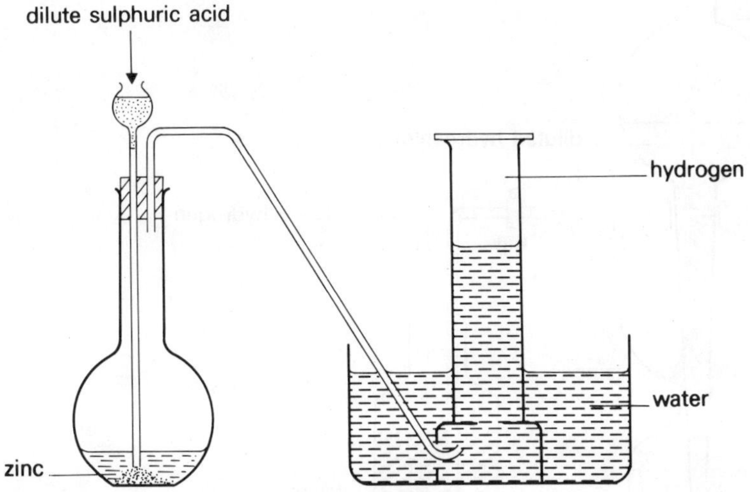

Fig. 5.2 Preparation of hydrogen

To prepare hydrogen

Slide (do not drop) granulated zinc into a flask arranged as in Fig. 5.2. The end of the thistle funnel must be near the bottom of the flask. Have no flames near during the preparation, otherwise there may be an explosion. Pour *cold* diluted sulphuric acid (1 acid : 5 water) or hydrochloric acid (1 acid : 3 water) down the funnel to cover the zinc. If the action is too slow (pure zinc reacts slowly) add a little copper(II) sulphate solution, which speeds up the reaction:

$$Zn(s) + 2H^+(aq) \rightarrow Zn^{2+}(aq) + H_2(g)$$

The diluted sulphuric acid is about 3 M. The final solution is warm enough and concentrated enough after filtering to deposit good crystals of zinc sulphate-7-water, $ZnSO_4 \cdot 7H_2O$. It is not possible to obtain zinc chloride crystals because this compound is very soluble and deliquescent. *Kipp's apparatus.* This (Fig. 5.3) is used so that a gas can be obtained readily. Add fairly large lumps of zinc to the middle bulb. Pour diluted hydrochloric acid (1 acid : 1 water) down through the top bulb or reservoir, with the tap open, until the acid just covers the zinc. Close the tap. The pressure of the gas forces the acid out of the middle bulb and into the top one. When the acid no longer touches the zinc, the reaction stops. It starts again when the tap is opened and acid rises to cover the zinc. Bubble the hydrogen through a wash bottle containing water, which removes tiny drops of hydrochloric acid carried over by the hydrogen.

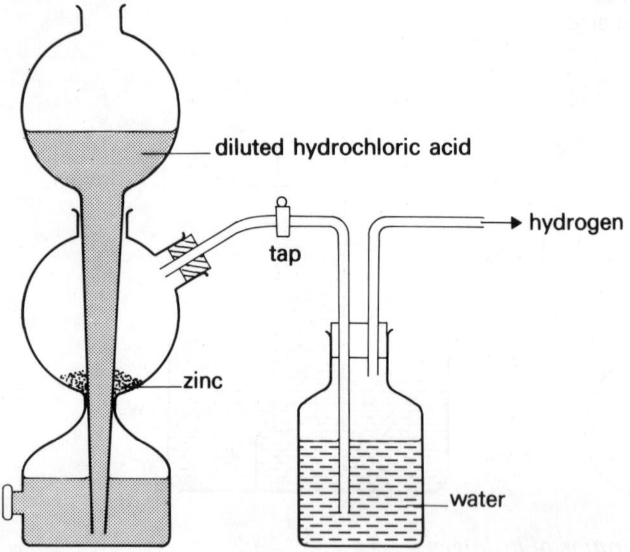

Fig. 5.3 Kipp's apparatus

Properties of hydrogen

Hydrogen is a colourless, odourless, tasteless gas (impurities often cause an unpleasant smell). It is slightly soluble in cold water (100 cm^3 dissolve about 2 cm^3 of the gas). It is neutral to litmus. It is the lightest gas known (air is 14.4 times denser than hydrogen). It diffuses faster than any other gas.

Density

a Stand one jar of hydrogen mouth upwards and hold a second jar mouth downwards (Fig. 5.4). Remove the covers at the same time, wait about 15 seconds, and then push burning splints into the jars. There is a slight explosion only in the jar held mouth downwards.
b *Soap bubble method*. Pass hydrogen into soap or detergent solution in a basin. Bubbles form and rise into the air (Fig. 5.5). (Place a burning splint near some of the bubbles.)

Burning splint

a Hold a jar of hydrogen mouth downwards. Remove the cover and push a long burning splint into the jar. The hydrogen *burns quietly* with a faint blue flame, and a film of water forms on the sides of the jar. The splint is extinguished.

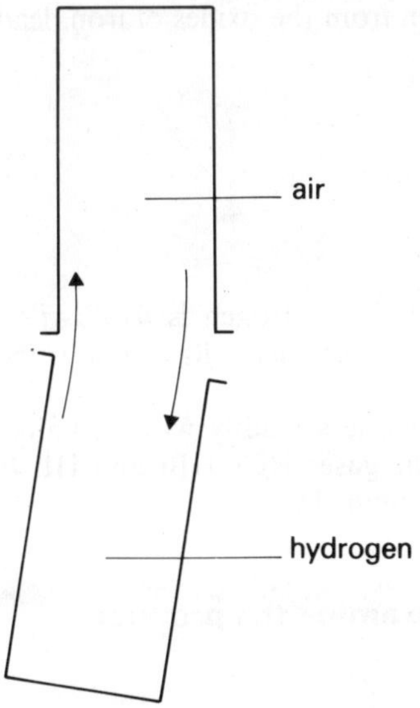

Fig. 5.4 Hydrogen is less dense than air

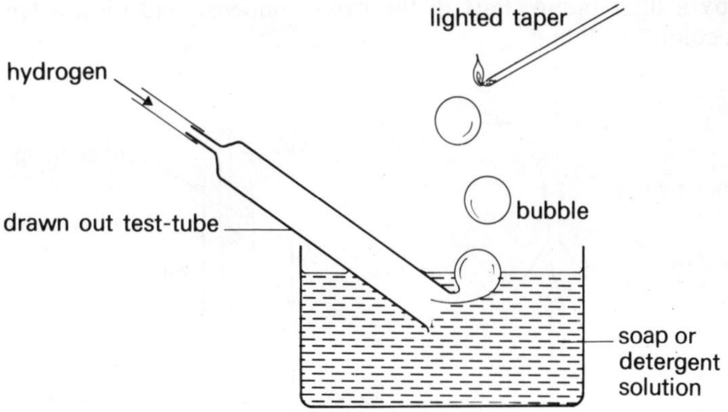

Fig. 5.5 Making and burning soap bubbles of hydrogen

b Remove the cover from a jar of hydrogen mixed with air. Put a flame near the gas. There is an explosion. If a hydrogen–oxygen mixture is used (in a soda-water bottle wrapped in cloth) there is a deafening explosion:

$$2H_2(g) + O_2(g) \rightarrow 2H_2O(g)$$

Test for hydrogen. A mixture of hydrogen and air explodes with a shrill noise when lit.

Reducing action. Hydrogen removes oxygen from the oxides of iron, lead and copper:

$$Fe_3O_4(s) + 4H_2(g) \rightarrow 3Fe(s) + 4H_2O(l)$$
$$CuO(s) + H_2(g) \rightarrow Cu(s) + H_2O(l)$$
$$PbO(s) + H_2(g) \rightarrow Pb(s) + H_2O(l)$$

The oxides are *reduced* to the metals and the hydrogen is *oxidized* to water. *Oxidation is the addition of oxygen to a substance. Reduction is the removal of oxygen from a substance.*

Hydrogen combines readily with chlorine, less readily with bromine, and less readily still with iodine to form the gases HCl, HBr and HI. It forms hydrides with nitrogen (NH_3) and sulphur (H_2S).

To burn dry hydrogen in air and to examine the product (synthesis of water)

Use hydrogen from a cylinder. If it is not available, use town gas or bottled gas. Light the hydrogen at the jet (Fig. 5.6). Let the flame burn so that hot gases from it are sucked up the funnel and through the cooled test-tube by a filter pump. Part of the gases condense and form a few drops of a colourless liquid.

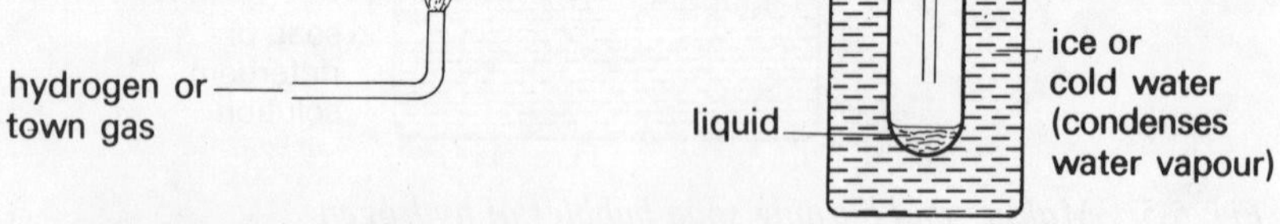

Fig. 5.6 Burning dry hydrogen or another gas in air

Testing the liquid for water.

a Dip neutral litmus paper into it; there is no action.
b Add to white anhydrous copper(II) sulphate; it turns blue.
c Find its boiling point; it is 100 °C. (Usually there is not enough liquid for this test.)

Synthesis and combination

Synthesis is the combination of two or more elements to form a compound, e.g.

$$2H_2(g) + O_2(g) \rightarrow 2H_2O(g \text{ then } l); Fe(s) + S(l) \rightarrow FeS(s)$$

Combination is the joining together of two or more substances to form a compound.

A synthesis is a combination between elements; examples of combinations which involve compounds are:

$$2SO_2(g) + O_2(g) \rightarrow 2SO_3(g \text{ then } s);$$
$$2NO(g) + O_2(g) \rightarrow 2NO_2(g)$$

To study the action of dry hydrogen on copper(II) oxide and lead(II) oxide

[Caution. This experiment is dangerous if air enters the apparatus and forms an explosive mixture with hydrogen. Town gas, mainly methane (CH_4), and 'bottled gas' are safe.]

Add copper(II) oxide to one porcelain boat and lead(II) oxide to another. Triiron tetraoxide, Fe_3O_4, can also be used. Arrange a combustion tube as in Fig. 6.3. Slope the tube downwards slightly so that water formed in the reaction does not run back on to the hot glass. Pass dry hydrogen from a cylinder, town gas or bottled gas, through the tube. Test to make sure that no air is in the apparatus. Heat the oxides.

The copper(II) oxide glows red-hot and changes to red-brown copper. The yellow lead(II) oxide changes to silver-like balls of molten lead. Water vapour is formed and condenses on the cold parts of the tube. When the changes are complete, stop heating the tube but continue to pass the gas until the metals are cold. The copper(II) sulphate test proves that the liquid formed contains water.

$$CuO(s) + H_2(g) \rightarrow Cu(s) + H_2O(g \text{ then } l);$$
$$PbO(s) + H_2(g) \rightarrow Pb(s) + H_2O(g \text{ then } l)$$

Uses of hydrogen

1 *Fuels and flames.* Hydrogen gives out much heat when it burns. Coal gas and water gas contain about 50 per cent hydrogen. The *oxyhydrogen flame* uses oxygen and hydrogen to form a hot flame (over

2000 °C) that can melt most metals. In the *atomic hydrogen flame*, hydrogen is passed through an electric arc; it absorbs energy and forms atoms. The atoms re-combine when out of the arc and their energy is evolved as heat.

2 *Hardening of oils.* Vegetable and animal oils (e.g. olive oil, whale oil, cotton-seed oil, palm oil) are liquids and usually have a distinctive taste and smell. Oils combine with hydrogen under pressure, in the presence of nickel or palladium as a catalyst, to form solid fats. The process is called the *hydrogenation or hardening of oils.* The fats are used for food, cooking, and making soap and candles. Margarine is a fat made from oils by the use of hydrogen, and is used instead of butter.

3 *Making petrol.* Petrol contains about 14 per cent of combined hydrogen and coal about 5 per cent. Coal and hydrogen react under certain conditions to form a liquid which contains petrol. The process is *hydrogenation of coal.* It is used in countries which have plenty of coal but no crude oil.

4 *Balloons and airships.* Hydrogen is the lightest gas known. Its density is only half that of the second lightest gas, helium. It is used for filling weather balloons and some balloons that are used during wars.

5 *Haber process.* Hydrogen and nitrogen are used to manufacture ammonia (p. 22).

Action of metals on water and steam

To study the actions of sodium and potassium on water

(Reaction between water and sodium can be violent and must be demonstrated by the teacher. Potassium is even more reactive and dangerous.) Pour cold water into a vessel. Do not wet the sides above the water level, otherwise the sodium will stick to them during the experiment. Take sodium out of a bottle with dry tongs; never touch sodium with your fingers. (It is stored under petrol or naphtha because it reacts rapidly with moist air.) Use a dry knife to cut small pieces, each about the size of a rice grain. Drop one piece into the water. Note everything that happens. Add more pieces, one at a time. (Float a filter paper on the water and place one piece of sodium on it. The sodium cannot move and the heat produced makes the hydrogen burn.) Feel the solution between the fingers. Dip litmus or Universal Indicator paper into the solution. Pour the solution into an evaporating basin and evaporate to dryness. Look at the solid residue.

Repeat the whole test with tiny pieces of potassium, which reacts more vigorously and dangerously than sodium. Note any differences between the two reactions.

Potassium. The reaction between potassium and water is like that between sodium and water. It is more reactive than sodium and the hydrogen formed burns with a purple (lilac) flame.

$$2K(s \text{ or } l) + 2H_2O(l) \rightarrow H_2(g) + 2KOH(aq)$$

Sodium. This is a white, silvery, shiny metal. Its density (0.97 g/cm^3) is low and it floats on water. Sodium first melts to a silvery ball, moves on the water, gives off hydrogen, and gradually becomes smaller as it reacts to form sodium hydroxide. The solution feels soapy and turns litmus blue. Much heat is formed, but not enough to light the hydrogen if the sodium is moving. If the sodium sticks against the vessel or is on floating filter paper, the hydrogen burns with a yellow flame:

$$2Na(s \text{ or } l) + 2H_2O(l) \rightarrow H_2(g) + 2NaOH(aq)$$

The silvery ball becomes colourless when very small—it is then molten sodium hydroxide; it breaks into pieces with a noise as the reaction finishes.

To collect hydrogen formed when sodium reacts with water

Cut small pieces of sodium as already described and wrap in wire gauze. Leave space for the sodium to move in the gauze. If it cannot move, there is danger of an explosion during the experiment. Fill a boiling-tube with water and invert it in a beaker of water. Drop the cage into the beaker and move the boiling-tube over it to collect any gas formed (Fig. 5.7). Test the gas with a burning splint.

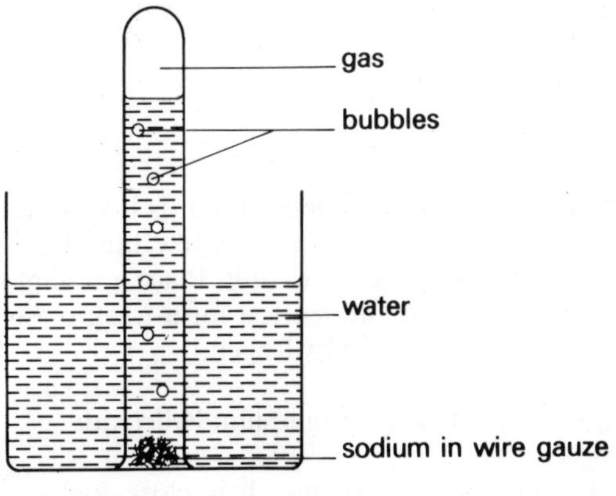

Fig. 5.7 Collecting the gas from sodium and water

To study the actions of calcium and magnesium on water

Calcium. Fill a beaker with water. Use tongs to drop calcium into the water. It sinks and reacts quickly to form hydrogen. Sometimes the gas makes some metal float. Test the solution with neutral litmus paper; this turns blue because the solution contains calcium hydroxide. The water becomes milky because the slightly soluble calcium hydroxide forms a suspension. Filter some of the suspension. Blow through glass tubing into the clear filtrate. It turns milky.

$$Ca(s) + 2H_2O(l) \rightarrow H_2(g) + Ca(OH)_2(aq)\text{, calcium hydroxide}$$

Collecting the gas. Add calcium to the beaker, cover with a filter funnel that has a short stem, and collect the gas formed in a boiling-tube (Fig. 5.8). Test it with a burning splint.

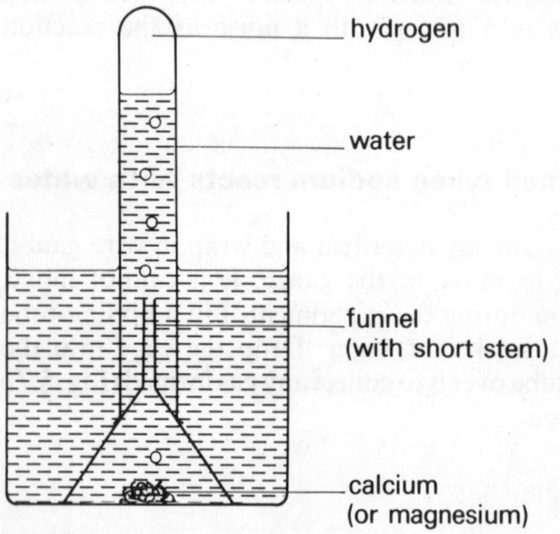

Fig. 5.8 Action of calcium or magnesium on water

Magnesium. Rub magnesium ribbon with sandpaper until it is bright and shiny, roll it into a ball and drop it into hot water. A few bubbles of hydrogen slowly form on the metal, which becomes dull. Place a boiling-tube filled with water over the magnesium and leave it for a week or so. Test any gas with a burning splint to prove it is hydrogen.

$$Mg(s) + 2H_2O(l) \rightarrow H_2(g) + Mg(OH)_2(aq)\text{, magnesium hydroxide}$$

Magnesium-copper couple. (A couple means two metals in close contact.) Dip one end of a short length of magnesium ribbon in copper(II) sulphate solution for a few seconds. Copper coats that end:

$$Mg(s) + Cu^{2+}(aq) \rightarrow Mg^{2+}(aq) + Cu(s)$$

Drop the ribbon into water. A steady stream of hydrogen bubbles form on the copper. After a few days the magnesium is covered with jelly-like magnesium hydroxide. (In the preparation of hydrogen, a zinc–copper couple, p. 49, reacts faster than zinc alone.)

Ionic equations for the above reactions are:

$$2Na(s) + 2H^+(aq) \rightarrow H_2(g) + 2Na^+(aq)$$
$$2K(s) + 2H^+(aq) \rightarrow H_2(g) + 2K^+(aq)$$
$$Ca(s) + 2H^+(aq) \rightarrow H_2(g) + Ca^{2+}(aq)$$
$$Mg(s) + 2H^+(aq) \rightarrow H_2(g) + Mg^{2+}(aq)$$

To study the action of steam on heated magnesium

Clean magnesium ribbon with sandpaper. Moisten but do not soak glass wool or sand with water. Arrange the apparatus as in Fig. 5.9 using a *wide* glass tube in the stopper. Heat the magnesium *strongly*. Heat conducted down the tube boils the water. The magnesium catches fire and burns brightly. Much heat is evolved (the tube usually swells or breaks) and the hot hydrogen may burn when it meets the air. (Light the hydrogen if necessary.) The residue is white magnesium oxide because the temperature is too high for the hydroxide:

$$Mg(s) + H_2O(g) \rightarrow H_2(g) + MgO(s), \text{ magnesium oxide}$$

(In the above experiment there is a slight danger of an explosion, and the stopper may be blown out if steam forms too fast. The following method avoids these dangers.)

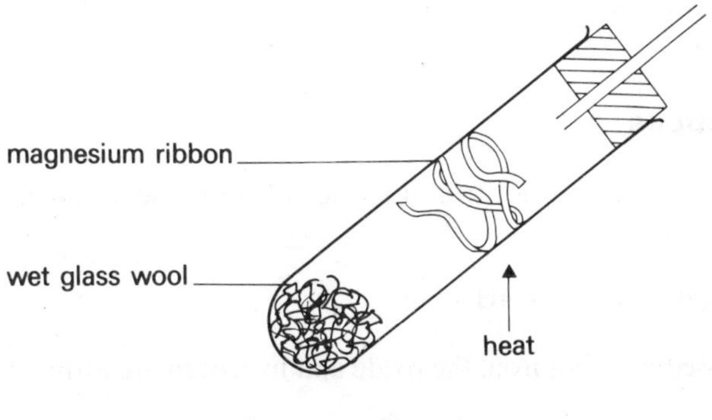

Fig. 5.9 Action of steam on heated magnesium

Alternative method. Use a small test-tube (75 × 10 mm) and no glass wool or stopper. Have water at the bottom of the tube and the magnesium near the top (otherwise the water boils away before reaction begins).

To study the action of steam on heated iron

Place iron powder in the middle part of a combustion tube. Arrange the apparatus as shown in Fig. 5.10 (but not with the gas-jar). Boil the water gently. Warm the end of the combustion tube where the steam enters so that it does not condense. When all the air is out of the apparatus, place the gas-jar in position. Heat the iron and pass steam *slowly*. The iron changes to blue-black triiron tetraoxide or iron(II) diiron(III) oxide and hydrogen collects in the jar:

$$3Fe(s) + 4H_2O(g) \rightleftharpoons 4H_2(g) + Fe_3O_4(s)$$

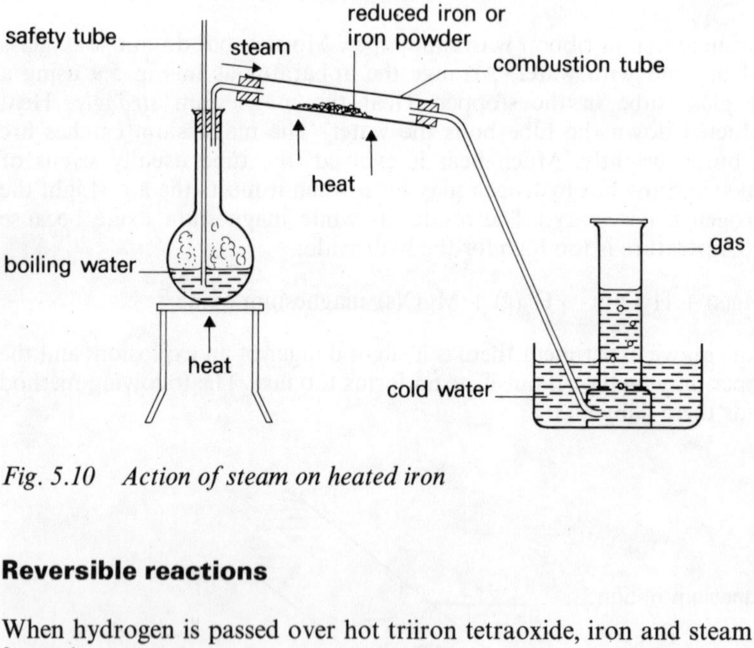

Fig. 5.10 Action of steam on heated iron

Reversible reactions

When hydrogen is passed over hot triiron tetraoxide, iron and steam are formed:

$$Fe_3O_4(s) + 4H_2(g) \rightarrow 3Fe(s) + 4H_2O(g)$$

When steam is passed over hot iron, the oxide and hydrogen are formed:

$$3Fe(s) + 4H_2O(g) \rightarrow Fe_3O_4(s) + 4H_2(g)$$

Clearly, the reaction is reversible.

A reversible reaction is one which can proceed in either direction depending on the conditions of temperature, pressure, concentration, etc., e.g.

$$A + B \rightleftharpoons C + D \text{ or } X \rightleftharpoons Y + Z$$

Examples of reversible reactions are:

$$2H_2(g) + O_2(g) \rightleftharpoons 2H_2O(g \text{ then } l);$$

$$CaCO_3(s) \rightleftharpoons CaO(s) + CO_2(g);$$

$$2SO_2(g) + O_2(g) \rightleftharpoons 2SO_3(g \text{ then } s);$$

$$NH_4Cl(s) \rightleftharpoons NH_3(g) + HCl(g)$$

Chemical equilibrium

If iron and steam are heated together *in a closed vessel*, they react to form triiron tetraoxide and hydrogen. As soon as these products are formed, they react to form iron and steam. After some time, the vessel contains definite amounts of iron, steam, triiron tetraoxide and hydrogen, which do not change if the temperature is constant. Chemical equilibrium exists. The rates of both forward and backward reactions are equal at equilibrium, which is *dynamic* and not static because the substances are still reacting.

Similarly, calcium carbonate decomposes completely if heated strongly in air so that carbon dioxide is allowed to escape. If heated *in a closed vessel*, it forms calcium oxide and carbon dioxide; these at once react to form calcium carbonate. Finally, an equilibrium exists and the amounts of calcium carbonate, calcium oxide and carbon dioxide do not change at constant temperature:

$$CaCO_3(s) \rightleftharpoons CaO(s) + CO_2(g)$$

Dynamic equilibrium

Bromine and water. Add a few cm^3 of bromine water to a beaker and stand it on white paper or a white tile. Use a teat pipette to add a few drops of bench sodium hydroxide to the bromine water, and observe any colour change. Now use a second pipette to add bench sulphuric acid and again observe any colour change. Add the alkali and acid alternately two or three times.

Bromine and water react reversibly to form hydrobromic acid, fully ionized, and the weakly acidic bromic(I) acid:

$$Br_2(aq) + H_2O(l) \rightleftharpoons H^+(aq) + Br^-(aq) + HBrO(aq)$$

The bromine is brown and the four other reactants in this equation are colourless. Addition of sodium hydroxide (i.e. of OH^- ions) removes the hydrogen ions. The forward reaction denoted by the top arrow takes place and the mixture becomes colourless. Addition of acid (i.e. of more H^+ ions) helps the backward reaction, denoted by the bottom arrow, to take place, and the mixture becomes brown again. This experiment shows that the reaction can go both ways. Under any given conditions there is an equilibrium; the rates of forward and backward reactions are equal. Changing the conditions (e.g. changing the hydrogen ion concentration in this experiment) alters the equilibrium, as the colour changes show clearly.

Iodine in two solvents. Iodine is soluble in potassium iodide solution (about M) and in trichloromethane (or tetrachloromethane). These two solvents do not mix and the potassium iodide solution floats on the denser trichloromethane.

To each of two test-tubes add a crystal of iodine; the crystals should be of about the same mass. To the first tube add aqueous potassium iodide solution (to a depth of about 2 cm); to the second tube add the same volume of trichloromethane or tetrachloromethane. Shake the tubes until the iodine dissolves, forming a brown solution with potassium iodide and a purple solution with the other solvent.

To the first tube add an equal volume of the trichloromethane and shake gently; the trichloromethane becomes slightly purple. To the second tube add an equal volume of aqueous potassium iodide and shake gently; the upper potassium iodide layer becomes slightly brown. This shows that the added solvent removes a little iodine from the original solvent in the tubes.

Now shake each tube vigorously (take care). Compare the colours of the potassium iodide solutions in the two tubes and of the trichloromethane solutions. The potassium iodide solutions should be the same brown colour and the other solutions should be the same purple colour. The experiment shows that the iodine distributes itself between the two solvents in the same way in the two tubes; equilibrium is reached:

$$I_2 \text{ (in KI)} \rightleftharpoons I_2 \text{ (in } CHCl_3 \text{ or } CCl_4\text{)}$$

The top arrow shows that iodine moved from the potassium iodide layer into the trichloromethane layer, and the bottom arrow indicates the reverse change. Both changes continue all the time, and at equilibrium the rate of the forward reaction equals the rate of the backward reaction.

Disturb the equilibrium in one tube as follows. Use a teat pipette to remove the upper potassium iodide layer. Now add an equal volume of fresh aqueous potassium iodide to this tube and shake. The new potassium iodide turns brown showing that it removes iodine from the lower trichloromethane layer. Repeat the process two or three times until almost all of the iodine has left the trichloromethane solution.

Reactivity series

Potassium displaces hydrogen most easily from water, and iron displaces it least easily. The list of metals, in order of their reactivity with water is: potassium, sodium, calcium, magnesium, and iron. We can add more metals by considering the action of acids on metals. Zinc reacts much faster than iron with dilute acids; lead forms hydrogen only with hot concentrated hydrochloric acid; copper never forms hydrogen. The list of common metals in order of their reactivity is:

1 Potassium	**5** Aluminium	**9** (Hydrogen)
2 Sodium	**6** Zinc	**10** Copper
3 Calcium	**7** Iron	**11** Mercury
4 Magnesium	**8** Lead	

This is called the *metal reactivity* or *activity series*. Remember the series by the 'words':

PoSo CaMAl ZIL(Hy)CoM. (Initials of the metals.)

Metal	Action on the metal of: Water	Steam	Acids	Air	Oxide
Potassium Sodium	Violent	Explosive	Explosive	React at once	Very soluble
Calcium	Moderate	Violent	Violent		Slightly soluble
Magnesium	Very slow	Rapid	Rapid	Burn readily to oxides	
Aluminium Zinc Iron	No action	Slow	Moderate		Insoluble in water
Lead Copper Mercury		No action	No action	Burn slowly to oxides	

To examine the action of an electric current on dilute sulphuric acid (the 'electrolysis of water')

Connect the apparatus (a coulometer) as in Fig. 5.11, but without liquid in it. The platinum electrode connected to the positive (red) terminal of the battery is the anode, and that connected to the negative (blue) terminal is the cathode. Pour distilled water into the coulometer. Adjust the rheostat (variable resistance) until its resistance is a maximum. Close

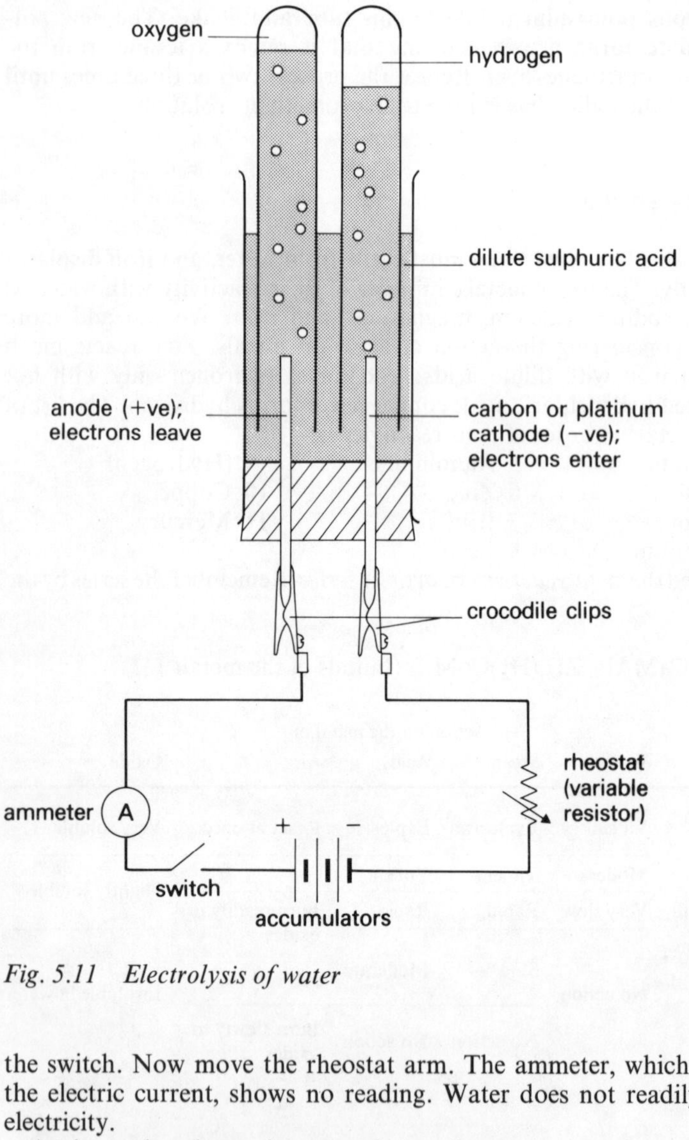

Fig. 5.11 Electrolysis of water

the switch. Now move the rheostat arm. The ammeter, which measures the electric current, shows no reading. Water does not readily conduct electricity.

Again make the resistance of the rheostat a maximum. Fill the coulometer with dilute sulphuric acid and adjust the rheostat. The ammeter shows a reading and gases form at the electrodes. Allow the gases to collect for some time. The volume of gas from the cathode is twice that from the anode (the ratio may not be exactly 2:1 because one gas is more soluble than the other). Test the gas formed at the anode with a glowing splint; it is oxygen. Test the gas formed at the cathode with a burning splint; it is hydrogen.

Commercial preparation of hydrogen

From natural gas, petroleum or water gas. Catalytic cracking (p. 304) of petroleum naphtha at about 700 °C produces a mixture of methane, hydrogen and other gases. Natural gas is mainly methane. Both the mixture and natural gas contain hydrogen sulphide and other sulphur compounds; they are removed because they would 'poison' the catalyst used later. The sulphur-free gases are mixed with steam and passed over a nickel catalyst; or are mixed with oxygen:

$$CH_4 + H_2O \rightarrow CO + 3H_2;$$

$$2CH_4 + O_2 \rightarrow 2CO + 4H_2$$

The product (or water gas, p. 209) and steam are then passed over an iron catalyst at 500 °C and more hydrogen is produced:

$$H_2O(g) + CO(g) \rightleftharpoons CO_2(g) + H_2(g) + \text{heat}$$

The process is repeated at about 200 °C and the final content of carbon monoxide is negligible. The carbon dioxide is removed by cooling the gases and dissolving it either in water under pressure or in hot potassium carbonate solution, which reacts with it to form the hydrogencarbonate. The final hydrogen is about 97% pure.
By electrolysis. Hydrogen is obtained by electrolysis of sodium hydroxide in countries where electricity is cheap and is a by-product in the manufacture of sodium hydroxide by the electrolysis of brine, p. 280.

Questions

1 How would you obtain a sample of the gases dissolved in tap water? Describe how you would determine accurately the percentage by volume of the two principal constituents of the sample. What kind of result would you expect, and how does it differ from the percentage of the same constituents in atmospheric air? (C.)

2 Draw a clear labelled diagram of the complete apparatus you would use to show that when dry hydrogen is burned in air a colourless liquid is formed. Indicate two ways in which you would satisfy yourself that the liquid obtained is water. State how, and under what conditions, the following react with water: (*a*) calcium; (*b*) coke; (*c*) ammonia. In each case name the products of the reaction. (N.)

3 Describe experiments which show how sodium, magnesium and iron react with water or steam (do not include experiments on the rusting of iron). The reaction with iron is said to be 'reversible'. Explain what is meant by this statement, and outline how you would show experimentally that it is true. (C.)

4 (*a*) Describe the commercial preparation of hydrogen from steam and coke. Give two commercial uses for hydrogen, excluding its use as a fuel. (*b*) How is oxygen manufactured? Give two different uses for oxygen. (*c*) How does distilled water differ from (i) rain water, and (ii) tap water? (L.)

5 What do you understand by a reversible reaction? Give three characteristics of a catalyst. Explain the meanings of the following terms, giving one example of each: efflorescence, deliquescence, and hygroscopic substance. (C.)

6 What is meant by the statement that hydrogen is a reducing agent? Describe an experiment which illustrates this property of hydrogen. How would you collect and identify the hydrogen compound that is formed? (N.)

7 Explain briefly how hydrogen can be obtained from water gas. Give labelled diagrams of apparatus (*a*) to show hydrogen diffuses more rapidly than air, (*b*) to find the composition of water by mass by passing dry hydrogen over heated copper(II) oxide. (N.)

6
The Nature of Matter

Dalton's Atomic Theory (1807)

Dalton (1766–1844), an English schoolmaster, put forward the first definite theory of atoms. His Atomic Theory is:

1 *Matter is made of tiny indivisible particles called atoms.*
2 *Atoms can be neither created nor destroyed.*
3 *All the atoms of one element are the same, especially in mass;* they are different from the atoms of all other elements.
4 *When atoms combine, they do so in small whole numbers* to form 'compound atoms' (molecules). The 'compound atoms' of one substance are the same.

Atoms and molecules

Many substances consist of tiny particles called molecules.

A molecule is the smallest electrically neutral particle of an element or compound which can exist on its own.

Elements and some groups of atoms form ions which are either positively or negatively charged. Therefore the words 'electrically neutral' are necessary in the definition.

There are about 90 naturally-occurring elements. If one piece of an element was divided over and over again, a tiny particle called an atom would finally be obtained.

An atom is the smallest electrically neutral indivisible particle of an element that can take part in a chemical change.

A molecule of a compound contains at least 2 atoms. The atoms of noble gases (helium, neon, argon, etc.) exist on their own; therefore, one of these atoms is also a molecule.

Atomicity of elements

The atomicity of an element is the number of atoms in one of its molecules.

The atomicity of the noble gases is 1; they are *monatomic*. The atomicity of oxygen, nitrogen, hydrogen is 2; they are *diatomic*. Ozone (O_3) is *triatomic* and phosphorus vapour (P_4) is *tetratomic*. Sulphur is S_8.

Motion of molecules

Brownian movement

Place a speck of Aquadag, diluted Indian ink (suspensions of carbon particles) or toothpaste, about the size of a pinhead, in about 5 cm^3 of water and stir well. Add one drop of the mixture to a microscope slide and cover with a cover-slip. Illuminate the slide from the side and focus on the liquid (use a 4 mm objective lens). Do the solid particles in the liquid move?

In 1827 an English botanist, Robert Brown, noticed that pollen grains in water burst to form tiny particles which continually moved. All tiny particles suspended in a liquid or gas show the same irregular *Brownian movement*.

The cause of the Brownian movement is bombardment of the particles by molecules of the liquid. It is evidence for the existence of molecules and for their perpetual motion. A large particle receives so many millions of blows each instant that there is no resultant force on it. A tiny particle momentarily receives more blows on one side than on its opposite side, and therefore it moves slightly. The resultant force continually changes direction and the movement of a tiny particle is zig-zag.

Diffusion of a gas or liquid or solute is the spreading movement of the substance due to the motion of its own molecules or ions.

To demonstrate the diffusion of liquids

Copper(II) sulphate solution. Drop a large crystal of copper(II) sulphate (or other coloured crystal) into a tall beaker of water. Leave the beaker for several weeks and do not move it. The crystal slowly dissolves and the *blue solution spreads or diffuses* through the water until the whole liquid is uniformly blue.

Copper(II) sulphate and ethanol. Pour copper(II) sulphate solution into a beaker. Use a pipette to run ethanol slowly down the inside of the beaker. The less dense ethanol forms a layer above the blue solution. Leave for several weeks. The two liquids gradually mix by diffusion.

To demonstrate the diffusion of gases

1 Invert a jar of hydrogen over a jar of air (which is 14.4 times denser) and leave for 5 minutes. Test both jars separately with a burning splint. The gas in both jars explodes, showing that some of the light hydrogen diffuses downwards.

Place a jar of air over a jar of carbon dioxide ($1\frac{1}{2}$ times denser) and leave for 5 minutes. Test the gas in both jars with calcium hydroxide solution which turns milky. Therefore, some of the dense carbon dioxide diffuses upwards.

2 Add one drop of starch solution (turned blue by iodine) to the middle of a filter paper. Put one iodine crystal in an evaporating basin and place the paper on the basin. The starch spot soon turns blue. This shows that iodine vapour (about 8 times denser than air) diffuses upwards in air.

These experiments show that *the molecules of liquids and gases move freely*. Two liquids that are soluble in each other finally mix to form a uniform solution, and a gas moves to fill the whole of the vessel in which it is placed. Diffusion of liquids is much slower than diffusion of gases.

To find if hydrogen diffuses faster than air

Close an unglazed porous pot with a rubber stopper fitted with a long U-tube containing coloured water. Invert a jar of hydrogen or town gas over the pot (Fig. 6.1). Watch the water levels in the U-tube. The liquid falls rapidly in the left hand tube. This shows that *hydrogen diffuses faster than air* through the tiny pores of the pot. Before the hydrogen is placed over the pot, air diffuses in and out through the pores. The volumes moving in and out are equal, and therefore the water levels do

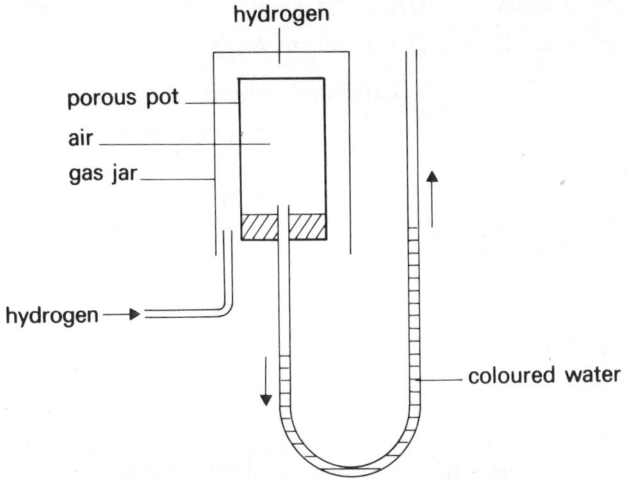

Fig. 6.1 Diffusion of gases

not change. When the hydrogen is over the pot, hydrogen diffuses in faster than air diffuses out. The pressure inside the pot rises and forces the water level down at one side and up at the other.

Remove the jar of hydrogen. The liquid now rises in the left hand tube, because the hydrogen inside the pot diffuses out faster than air diffuses in. Finally the levels become equal.

To find if carbon dioxide diffuses faster than air

Repeat the above experiment, using carbon dioxide instead of hydrogen. As carbon dioxide is denser than air, it is necessary to use a cardboard cover to keep the gas in the jar. The results are the opposite of those obtained when using hydrogen, showing that *air diffuses faster than carbon dioxide.*

Graham's Law of Diffusion

Graham's Law states that the rate of diffusion of a gas is inversely proportional to the square root of its density.

Oxygen is 16 times denser than hydrogen; therefore hydrogen diffuses 4 times faster than oxygen. Hydrogen, the lightest gas known, diffuses faster than any other gas.

$$\frac{\text{Rate of diffusion of gas A}}{\text{Rate of diffusion of gas B}} = \sqrt{\frac{\text{Density of gas B}}{\text{Density of gas A}}}$$

$$= \sqrt{\frac{\text{Relative molecular mass of gas B}}{\text{Relative molecular mass of gas A}}}$$

(See p. 79.) Densities can be either g/cm^3, g/dm^3 or vapour densities.

If equal volumes of gases diffuse, the rates of diffusion are inversely proportional to the time, i.e.

$$\frac{\text{Time of diffusion of gas A}}{\text{Time of diffusion of gas B}} = \sqrt{\frac{\text{Density of gas A}}{\text{Density of gas B}}}$$

Use the above formulae to show that (*a*) if equal volumes of hydrogen and air diffuse through a porous plug in 82 and 310 seconds respectively, air is about 14.3 times denser than hydrogen, and (*b*) if oxygen (relative molecular mass 32) diffuses 1.22 times faster than ozone, the relative molecular mass of ozone is 48.

Laws of chemical combination of elements

Law of Conservation of Mass (1774)

Matter is neither created nor destroyed in a chemical reaction.

This law is also called the *Law of Indestructibility of Matter*. It means that the mass of the substances before chemical reaction (reactants) is exactly equal to the mass of the substances after reaction (products). We can illustrate this law by finding the mass of two chemicals, letting them react, and finding the mass of the products. There should be no change in mass.

Explanation of conservation of mass

Matter is made up of atoms. Atoms can be neither created nor destroyed. Therefore, matter can be neither created nor destroyed.

To illustrate the Law of Conservation of Mass

Arrange the apparatus as in Fig. 6.2. The two reactants must not mix. Find the mass of the whole apparatus. Touch only the rim of the flask with the tips of clean fingers, to avoid adding moisture or dust to it. Open the stopper for a moment so that the thread is free; the test-tube drops and the two solutions mix, forming a white precipitate:

$$BaCl_2(aq) + H_2SO_4(aq) \rightarrow BaSO_4(s) + 2HCl(aq)$$

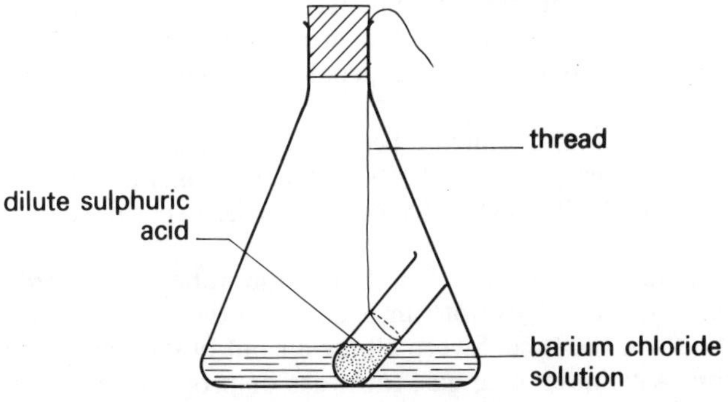

Fig. 6.2 To illustrate the Law of Conservation of Mass

Again find the mass of the whole apparatus. It is the same.

Other pairs of substances can be used, and equations of some examples are below. Each pair forms a precipitate but *no gases are evolved* and *there is little heat change* otherwise water may evaporate.

$$CuSO_4(aq) + 2NaOH(aq) \rightarrow Cu(OH)_2(s) + Na_2SO_4(aq)$$

$$Pb(NO_3)_2(aq) + H_2SO_4(aq) \rightarrow PbSO_4(s) + 2HNO_3(aq)$$

$$Pb(NO_3)_2(aq) + 2HCl(aq) \rightarrow PbCl_2(s) + 2HNO_3(aq)$$

$$AgNO_3(aq) + HCl(aq) \rightarrow AgCl(s) + HNO_3(aq)$$

Law of Definite Proportions

A compound always contains the same elements combined together in the same proportions by mass.

Explanation of definite proportions (constant composition)

A compound is made of molecules which are the same. Each molecule contains the same elements and the same number of atoms of each element. All atoms of an element have the same mass. Therefore, a compound contains the same elements combined in the same proportions by mass.

To illustrate the Law of Definite Proportions

We can illustrate this law by preparing copper(II) oxide, or lead(II) oxide, by different methods and then finding the proportions of metal and oxygen in the samples by passing hydrogen, coal gas, town gas, propane or bottled gas over them.

The experiment is long and difficult because nine masses must be determined: masses of three porcelain boats, porcelain boats plus metal oxide, and porcelain boat plus metal. Demonstrate the experiment but omit the weighings.

Arrange the apparatus as in Fig. 6.3. Slope the tube downwards slightly so that water formed does not run back on to the hot glass and crack it. Put the boats in the tube. Sweep all the air out of the apparatus with hydrogen from a cylinder, coal gas, town gas or propane and then light the gas at the jet. Heat the boats, using a flame spreader. The black copper(II) oxide is reduced to red-brown copper, and drops of water condense on the cold parts of the combustion tube:

$$CuO(s) + H_2(g) \rightarrow Cu(s) + H_2O(g \text{ or } l)$$
$$CuO(s) + CO(g) \rightarrow Cu(s) + CO_2(g)$$
$$3CuO(s) + CH_4(g) \rightarrow 3Cu(s) + CO(g) + 2H_2O(g \text{ or } l)$$

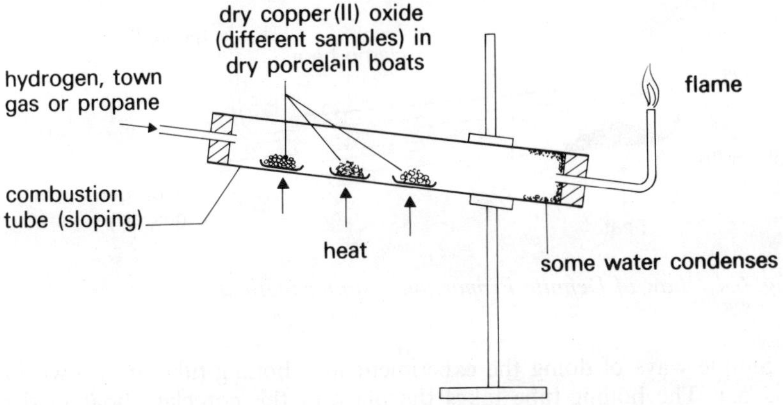

Fig. 6.3 To illustrate the Law of Definite Proportions

When the changes appear to be complete, stop heating the tube but continue to pass gas over the boats, otherwise air may enter and oxidize the hot copper. [In a hot Bunsen flame methane reduces copper(II) oxide completely, partially reduces iron(III) oxide, and does not reduce lead(II) oxide.]

			Copper oxide sample	
		1	2	3
1	Mass of porcelain boat	$= a$		
2	Mass of porcelain boat and copper oxide	$= b$		
3	Mass of porcelain boat and copper	$= c$		
2–3	Mass of OXYGEN	$= (b-c)$		
3–1	Mass of copper	$= (c-a)$		
	Mass of copper which combines with 1 g of oxygen	$= \dfrac{(c-a)}{(b-c)}$		

If the three masses of copper, $\dfrac{(c-a)}{(b-c)}$, are the same, within experimental uncertainty, the results illustrate the law.

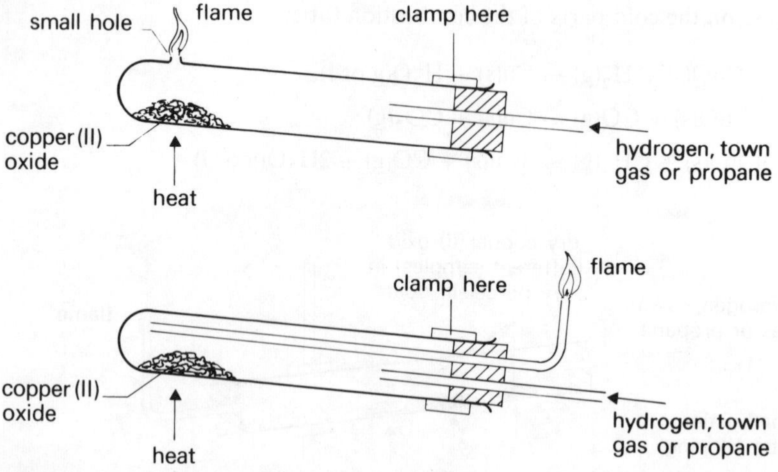

Fig. 6.4 Law of Definite Proportions (simple method)

Simple ways of doing the experiment in a boiling-tube are shown in Fig. 6.4. The boiling-tube takes the place of the porcelain boat in the readings and results.

No one-hole stopper and delivery tube is required if small test-tubes (75 × 10 mm) are used. The rubber tubing from the gas supply fits into the mouth of this size tube (and can be held instead of using a clamp). Take care that the flame used to heat the oxide does not burn the rubber.

Law of Multiple Proportions (1803)

If elements A and B combine to form more than one compound, then the masses of A which separately combine with a fixed mass of B are in a simple ratio.

To illustrate the Law of Multiple Proportions

We can illustrate the law by using black copper(II) and red copper(I) oxide. The masses of copper which combine with 1 g of oxygen can be determined by reducing with gas, and the masses should be in a simple ratio, e.g. 2 : 1, 3 : 2, 3 : 4, etc. The three oxides of lead [lead(II) oxide, PbO, red lead oxide, Pb_3O_4, and lead(IV) oxide, PbO_2] can be used instead of copper oxides.

Demonstrate the experiment but omit the six weighings. Add black copper oxide [copper(II) oxide, CuO] to one porcelain boat and red copper oxide [copper(I) oxide, Cu_2O] to another. Find the masses of the boats and contents. Heat them in a combustion tube and pass gas over them as described in the previous experiment. Finally, find the masses of the cold boats and copper.

$$Cu_2O + H_2 \rightarrow 2Cu + H_2O; CuO + H_2 \rightarrow Cu + H_2O$$

			Black copper(II) oxide	Red copper(I) oxide
1	Mass of boat	$= a$		
2	Mass of boat and oxide	$= b$		
3	Mass of boat and copper	$= c$		
3–1	Mass of copper	$= (c-a)$		
2–3	Mass of OXYGEN	$= (b-c)$		
	Mass of copper which combines with 1 g of oxygen	$= \dfrac{(c-a)}{(b-c)}$		

If the masses $\dfrac{(c-a)}{(b-c)}$ are in a simple ratio within experimental uncertainty, the results illustrate the law.

Masses of atoms and molecules

One gram of hydrogen contains six hundred thousand million, million, million atoms. Clearly it is useless to measure the mass of atoms or molecules in grams or any other unit of mass. Originally, the mass of a hydrogen atom, which is the lightest atom, was taken as the standard and the masses of other atoms and molecules were compared with it. Nowadays, one-twelfth of an atom of carbon-12 is taken as the standard mass, and the definitions are:

The relative atomic mass of an element is the mass of one atom of the element divided by the mass of one-twelfth of an atom of carbon-12.

The relative molecular mass of an element or compound is the mass of one molecule divided by the mass of one-twelfth of an ATOM of carbon-12.

$$\text{Relative atomic mass} = \frac{\text{Mass of 1 atom of element}}{\frac{1}{12} \times \text{mass of 1 atom of carbon-12}}$$

$$\text{Relative molecular mass} = \frac{\text{Mass of 1 molecule of substance}}{\frac{1}{12} \times \text{mass of 1 ATOM of carbon-12}}$$

By these definitions, the relative atomic mass of hydrogen is 1.008 and its relative molecular mass is 2.016. The symbols for relative atomic and molecular masses are A_r and M_r respectively.

Formula mass is used instead of molecular mass for substances which do not exist as molecules, e.g. ionic compounds.

One mole is the amount of substance of a system which contains as many elementary units (atoms, molecules, ions or electrons) as there are carbon atoms in 12 g of carbon-12.

The *molar mass M* of a substance is the mass of one mole. Its SI unit is $kg\,mol^{-1}$ but in this book we shall use $g\,mol^{-1}$. The molar mass of:

oxygen atoms is 16 g (formerly called 1 *g-atom*),
oxygen molecules is 32 g (formerly called 1 *g-molecule*),
hydroxide ions, OH^-, is 17 g (formerly called 1 *g-ion*),
sodium chloride, $(Na^+ + Cl^-)$, is 58.5 g,
sulphuric acid, H_2SO_4, is 98 g,
sulphuric acid, $\frac{1}{2}H_2SO_4$, is 49 g,
calcium hydroxide, $Ca(OH)_2$ is 74 g, and of
calcium hydroxide, $\frac{1}{2}Ca(OH)_2$, is 37 g.

The species $\frac{1}{2}H_2SO_4$ and $\frac{1}{2}Ca(OH)_2$ are useful because their molar masses produce 1 mole of $H^+(aq)$ and $OH^-(aq)$ respectively.

Whatever the mass of the atom or molecule, one mole or one molar mass always contains the same number of atoms or molecules. This is the *Avogadro constant L*, which is $6.022 \times 10^{23}\,mol^{-1}$.

Molecular theory of gases

Gay-Lussac's Law

In 1781 Cavendish showed that hydrogen and oxygen react in the ratio of 2:1 by volume. In about 1802 Gay-Lussac obtained results like these:

1 volume of hydrogen reacts with 1 volume of chlorine to form 2 volumes of hydrogen chloride;

2 volumes of carbon monoxide react with 1 volume of oxygen to form 2 volumes of carbon dioxide.

Gay-Lussac's Law states that when gases react, they do so in volumes which bear a simple ratio to one another, and to the volume of the gaseous products, provided all the volumes are measured at the same temperature and pressure.

More examples of the law are:

2 volumes of ammonia decompose to form 1 volume of nitrogen and 3 volumes of hydrogen;

Carbon, a solid, reacts with 1 volume of oxygen to form 1 volume of carbon dioxide.

The Gas Laws

Boyle's Law states that the volume of a given mass of gas is inversely proportional to its pressure, if the temperature is constant.

The law means that the volume of a gas doubles if its pressure halves, and so on. If V is the volume of a given mass of gas at pressure P (temperature constant):

$$V \propto \frac{1}{P} \quad \text{and} \quad P \propto \frac{1}{V}$$

i.e. PV = a constant (at constant temperature)

A volume V_1 measured at pressure P_1 can be converted to volume V_2 at any other pressure P_2 because

$$P_1V_1 = P_2V_2 \text{ (at constant temperature)}$$

The *absolute scale of temperature* is related to the Celsius scale by the formula:

Absolute temperature = 273 + Celsius temperature

e.g. $0\,°C = 273 + 0 = 273\,K$ (kelvin)

$30\,°C = 273 + 30 = 303\,K$

$-20\,°C = 273 + (-20) = 253\,K$

Charles' Law states that the volume of a given mass of gas is directly proportional to its absolute temperature, if the pressure is constant.

The law means that the volume of a gas doubles if its absolute temperature doubles, and so on. If V is the volume of a given mass of gas at absolute temperature T (pressure constant):

$$V \propto T, \text{ i.e. } \frac{V}{T} = \text{a constant}$$

A volume V_1 measured at absolute temperature T_1 can be converted to volume V_2 at any other absolute temperature T_2 because

$$\frac{V_1}{T_1} = \frac{V_2}{T_2} \text{ (at constant pressure)}$$

The gas laws combine to give the *gas equation*:

$$\frac{P_1V_1}{T_1} = \frac{P_2V_2}{T_2}$$

The volume and density of a gas depend on its temperature and pressure. Usually they are given at *Standard Temperature and Pressure* (*s.t.p.*) which is 0 °C (273 K) and 760 mmHg or 101 325 pascal (Pa) or 1 atmosphere (1 atm) pressure. (More exactly, 273 K should be 273.15 K.)

Effect of water vapour

Usually a gas is collected over water before its volume is measured. The gas is saturated with water vapour. The total pressure is due to the gas and the water vapour:

Atmospheric pressure = Pressure of gas + Vapour pressure of water

i.e. Pressure of gas = Atmospheric pressure – Vapour pressure of water

The vapour pressure of water at any temperature is obtained from tables in reference books.

Calculation on the gas laws

The volume of a given mass of gas is 360 cm³ at 50 °C and 700 mmHg pressure. What will be the volume at s.t.p.?

Using the gas equation:

$$\frac{P_1V_1}{T_1} = \frac{P_2V_2}{T_2}$$

$$\therefore \frac{700 \times 360}{273+50} = \frac{760 \times V_2}{273}$$

$$V_2 = \frac{700 \times 360 \times 273}{323 \times 760}$$

$$= 280.2\,\text{cm}^3$$

(Note that in such calculations, one of the numbers 273 and 760 is in the numerator and one in the denominator.) It is interesting to note that the volume at s.t.p. is the same as at the following:

T (°C)	–5	4	14	18	23	27
P (mmHg)	746	771	799	810	824	835

Avogadro's Principle or Law (1811)

The molar volume of a gas is the volume occupied by one mole of the gas at standard temperature and pressure (s.t.p.).

Use a book of data to calculate molar volumes (molar mass/density) at s.t.p. of various gases. Examples are:

	Molar mass	Density at s.t.p. (g/dm^3)	Molar volume (cm^3)
Hydrogen	2.016	0.089 88	22 430
Oxygen	32.00	1.429	23 390
Nitrogen	28.01	1.251	23 370
Ammonia	17.03	0.762 1	22 350

Avogadro's Principle states that 1 mole of any gas occupies the same volume at the same temperature and pressure, or that equal volumes of all gases under the same conditions of temperature and pressure contain equal numbers of molecules.

The value of this principle is that we can write *molecules* instead of *volumes* in any reaction concerning gases, e.g.

2 volumes of hydrogen + 1 volume of oxygen → 2 volumes of steam

∴ 2 *molecules* of hydrogen + 1 *molecule* of oxygen → 2 *molecules* of steam

It is assumed that the volume of one mole of a gas is 22 400 cm^3 or 22.4 dm^3 at s.t.p. and approximately 24 dm^3 at room temperature and pressure. The exact value, based on an ideal gas, at s.t.p. is 22 414 cm^3.

Deductions from Avogadro's Principle or Law

1 *The hydrogen molecule contains two atoms.*

a 1 volume of hydrogen + 1 volume of chlorine → 2 volumes of hydrogen chloride

Therefore, by Avogadro's Principle:

x molecules of hydrogen + x molecules of chlorine → $2x$ molecules of hydrogen chloride

i.e. $\frac{1}{2}$ molecule of hydrogen + $\frac{1}{2}$ molecule of chlorine → 1 molecule of hydrogen chloride

1 molecule of hydrogen chloride must contain a whole number of hydrogen atoms, because atoms are indivisible.

∴ $\frac{1}{2}$ molecule of hydrogen contains 1, 2 or 3, etc. atoms,
i.e. 1 molecule of hydrogen contains 2, 4 or 6, etc. atoms.

A molecule of hydrogen contains at least 2 *atoms* and its formula is H_2, H_4, or H_6, etc.
b Experiments indicate that 1 *volume of hydrogen never forms more than* 2 *volumes of a gaseous compound*. Therefore 1 molecule of hydrogen probably contains only 2 atoms and its formula is H_2.

$$\begin{matrix} H \\ | \\ H \end{matrix} + \begin{matrix} Cl \\ | \\ Cl \end{matrix} \rightarrow \begin{matrix} H \\ | \\ Cl \end{matrix} + \begin{matrix} H \\ | \\ Cl \end{matrix}$$

If its formula was H_4 we would expect 1 volume of hydrogen to form 4 volumes of a gas on occasions, e.g.

$$\underset{(1\ \text{volume})}{H_4} + X_4\ (\text{or } 2X_2) \rightarrow \underset{(4\ \text{volumes})}{4HX}$$

c *Hydrogen chloride forms only one sodium compound*, which contains no hydrogen. If the formula of hydrogen chloride was H_2Cl_2 we would expect two salts: $NaHCl_2$ and Na_2Cl_2. Therefore the formula is probably HCl and not H_2Cl_2, H_3Cl_3, etc., and 1 molecule contains only 1 atom of hydrogen. However, 1 molecule contains $\frac{1}{2}$ molecule of hydrogen (proved above).

$\therefore$ $\frac{1}{2}$ molecule of hydrogen = 1 atom only,
i.e. 1 molecule of hydrogen = 2 atoms only.

2 *Relative molecular mass of a gas is twice its vapour density.*

$$\text{The vapour density of a gas} = \frac{\text{Mass of any volume of the gas}}{\text{Mass of the same volume of hydrogen}}$$

(at the same temperature and pressure).

(by Avogadro's Principle)

$$= \frac{\text{Mass of 1 molecule of the gas}}{\text{Mass of 1 molecule of hydrogen}}$$

$$= \frac{\text{Mass of 1 molecule of the gas}}{\text{Mass of 2 atoms of hydrogen}}$$

(since hydrogen is diatomic)

$$= \tfrac{1}{2} \times \frac{\text{Mass of 1 molecule of the gas}}{\text{Mass of 1 atom of hydrogen}}$$

$$= \tfrac{1}{2} \times \text{Relative molecular mass}$$

(if H = 1), or

$$\frac{1}{2.016} \times \text{Relative molecular mass}$$

(if C = 12, i.e. H = 1.008)

Therefore,

Relative molecular mass = 2 × Vapour density (H = 1)

or Relative molecular mass = 2.016 × Vapour density (C = 12)

We shall use the simpler relation unless otherwise stated.

	Formula	Molecular mass	Vapour density
Oxygen	O_2	32	16
Carbon dioxide	CO_2	44	22
Hydrogen chloride	HCl	36.5	18.25
Ammonia	NH_3	17	8.5
Air	—	—	14.4

If a gas has a vapour density more than 14.4 it is denser than air. For example, carbon dioxide is $22 \div 14.4$ (about $1\frac{1}{2}$) times denser than air, and air is $14.4 \div 8.5$ (about 2) times denser than ammonia.

To estimate the length of a molecule

The area of water surface covered by a known volume of acid is measured. A solution of the acid in benzene or petroleum ether is used. The solvent evaporates quickly and leaves a film of acid, assumed to be one molecule thick. Suitable acids are stearic, palmitic and oleic acids.

Clamp a large filter funnel (minimum diameter 15 cm) over a sink. Use rubber tubing to connect the funnel stem to a water tap, Fig. 6.5. Fill the funnel with water until it runs over the rim in order to clean it. Turn off the tap.

Use a small beaker or tube to remove a little water from the funnel; the water level is just below the rim and it is possible to add acid solution later. Do not touch the water with your fingers; grease or impurity spoils the results.

Dissolve $0.1\,cm^3$ (0.1 g) of the acid in $1\,dm^3$ of benzene or petroleum ether. Add a few cm^3 of solution to a burette (or teat pipette with a fine point) with its end about 1 cm above the water.

Sprinkle fine sulphur powder (or chalk dust, powdered talc or lycopodium powder) over the water surface. Add one drop of acid solution to the centre of the water; observe how it pushes away the powder. Add one or two more drops until the solution covers most of the water surface. Measure the diameter of the film of acid and calculate its area.

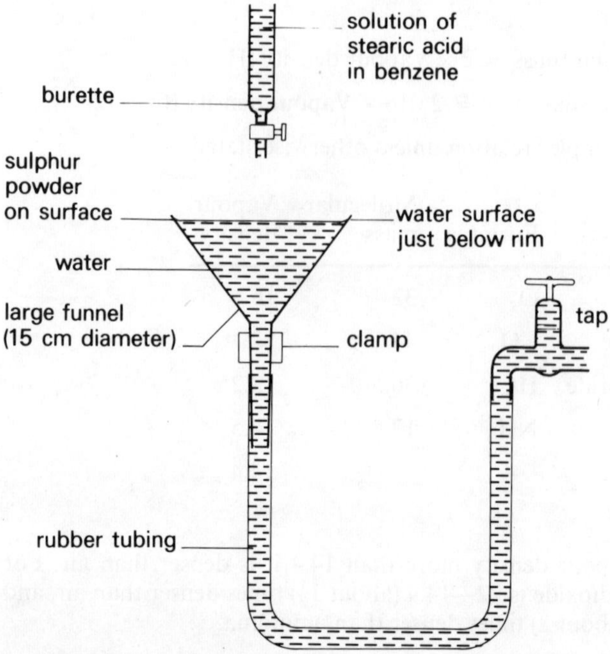

Fig. 6.5 Measuring the length of a molecule of acid

Finally estimate the volume of one drop of acid solution by dropping $1\,cm^3$ into a beaker and counting the drops added.

Area of acid film $= A\ (cm^2)$

Number of drops in $1\,cm^3 = n$

$1000\,cm^3$ of solution contain $0.1\,cm^3$ of acid.

$\therefore$ $1\,cm^3$ of solution contains $0.000\,1\,cm^3$ of acid.

$\therefore$ 1 drop of solution contains $\frac{0.000\,1}{n}\,cm^3$ of acid.

If the thickness of the acid film $= t$ cm (which we assume to be the length of one molecule) the volume of acid in one drop = thickness × area $= tA$.

$tA = 0.000\,1/n$. Calculate t.

Its value is about 2 nanometre or 2×10^{-7} cm.

Questions

(Where necessary assume that 1 cm^3 of hydrogen at s.t.p. has a mass of 0.000 09 g.)

1 State the law of definite proportions. In an experiment 1.288 g of copper oxide were obtained from 1.03 g of copper. In another experiment, 3.672 g of copper oxide gave, on reduction, 2.938 g of copper. Show that these figures are in accordance with the law of definite proportions. (C.)

2 4.90 g of copper oxide yielded 3.92 g of copper when reduced by town gas. Calculate the mass of copper oxide required to yield (*a*) 4 g and (*b*) 3.64 g of copper. State the law you make use of in your calculations. (N.)

3 Three oxides of a metal contain respectively 7.15, 9.35 and 13.4 per cent of oxygen. Show that these figures illustrate a chemical law, and state this law. (C.)

4 State the law of multiple proportions and describe one experiment you could do to test it. State all the precautions that should be taken to ensure an accurate result. Two oxides of a metal contain 22.2 and 30 per cent of oxygen respectively. Show that these figures support the above law. (C.)

5 1.60 g of oxide of a metal were reduced and formed 1.44 g of a lower oxide, which on further reduction gave 1.12 g of the metal. Show that these figures agree with a chemical law, and name the law. Two chlorides contain 38.17 and 48.08 per cent of chlorine; show that these results illustrate the same law. (L.)

6 What is meant by water of crystallization? Name and give the formulae of three hydrates and three anhydrous salts. A salt forms two hydrates. They contain 36.14 and 10.17 per cent of water of crystallization respectively. Find if these figures illustrate a chemical law. (C.)

7 What do you understand by the terms (*a*) molecule, (*b*) atomicity? Describe experiments to show (*c*) that gases in contact mix completely, (*d*) that the rate of diffusion of a gas depends on its density. Explain what the results of these experiments are thought to indicate with regard to gases. (L.)

8 The gaseous oxide of a non-metal X contains 50 per cent by mass of oxygen; what is the mass of X which combines with 1 mole (16 g) of oxygen? Under the same conditions, oxygen diffuses 1.414 times as fast as the oxide of X. Show that the relative molecular mass of the oxide is 64 and the relative atomic mass of X is probably 32. (L.)

9 Calculate the volume at s.t.p. of a gas whose volume is
(*a*) 198.0 cm^3 at 24 °C and 740 mmHg pressure.
(*b*) 340.0 cm^3 at 15 °C and 735 mmHg pressure.
(*c*) 200.0 cm^3 at 27 °C and 700 mmHg pressure.

10 The mass of 509 cm^3 of dinitrogen oxide, measured at s.t.p. is 1 g. The mass of 250 cm^3 of hydrogen sulphide at 17 °C and 740 mmHg pressure is 0.35 g. Show clearly that the relative molecular masses of the gases are 44 and 34 respectively.

11 1.00 g of a metal displaces 340 cm^3 of hydrogen, measured at s.t.p., from a dilute acid. Calculate the mass of metal which displaces 1 mole (1 g) of hydrogen atoms.

12 0.20 g of a metal reacted with an acid to form 265 cm^3 of hydrogen measured at 0 °C and 760 mmHg pressure. Calculate the mass of metal which displaces 1 mole (1 g) of hydrogen atoms. (N.)

7
Formulae and Equations

Symbols

The symbol of an element is one or two letters which mean one atom (or one mole, sometimes) of the element.

Symbols for some elements are:

Aluminium	Al	Hydrogen	H	Oxygen	O
Argon	Ar	Iodine	I	Phosphorus	P
Barium	Ba	Iron	Fe	Potassium	K
Bromine	Br	Lead	Pb	Silver	Ag
Calcium	Ca	Magnesium	Mg	Sodium	Na
Carbon	C	Manganese	Mn	Sulphur	S
Chlorine	Cl	Mercury	Hg	Tin	Sn
Copper	Cu	Nitrogen	N	Zinc	Zn

Chemical formulae

The formula 2O means '2 atoms of oxygen not combined together'; O_2 means '1 molecule of oxygen, which contains 2 atoms'. H_2O means 1 molecule of water containing 2 atoms of hydrogen and 1 atom of oxygen.

The formula of an element or compound is the symbols and numbers which mean one molecule (or, sometimes, one mole).

The number in front of a formula shows the number of molecules, e.g. $2CO_2$ means 2 molecules of carbon dioxide. Some substances, e.g. NaCl, do not exist as molecules; the formula represents the simplest entity or particle in the substance.

Radicals

All sulphates contain the group SO_4, nitrates contain NO_3, and ammonium compounds contain NH_4. These groups are examples of radicals.

A radical is a group of atoms that exists in several compounds but does not exist on its own.

	Valency 1		Valency 2		Valency 3	
Metals	Potassium	K	Calcium	Ca	Aluminium	Al
	Ammonium	NH_4	Magnesium	Mg	Iron(III)	Fe
	Sodium	Na	Barium	Ba		
	Silver	Ag	Zinc	Zn		
			Iron(II)	Fe		
			Lead(II)	Pb		
			Copper(II)	Cu		
			Mercury(II)	Hg		
Non-metals	Hydrogen	H	Oxygen	O	Nitrogen	N
	Chlorine	Cl	Sulphur	S	Phosphorus	P
Radicals	Hydroxide	OH	Oxide	O	Phosphate	PO_4
	Chloride	Cl	Carbonate	CO_3		
	Nitrate	NO_3	Sulphate	SO_4		
	Hydrogen-carbonate	HCO_3	Sulphite	SO_3		
	Hydrogen-sulphate	HSO_4				
	Nitrite	NO_2				

Hydrogen compound		Radical		
Name	Formula	Name	Formula	Valency
Water	$H \cdot OH$	Hydroxide	$-OH$	1
Hydrochloric acid	HCl	Chloride	$-Cl$	1
Nitric acid	HNO_3	Nitrate	$-NO_3$	1
Carbonic acid	$H \cdot HCO_3$	Hydrogencarbonate	$-HCO_3$	1
Sulphuric acid	$H \cdot HSO_4$	Hydrogensulphate	$-HSO_4$	1
Water	H_2O	Oxide	$-O$	2
Carbonic acid	H_2CO_3	Carbonate	$-CO_3$	2
Sulphuric acid	H_2SO_4	Sulphate	$-SO_4$	2

Valency (combining number)

Combining number or *valency* is a measure of the power of an element or radical to combine with others. Hydrogen is the standard and its valency is 1.

The valency of an element (or radical) is the number of hydrogen atoms which combine with or displace one atom of the element (or one group of the radical).

The valency of chlorine is 1 because 1 atom of hydrogen combines with 1 atom of chlorine to form HCl. The valency of oxygen is 2 because 2 atoms of hydrogen combine with 1 atom of oxygen. The valency of zinc is 2 because 1 atom of zinc displaces 2 atoms of hydrogen from dilute acids.

Variable valencies

The valency of copper can be 1 or 2, and the valency of iron can be 2 or 3. The different valencies are shown by roman numerals:
Iron(II) chloride $FeCl_2$ Iron(III) chloride $FeCl_3$
Copper(I) oxide Cu_2O Copper(II) oxide CuO
Metals have a valency of 2, *except:*
Potassium, Ammonium, Sodium, Silver 1
Aluminium, Iron(III) 3
(The initials PASS and ALIR may help to recall these.) The ammonium radical NH_4 is not a metal, but its compounds are similar to those of sodium and potassium.
Elements with higher valencies are: carbon and silicon (4) and phosphorus and nitrogen (sometimes 5, as in P_2O_5 and HNO_3).
It is easy to deduce the valency of a non-metal if the formula of its hydrogen compound is known:

Writing formulae

We use symbols, radicals and valencies to write formulae of compounds. The rules are as follows, sodium sulphate and copper(II) chloride being examples:

1 Write the symbols for the elements and radicals:
Na SO_4; Cu Cl

2 Write valencies above and right of the symbols:
Na^1 SO_4^2; Cu^2 Cl^1

3 Write the symbols again, reversing the valencies and writing the numbers (but not 1) below and to the right:
Na_2 SO_4; Cu Cl_2
i.e. Na_2SO_4 $CuCl_2$

Other examples make the method clear:

	Rules				
	1 and 2		3		Formula
Sodium chloride	Na^1	Cl^1	Na	Cl	NaCl
Potassium hydroxide	K^1	OH^1	K	OH	KOH
Calcium chloride	Ca^2	Cl^1	Ca	Cl_2	$CaCl_2$
Copper hydroxide	Cu^2	OH^1	Cu	$(OH)_2$	$Cu(OH)_2$
Zinc nitrate	Zn^2	NO_3^1	Zn	$(NO_3)_2$	$Zn(NO_3)_2$
Iron(III) chloride	Fe^3	Cl^1	Fe	Cl_3	$FeCl_3$
Ammonium sulphate	NH_4^1	SO_4^2	$(NH_4)_2$	SO_4	$(NH_4)_2SO_4$
Copper(II) oxide	Cu^2	O^2	Cu_2	O_2	CuO
Zinc sulphate	Zn^2	SO_4^2	Zn_2	$(SO_4)_2$	$ZnSO_4$

Note that the simplest formula is used in the last two examples, i.e. the formula for copper(II) oxide is CuO and not Cu_2O_2.

Chemical equations

A chemical equation represents a chemical change by means of symbols and formulae, e.g. $Fe + S \rightarrow FeS$ means that '1 atom of iron reacts with 1 atom of sulphur to form 1 molecule of iron(II) sulphide'.

The process of making the number and kind of atoms equal on both sides of an equation is called balancing the equation.

The rules for writing chemical equations are:

1 Write the formulae of the reactants on the left hand side and the formulae of the products on the right, e.g.

$$Zn + HCl \rightarrow ZnCl_2 + H_2;$$
$$Mg + O_2 \rightarrow MgO$$

2 Balance the equation, if necessary, by writing numbers in front of the formulae, e.g.

$$Zn + 2HCl \rightarrow ZnCl_2 + H_2;$$
$$2Mg + O_2 \rightarrow 2MgO$$

Sometimes it is easier to balance an equation by using fractions of a molecule and then multiplying the whole equation to remove the fraction, e.g.

Rule 1 $KClO_3 \rightarrow KCl + O_2$

Rule 2 $KClO_3 \rightarrow KCl + 1\frac{1}{2}O_2$

i.e. $2KClO_3 \rightarrow 2KCl + 3O_2$

Ionic equations

Many chemical reactions take place between ions and not molecules. The equations are simpler if the ions are shown. For example, by writing down all the ions the equation:

$Zn(s) + 2HCl(aq) \rightarrow ZnCl_2(aq) + H_2(g)$

becomes:

$Zn(s) + 2H^+(aq) + 2Cl^-(aq) \rightarrow Zn^{2+}(aq) + 2Cl^-(aq) + H_2(g)$

By omitting the ions that are on both sides, we have:

$Zn(s) + 2H^+(aq) \rightarrow Zn^{2+}(aq) + H_2(g)$

This is an ionic equation. *The charges on both sides must be equal.* Other examples are:

Acid on hydroxides and oxides:

$H^+(aq) + OH^-(aq) \rightarrow H_2O(l)$;

$2H^+(aq) + O^{2-}(s) \rightarrow H_2O(l)$

Acid on carbonates:

$2H^+(aq) + CO_3^{2-}(s) \rightarrow CO_2(g) + H_2O(l)$

Precipitation:

$Cu^{2+}(aq) + 2OH^-(aq) \rightarrow Cu(OH)_2(s)$;

$Cu^{2+}(aq) + CO_3^{2-}(aq) \rightarrow CuCO_3(s)$

Calculations from formulae and equations

The empirical formula of a compound is the simplest formula which expresses its composition by mass. The molecular formula of a compound is the formula which shows the number of each kind of atom present in one molecule of the compound.

Some examples are:

	Empirical formula	Molecular formula
Water	H_2O	H_2O
Hydrogen peroxide	HO	H_2O_2
Dinitrogen tetraoxide	NO_2	N_2O_4
Ethene	CH_2	C_2H_4
Glucose	CH_2O	$C_6H_{12}O_6$

Calculation of empirical formulae

1 Sodium sulphate has the following composition by mass: sodium, 32.4 per cent; sulphur, 22.5 per cent; and oxygen, 45.1 per cent. What is its empirical formula?

	Sodium	Sulphur	Oxygen
Relative masses	32.4	22.5	45.1
Relative numbers of atoms	$\frac{32.4}{23}$	$\frac{22.5}{32}$	$\frac{45.1}{16}$
$\left(\text{i.e. } \frac{\text{relative mass}}{\text{relative atomic mass}}\right)$	$=1.41$	$=0.70$	$=2.82$
Divide by smallest number	$\frac{1.41}{0.70}$	$\frac{0.70}{0.70}$	$\frac{2.82}{0.70}$
	$=2$	$=1$	$=4$

The empirical formula is Na_2SO_4.

Percentage composition from formula

2 Calculate the percentage of iron by mass in iron(II) sulphate crystals, $FeSO_4 \cdot 7H_2O$.
The relative molecular (formula) mass of $FeSO_4 \cdot 7H_2O$ is

$$56 + 32 + (4 \times 16) + (7 \times 18) = 278$$

There are 56 parts of iron in 278 parts of compound.

$$\text{Percentage of iron by mass} = \frac{56 \times 100}{278} = 20.1 \text{ per cent.}$$

Calculations of masses from equations

3 Calculate the loss in mass when 100 g of calcium carbonate are heated to constant mass.
The equation is:

$CaCO_3(s)$	$\rightarrow CaO(s) +$	$CO_2(g)$
$40 + 12 + 48$		$12 + 32$
$= 100$		$= 44$

When 100 g of calcium carbonate are heated, 44 g of carbon dioxide are evolved. The loss in mass is 44 g.

4 Calculate the mass of ammonium chloride that will just react completely with 14.8 g of calcium hydroxide.

$2NH_4Cl$	$+ Ca(OH)_2$	$\rightarrow 2NH_3 + CaCl_2 + 2H_2O$
$2(14+4+35.5)$	$40 + 2(16+1)$	
$= 107$	$= 74$	

74 g of calcium hydroxide react with 107 g of chloride

$\therefore$ 14.8 g of calcium hydroxide react with $\frac{14.8 \times 107}{74}$ g of chloride $= 21.4$ g.

To determine the number of molecules of water of crystallization in copper(II) sulphate crystals

Let the number be y, i.e. the formula of the crystals is $CuSO_4 \cdot yH_2O$. Using relative atomic masses:

$CuSO_4$	yH_2O
$63.5 + 32 + 64$	$18y$
$= 159.5$	

i.e. $$\frac{\text{Mass of water of crystallization}}{\text{Mass of anhydrous copper(II) sulphate}} = \frac{18y}{159.5}$$

Determine the mass of water of crystallization $(b-c)$ in a known mass $(b-a)$ of crystals as described on p. 8.

$$\frac{\text{Mass of water}}{\text{Mass of anhydrous salt}} = \frac{18y}{159.5} = \frac{(b-c)}{(c-a)}$$

The value of y can be calculated from the three masses a, b and c made during the experiment.

Meaning of an equation

Consider this equation:

$Zn(s) +$	$H_2SO_4(aq)$ $\rightarrow$	$ZnSO_4(aq)$	$+ H_2(g)$
65	$2 + 32 + 64$	$65 + 32 + 64$	2 g or
	$= 98$ g	$= 161$ g	$22.4\,dm^3$ at s.t.p.

It expresses the following facts:

1 *About each compound.*

a 1 molecule of sulphuric acid contains 2 atoms of hydrogen, 1 of sulphur and 4 of oxygen.

b 1 molecule of zinc sulphate contains 1 atom of zinc, 1 of sulphur and 4 of oxygen.

c 1 molecule of hydrogen contains 2 atoms.

d 98 g of sulphuric acid contains 2 g of hydrogen, 32 g of sulphur and 64 g of oxygen.

e 161 g of zinc sulphate contains 65 g of zinc, 32 g of sulphur and 64 g of oxygen.

2 *About the whole reaction.*

a Solid zinc reacts with aqueous sulphuric acid to form aqueous zinc sulphate and gaseous hydrogen.

b 1 atom of zinc reacts with 1 molecule of sulphuric acid to form 1 molecule of zinc sulphate and 1 molecule of hydrogen.

c 1 mole of zinc reacts with 1 mole of sulphuric acid to form 1 mole of zinc sulphate and 1 mole of hydrogen.

d 65 g of zinc reacts with 98 g of sulphuric acid to form 161 g of zinc sulphate and 2 g (or $22.4\,dm^3$ at s.t.p.) of hydrogen.

A plain equation does not give:

1 The conditions under which the reaction occurs, e.g. whether or not heat or a catalyst is required.

2 The speed of the reaction.

3 The heat of reaction, i.e. if heat is given out or absorbed; however, this can be added, if required, e.g.

$$2SO_2 + O_2 \rightleftharpoons 2SO_3 \quad \Delta H = -109\,kJ$$ (chapter 15, p. 173)

Questions

(Relative atomic masses are on pp. 352–3.)

1 Calculate the maximum mass of barium sulphate that could be precipitated by a solution containing 7.1 g of sodium sulphate. What is the percentage of nitrogen in ammonium sulphate? (C.)

2 State Gay-Lussac's Law and Avogadro's Law. (*a*) 10 cm^3 of carbon monoxide were mixed with 15 cm^3 of oxygen and exploded. After cooling to the original temperature the volume was 20 cm^3, and after shaking with aqueous potassium hydroxide the volume was reduced to 10 cm^3. Show that these figures agree with Gay-Lussac's Law. (*b*) When 5.0 g of solid were heated the residue weighed 2.8 g and 1120 cm^3 of a gas, measured at s.t.p., were evolved. Calculate the relative molecular mass of the gas. (C.)

3 What is the percentage by mass of sulphur in iron(III) sulphate, $Fe_2(SO_4)_3$? Calculate (*a*) the mass of calcium hydroxide needed to decompose 2.14 g of ammonium chloride (*b*) the volume of ammonia at s.t.p. formed from 4.28 g of ammonium chloride. (C.)

4 If 5.0 g of copper(II) sulphate crystals lose 1.8 g of water when heated to the anhydrous salt, what is the formula of the hydrated copper sulphate? Describe in detail an experiment by which you would determine the number of molecules of water of crystallization in one molecule of hydrated barium chloride. (L.)

5 Using 24 g of copper, what mass of copper(II) nitrate will be formed in the reaction:

$$3Cu + 8HNO_3 \rightarrow 3Cu(NO_3)_2 + 2NO + 4H_2O$$

What mass of water of crystallization is present in that mass of sodium thiosulphate crystals, $Na_2S_2O_3 \cdot 5H_2O$, which contains 8 g of sulphur? (L.)

6 50 cm^3 of a gas mixture containing carbon monoxide, carbon dioxide and nitrogen were shaken with aqueous potassium hydroxide and the residual volume was 36 cm^3. To this residual mixture of gases was added 20 cm^3 (an excess) of oxygen and it was exploded by sparking. The new volume after cooling was 48 cm^3. Assuming all volumes were measured at the same room temperature and pressure, calculate the composition of the original mixture. (L.)

7 Taking the reaction expressed by the equation

$$Mg + H_2SO_4 + 7H_2O = MgSO_4 \cdot 7H_2O + H_2$$

state all that you can that is indicated by the equation. Describe in detail how you would prove experimentally that the equation correctly represents the amount of hydrogen obtainable using a given mass of magnesium (Mg 24, H 1, S 32, O 16). (L.)

8 State (*a*) Gay-Lussac's Law of Volumes, (*b*) Avogadro's hypothesis (law). Describe one experiment which illustrates the law of volumes. Calor gas consists of 95 per cent butane (C_4H_{10}) and 5 per cent pentane (C_5H_{12}) by volume. Assuming that air contains 20 per cent of oxygen by volume, calculate the volume of air needed for the complete combustion of 100 dm^3 of Calor gas. All measurements are made at the same temperature and pressure. (L.)

8
The Structure of Matter

Radioactivity

In 1896, Becquerel left uranium ore on a packet of unexposed photographic plates. He found that the plates were affected and became 'fogged' although no light could pass through their wrappings of black paper. It was found that the cause was the splitting up of some uranium atoms; they formed other atoms and gave off rays that could pass through paper and even metal. In 1898, Pierre and Marie Curie discovered two new elements, polonium and radium, in the ore pitchblende from which uranium was extracted. Radium glowed in the dark and kept itself warmer than its surroundings. Some radium atoms split up to form the noble gas radon, which in turn splits up into radium and finally into lead. These discoveries proved that atoms are not indivisible and indestructible. *Radioactivity is the spontaneous splitting up of the atoms of certain elements.* The rate at which radioactivity occurs does not depend on temperature or any other physical or chemical factor, and therefore radioactive changes are different from chemical changes.

Three kinds of radiation. Radium atoms are unstable. They emit alpha and beta particles and gamma rays (the first three letters of the Greek alphabet: α, β, γ). The two particles are deflected in different directions by magnetic or electrical forces, and therefore they have different charges.

An *alpha particle* is positively charged. It is a helium atom minus 2 electrons (i.e. a helium ion He^{2+}).

A *beta particle* is negatively charged. It is an electron moving at a very high speed.

Gamma rays are electromagnetic waves. They are similar to light but their frequency is 100 000 times higher, and is even 100 times higher than that of X-rays. They can penetrate solid objects more readily than X-rays.

Radium (and other radioactive elements) disintegrates at a steady rate that cannot be affected by any known means. In every 1620 years half the atoms of radium split up, i.e. the formation of rays is reduced to one-half every 1620 years. This time is called the *half-life*. There are many radioactive elements, including many made artificially, and each has a characteristic half-life. This varies from a few millionths of a second to millions of years. The half-life of uranium is 700 million years. We now know that *radioactivity is due to decomposition of the nuclei* of radioactive atoms.

What is inside atoms?

In 1859 it was found that electricity flows between electrodes placed in gases under very low pressure. *Cathode rays* move in straight lines from the negative electrode. The 'rays' are actually negatively charged particles. In 1897 Thomson proved that the particles were the same whatever the gas and electrodes were made of. Therefore, they are fundamental particles present in all atoms, and are called *electrons*. Cathode rays are electrons moving at speeds about one-tenth that of light. In 1920, Rutherford discovered positively charged particles, *protons*, and in 1932 Chadwick discovered particles with no electric charge, *neutrons*. All atoms contain electrons, protons and neutrons (except the ordinary hydrogen atom, which contains no neutrons).

	Mass/kg	Relative masses
Electron	9.109×10^{-31}	0.000 549
Proton	1.672×10^{-27}	1.007 275
Neutron	1.674×10^{-27}	1.008 665

The relative masses are on the carbon-12 scale. The mass of a neutron is slightly greater than that of a proton and is about 1840 times that of an electron. The positive charge on a proton equals the negative charge of an electron.

The nucleus

An atom consists of electrons moving around a nucleus in the centre of the atom. The diameter of an atom is about 10 000 times larger than that of its nucleus.

The nucleus of ordinary hydrogen is a proton; the nuclei of other atoms consist of protons and neutrons. The number of protons (*proton number Z*) varies from 1 to 92, e.g. hydrogen has 1, helium 2, lithium 3, and so on up to uranium with 92—uranium is the heaviest natural atom. Many elements with more than 93 protons have been made artificially, and they are all radioactive.

The *neutron number N* is the number of neutrons in the nucleus of an atom. Protons and neutrons are called *nucleons*, and their total in an atom is its *nucleon number* or *mass number*, A. ($A = Z + N$).

	Protons (atomic number)	Neutrons	Mass number
Hydrogen	1	0	1
Carbon	6	6	12
Nitrogen	7	7	14
Sodium	11	12	23

Protons are positively charged and neutrons are neutral, therefore a nucleus is positively charged and the charge is equal to the number of protons in it.

Explanation of radioactivity. Radioactivity is the spontaneous decomposition of unstable nuclei of an element. Particles are emitted from the nuclei and the element changes to a different element or to lighter atoms of the same element (an isotope):

	Radium →	Radon +	Helium ion + Energy
Protons	88	86	2
Neutrons	138	136	2

In a second kind of radioactivity, a neutron changes to a proton and an electron, the proton remains in the nucleus and the electron is emitted:

	Radioactive lead →	Bismuth + Electron
Protons	82	83
Neutrons	128	127

Electrons in an atom

Electrons move in *orbits* (sometimes called *shells* or *energy levels*) around the nucleus. An atom is neutral; therefore the number of electrons (−ve) equals the number of protons (+ve) in a nucleus. *The chemical properties of an atom depend on the number and arrangement of its extra-nuclear electrons.*

Electronic structures of elements. The electrons move in orbits around the nucleus. Hydrogen, the lightest element, has 1 electron. Helium has 2 electrons (a *duplet*). Neon, another noble gas, has 10 electrons, 2 in the first orbit and 8 (an *octet*) in the second, farther away from the nucleus.

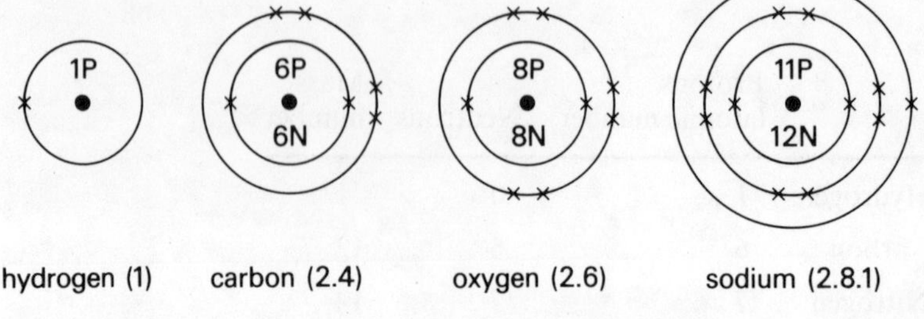

Fig. 8.1 Structures of some atoms (in cross-section)

Argon has 18 electrons, in orbits of 2, 8 and 8. The first 2 electrons or duplet and *an octet of electrons* are very stable. The first 20 elements have 1 to 20 protons and 1 to 20 electrons in each atom; the electrons in each orbit (*electron configuration*) are:

Hydrogen	1				
Helium	2	Neon	2.8	Argon	2.8.8
Lithium	2.1	Sodium	2.8.1	Potassium	2.8.8.1
Beryllium	2.2	Magnesium	2.8.2	Calcium	2.8.8.2
Boron	2.3	Aluminium	2.8.3		
Carbon	2.4	Silicon	2.8.4		
Nitrogen	2.5	Phosphorus	2.8.5		
Oxygen	2.6	Sulphur	2.8.6		
Fluorine	2.7	Chlorine	2.8.7		

Note that an alkali metal atom (Li, Na, K) has 1 electron in its outer orbit; a halogen atom (F, Cl) has 7, and an alkaline earth metal atom (Be, Mg, Ca) has 2. *Noble gases have* 2 *or* 8.

Isotopes

All atoms of one element have the same number of protons and electrons but may have different numbers of neutrons and therefore different masses. The chemical properties of the atoms are the same, because they depend on the electrons.

Isotopes are different atoms of the same element; they have the same chemical properties but different numbers of neutrons and therefore different relative atomic masses.

Hydrogen isotopes. A hydrogen atom has 1 proton, 1 electron and 0, 1 or 2 neutrons and therefore has three isotopes:

	Hydrogen	Deuterium (heavy hydrogen)	Tritium
Protons	1	1	1
Electrons	1	1	1
Neutrons	0	1	2
Mass number	1	2	3

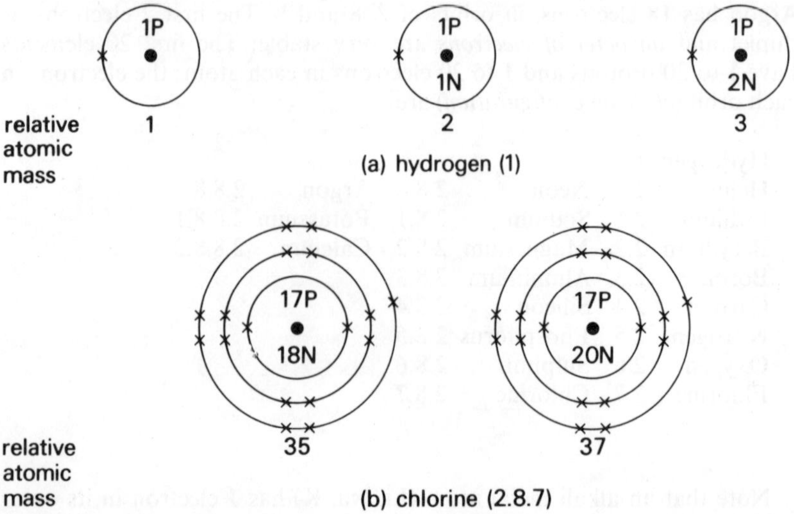

Fig. 8.2 Isotopes

The relative atomic mass of natural hydrogen is 1.008 because it contains a small amount of deuterium and tritium. *Heavy water* is the oxide of deuterium, i.e. D_2O.

Chlorine isotopes. A chlorine atom has 17 protons, 17 electrons and 18 or 20 neutrons. The relative atomic masses are either 35 (17+18) or 37 (17+20). Since there are about three times as many chlorine-35 atoms as chlorine-37 atoms the average relative atomic mass of ordinary chlorine is 35.5. The two isotopes are:

	Protons	Electrons	Neutrons	Mass number
(i)	17	17	18	35
(ii)	17	17	20	37

Most elements have isotopes, e.g. carbon has two and oxygen has three. They are usually present in definite proportions in any one element, and so the average relative atomic mass of an element is constant.

Electronic theory of valency

The electron configurations in noble gases are very stable, e.g. helium 2, neon 2.8, and argon 2.8.8. They have the stable octet of electrons (duplet in helium) in the outer orbit. Atoms combine in order to have one of these electron configurations, and they do so by the transfer or the sharing of electrons.

Electrovalency—transfer of electrons

Sodium chloride. A sodium atom has 11 electrons (2.8.1) or 1 more than neon; a chlorine atom has 17 electrons (2.8.7) or 1 less than argon. They combine by the transfer of 1 electron from the sodium atom to the chlorine atom. The atoms become ions, Na^+ (2.8) and Cl^- (2.8.8). The ions have opposite charges and therefore attract each other; the bond between them is *ionic* or *electrovalent*. We write the formula as $(Na^+ + Cl^-)$ which represents

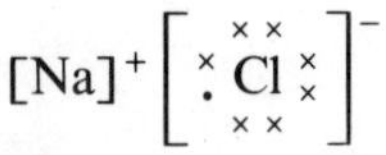

This is a 'dot and cross' diagram in which · represents the electron transferred from sodium to chlorine and × an electron of the chlorine atom.

Electrons in the complete inner orbits, i.e. the 2.8 of sodium (2.8.1) and of chlorine (2.8.7) take no part in forming bonds and are not shown. The complete electronic structure is shown in Fig. 8.3.

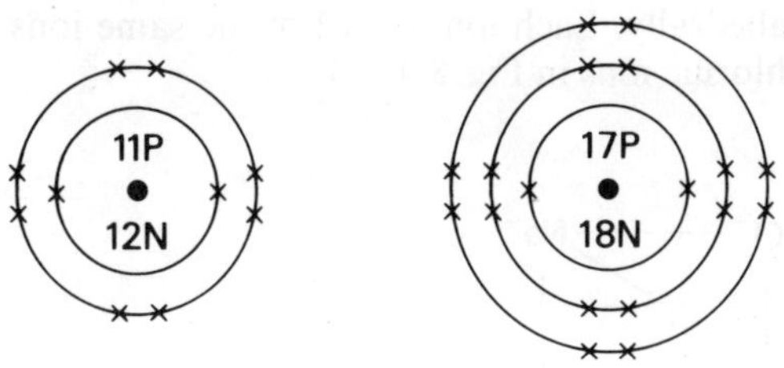

Na^+ (2.8) Cl^- (2.8.8)

Fig. 8.3 Sodium chloride

An ionic bond is one due to the transfer of one or more electrons from one atom (or radical) to another.

The electrovalency of an atom or radical is the number of electrons which it transfers or receives.

Metals (and hydrogen) can transfer 1, 2 or 3 electrons from the outer orbit of an atom to the outer orbit of a non-metal. Some electrovalencies are: H, Na, K, 1; Ca, Mg, 2; Fe, 2 or 3; Cl, 1; S, O, 2. In the examples below note the complete octet in the outer orbit of all the ions except hydrogen, which is a single proton (always hydrated, usually to H_3O^+).

Hydrochloric acid ($H^+ + Cl^-$)

$$H^{\bullet} + {}^{\times}\underset{\times\times}{\overset{\times\times}{Cl}}\,{}^{\times}_{\times} \rightarrow [H]^+ \left[{}^{\bullet}_{\times}\underset{\times\times}{\overset{\times\times}{Cl}}\,{}^{\times}_{\times} \right]^-$$

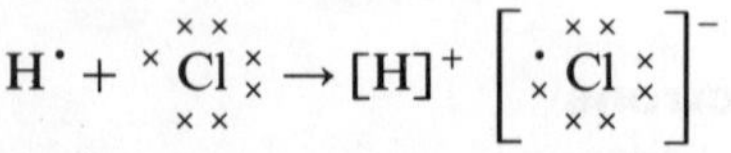

Calcium chloride ($Ca^{2+} + 2Cl^-$)

$$Ca\colon + 2\,{}^{\times}\underset{\times\times}{\overset{\times\times}{Cl}}\,{}^{\times}_{\times} \rightarrow [Ca]^{2+}\; 2\left[{}^{\times}_{\bullet}\underset{\times\times}{\overset{\times\times}{Cl}}\,{}^{\times}_{\times} \right]^-$$

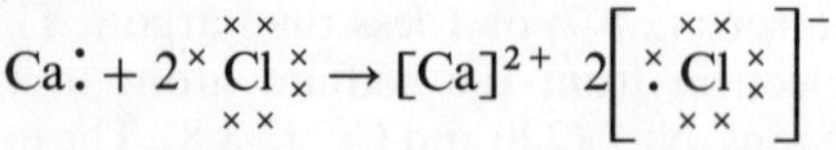

Calcium oxide ($Ca^{2+} + O^{2-}$)

$$Ca\colon + \underset{\times\times}{\overset{\times\times}{O}}\,{}^{\times}_{\times} \rightarrow [Ca]^{2+} \left[\colon\underset{\times\times}{\overset{\times\times}{O}}\,{}^{\times}_{\times} \right]^{2-}$$

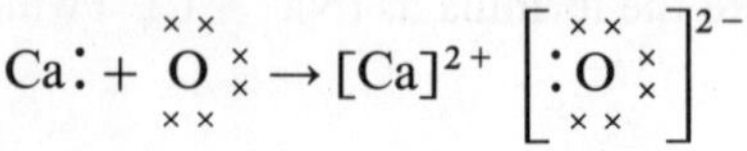

Crystals from ions

Solid sodium chloride consists of sodium and chlorine ions, and there is electrostatic attraction between the oppositely charged ions. One sodium ion is not combined or attached to any particular chlorine ion, and *there is no sodium chloride molecule NaCl*. Each crystal is one *giant structure*. Each sodium ion has 6 equidistant chlorine ions around it and arranged octahedrally, and each chlorine ion has 6 equidistant sodium ions around it, also arranged octahedrally. Each ion has 12 of the same ions equidistant from it, e.g. the chlorine ions in Fig. 8.4.

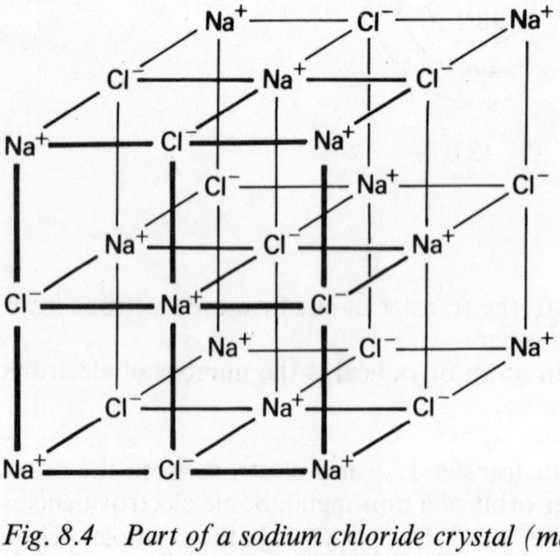

Fig. 8.4 Part of a sodium chloride crystal (magnesium oxide is similar)

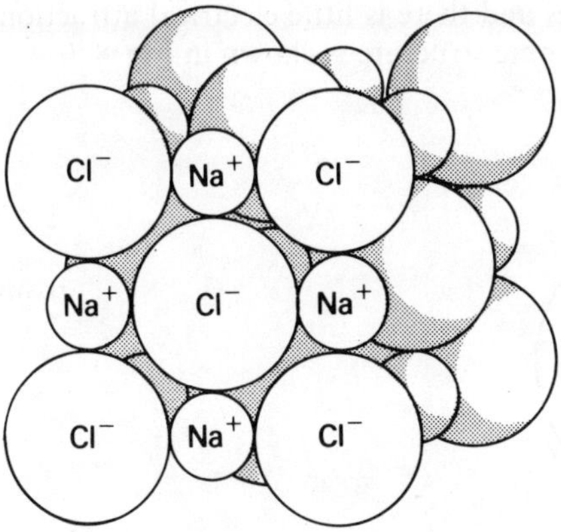

Fig. 8.5 Packing of the ions in sodium chloride

Covalency—sharing of electrons

Hydrogen. Two hydrogen atoms combine by sharing their electrons (Fig. 8.6). The two shared electrons (a *shared-pair* or *electron-pair*) revolve around both atoms, which in effect have the stable helium duplet. The shared-pair is a covalent bond, represented by

$$H\overset{\times}{\cdot}H \quad \text{or} \quad H—H$$

where · and × represent the single electrons from the two atoms and the valency line (—) represents one covalent bond of two electrons, one from each atom.

Chlorine. Two chlorine atoms combine by sharing two electrons, one from each atom. Each atom then has 6 electrons of its own in the outer orbit plus the shared-pair, which revolves around both atoms, i.e. they each have a complete outer octet and the stable argon structure 2.8.8.

$$:\!\underset{\cdot\cdot}{\overset{\cdot\cdot}{Cl}}\,\overset{\cdot}{\underset{\times}{}}\,\underset{\times\times}{\overset{\times\times}{Cl}}\,\overset{\times}{\underset{\times}{}} \qquad Cl—Cl$$

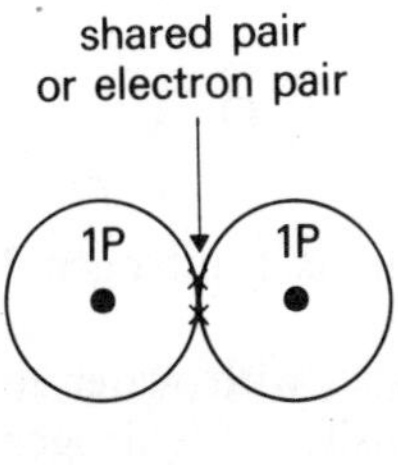

Fig. 8.6 Hydrogen molecule

Note that chlorine forms molecules and there is little electrical attraction between them. The complete electronic structure is shown in Fig. 8.7.

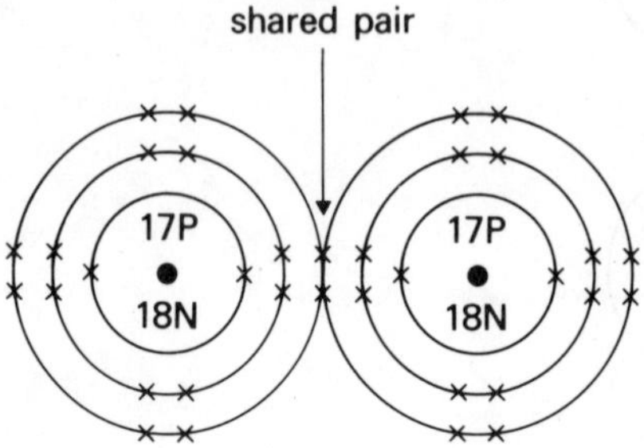

Fig. 8.7 Chlorine molecule

A covalent bond is one due to the sharing of two electrons, one from each atom.

The covalency of an atom is the number of electron-pairs which it shares.

Simple electronic formulae of some covalent compounds are given below. The complete inner orbits are omitted. The old method of writing these formulae is still useful as the valency line (—) represents a covalent bond of 2 electrons, one from each atom. Four shared electrons is a double bond, as in carbon dioxide, and six shared electrons is a triple bond, as in nitrogen.

Oxygen	O=O
Hydrogen chloride	H—Cl
Ammonia	H—N—H with H bonded below N
Nitrogen	N≡N
Carbon dioxide	O=C=O

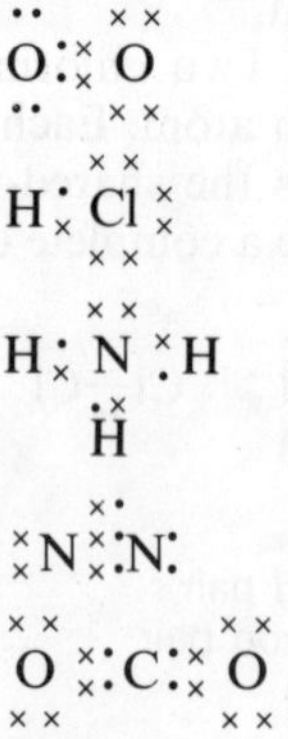

The covalency of oxygen is 2, of hydrogen and chlorine is 1, nitrogen 3 and carbon 4.

Hydrogen chloride is a covalent compound. It reacts with water to form hydrochloric acid, which is electrovalent and consists of hydrogen and chlorine ions. Some compounds contain both electrovalent and covalent bonds, e.g. sodium hydroxide:

$[Na]^+[O—H]^-$ or $[Na]^+$ 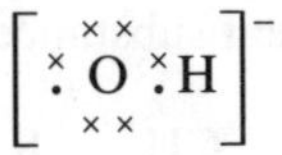

One . represents the electron transferred from the sodium (electrovalent bond) and the other . represents the electron of the hydrogen in the shared-pair (covalent bond).
Two or more covalent bonds in one molecule are arranged in definite directions. For example the atoms in a water molecule are:

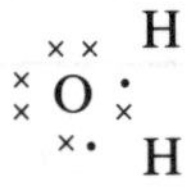

or

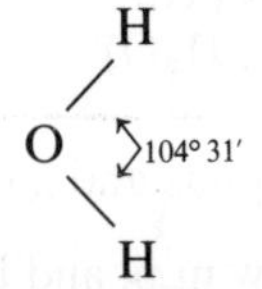

The angle between the N—H bonds in ammonia is 107°. Refer to the bonds in methane, p. 315.

The molecule of methane, CH_4, is symmetrical and the angle between the C—H bonds is $109\frac{1}{2}°$, the angle of a regular tetrahedron. An ammonia molecule is not symmetrical and it has two unshared electrons, a *lone pair*, in one tetrahedral position. This lone pair repels the shared electrons which constitute the three N—H covalent bonds, and decreases the bond angle by more than 2° to only 107°. A water molecule has two lone pairs and these have an even greater repelling force on the two O—H bonds; the bond angle is decreased by 5° to only $104\frac{1}{2}°$.

Properties of ionic and covalent substances

Strong electrostatic forces hold together the ions in ionic compounds. Great energy is needed to break the bonds and therefore the melting and boiling points are high, e.g.

	NaCl	KBr	NaI	$MgCl_2$
M.p. (°C)	808	735	662	714
B.p. (°C)	1465	1435	1304	1418

The molar latent heats of fusion and vaporization (the heat required to break the bonds in 1 mole of cations and anions in the solid and liquid respectively) are also high. The solids do not conduct electricity, but the ions can move freely in solution and in the molten compounds, which are good conductors.

The forces between covalent molecules are weak. Many covalent substances are gases or liquids. The melting and boiling points and molar latent heats of covalent substances are low:

	H_2	O_2	CH_4	S	H_2O
M.p. (°C)	−259	−219	−182	120	0
B.p. (°C)	−253	−183	−161	444	100

Electrovalent (e.g. $Na^+ + Cl^-$)	Covalent (e.g. H_2O)
Crystalline solids	Liquids and gases
High m.p. and b.p. (i.e. non-volatile)	Low m.p. and b.p. (i.e. volatile)
Consist of ions	Consist of molecules
Electrolytes. Conduct electricity when melted or dissolved	Non-electrolytes. Do not conduct electricity
Insoluble in organic solvents, e.g. ethanol, ether	Soluble in organic solvents

Unequal sharing of covalent bond electrons

A covalent bond is a pair of shared electrons. If the bond is between two identical atoms, e.g. H—H or Cl—Cl, the electrons are shared equally and the bond is 100 per cent covalent. If the atoms are not the same, e.g. H—Cl, the two electrons are not shared equally. The chlorine atom of a hydrogen chloride molecule has a stronger attraction for the shared electrons of the bond. The electrons are displaced slightly and cause the equal positive charge: $\overset{+}{H}—\overset{-}{Cl}$. In other words, the covalent bond has some ionic character. The amount of ionic character in the H—Cl bond is about 17 per cent. It is also 17 per cent in the $\overset{+}{H}—\overset{-}{N}$ bonds of ammonia, and 30 per cent in the $\overset{+}{H}—\overset{-}{O}$ bonds of water.

Atomic energy

Uranium has two important isotopes with relative atomic masses of 235 and 238. In 1939, it was observed that a uranium 235 atom can split into two parts and set free energy. This is an example of *nuclear fission* or *atomic fission*. Matter is destroyed and energy equivalent to this matter is set free.

> Nuclear fission is the process in which one atom produces two or more simpler atoms and energy.

The loss in mass in a nuclear fission is about 0.1 per cent or 1 g per kilogram. In a chemical change only the electrons around the nuclei are rearranged and the loss in mass is about 1 g per thousand million kilograms. The destruction of 1 kilogram of matter yields 9×10^{16} joules. Nuclear fission can be kept under control in atomic reactors, in which uranium is put in large blocks of graphite which prevents explosion. The energy is released steadily and can generate electricity.

Nuclear fusion. In the sun at temperatures of millions of degrees, 4 hydrogen atoms join to form 1 helium atom. Some mass is lost and energy is liberated:

4 hydrogen atoms $\rightarrow$	1 helium atom
4.032	4.003

> Nuclear fusion is the process in which two or more atoms combine to form one atom.

Molecular crystals

Covalent substances that form molecular crystals include iodine, solid carbon dioxide, sulphur, and many organic compounds, e.g. sugar and naphthalene. There are no bonds between the molecules, but there are weak intermolecular forces. Since little energy is needed to break the weak forces, the substances are soft. Melting points and boiling points are low. Molar latent heat (the heat required to separate 1 mole of the molecules) is also low. The crystals are non-conductors of electricity.

Metallic crystals

The fact that metals are good conductors of heat and electricity indicates that their electrons can move freely. Most common metals, e.g. iron, copper, aluminium, etc. have high melting points and boiling points; this suggests their bonds are ionic in nature. A metal consists of positively charged ions surrounded by a cloud of valency electrons which are free to move about within the solid. The ions are close-packed and this accounts for the high densities of most metals. Molar heats of vaporization of metals are high because the energy required to separate their particles is great.

A lump of metal consists of crystals or grains. Its strength and ductility depends on their size, which can be altered by heating the metal and by rolling, pressing or stretching the hot metal. There is no unit of structure within the metal except the crystals or grains, which are of variable size. Therefore, a metal has a *giant structure* (and so have electrovalent compounds such as sodium chloride, and covalent graphite and diamond, pp. 98 and 199).

Dalton's Theory amended

1 Matter is made of atoms. *Atoms are made of electrons, protons and neutrons.*

2 Atoms can be neither created nor destroyed in a chemical change. *Atoms are created or destroyed in special changes such as radioactivity, nuclear fission and fusion.*

3 The atoms of one element all contain the same number of protons in their nuclei, but they can have different relative atomic masses. The *average mass* of an atom of one element is constant. The isotopes of an element have the same chemical properties.

4 Atoms (*except carbon*) combine in small whole numbers. Carbon can form very large carbon chains or rings in organic compounds. However, even in these compounds *each atom is united to a small number of others.*

Oxidation number

The oxidation state of an element can be expressed by a number. The oxidation number of atoms of free elements is zero. The number for an element in an ionic compound equals the charge on the ion, e.g. sodium is +1 and chlorine is −1 in sodium chloride, $Na^+ + Cl^-$. Elements in covalent compounds are given numbers by regarding the covalent bonds as ionic, e.g. the oxidation number of hydrogen in HCl is +1 and of oxygen in H_2O is −2.

Remember these important oxidation numbers: all free elements 0, e.g. chlorine in Cl_2 is 0; in compounds, fluorine is always −1; hydrogen is always +1 (except in metallic hydrides such as NaH and CaH_2, where it is −1); and oxygen is always −2 (except in peroxides such as H_2O_2 and Na_2O_2, where it is −1).

Examples of oxidation numbers follow; note that in an uncharged compound the sum of the numbers is zero and in an ion the sum of the numbers equals the charge on the ion:

+1 −1	+1 −2	−3 +1	−3 +1	+4 −1	+4 −2
HCl	H_2O	NH_3	NH_4^+	CCl_4	CO_2

When an element is oxidized its oxidation number increases, and when it is reduced its number decreases:

$$2Fe^{2+}(aq) + Cl_2(g) \rightarrow 2Fe^{3+}(aq) + 2Cl^-(aq)$$
$$2 \qquad 0 \qquad 3 \qquad -1$$

Questions

1 By means of simple electronic diagrams show the structure of (*a*) the calcium atom, (*b*) the chlorine atom, (*c*) calcium chloride. Give a key to your diagrams. State differences between the properties of covalent and electrovalent compounds. (O.)

2 Outline briefly the evidence that atoms are not indivisible. Explain the structures of the first 20 elements from hydrogen to calcium. What is the difference between the structures of hydrogen chloride and hydrochloric acid?

3 Explain the difference between electrovalency and covalency. Of which of these two types of valency is ammonia an example? By a simple electronic diagram show the structure of an ammonia molecule. (N.)

4 Explain the differences between the properties of electrovalent and covalent compounds, using sodium chloride and water as examples. Draw diagrams showing the complete structure of one atom of an element with atomic number 18 and relative atomic mass 40.

5 Chlorine consists of isotopes chlorine-35 and chlorine-37. Their relative abundance by number of atoms is 754:246. Show that the relative atomic mass of chlorine is 35.492. The relative atomic mass of fluorine is 19.00; explain why you consider that this fact indicates that fluorine consists of only one kind of atom (nuclide).

6 Silicon (atomic number 14) consists of three isotopes:

Isotopic mass	Percentage abundance by numbers of atoms
28.0	92.2
29.0	4.7
30.0	3.1

Show that the relative atomic mass of silicon is about 28.1. Describe the structure of the three nuclei of the isotopes.

7 Magnesium has a volume of 14 cm^3 per mole (24 g). Oxygen at room temperature and pressure has a volume of 22 $dm^3\,mol^{-1}$. 24 g of magnesium and 16 g of oxygen can combine to form 40 g of magnesium oxide. The volume of solid magnesium oxide is 11 $cm^3\,mol^{-1}$. Use the structures of solids and gases to explain these facts.

9
Oxides. Oxidation and Reduction. Hydrogen Peroxide

Preparation of oxides

1 *Heat the element in air or oxygen.*
2 *Heat the metallic hydroxide, carbonate or nitrate.*

$$Pb(OH)_2(s) \rightarrow PbO(s) + H_2O(g)$$
$$ZnCO_3(s) \rightarrow ZnO(s) + CO_2(g)$$
$$2Cu(NO_3)_2(s) \rightarrow 2CuO(s) + 4NO_2(g) + O_2(g)$$

To prepare copper(II) oxide by several methods

From copper(II) sulphate (*or hydroxide*). Pour copper(II) sulphate solution into a beaker, add excess sodium hydroxide, and shake. A blue jelly-like precipitate forms:

$$Cu^{2+}(aq) + 2OH^- \rightarrow Cu(OH)_2(s), \text{ copper(II) hydroxide}$$

Boil gently for some minutes. The precipitate changes to black copper(II) oxide (more exactly, to a hydrated oxide):

$$Cu(OH)_2(s) \rightarrow CuO(s) + H_2O(l)$$

Let the precipitate settle and decant the liquid. Boil the precipitate with water to remove any soluble substances. Filter, and dry the copper(II) oxide by heating in an oven or crucible.
From copper(II) carbonate. Heat copper carbonate in a crucible. Carbon dioxide is evolved, and the green solid becomes black:

$$CuCO_3(s) \rightarrow CuO(s) + CO_2(g)$$

From copper(II) nitrate. Place the blue hydrated crystals in a crucible, and heat near an open window or in a fume cupboard. They change to the green anhydrous salt and then to the black oxide; reddish-brown nitrogen dioxide (poisonous) and oxygen are evolved:

$$2Cu(NO_3)_2(s) \rightarrow 2CuO(s) + 4NO_2(g) + O_2(g)$$

From copper. Add concentrated nitric acid to copper in a dish. Do this in a fume cupboard or near an open window. Use the *minimum* amount of acid. Green copper(II) nitrate solution and reddish-brown nitrogen dioxide are formed:

$$Cu + 4HNO_3 \rightarrow Cu(NO_3)_2(aq) + 2NO_2(g) + 2H_2O(l)$$

Evaporate the copper(II) nitrate solution to dryness, and heat the solid nitrate strongly, as before.

Properties of metallic oxides

Solubility. The oxides of lithium, potassium, sodium, calcium and magnesium react with water to form alkalis:

$$CaO(s) + H_2O(l) \rightarrow Ca(OH)_2(aq)$$

Oxides of other metals are insoluble in water.
Heat. Oxides of potassium and sodium (top of the activity series) form peroxides (e.g. Na_2O_2) on heating. Mercury(II) oxide (bottom of the series) decomposes to mercury and oxygen; other oxides do not change.
Reduction to metal. Carbon and hydrogen reduce the oxides of iron and of other metals lower in the activity series; hydrogen also reduces zinc oxide.

$$ZnO(s) + H_2(g) \rightarrow Zn(s) + H_2O(l)$$

$$Fe_2O_3(s) + 3C(s) \rightleftharpoons 2Fe(s) + 3CO(g)$$

Classification of oxides

1 *Acidic oxides are oxides of non-metals which form acids with water.* They are also called *acid anhydrides*. Examples are SO_2, SO_3, CO_2, P_2O_5. They react with alkalis to form a salt and water only.

$$SO_3(s) + H_2O(l) \rightarrow H_2SO_4(aq)$$

$$SO_3(s) + 2NaOH(aq) \rightarrow Na_2SO_4(aq) + H_2O(l)$$

Dinitrogen tetraoxide is a *mixed anhydride* because it forms two acids with water:

$$N_2O_4(g) + H_2O(l) \rightarrow \underset{\text{nitric acid}}{HNO_3(aq)} + \underset{\text{nitrous acid}}{HNO_2(aq)}$$

2 *Basic oxides are oxides of metals which react with acids to form a salt and water only* (e.g. CaO, MgO).

$$CuO(s) + H_2SO_4(aq) \rightarrow CuSO_4(aq) + H_2O(l)$$

Some basic oxides (e.g. Fe_2O_3) do not react with water and do not affect litmus. The oxides of metals high in the activity series (Li, K, Na, Ca, Mg) form alkalis with water:

$$Na_2O(s) + H_2O(l) \rightarrow 2NaOH(aq);$$

$$CaO(s) + H_2O(l) \rightarrow Ca(OH)_2(aq)$$

3 *Neutral oxides are oxides which have neither acidic nor basic properties.* They are usually the lower oxides of non-metals, e.g. H_2O, CO, dinitrogen oxide, N_2O, nitrogen oxide, NO.

4 *Amphoteric oxides are oxides which have both acidic and basic properties*, e.g. oxides of aluminium, zinc and lead. They form salts with acids and complex salts with alkalis:

$$ZnO(s) + 2HCl(aq) \rightarrow H_2O(l) + ZnCl_2(aq)$$

$$Al_2O_3(s) + 3H_2O(l) + 2OH^-(aq) \rightarrow 2Al(OH)_4^-(aq), \text{ aluminate ion}$$

$$ZnO(s) + H_2O(l) + 2OH^-(aq) \rightarrow Zn(OH)_4^{2-}(aq), \text{ zincate ion}$$

$$PbO(s) + H_2O(l) + 2OH^-(aq) \rightarrow Pb(OH)_4^{2-}(aq), \text{ plumbate ion}$$

5 *Peroxides and (IV) oxides are oxides which contain twice as much oxygen as expected from the usual valency of the other elements in the oxides. Peroxides contain the O_2^{2-} ion and react with dilute acids to form hydrogen peroxide.* Examples are sodium peroxide, Na_2O_2, and barium peroxide, BaO_2:

$$O_2^{2-}(s) + 2H^+(aq) \rightarrow H_2O_2(aq)$$

They are true salts of hydrogen peroxide, a weak acid.

(IV) oxides do not react with dilute acids to form hydrogen peroxide. Examples are lead(IV) oxide, PbO_2, and manganese(IV) oxide, MnO_2. They oxidize concentrated hydrochloric acid to chlorine:

$$MnO_2(s) + 4HCl(aq) \rightarrow Cl_2(g) + MnCl_2(aq) + 2H_2O$$

6 *Mixed oxides are oxides which react like a mixture of two simpler oxides.* Trilead tetraoxide (red lead oxide), Pb_3O_4, reacts like a mixture of 2PbO and PbO_2; triiron tetraoxide, Fe_3O_4, reacts like FeO and Fe_2O_3; and dinitrogen tetraoxide, N_2O_4, reacts like N_2O_3 and N_2O_5. [The recommended names for Fe_3O_4 and Pb_3O_4 are iron(II) diiron(III) oxide and dilead(II) lead(IV) oxide respectively. This book uses the simpler names just given above.]

To classify oxides

1 *Litmus.* Shake with water, then test with neutral litmus.

Litmus turns blue	Basic or peroxide
Litmus turns red	Acidic

2 *Sodium hydroxide*. Warm with dilute sodium hydroxide.
Oxide dissolves — Acidic or amphoteric

3 *Dilute acid*. Warm with dilute nitric acid.
Oxide dissolves — Basic or amphoteric

4 *Heat*. Heat, and test for oxygen with a glowing splint.
Splint re-lights — Peroxide or (IV) oxide (also oxide of mercury)

5 *Concentrated hydrochloric acid*. Heat with the acid and test for chlorine with damp litmus paper.
Litmus bleached — Peroxide or (IV) oxide
Oxide dissolves; no chlorine — Basic or amphoteric

Oxides of metals

Sodium oxide, Na_2O, and **potassium oxide**, K_2O, are not important. They are white solids and react vigorously with water:

$$Na_2O(s) + H_2O(l) \rightarrow 2NaOH(aq)$$

Calcium oxide, CaO. See p. 281.

Magnesium oxide, MgO, is a white solid made by heating the carbonate or nitrate. It combines slowly with water:

$$MgO(s) + H_2O(l) \rightarrow Mg(OH)_2(aq)$$

Aluminium oxide, Al_2O_3, is a white insoluble solid prepared by heating aluminium strongly in air, or from the hydroxide and nitrate (aluminium carbonate does not exist):

$$2Al(OH)_3(s) \rightarrow Al_2O_3(s) + 3H_2O(g)$$

It reacts with both acids and alkalis, i.e. it is amphoteric:

$$Al_2O_3(s) + 6HCl(aq) \rightarrow 3H_2O(l) + 2AlCl_3(aq)$$

$$Al_2O_3(s) + 2NaOH(aq) + 3H_2O(l) \rightarrow \underset{\text{sodium aluminate}}{2NaAl(OH)_4(aq)},$$

Coloured by impurities, it occurs naturally in rubies, sapphires and other gems, and in emery.

Zinc oxide, ZnO, is a white powder (yellow when hot) made by heating the hydroxide, nitrate or carbonate. It is amphoteric. It is used in zinc ointment and in some paints. Air containing hydrogen sulphide blackens lead paints by forming black lead(II) sulphide; zinc paints do not change colour because zinc sulphide is white.

Iron(III) oxide, Fe_2O_3, is a red powder prepared by heating the hydroxide or iron(II) sulphate (an unusual reaction):

$$2FeSO_4(s) \rightarrow Fe_2O_3(s) + SO_2(g) + SO_3(g)$$

It is used in cosmetics and, as *jeweller's rouge*, for polishing jewellery and steel cutlery.
Lead(II) oxide, PbO, is a yellow or orange solid (red-brown when hot) made by heating the hydroxide, carbonate or nitrate. It is amphoteric:

$$PbO(s) + 2HNO_3(aq) \rightarrow H_2O(l) + Pb(NO_3)_2(aq)$$

$$PbO(s) + 2NaOH(aq) + H_2O(l) \rightarrow \underset{\text{sodium plumbate}}{Na_2Pb(OH)_4(aq)},$$

It does not react readily with hydrochloric and sulphuric acids because lead(II) chloride and sulphate form an insoluble film around it and stop further action. It is used for making flint glass and for glazing pottery.
Copper(II) oxide, CuO, is a hygroscopic black powder.
Mercury(II) oxide, HgO, is a red powder.
Iron(II) diiron(III) oxide or triiron tetraoxide, Fe_3O_4, occurs naturally as *magnetite* and *lodestone*. It is made by heating iron in air, oxygen or steam:

$$3Fe(s) + 2O_2(g) \rightarrow Fe_3O_4(s);$$

$$3Fe(s) + 4H_2O(g) \rightleftharpoons Fe_3O_4(s) + 4H_2(g)$$

It is a *mixed oxide* and forms iron(II) and iron(III) salts with acids.
Red lead oxide or **trilead tetraoxide**, Pb_3O_4, is a red powder made by heating lead(II) oxide in air at 450 °C for a long time. It is a *mixed oxide*, and reacts with dilute nitric acid to form a dark-brown precipitate of lead(IV) oxide. Red lead oxide is a paint used on iron and steel to prevent rusting. Other paints are then put over the red lead paint.

To prepare lead(IV) oxide from red lead oxide, Pb_3O_4

Add read lead oxide, a little at a time, to warm dilute nitric acid in a beaker. A dark-brown precipitate settles:

$$Pb_3O_4(s) + 4HNO_3(aq) \rightarrow PbO_2(s) + 2Pb(NO_3)_2(aq) + 2H_2O(l)$$

Either filter off or decant the liquid, which contains lead nitrate and excess nitric acid. Wash the precipitate with dilute nitric acid (to remove red lead oxide still in it) and then with hot distilled water to remove acid. Dry in sunshine or an oven.

Properties of lead(IV) oxide and red lead oxide

Heat. They both form lead(II) oxide (yellow when cold, reddish-brown when hot) and oxygen:

$$2Pb_3O_4(s) \rightarrow 6PbO(s) + O_2(g); 2PbO_2(s) \rightarrow 2PbO(s) + O_2(g)$$

Concentrated hydrochloric acid. Both oxidize the warm acid to chlorine, and white lead chloride is precipitated:

$$PbO_2(s) + 4HCl(aq) \rightarrow PbCl_2(s) + Cl_2(g) + 2H_2O(l)$$

Concentrated sulphuric acid. The warm acid forms oxygen and a white precipitate of lead sulphate:

$$2PbO_2(s) + 2H_2SO_4(aq) \rightarrow 2PbSO_4(s) + O_2(g) + 2H_2O(l)$$

Oxidation and reduction

The simple meanings are: oxidation is addition of oxygen to a substance and reduction is removal of oxygen. Hydrogen seems to be the chemical opposite of oxygen (the two elements combine readily, and are evolved at opposite electrodes during electrolysis). Removal of hydrogen is similar to addition of oxygen; addition of hydrogen is similar to removal of oxygen. Fuller meanings are therefore: *Oxidation is the addition of oxygen to, or the removal of hydrogen from, a substance. Reduction is the removal of oxygen from, or the addition of hydrogen to, a substance.*

$$2SO_2(g) + O_2(g) \rightleftharpoons 2SO_3(\text{g then s})$$ (oxidation of SO_2; addition of oxygen)

$$PbO(s) + H_2(g) \rightarrow Pb(s) + H_2O(l)$$ (reduction of PbO; removal of oxygen)

$$Cl_2(g) + H_2(g) \rightarrow 2HCl(g)$$ (reduction of Cl_2; addition of hydrogen)

$$H_2S(g) + Cl_2(g) \rightarrow S(s) + 2HCl(g)$$ (oxidation of H_2S; removal of hydrogen)

The words now are applied to reactions in which neither oxygen nor hydrogen is involved. The change of iron(II) oxide to iron(III) oxide is obviously oxidation; the change of any iron(II) compound to an iron(III) compound is also an oxidation [and a change of iron(III) to iron(II) is reduction].

Electrons in oxidations and reductions

The equations for the oxidation of iron(II) chloride are:

$$2FeCl_2(aq) + Cl_2(g) \rightarrow 2FeCl_3(aq)$$

or $$2Fe^{2+}(aq) + Cl_2(g) \rightarrow 2Fe^{3+}(aq) + 2Cl^-(aq)$$

The oxidation involves a change of iron(II) ions to iron(III) by loss of electrons (e) and of chlorine to chlorine ions by gain of electrons:

$Fe^{2+} - e \rightarrow Fe^{3+}$ (oxidation); $Cl_2 + 2e \rightarrow 2Cl^-$ (reduction)

Oxidation is the removal of electrons from a substance. Reduction is the addition of electrons to a substance. An oxidizing agent is a substance that accepts electrons. A reducing agent is a substance that supplies electrons.

(Remember ORE—Oxidation is Removal of Electrons.) Note that when one substance is oxidized (loses electrons) in a reaction another substance is reduced (gains electrons), i.e. oxidation and reduction occur together and are called *redox* reactions. A redox reaction may be considered in two parts: an oxidizing agent removes electrons from the substance oxidized, and a reducing agent supplies electrons to the substance reduced. Each is a *half reaction*; some examples are:

Oxidizing agents (remove electrons)

1 Cl_2 — Cl_2(g or aq) + 2e → $2Cl^-$(aq)

2 HNO_3 — $2HNO_3 + e \rightarrow NO_3^-$(aq) + NO_2(g) + H_2O

3 H_2SO_4 — $2H_2SO_4 + 2e \rightarrow SO_4^{2-}$(aq) + SO_2(g) + $2H_2O$

4 $FeCl_3$ — Fe^{3+}(aq) + e → Fe^{2+}(aq)

Potassium manganate(VII) and potassium dichromate(VI), both acidified with dilute sulphuric acid, are common oxidizing agents, but example equations are not necessary.

Reducing agents (supply electrons)

1 HCl — $2Cl^-$(aq) → Cl_2(aq or g) + 2e

2 SO_2 — SO_2(g) + $2H_2O \rightarrow SO_4^{2-} + 4H^+$(aq) + 2e

3 H_2S — S^{2-}(aq) → S(s) + 2e

4 Metals — Zn(s) → Zn^{2+} + 2e

5 $FeSO_4$ — Fe^{2+}(aq) → Fe^{3+}(aq) + e

Tests for oxidizing agents

To classify substances as oxidizing and reducing agents

1 *Heat*. Some oxidizing agents evolve oxygen on warming.
2 *Concentrated hydrochloric acid*. Heat with the acid. Chlorine (which bleaches litmus paper) is evolved.

3 *Potassium iodide*. Add the substance to potassium iodide solution, acidified with dilute sulphuric acid, and then add starch solution. Oxidizing agents liberate iodine, which turns the solution brown and forms a blue colour with starch.
4 *Sulphur dioxide*. Bubble sulphur dioxide through an aqueous solution of the substance. Test for the formation of a sulphate by adding dilute nitric acid and barium nitrate solution.

Tests for reducing agents

1 *Acidified potassium manganate(VII)*. Acidify potassium manganate(VII) solution with dilute sulphuric acid. Add the mixture drop by drop to the substance. The purple solution is turned colourless.
2 *Acidified potassium dichromate(VI)*. Repeat with this solution. Its orange or yellow colour is turned green.
3 *Bromine water or iodine solution*. Add a few drops of one of these to a solution of the substance. The red bromine or brown iodine is turned colourless.
4 *Concentrated nitric acid*. Warm with a little of this acid. Brown nitrogen dioxide is formed.

Hydrogen peroxide, H_2O_2

To prepare hydrogen peroxide

Pour dilute sulphuric acid into a beaker and cool by adding ice. Moisten hydrated barium peroxide ($BaO_2 \cdot 8H_2O$) with water and add it a little at a time to the ice-cold acid until the final mixture is only weakly acidic:

$$O_2^{2-}(aq) + 2H^+(aq) \rightarrow H_2O_2(aq)$$

Allow the white barium sulphate to settle and decant or filter the solution. The liquid is very dilute hydrogen peroxide.

Properties of hydrogen peroxide

It is a syrupy, explosive liquid when pure (m.p. 0 °C, b.p. 50 °C, and density 1.4 g/cm^3) but usually it is used in dilute aqueous solution. It is a weak acid.
Heat. It forms oxygen and steam, which prevents the oxygen re-lighting a glowing splint:

$$2H_2O_2(aq) \rightarrow 2H_2O(l) + O_2(g)$$

Manganese(IV) oxide and platinized asbestos. Effervescence occurs when either is added to hydrogen peroxide, and oxygen is evolved rapidly. The substances are catalysts.

Oxidizing reactions

Hydrogen peroxide is a strong oxidizing agent because it supplies oxygen for oxidation or removes electrons:

$$H_2O_2(aq) \rightarrow H_2O(l) + O \text{ (used for oxidizing)}$$

$$\text{or } H_2O_2(aq) + 2H^+(aq) + 2e \rightarrow 2H_2O(l)$$

Potassium iodide. Acidify potassium iodide solution with dilute sulphuric acid and add hydrogen peroxide; then add starch solution. (Alternatively, use starch-iodide paper.) The brown colour of iodine appears first, and the starch turns blue:

$$2KI + H_2SO_4 + H_2O_2 \rightarrow I_2(\text{aq or s}) + 2H_2O + K_2SO_4$$

$$\text{ionically, } 2I^- + 2H^+ + H_2O_2 \rightarrow I_2(\text{aq or s}) + 2H_2O$$

Lead(II) sulphide. Dip filter paper in lead(II) ethanoate or nitrate solution, and then hold it in hydrogen sulphide. A shiny black precipitate of lead(II) sulphide forms. Drop the paper into hydrogen peroxide (alternatively, let it dry and write on it with a glass rod dipped in the peroxide). The black precipitate changes to white lead(II) sulphate:

$$PbS(s) + 4H_2O_2(aq) \rightarrow PbSO_4(s) + 4H_2O$$

Hydrogen peroxide oxidizes *iron(II) salts* to iron(III), *sulphurous* to sulphuric acid, and *hydrogen sulphide* to sulphur:

$$2FeCl_2(aq) + 2HCl(aq) + H_2O_2(aq) \rightarrow 2FeCl_3(aq) + 2H_2O(l)$$

$$H_2SO_3(aq) + H_2O_2(aq) \rightarrow H_2SO_4(aq) + H_2O(l)$$

$$H_2S(g) + H_2O_2(aq) \rightarrow S(s) + 2H_2O(l)$$

Its *bleaching action* (see later) is also an oxidation.

Reducing reactions

Hydrogen peroxide removes oxygen from a substance, forming gaseous oxygen, or it supplies electrons:

$$H_2O_2(aq) + O \rightarrow H_2O(l) + O_2(g)$$

$$\text{or } \quad H_2O_2(aq) \rightarrow 2H^+(aq) + O_2(g) + 2e$$

Lead(IV) oxide. Suspend the oxide in dilute nitric acid and add hydrogen peroxide. Vigorous effervescence (oxygen) occurs and a colourless solution of lead(II) nitrate forms.

$$PbO_2(s) + 2HNO_3(aq) + H_2O_2(aq) \rightarrow Pb(NO_3)_2(aq) + 2H_2O(l) + O_2(g)$$

Chlorine. This is reduced to hydrochloric acid:

$$H_2O_2(aq) + Cl_2(aq) \rightarrow 2HCl(aq) + O_2(g)$$

Purple acidified *potassium manganate(VII)* is turned colourless (oxygen is evolved), and orange acidified *potassium dichromate(VI)* is turned green (a deep blue solution forms for a few seconds).

Uses of hydrogen peroxide

The solution *kills germs* rapidly, and is therefore used as a mouth wash and for cleansing wounds. It *bleaches* hair, silk, teeth, feathers and other delicate materials which are damaged by chlorine or sulphur dioxide. It bleaches by oxidation and forms water, whereas chlorine and sulphur dioxide both form acids:

$$H_2O_2(aq) + \text{dye} \rightarrow H_2O(l) + (\text{dye} + O), \text{ colourless}$$

Hydrogen peroxide is used in rockets moving outside the earth's atmosphere, and *provides oxygen* for the burning of the fuel. It also provides oxygen for the burning of diesel oil in the engines of submerged submarines, which cannot use air.

The solution is usually sold as '10 volume' or '20 volume' peroxide; '100 volume' peroxide is occasionally used in laboratories. 'x volume' peroxide means that 1 volume of hydrogen peroxide yields x volumes of oxygen (measured at s.t.p.) on heating. All solutions slowly decompose when stored. 1000 cm^3 of '10 volume' hydrogen peroxide contains 30.4 g of hydrogen peroxide; prove this by calculation.

Questions

1 Name four classes of oxides, giving the name, formula and one property of a typical member of each class. The property given must identify the oxide concerned as a member of its class. Giving your reasons, classify the following oxides: calcium oxide, nitrogen dioxide (dinitrogen tetraoxide), manganese(IV) oxide. (L.)

2 Describe the appearance of the three oxides of lead: PbO, Pb_3O_4, and PbO_2. Describe what (if anything) happens when each oxide is warmed with (*a*) dilute nitric acid, (*b*) dilute hydrochloric acid. How can the two higher oxides be prepared from lead(II) oxide? (O.)

3 Define oxidation and reduction. How would you oxidize (*a*) hydrochloric acid to chlorine, (*b*) copper to copper(II) oxide? How would you reduce (*c*) copper(II) oxide to copper, (*d*) steam to hydrogen? (C.)

4 Describe briefly two methods in each case for the detection of (*a*) an oxidizing agent, (*b*) a reducing agent. In which class would you place (i) nitric acid, (ii) hydrochloric acid, (iii) potassium chlorate, (iv) zinc dust in dilute hydrochloric acid? Give one reason in each case. (C.)

5 In each of the following reactions state (*a*) the substance being oxidized, (*b*) the product of the oxidation:

$$2Cl_2(g) + 2H_2O(l) \rightarrow 4HCl(aq) + O_2(g)$$

$$2FeCl_2(aq) + 2HCl(aq) + H_2O_2(aq) \rightarrow 2FeCl_3(aq) + 2H_2O(l)$$

$$4HCl(aq) + MnO_2(s) \rightarrow Cl_2(g) + MnCl_2(aq) + 2H_2O(l)$$

$$3CuO(s) + 2NH_3(g) \rightarrow 3Cu(s) + 3H_2O(l) + N_2(g)$$

State the conditions under which each reaction takes place. (N.)

6 Describe three different methods by which metallic oxides can be prepared in a reasonably pure state. Describe, giving reasons for your choice, which of these methods you would use to prepare an oxide from (i) copper, (ii) magnesium, (iii) iron(III) chloride. (N.)

7 Describe how you would prepare a solution of hydrogen peroxide. State and explain three reactions of hydrogen peroxide. What is meant by '100 volume hydrogen peroxide'? (L.)

8 Describe what takes place when hydrogen peroxide is added to (*a*) acidified potassium manganate(VII) solution, (*b*) lead(II) sulphide, (*c*) manganese(IV) oxide. Give equations for the reactions in (*b*) and (*c*). How you would prepare several gas-jars of oxygen from hydrogen peroxide? (L.)

10
Acids, Salts and Bases

Acids

Some non-metals burn in air or oxygen to form oxides, which are acidic oxides because they form acids with water.

$CO_2(g) + H_2O(l) \rightleftharpoons H_2CO_3(aq)$ carbonic acid

$SO_2(g) + H_2O(l) \rightleftharpoons H_2SO_3(aq)$ sulphurous acid

Properties of acids

1 *Taste*. Acids have a sour, sharp taste.

2 *Indicators*. (An indicator is a substance that has different colours in acid and alkaline solutions.) Acids turn litmus red, methyl orange red, and phenolphthalein colourless. Carbonic acid, sulphurous acid and hydrogen sulphide and a few other acids are so weak that they only turn litmus pale red.

Litmus is extracted from lichen. Home-made indicators can be obtained from coloured fruit or plant material (e.g. rose petals, red cabbage leaves, beetroot, etc.). Crush the material in a mortar, add to a small plastic beaker, cover with a solution of ethanol-water (1:5 by volume), and warm by placing in a beaker of hot water. Stir well for 5 minutes, and then filter the mixture and collect the coloured filtrate, which is an indicator.

Universal Indicators show a series of colour changes as the acidity or alkalinity of a solution changes.

3 *Carbonates and hydrogencarbonates*. Most react and bubbles of carbon dioxide are evolved:

$$2H^+(aq) + CO_3^{2-}(s) \rightarrow CO_2(g) + H_2O(l)$$

$$H^+(aq) + HCO_3^-(s) \rightarrow CO_2(g) + H_2O(l)$$

4 *Oxides and hydroxides*. Acids react with oxides and hydroxides of metals to form salts and water only:

$$H_2SO_4(aq) + CuO(s) \rightarrow CuSO_4(aq) + H_2O(l),$$

i.e. $2H^+(aq) + O^{2-}(s) \rightarrow H_2O(l)$

$$HCl(aq) + NaOH(aq) \rightarrow NaCl(aq) + H_2O(l),$$

i.e. $H^+(aq) + OH^-(aq) \rightarrow H_2O(l)$

5 *Metals*. Acids and many metals form hydrogen:

$$Zn(s) + 2H^+(aq) \rightarrow Zn^{2+}(aq) + H_2(g)$$

Magnesium displaces hydrogen from very dilute nitric acid. Copper and mercury do not displace hydrogen from any acid.

Meaning of acid

The characteristic properties of acids are those of hydrated hydrogen ions, represented by $H^+(aq)$. Most are *oxonium ions*, H_3O^+ or $H(H_2O)^+$ but some are H_9O_4 or $H(H_2O)_4^+$. Whenever H^+ occurs in equations in this book, its full meaning is the hydrated ion, $H^+(aq)$ or H_3O^+:

$$HCl(g) + \text{water} \rightarrow H^+(aq) + Cl^-(aq) \text{ or}$$

$$HCl(g) + H_2O \rightarrow H_3O^+ + Cl^-(aq)$$

Hydrogen chloride gas and its solution in methylbenzene have no acidic properties (p. 259). Butanoic acid is readily obtained pure; it has no action on litmus, Universal Indicator paper or magnesium until water is added and forms $H^+(aq)$.

An acid is a compound which, when dissolved in water, forms hydrogen ions as the only positively charged ions.

The basicity of an acid is the number of hydrogen ions that can be formed from one molecule of the acid.

Hydrochloric acid	$HCl \rightarrow H^+ + Cl^-$	Monobasic
Nitric acid	$HNO_3 \rightarrow H^+ + NO_3^-$	Monobasic
Sulphuric acid	$H_2SO_4 \rightarrow 2H^+ + SO_4^{2-}$	Dibasic

These are *strong acids* because dilute solutions are completely ionized. *Weak acids* are only slightly ionized in dilute solution and exist largely as molecules and their ionization is reversible, e.g.

Carbonic acid $H_2CO_3 \rightleftharpoons H^+ + HCO_3^- \rightleftharpoons 2H^+ + CO_3^{2-}$

Sulphurous acid $H_2SO_3 \rightleftharpoons H^+ + HSO_3^- \rightleftharpoons 2H^+ + SO_3^{2-}$

Phosphoric acid $H_3PO_4 \rightleftharpoons H^+ + H_2PO_4^- \rightleftharpoons 2H^+ + HPO_4^{2-} \rightleftharpoons 3H^+ + PO_4^{3-}$

Phosphoric acid is tribasic. All the hydrogen of the above acids can exist as ions, but only part of the hydrogen of some acids can do so, e.g.

Methanoic acid $HCOOH \rightleftharpoons HCOO^- + H^+$

Ethanoic acid $CH_3COOH \rightleftharpoons CH_3COO^- + H^+$

Some everyday acids are: *citric acid* in lemons and limes, *tartaric acid* in baking powder and health salts, *carbonic acid* in soda water, and *acetic* (ethanoic) *acid* in vinegar.

Preparation of acids

1 By the action of water on an acid anhydride (the acidic oxide of a non-metal) e.g. SO_2, SO_3, CO_2, P_2O_5:

$$H_2O(l) + SO_3(s) \rightarrow H_2SO_4(aq)$$

2 Displace a volatile acid by a less volatile one (e.g. concentrated sulphuric acid):

$$H_2SO_4(l) + NaCl(s) \rightarrow HCl(g) + NaHSO_4(s)$$

$$H_2SO_4(l) + KNO_3(s) \rightarrow HNO_3(l) + KHSO_4(s)$$

3 Synthesis (direct combination of elements):

$$H_2(g) + Cl_2(g) \rightarrow 2HCl(g)$$

Salts

A salt is the substance formed when either all or part of the ionizable hydrogen of an acid is replaced by a metallic ion or ammonium ion.

Formula of acid	Salt	
HCl	$NaCl$,	Sodium chloride
HCl	NH_4Cl,	Ammonium chloride
HNO_3	$Pb(NO_3)_2$,	Lead(II) nitrate
H_2SO_4	$ZnSO_4$,	Zinc sulphate

If all the ionizable hydrogen is replaced, the salts are *normal salts*, e.g. Na_2SO_4 and $CaCO_3$; if only part is replaced, the salts are *acid salts*, e.g. $NaHSO_4$ and $NaHCO_3$. A monobasic acid cannot form acid salts. Sodium ethanoate, CH_3COONa, is a normal salt because the hydrogen it contains does not form ions and cannot be replaced by a metal.

Acid salts		Normal salts	
Hydrogensulphate	$KHSO_4$	Potassium sulphate	K_2SO_4
Hydrogencarbonate	$NaHCO_3$	Sodium carbonate	Na_2CO_3
Hydrogencarbonate	$Ca(HCO_3)_2$	Calcium carbonate	$CaCO_3$
Hydrogensulphite	$NaHSO_3$	Sodium sulphite	Na_2SO_3

pH scale of acidity and alkalinity

Pure water is only slightly ionized: $H_2O \rightleftharpoons H^+ + OH^-$. $1000\,cm^3$ of water contains 10^{-7} moles of $H^+(aq)$ and of $OH^-(aq)$. The pH scale is a scale of numbers, from about 0 to 14, to express acidity and alkalinity. Water and any neutral solution has a pH of 7, a solution with a pH greater than 7 is alkaline, and one with a pH smaller than 7 is acid. Some pH values are: 0.1 M hydrochloric acid 1 (refer to p. 325 for the meaning of M); vinegar 3–4; baking powder 9; washing soda 11; 0.1 M sodium hydroxide 13. pH values apply only to fairly dilute aqueous solutions, and we cannot give a true pH value for concentrated sulphuric acid for example.

Measure the pH values of various solutions by adding Universal Indicator to them.

	0–4	5	6	7	8	9	10–14
Colour:	red	orange	yellow	green	blue	indigo	violet

Bases and alkalis

A base is a compound which contains oxide (O^{2-}) or hydroxide (OH^-) ions and reacts with an acid to form a salt and water only.

An alkali is a compound which, when dissolved in water, forms hydroxide ions as the only negatively charged ions.

Neutralization is the combination of the oxide or hydroxide ions of a base with the hydrogen ions of an acid to form water, and a salt is also formed.

For example,

$$HCl(aq) + NaOH(aq) \rightarrow H_2O(l) + NaCl(aq)$$

ionically,

$$H^+(aq) + Cl^-(aq) + Na^+(aq) + OH^-(aq) \rightarrow H_2O(l) + Na^+(aq) + Cl^-(aq)$$

By omitting ions common to both sides we have:

$$H^+(aq) + OH^-(aq) \rightarrow H_2O(l)$$

$$H_2SO_4(aq) + CuO(s) \rightarrow H_2O(l) + CuSO_4(aq)$$

i.e. $2H^+(aq) + O^{2-}(aq) \rightarrow H_2O(l)$

Strong and weak alkalis

Chemical name	Common name	Formula Ions
Sodium hydroxide	Caustic soda	$NaOH \rightarrow Na^+ + OH^-$
Potassium hydroxide	Caustic potash	$KOH \rightarrow K^+ + OH^-$
Calcium hydroxide	Slaked lime	$Ca(OH)_2 \rightarrow Ca^{2+} + 2OH^-$
Aqueous ammonia	Ammonia solution	$NH_3(aq) \rightleftharpoons NH_4^+ + OH^-$

All the above ions are hydrated. Sodium hydroxide and potassium hydroxide are strong alkalis; they are completely ionized even in the solid state, and contain no molecules. Calcium hydroxide is only slightly soluble, but since it is completely ionized it is a strong alkali. Aqueous ammonia is a weak alkali; it exists as molecules with only a few ions, and its ionization is reversible.

The alkalis are more useful than insoluble bases because many reactions occur only in solution. Sodium and potassium hydroxides react with skin and are *caustic* alkalis (caustic means corrosive or burning).

Preparation of bases

1 Burn a metal in air or oxygen:

$$2Mg(s) + O_2(g) \rightarrow 2MgO(s)$$

2 Add water to a metal or oxide:

$$2Na(l) + 2H_2O(l) \rightarrow 2NaOH(aq) + H_2(g)$$

$$CaO(s) + H_2O(l) \rightarrow Ca(OH)_2(aq)$$

3 Heat the hydroxide, carbonate or nitrate of any metal (except sodium and potassium):

$$Cu(OH)_2(s) \rightarrow CuO(s) + H_2O(g)$$

$$CaCO_3(s) \rightarrow CaO(s) + CO_2(g)$$

$$2Pb(NO_3)_2(s) \rightarrow 2PbO(s) + 4NO_2(g) + O_2(g)$$

4 Add aqueous sodium hydroxide, potassium hydroxide or ammonia to a solution of a salt:

$$Cu^{2+}(aq) + 2OH^{-}(aq) \rightarrow Cu(OH)_2(s)$$

$$Fe^{3+}(aq) + 3OH^{-}(aq) \rightarrow Fe(OH)_3(s)$$

Properties of alkalis

1 *Feel and taste.* Alkalis feel soapy and taste bitter.
2 *Indicators.*

Indicator	Acids	Alkalis
Litmus	Red	Blue
Methyl orange	Red	Yellow
Phenolphthalein	Colourless	Red

3 *Ammonium salts.* Alkalis (and bases) react with ammonium salts to form ammonia, which has a choking smell and turns litmus blue:

$$NH_4^+(aq) + OH^-(aq) \rightleftharpoons NH_3(g) + H_2O(l)$$

4 *Acids.* Alkalis neutralize acids to form a salt and water.
5 *Salts.* Alkalis precipitate many insoluble hydroxides from solutions of salts. The colours of the precipitates and equations are on p. 340.
6 *Air.* Sodium hydroxide is deliquescent. It quickly becomes wet and soon forms a solution, which then absorbs carbon dioxide and forms white crystalline sodium carbonate:

$$2NaOH(aq) + CO_2(g) \rightarrow Na_2CO_3(aq\ or\ s) + H_2O(l)$$

Stoppers of bottles containing sodium hydroxide must be rubber because glass would soon be fixed tight by carbonate formed around it. Potassium hydroxide is deliquescent, but potassium carbonate is also deliquescent.

Proton theory of acids and bases

The ionic theory of acids and bases refers only to aqueous solutions and gives too much importance to the ions $H^+(aq)$ or H_3O^+ and $OH^-(aq)$.

The theory does not explain (i) why ammonium chloride dissolved in liquid ammonia is acidic just as hydrogen chloride in water is:

$HCl \rightarrow Cl^- + H^+$ (acidic); $NH_4Cl \rightarrow Cl^- + NH_4^+$ (acidic)

(ii) why sodium or potassium reacts with liquid ammonia to form hydrogen and an alkaline solution:

$2Na + 2H_2O \rightarrow H_2 + 2Na^+ + 2OH^-$ (alkaline)

$2Na + 2NH_3 \rightarrow H_2 + 2Na^+ + 2NH_2^-$ (alkaline)

and (iii) why solutions of salts in liquid ammonia conduct electricity and are electrolysed.

On a wider theory of acids and bases (1922):
A base is a substance that will combine with protons. An acid is a substance that will give up protons to a base.
This theory does not mention any solvent but it does mention a base. An acid is a proton-donor and a base is a proton-acceptor:

Acid $\rightleftharpoons$ Base + Proton (i.e. H^+)

Some acids and their corresponding bases (called a *conjugate pair*) and which can be molecules, radicals or ions are:

Acid	Base	Acid	Base
HCl	Cl^-	H_2CO_3	HCO_3^-
HNO_3	NO_3^-	CH_3COOH	CH_3COO^-
H_2O	OH^-	H_3O^+	H_2O
NH_3	NH_2^-	NH_4^+	NH_3
H_2SO_4	HSO_4^-	HSO_4^-	SO_4^{2-}

Note that water and ammonia (and also HSO_4^-, HCO_3^- and HS^-) can act as either an acid or a base:

$NH_3 + NH_3 \rightleftharpoons NH_4^+ + NH_2^-$

$H_2O + H_2O \rightleftharpoons H_3O^+ + OH^-$

Acid Base Acid Base

Preparation of salts

Soluble salts are obtained by preparing them in solution, evaporating and crystallizing. Insoluble salts are obtained by precipitation:

Soluble	Insoluble
All sodium, potassium and ammonium salts.	
All nitrates.	
All chlorides, except	lead(II) and silver chlorides [lead(II) chloride is soluble in hot water].
All sulphates, except	lead(II) and barium sulphates (calcium sulphate is only slightly soluble).
Carbonates of lithium, sodium, potassium and ammonium.	All other carbonates.
Oxides and hydroxides of lithium, sodium, potassium, calcium and ammonium.	All other oxides and hydroxides (calcium and magnesium hydroxides are only slightly soluble).

Salts are prepared by:

a Synthesis (direct combination of elements):

$$Zn + S \rightarrow ZnS \text{ (p. 18)}$$

$$2Fe + 3Cl_2 \rightarrow 2FeCl_3 \text{ (p. 268)}$$

b The action of an acid on (i) a metal, (ii) an insoluble oxide or hydroxide or carbonate, and (iii) an alkali or soluble carbonate.

c Precipitation:

$$Pb(NO_3)_2(aq) + 2HCl(aq) \rightarrow PbCl_2(s) + 2HNO_3(aq)$$

i.e. $$Pb^{2+}(aq) + 2Cl^-(aq) \rightarrow PbCl_2(s)$$

To prepare zinc sulphate crystals from zinc

Action of an acid on a metal

Refer to p. 49. Add diluted sulphuric acid (1 acid: 5 water) mixed with a little copper(II) sulphate solution to zinc in a beaker. Filter off the excess zinc and any solid impurities [usually black pieces of carbon that were in the zinc, and copper formed from the copper(II) sulphate]. Collect the colourless filtrate in a beaker. Let the hot solution crystallize slowly.

Good crystals form slowly; crystals that form quickly are small. Filter off the crystals, which are white needles of zinc sulphate-7-water, $ZnSO_4 \cdot 7H_2O$. Wash them twice with a *little* cold distilled water. Dry by pressing gently between two pieces of filter paper or by leaving them on a porous plate or in sunshine..

Iron(II) sulphate-7-water, $FeSO_4 \cdot 7H_2O$, can be prepared in the same way from iron filings:

$$Fe(s) + H_2SO_4(aq) \rightarrow FeSO_4(aq) + H_2(g)$$

Iron filings react very slowly with bench sulphuric acid; use diluted acid (1 conc. acid: 5 water). Do not evaporate iron(II) sulphate solution too much because it readily turns brown due to atmospheric oxidation.

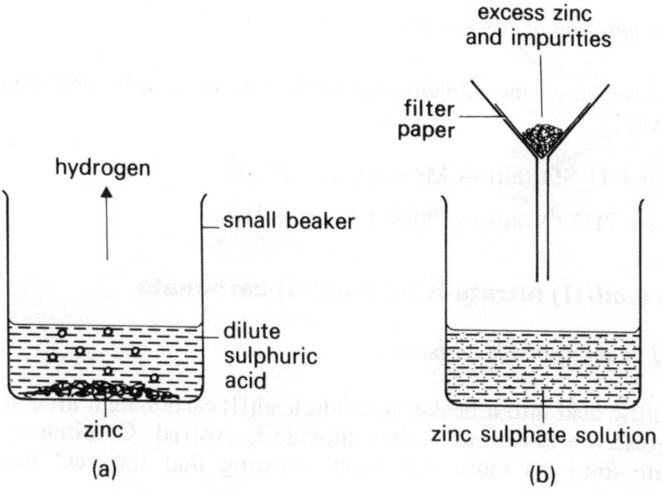

Fig. 10.1 Preparation of zinc sulphate

To prepare copper(II) sulphate from copper(II) oxide

Action of acid on an insoluble oxide or hydroxide

Pour dilute sulphuric acid into a beaker and warm gently but *do not boil.* Add copper(II) oxide to the warm acid, a little at a time (Fig. 10.2). It reacts without effervescence and forms a blue solution. Continue to add the oxide until no more reacts, showing that all the acid has been neutralized:

$$CuO(s) + H_2SO_4(aq) \rightarrow CuSO_4(aq) + H_2O(l)$$

Filter off the excess copper(II) oxide. Evaporate the blue filtrate in a beaker and test now and then to find if it will form crystals when it cools. Obtain copper(II) sulphate-5-water crystals, $CuSO_4 \cdot 5H_2O$, as in the previous experiment.

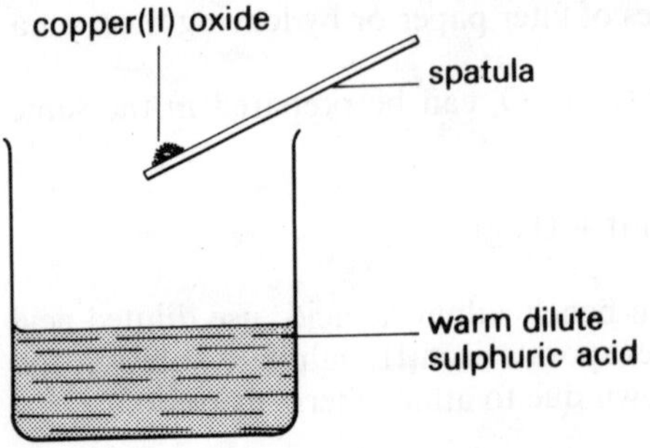

Fig. 10.2 Preparation of copper(II) sulphate

Magnesium sulphate, zinc sulphate and lead(II) nitrate can be prepared in the same way:

$$Mg(OH)_2(s) + H_2SO_4(aq) \rightarrow MgSO_4(aq) + 2H_2O$$
$$PbO(s) + 2HNO_3(aq) \rightarrow Pb(NO_3)_2(aq) + H_2O$$

To prepare lead(II) nitrate from lead(II) carbonate

Action of acid on an insoluble carbonate

Pour dilute nitric acid into a beaker and add lead(II) carbonate a little at a time. Effervescence occurs as carbon dioxide is evolved. Continue to add carbonate until no more will react, showing that the acid has reacted:

$$PbCO_3(s) + 2HNO_3(aq) \rightarrow Pb(NO_3)_2(aq) + CO_2(g) + H_2O$$

Filter off excess carbonate. Evaporate the colourless filtrate and obtain white crystals as in the previous experiments.

Copper(II) sulphate and nitrate, magnesium sulphate, zinc sulphate, and calcium chloride and nitrate can be prepared by this method. Calcium chloride and nitrate are deliquescent and do not form crystals; their solutions must be evaporated to dryness.

$$ZnCO_3(s) + H_2SO_4(aq) \rightarrow ZnSO_4(aq) + CO_2(g) + H_2O$$
$$CaCO_3(s) + 2HCl(aq) \rightarrow CaCl_2(aq) + CO_2(g) + H_2O$$

Action of acid on a soluble hydroxide or carbonate

Sodium, potassium and ammonium salts can be made from solutions of their hydroxides or carbonates. Methyl orange must be used as indicator with sodium carbonate, potassium carbonate and aqueous ammonia. Sodium and ammonium nitrates are very soluble and do not form crystals easily.

$$Na_2CO_3(aq) + H_2SO_4(aq) \rightarrow Na_2SO_4(aq) + CO_2(g) + H_2O$$
$$NH_3(aq) + HCl(aq) \rightarrow NH_4Cl(aq)$$

To prepare sodium sulphate

Fix a burette in its stand. Place a funnel in the burette and add dilute sulphuric acid until it is at or below the zero mark. Note the reading (it is easier to see the meniscus if white paper is held behind it).

Use a measuring cylinder to add 25 cm^3 of sodium hydroxide or sodium carbonate to a beaker. Add 2 drops of litmus solution. Add acid from the burette to the alkali, adding about 1 cm^3 at a time and shaking carefully after each addition. When the colour of the litmus shows signs of changing to red, add the acid *one drop at a time* until the colour is purple or just red, i.e. the solution is neutral or just acid.

$$2NaOH(aq) + H_2SO_4(aq) \rightarrow Na_2SO_4(aq) + 2H_2O$$
$$Na_2CO_3(aq) + H_2SO_4(aq) \rightarrow Na_2SO_4(aq) + H_2O + CO_2(g)$$

Read the burette once again; the difference between the two readings is the volume of acid needed to neutralize 25 cm^3 of the alkali. Throw away the solution as the litmus would colour the salt obtained from it. (Keep the solution if you are using the charcoal method below.)

Repeat the whole process using exactly the same volumes of the acid and alkali, but do not add litmus. Evaporate the solution and allow it to crystallize slowly on cooling.

Note. Remove the litmus from the neutral solution by boiling it for 5 minutes with animal charcoal and then filtering. The charcoal absorbs the litmus and the filtrate is colourless. If this method is used, no burette readings are necessary.

To prepare lead(II) sulphate

Precipitation

Add dilute sulphuric acid (or a solution of any soluble sulphate) to lead(II) nitrate solution in a beaker, stirring all the time. A white precipitate forms:

$$Pb^{2+}(aq) + SO_4^{2-}(aq) \rightarrow PbSO_4(s)$$

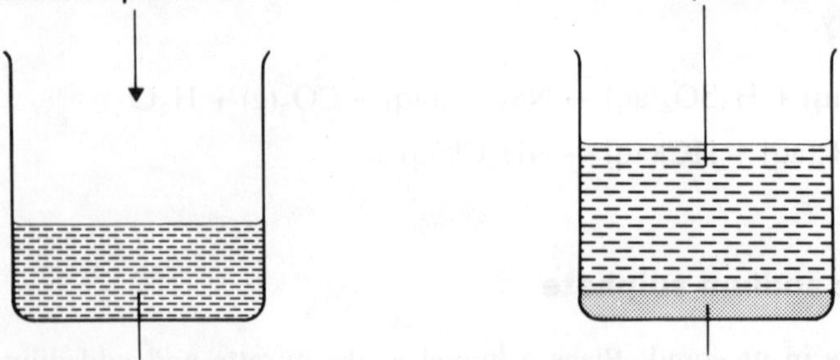

Fig. 10.3 Preparation of lead(II) sulphate

Either filter off the precipitate or allow it to settle and decant the liquid. Wash the precipitate with hot distilled water to remove acid and dry in an oven or in air.

To prepare lead(II) chloride

Add dilute hydrochloric acid (or a solution of any soluble chloride) to lead(II) nitrate solution in a beaker, stirring all the time. A white precipitate forms:

$$Pb^{2+}(aq) + 2Cl^-(aq) \rightarrow PbCl_2(s)$$

Filter off the precipitate or allow it to settle and decant the liquid. Wash the precipitate twice with *a little* cold distilled water to remove any acid. Dissolve the lead(II) chloride in the *smallest amount* of hot water. Allow the solution to cool slowly. Filter off and dry the crystals.

Silver chloride, barium sulphate and calcium sulphate are white insoluble salts usually prepared by precipitation; they do not form crystals:

$$AgNO_3(aq) + HCl(aq) \rightarrow AgCl(s) + HNO_3(aq)$$

i.e. $$Ag^+(aq) + Cl^-(aq) \rightarrow AgCl(s)$$

$$BaCl_2(aq) + H_2SO_4(aq) \rightarrow BaSO_4(s) + 2HCl(aq)$$

i.e. $$Ba^{2+}(aq) + SO_4^{2-}(aq) \rightarrow BaSO_4(s)$$

Other preparations are described in this book:

Iron(II) sulphide p. 18
Sodium hydrogencarbonate p. 189
Sodium carbonate p. 189

Zinc sulphide p. 18
Copper(II) sulphate p. 253
Sodium carbonate p. 190
Sodium hydrogencarbonate p. 189
Iron(III) chloride p. 268
Iron(II) chloride p. 269

Special preparations of salts

To prepare an insoluble salt from an insoluble substance [e.g. lead(II) sulphate from lead or lead(II) carbonate, calcium sulphate from calcium carbonate] first dissolve the substance in nitric acid and then precipitate the salt, e.g.

$$\underset{\text{insoluble}}{PbCO_3(s)} + 2HNO_3(aq) \rightarrow \underset{\text{soluble}}{Pb(NO_3)_2(aq)} + CO_2(g) + H_2O$$

$$Pb(NO_3)_2(aq) + H_2SO_4(aq) \rightarrow PbSO_4(s) + 2HNO_3(aq)$$

Remember that sulphuric acid hardly reacts with lead, lead carbonate or calcium carbonate.

To prepare a soluble salt from another soluble salt [e.g. copper(II) nitrate from copper(II) sulphate], first prepare the insoluble hydroxide and dissolve it in acid:

$$CuSO_4(aq) + 2NaOH(aq) \rightarrow Cu(OH)_2(s) + Na_2SO_4(aq)$$

$$Cu(OH)_2(aq) + 2HNO_3(aq) \rightarrow Cu(NO_3)_2(aq) + 2H_2O$$

Questions

1 What properties do you regard as characteristic of (*a*) an acid, (*b*) a base? Include as many properties as possible. Describe in detail how you would (i) convert some metallic copper completely to a base, and (ii) form crystals of a copper salt from the base so obtained. (C.)

2 What is a salt? Distinguish between (*a*) acid salts and normal salts, (*b*) hydrated salts and anhydrous salts. Outline three different methods of making normal salts and illustrate these methods by describing how you would make fairly pure samples of (i) magnesium sulphate, (ii) sodium nitrate, (iii) silver chloride. (L.)

3 Write down four properties you expect an acid to possess. Describe in detail how you would prepare in the laboratory crystals of (*a*) zinc sulphate from zinc, (*b*) potassium nitrate from potassium hydroxide solution, (*c*) sodium carbonate from sodium. (C.)

4 State briefly three general methods for the preparation of salts and illustrate each by a chemical equation. Select any one of these methods and give complete details for the preparation of a pure dry sample of a salt. (N.)

5 What is the chemical name for caustic soda? Describe the solid form in which it is usually found in the laboratory. State two properties and indicate briefly two uses of this compound. Describe fully the action of potassium hydroxide solution on ammonium chloride and on copper(II) sulphate solution. (N.)

6 Give three characteristic properties of a base. Explain the meaning of the term 'basicity' of an acid. Describe how you would prepare (*a*) a base from copper(II) sulphate solution, (*b*) an acid from sodium nitrate, (*c*) crystals of a normal salt from sulphuric acid. (L.)

7 What are basic oxides and acidic oxides? Describe in detail how you would prepare crystals of copper(II) sulphate from copper(II) oxide. Describe how you would obtain a specimen of copper(II) hydroxide from copper(II) sulphate solution. (O.)

8 State clearly how you would prepare in the laboratory: (*a*) iron from powdered iron(III) oxide, (*b*) iron(III) oxide from iron(III) hydroxide, (*c*) iron(III) hydroxide from iron(III) chloride solution, (*d*) iron(II) sulphate-7-water, $FeSO_4 \cdot 7H_2O$, from iron filings. (L.)

9 What do you understand by the term 'salts' as applied to a class of compounds? Chlorides may be prepared by (*a*) direct combination, (*b*) precipitation, (*c*) neutralization. Selecting a suitable yet different method for each salt, briefly describe the preparation of (i) silver chloride, (ii) sodium chloride, (iii) iron(III) chloride. (L.)

10 Describe how you would prepare specimens of (*a*) calcium sulphate (insoluble) from calcium carbonate, and (*b*) copper from copper(II) sulphate (not by electrolysis). (C.)

11 Masses and Numbers of Reacting Particles

In the experiments that follow, you will determine the masses of, and numbers of atoms, molecules or ions that react together, and will then be able to write the formulae of simple substances and chemical equations. Similar experiments had to be done before any formulae and chemical equations could be written.

To find the formula of magnesium oxide by direct combination of magnesium and oxygen

Find the mass of a clean crucible and lid. Use sandpaper to clean magnesium ribbon and add it, or magnesium powder, to the crucible. Convert the metal to its oxide by heating as described on p. 30. Allow the crucible to cool. Find the mass of the crucible, lid and oxide. (In accurate work, leave the crucible and lid in a desiccator before weighing, and also allow the apparatus to cool in a desiccator before the final weighing. This ensures that the apparatus is quite dry.)

1	Mass of crucible and lid	$= a$ g
2	Mass of crucible, lid and magnesium	$= b$ g
3	Mass of crucible, lid and magnesium oxide	$= c$ g
2–1	Mass of magnesium	$= (b-a)$ g
3–2	Mass of oxygen	$= (c-b)$ g

Mass $(c-b)$ g of oxygen combines with mass $(b-a)$ g of magnesium.

$$\therefore\ 16\,\text{g of oxygen combine with } 16\frac{(b-a)}{(c-b)}\,\text{g of magnesium.}$$

Accurate experiments show that 16 g of oxygen (i.e. 1 mole) combine with 24 g of magnesium (1 mole). Therefore 1 atom of oxygen combines with 1 atom of magnesium and the formula of magnesium oxide is MgO. The equation must be:

$$2Mg(s) + O_2(g) \rightarrow 2MgO(s)$$

Some textbooks recommend lining the crucible with heat resistant paper to stop the magnesium reacting with the procelain. This is not advisable because the heat resistant paper loses moisture and causes errors. The magnesium may form a little nitride, Mg_3N_2, but it is negligible.

To oxidize copper and find the formula of copper(II) oxide

Place a plug of glass wool loosely in the mouth of a clean test-tube and find the total mass. Remove the wool, add copper to the tube, replace the wool, and find the mass again. Remove the wool and to the copper add 5 drops of water and then concentrated nitric acid, drop by drop. Do this in a fume cupboard or near an open window. Reddish-brown fumes of

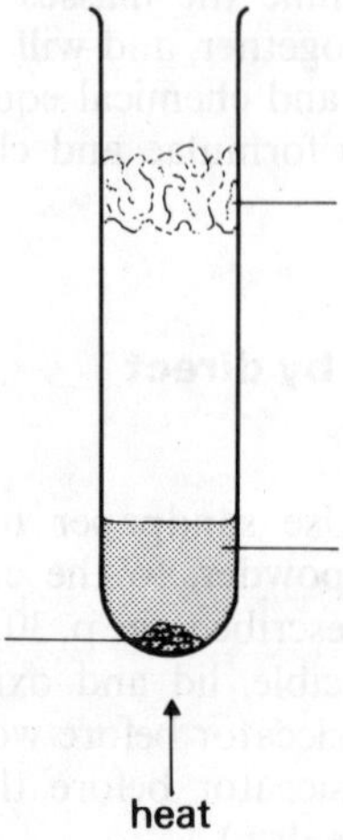

Fig. 11.1 Preparation of copper(II) oxide by indirect oxidation

nitrogen dioxide (poisonous) are evolved and a blue or green copper(II) nitrate solution remains:

$$Cu(s) + 4HNO_3(aq) \rightarrow Cu(NO_3)_2(aq) + 2NO_2(g) + 2H_2O(l)$$

Use the minimum amount of acid because any excess forms noxious fumes when evaporated later.

Push the glass wool down the test-tube. Evaporate the liquid *carefully* in a fume cupboard. The wool prevents any solution 'spitting' out of the tube. Greenish copper(II) nitrate is the solid first formed, and then it decomposes to black copper(II) oxide. More reddish-brown fumes are evolved:

$$2Cu(NO_3)_2(s) \rightarrow 2CuO(s) + 4NO_2(g) + O_2(g)$$

Find the mass of the test-tube and contents when cool. If necessary, repeat the heating until a constant mass is reached.

1	Mass of test-tube and glass wool	$= a$ g
2	Mass of test-tube, glass wool and copper	$= b$ g
3	Mass of test-tube, glass wool and copper(II) oxide	$= c$ g
2–1	Mass of copper	$= (b - a)$ g
3–2	Mass of oxygen	$= (c - b)$ g

Mass $(c - b)$ g of oxygen combines with mass $(b - a)$ g of copper.

$\therefore$ 16 g of oxygen combine with $16\dfrac{(b-a)}{(c-b)}$ g of copper.

16 g (1 mole) of oxygen combines with 63.5 g (1 mole) of copper. The formula of copper(II) oxide is therefore CuO.

The experiment can be done with magnesium, zinc or lead instead of copper. Instead of the test-tube and glass wool, an evaporating basin covered with a clock-glass can be used. The clock-glass prevents loss of nitrate solution by 'spitting' during the evaporation. See Fig. 11.2.

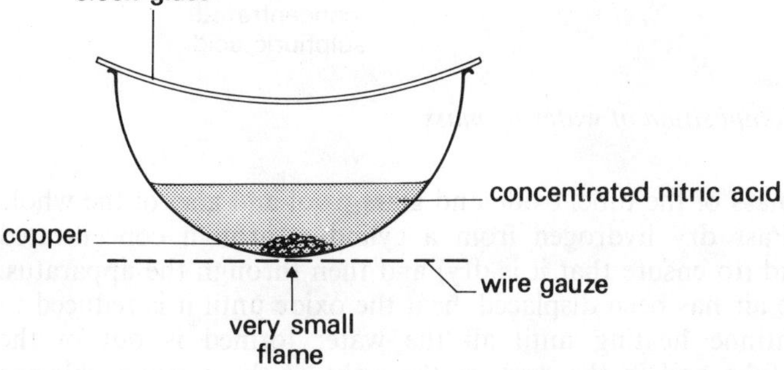

Fig. 11.2 Formula of copper(II) oxide by indirect oxidation

Composition of water by mass

This was first determined by Dumas in 1842. A similar experiment to his is to pass hydrogen over heated copper(II) oxide, and find the mass of water formed. The mass of oxygen is equal to the loss in mass of the copper(II) oxide:

$$CuO(s) + H_2(g) \rightarrow Cu(s) + H_2O(g)$$

Since hydrogen is used in this experiment, there is some danger of an explosion unless care is taken. A plastic safety screen must be used.

Arrange the apparatus as in Fig. 11.3 and dry it in an oven at 100 °C. The glass wool keeps the dry wire-form copper(II) oxide in position in the combustion tube.

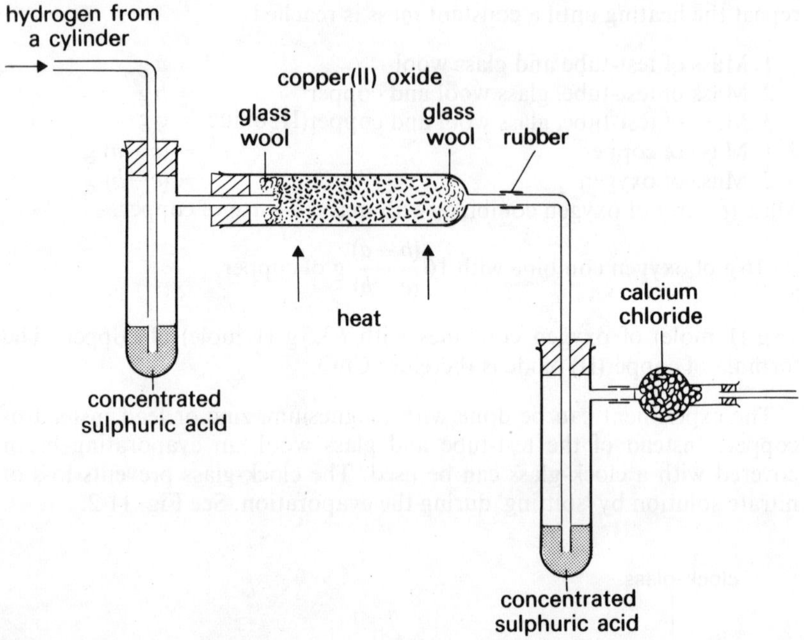

Fig. 11.3 Composition of water by mass

Find the mass of the tube, oxide and glass wool and also of the whole apparatus. Pass dry hydrogen from a cylinder through concentrated sulphuric acid (to ensure that it is dry) and then through the apparatus. When all the air has been displaced, heat the oxide until it is reduced to copper. Continue heating until all the water formed is out of the combustion tube and in the acid on the right or the calcium chloride tube. Turn off the flame and pass hydrogen until the apparatus is cool.

Find the mass of the whole apparatus, and then of the tube, copper and glass wool.

1 Mass of tube, oxide and wool $= a$ g
2 Mass of whole apparatus at start $= b$ g
3 Mass of whole apparatus at end $= c$ g
4 Mass of tube, copper and wool $= d$ g

Therefore, the mass of hydrogen is $(c-b)$ g and the mass of oxygen in the water formed is $(a-d)$ g.

$$\frac{\text{Mass of hydrogen}}{\text{Mass of oxygen}} = \frac{(c-b)}{(a-d)}$$

This ratio is about 1:8.

(The ratio of hydrogen: oxygen by moles is $\frac{1}{1}:\frac{8}{16}$ which is 2:1, and therefore the formula of water is H_2O.)

The composition by volume and formula of hydrogen chloride are on p. 267.

Replacement of one metal by another

Add zinc foil to concentrated copper(II) sulphate solution in an evaporating basin. Tap the zinc gently with a glass rod (Fig. 11.4) to knock off copper which forms on the outside.

$$\frac{\text{Mass of zinc used}}{\text{Mass of copper replaced}} = \frac{\text{Reacting mass of zinc}}{\text{Reacting mass of copper}}$$

If the relative atomic masses of copper and zinc (63.5 and 65.4 respectively) are assumed, the equation for the reaction between zinc and copper(II) sulphate can be determined from the above reaction.

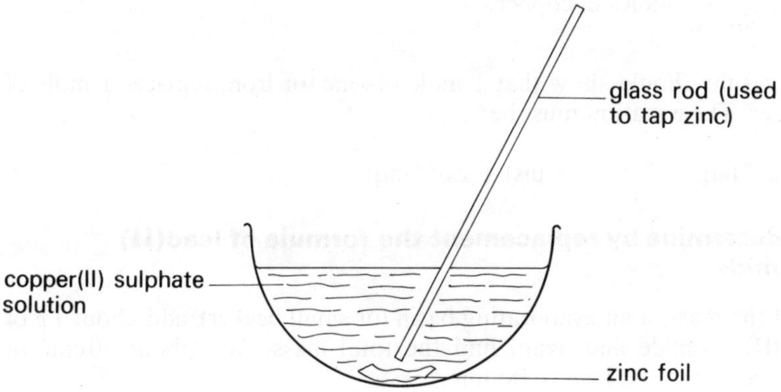

Fig. 11.4 Replacement of copper by zinc

To determine by replacement the equation for the reaction between a metal (zinc or iron) and a salt (copper(II) sulphate)

Find the mass of an evaporating basin, add about 0.5 g of zinc foil (or iron filings) and again find the total mass.

Dissolve about 3 g (i.e. excess) of copper(II) sulphate-5-water in a test-tube half full of hot distilled water. Add the hot solution to the metal in the basin. Tap the foil with a glass rod so that copper which forms on the outside falls off and the solution can react with the zinc inside the foil.

(Stir the iron filings with a glass rod to ensure that reaction is complete; the reaction stops if a copper coating forms around each filing.) Usually reaction is complete in less than 5 minutes.

Let the copper powder settle to the bottom of the basin. Carefully pour away the solution [excess copper(II) sulphate with zinc(II) or iron(II) sulphate], wash the copper with distilled water to remove traces of solution, and finally wash with propanone or ethanol. Pour away most of the propanone or ethanol, and then dry the basin and copper in an oven or sunshine. Propanone and ethanol are volatile and soon evaporate.

When cool, find the mass of the basin and dry copper.

1 Mass of evaporating basin $= a$ g
2 Mass of basin + zinc (or iron) $= b$ g
3 Mass of basin + copper $= c$ g

Mass $(b-a)$ g of zinc replaces mass $(c-a)$ g of copper.

$\therefore$ mass 65.4 g (1 mole) of zinc replaces $\dfrac{65.4(c-a)}{(b-a)}$ g of copper

$$= \frac{65.4(c-a)}{63.5(b-a)} \text{ moles of copper.}$$

The results should show that 1 mole of zinc (or iron) replaces 1 mole of copper. The equation must be:

$$Cu^{2+}(aq) + Zn(s) \rightarrow Cu(s) + Zn^{2+}(aq)$$

To determine by replacement the formula of lead(II) bromide

Find the mass of an evaporating basin (or small beaker), add about 1 g of lead(II) bromide and again find the total mass. Add about 50 cm^3 of distilled water and heat to boiling.

Remove the basin or beaker from the heat. Add about 0.1 g of aluminium powder and boil gently for 10 minutes. The aluminium replaces the lead. Excess aluminium remains; add about 20 cm^3 of bench sodium hydroxide solution (about 2 M, p. 325) to dissolve this aluminium. Carefully pour away the solution but not the lead.

Clean the lead with distilled water and propanone or ethanol (as in the previous experiment), and dry the basin and lead.

When cool, find the mass of the basin and lead.

1 Mass of basin (or beaker) $= a$ g
2 Mass of basin + lead(II) bromide $= b$ g
3 Mass of basin + lead $= c$ g

Mass $(b-a)$ g of lead(II) bromide contains mass $(c-a)$ g of lead. Therefore it also contains $(b-a)$ g $-(c-a)$ g of bromine.

(Assume that the relative atomic masses of lead and bromine are 207 and 80 respectively.)

Mass $(c-a)$ g of lead combines with mass $(b-a)\,\text{g}-(c-a)\,\text{g}$ of bromine.

$\therefore$ mass 207 g (1 mole) of lead combines with $\dfrac{207[(b-a)-(c-a)]}{80(c-a)}$ moles of bromine.

The results should show that 1 mole of lead combines with 2 moles of bromine. The formula of lead(II) bromide is $PbBr_2$.

Reaction involving a gas

In this experiment, we measure the maximum volume of gas, carbon dioxide, produced when increasing volumes of one solution (2 M hydrochloric acid, p. 328) reacts with a fixed volume of another solution (M sodium carbonate). The special flask, Fig. 11.5 prevents the solutions mixing until required. If it is not available, use a flask and test-tube as in Fig. 6.2.

Use graduated pipettes to add 4.0 cm^3 of M sodium carbonate in one side of the flask (or the test-tube) and 1.0 cm^3 of 2 M hydrochloric acid to the other. Connect the flask to a syringe, and note the reading. Mix the solutions. Note the new reading and therefore the volume of carbon dioxide evolved. Repeat with 2, 3, 4, 5 and 6 cm^3 of acid.

Acid (cm^3)	1.0	2.0	3.0	4.0	5.0	6.0
Gas (cm^3)						

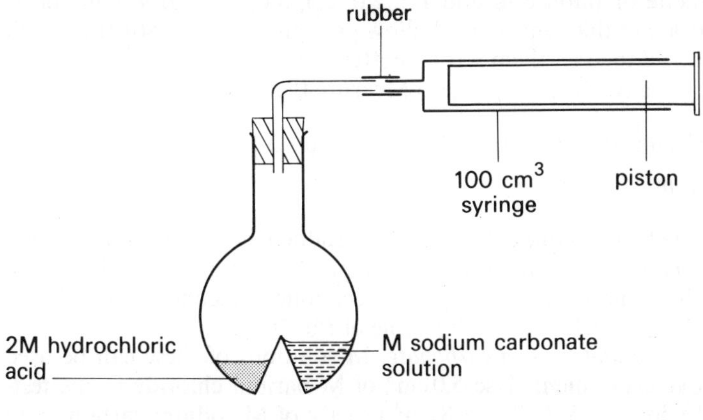

Fig. 11.5 Equation for a reaction involving a gas

You should find that 4 cm^3 of acid react completely with 4 cm^3 of sodium carbonate (the volumes of gas increase but are the same, about 100 cm^3, for 4, 5 or 6 cm^3 of acid).

1000 cm^3 of M hydrochloric acid contain 1 mole of acid.

$\therefore$ 4 cm^3 of 2 M hydrochloric acid contain $\frac{4 \times 2}{1000} = 0.008$ mole of acid.

4 cm^3 of 2 M hydrochloric acid (0.008 mole) reacts completely with 4 cm^3 of M sodium carbonate (0.004 mole) to form about 100 cm^3 of carbon dioxide at room temperature and pressure.

A volume of 24 000 cm^3 of carbon dioxide at room temperature and pressure is 1 mole (p. 77), and 100 cm^3 of the gas is $\frac{100}{24\,000} = 0.004\,2$ mole. Therefore, 0.008 mole of hydrochloric acid react with 0.004 mole of sodium carbonate to form about 0.004 mole of carbon dioxide.

Therefore 1 mole of sodium carbonate (Na_2CO_3) reacts with 2 moles of hydrochloric acid (2HCl) to form 1 mole of carbon dioxide (CO_2), and the equation must be:

$$CO_3^{2-}(aq) + 2H^+(aq) \rightarrow CO_2(g) + H_2O$$

Reaction involving a precipitate

Increasing volumes of M lead(II) nitrate are added separately to equal volumes of M potassium iodide in six similar test-tubes. Precipitates are formed and their heights in the tubes measured. The height reaches a maximum and does not increase when excess lead nitrate is added.

Use a graduated pipette or burette to add 5.0 cm^3 of M potassium iodide to each of six uniform test-tubes (125 × 16 mm) in a rack. Use a second pipette or burette to add 1.5, 2.0, 2.5, 3.0, 3.5 and 4.0 cm^3 of M lead(II) nitrate to different tubes. Yellow precipitates form. Stir them with a glass rod and then let them settle. (Better results are obtained by using a centrifuge to settle the precipitates.) Measure their heights.

M lead(II) nitrate/cm^3	1.5	2.0	2.5	3.0	3.5	4.0
Height/mm						

Plot a graph of the volume of lead(II) nitrate added (horizontal axis) against the height of the precipitate. What is the minimum volume of lead(II) nitrate which produces the maximum height of precipitate? Calculate the number of moles of I^-(aq) which react with 1 mole of Pb^{2+}(aq).

Barium chloride and sodium carbonate. M solutions of these can be used in the above experiment. Use 5.0 cm^3 of M barium chloride in the test-tubes and add 3, 4, 5, 6, 7 and 8 cm^3 exactly of M sodium carbonate to different tubes. The white precipitates do not settle easily when cold.

Warm them by placing the six test-tubes in a beaker of hot water, stirring well, and then allowing to cool in the rack. Measure the heights of the precipitates.

Specimen results are:

M Ba^{2+}(aq) (cm^3)	5	5	5	5	5	5
M CO_3^{2-}(aq) (cm^3)	3	4	5	6	7	8
Height (mm)	19	24	30	28	31	29

The reaction is complete with 5 cm^3 of sodium carbonate as further addition forms no more precipitate.

$$5\,cm^3\ M\ Ba^{2+}(aq) \equiv 5\,cm^3\ M\ CO_3^{2-}$$

$$\therefore\quad 1\ mole\ Ba^{2+}(aq) \equiv 1\ mole\ CO_3^{2-}$$

and the equation must be:

$$Ba^{2+}(aq) + CO_3^{2-}(aq) \rightarrow BaCO_3(s)$$

(A solution of 0.5 M barium chloride and increasing volumes of 0.5 M potassium chromate(VI) may also be used. The colour of the liquid above the precipitate changes and also indicates when reaction is complete.)

Questions

(Where necessary assume that 1 cm^3 of hydrogen at s.t.p. has a mass of 0.000 09 g.)

1 Draw a labelled diagram of the apparatus you would use to make a reasonably accurate determination of the mass of zinc or magnesium which displaces 1 g of hydrogen from dilute sulphuric acid. Mention two necessary precautions. 0.52 g of a metal liberated 179.2 cm^3 of hydrogen, measured at s.t.p. Find the mass of metal which displaces 1 mole (1 g) of hydrogen atoms. (C.)

2 Iron will displace copper from copper(II) sulphate solution. Describe how you would find the mass of iron which displaces 1 mole (64 g) of copper. In such an experiment the following results were obtained: Mass of iron, 2.31 g; mass of copper displaced, 2.64 g. Calculate the reacting mass of iron (Cu = 64). (C.)

3 1 g of mixture of zinc and zinc oxide formed 177 cm^3 of hydrogen measured at s.t.p. Calculate the percentage of zinc oxide in the mixture. (32.5 g of zinc form 11 200 cm^3 of hydrogen at s.t.p.) (N.)

4 Copper(II) oxide was reduced in hydrogen. 1.00 g of water was formed from 4.44 g of the oxide. Calculate the mass of copper which combines with 1 mole (16 g) of oxygen.

5 Explain what is meant by the 'molar mass' of an element. When 0.12 g of a metal was dissolved in excess of dilute sulphuric acid, 112 cm^3 of dry hydrogen were evolved, measured at s.t.p. Calculate the mass of metal which displaces 1 g of hydrogen. The density of hydrogen at s.t.p. is 0.090 g per dm^3. Describe in detail how you would carry out the above determination in the laboratory. (L.)

6 Describe what you would see, and explain the chemistry of the reactions involved when: (*a*) concentrated nitric acid is added a little at a time to copper turnings in a beaker until no further change takes place; (*b*) the solution from (*a*) is carefully evaporated to dryness, after which the residue is strongly heated until no further change occurs; (*c*) part of the residue from (*b*) is heated in a stream of hydrogen until there is no further change; (*d*) the remainder of the residue from (*b*) is added a little at a time to dilute sulphuric acid, the mixture being warmed and stirred, until the residue is present in excess. The excess is then filtered off; (*e*) to the filtrate from (*d*) pieces of zinc foil are added and the mixture is well stirred. (L.)

7 Various volumes of M lead(II) nitrate and M potassium iodide were mixed in identical test-tubes. Each precipitate was centrifuged and its height in the tube was measured.

Volume KI (cm^3)	10	10	10	10	10	10	10	10
Volume nitrate (cm^3)	3	4	5	6	7	8	9	10
Height of ppt. (mm)	12	16	20	19	21	20	19	20.5

Use these results to suggest an equation for the reaction that occurs, and explain your answer fully.

8 1.00 M nitric acid was added 1 cm^3 at a time to 50 cm^3 of 0.10 M sodium carbonate. Effervescence occurred until 10.0 cm^3 of acid had been added and after that no further effervescence was observed. Write the left hand side of the equation for the reaction that occurs, using these results, and give your reasons. 0.848 g (0.008 mole) of anhydrous sodium carbonate reacted with excess dilute nitric acid and produced 196 cm^3 of gas (measured at s.t.p.). Use this result to complete the equation, and explain your reasoning.

9 What maximum mass of aluminium(III) oxide could be obtained by heating 7.8 g of pure aluminium hydroxide? Explain what is meant by the Avogadro constant.

10 A metal forms two chlorides containing 55.95 and 65.5 per cent of chlorine by mass. Calculate the masses of metal which combine with 1 mole (35.5 g) of chlorine atoms. Suggest valencies of the metal in the chlorides and possible formulae for the chlorides. What is the probable relative atomic mass of the metal?

11 A compound may be represented by an empirical formula and by a molecular formula. Distinguish between the two, giving an example of a compound where they differ. A volatile compound contains 40.0 per cent carbon, 6.67 per cent hydrogen, and 53.33 per cent oxygen. Its vapour density is 30. Show that its empirical formula is CH_2O and its molecular formula is $C_2H_4O_2$. (L.)

12
Rates of Reactions

Temperature, concentration, surface area of solid reactants (or particle size) and catalysts affect rates of reactions. Explosive reactions are complete in a fraction of a second, corrosion of iron and other metals takes place over months or years, but we will study rates of reactions that are complete in a few minutes. The decomposition of hydrogen peroxide is suitable because oxygen is evolved and we can measure its volume at various times. Fig. 12.1 shows the typical graph obtained when plotting the volume of oxygen against time.

$$\text{Rate of reaction} = \frac{\text{Volume of oxygen}}{\text{Time interval}}$$

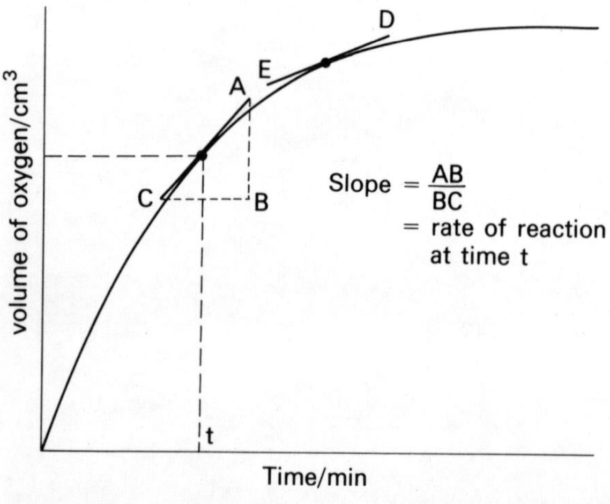

Fig. 12.1 Oxygen/time graph when hydrogen peroxide decomposes

Students who understand the mathematics of graphs know that the rate at any time *t* is given by the slope of the tangent AC of the graph at that time. The slope of tangent DE is less than that of AC; the rate of reaction decreases with time and is slowest near the end of the reaction.

To study the rate of decomposition of hydrogen peroxide

Effect of a catalyst. Arrange a syringe apparatus, Fig. 12.2. Dilute $2\,cm^3$ of 20 volume hydrogen peroxide with water. Add a little manganese(IV)

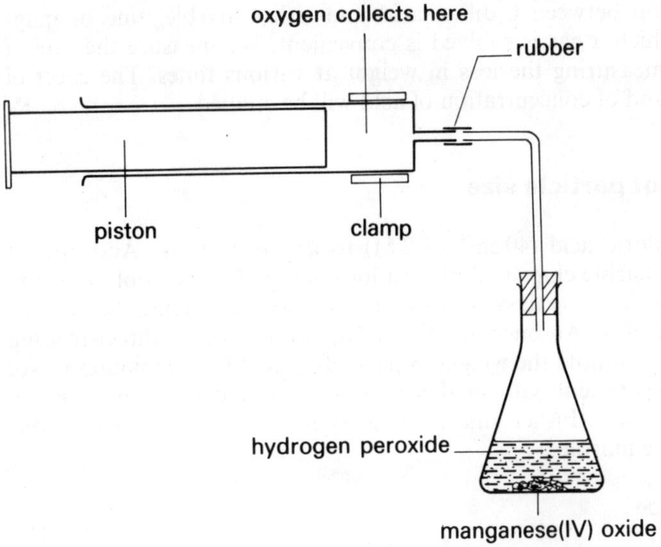

Fig. 12.2 The effect of a catalyst on reaction rate

oxide and observe the volume of oxygen produced at intervals of 1 minute. (The rate at which oxygen is produced when no catalyst is present is negligible.)

(Instead of a syringe, you can use a burette filled with water and clamped upside down in a small trough of water. Oxygen passes through a delivery tube from the conical flask to the burette, and its volume can be measured.)

Effect of concentration. Take four conical flasks. To three of them add 70, 30 and 10 cm^3 of water. Now add 10 cm^3 of hydrogen peroxide solution to each flask, making the total volumes of solution 80, 40, 20 and 10 cm^3. The concentrations of the peroxide are in the ratio 1:2:4:8.

Add a known mass of manganese(IV) oxide to one flask. Use the apparatus of Fig. 12.2 to observe the time taken for a certain volume of oxygen to be evolved. Repeat with the other three flasks, using the same mass of manganese(IV) oxide each time.

Plot graphs of (*a*) concentration of hydrogen peroxide against the time taken for the oxygen to be evolved, and (*b*) concentration against $time^{-1}$ (i.e. 1/time) which is proportional to the rate of reaction. (The longer the time taken, the slower the rate of reaction.)

Effect of temperature. Add 50 cm^3 of hydrogen peroxide solution to a flask and warm it quickly to 40 °C. Use the apparatus of Fig. 12.2 to observe the time taken for a certain volume of oxygen to be evolved. Repeat with the same volume of the same solution at 50 °C, and then at other convenient temperatures.

Plot a graph of the temperature against $time^{-1}$ (i.e. rate of reaction).

The reaction between a dilute acid and either marble, zinc or magnesium, in which a gas is evolved is convenient. We measure the rate of reaction by measuring the loss in weight at various times. The effect of particle size and of concentration of acid will be studied.

The effect of particle size

Add hydrochloric acid (40 cm^3 of 2 M) to a conical flask. Add 20 g of medium size marble chips and place a loose plug of glass wool or cotton wool in the neck of the flask to prevent acid spray damaging the balance used, Fig. 12.3(a). At once weigh the apparatus on a direct-reading balance, and then note the weight every half-minute for 10 minutes or so. Repeat the experiment with smaller marble chips and then with calcium carbonate powder. (Either zinc or magnesium of different particle sizes can replace the marble.)

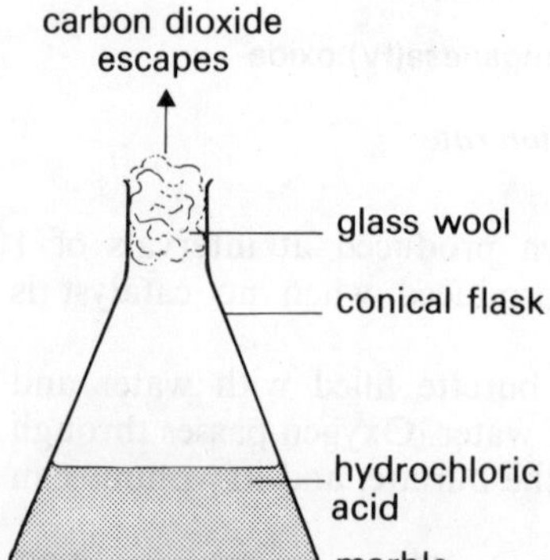

Fig. 12.3 Effect of particle size on rate of reaction: weigh every $\frac{1}{2}$ minute

Obtain typical rate curves by plotting loss of weight (i.e. the extent of reaction) against time. Compare the slopes of the three graphs. How does the rate of reaction vary with particle size?

To determine the *effect of concentration* of the acid on the reaction rate, repeat the above experiment using the same mass of the same solid but using M, then 2 M, and then 3 M hydrochloric acid respectively. How does the rate vary with concentration?

The effect of concentration and also of temperature can be shown more easily by using the reaction between sodium thiosulphate and hydrochloric acid. Demonstrate the reaction by adding acid to sodium thiosulphate solution in a beaker. At first there is no visible reaction but after a *time interval t* pale yellow sulphur is precipitated sharply:

$$S_2O_3^{2-}(aq) + 2H^+(aq) \rightarrow S(s) + SO_2(g) + H_2O(l)$$

The longer the time interval, the slower is the reaction rate. In other words, rate of reaction is proportional to $1/t$ or t^{-1}.

The effect of concentration

Sodium thiosulphate and hydrochloric acid. Take four conical flasks. To three add 10, 20 and 30 cm^3 of water. Make the total volume in each flask 40 cm^3 by adding 40, 30, 20 and 10 cm^3 of sodium thiosulphate solution (40 g/dm^3). The concentrations of solution are in the ratio 1:2:3:4.

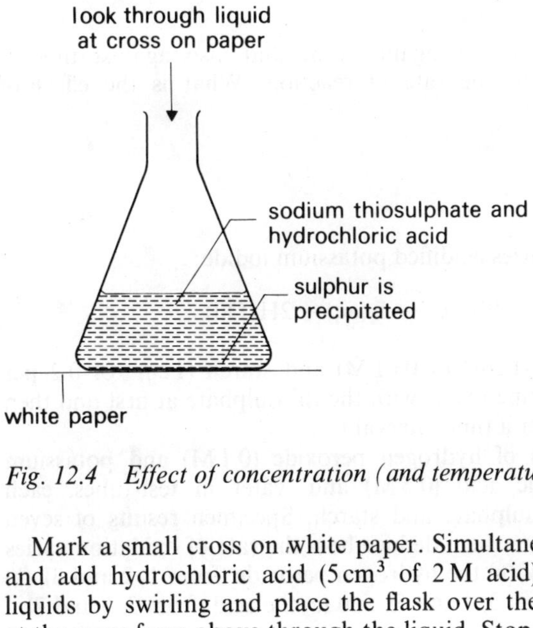

Fig. 12.4 Effect of concentration (and temperature) on rate of reaction

Mark a small cross on white paper. Simultaneously start a stopwatch and add hydrochloric acid (5 cm^3 of 2 M acid) to one flask. Mix the liquids by swirling and place the flask over the cross, Fig. 12.4. Look at the cross from above through the liquid. Stop the watch when the fine sulphur precipitate just makes the cross invisible. Note the time interval. Repeat with the other three flasks.

Concentration	1	2	3	4
Time interval (s)				
$Time^{-1}$ (s^{-1})				

Plot graphs of (*a*) concentration against time, and (*b*) concentration against 1/time ($time^{-1}$), which is proportional to the rate of reaction. Deduce how the reaction rate varies with the concentration.

The effect of temperature

Use a measuring cylinder to add 50 cm^3 of sodium thiosulphate to a conical flask. Warm the solution to about 32 °C (when cold acid is added later the temperature will be about 30 °C). Mark a small cross on white paper. Simultaneously start a stopwatch and add hydrochloric acid (5 cm^3) to the warm solution. Observe the time interval as above. Repeat the test at about 40, 50 and 60 °C.

Temperature (°C) e.g.	29	41	52	61
Time interval (s)				
$Time^{-1}$ (s^{-1})				

Plot graphs of temperature against time and also against $time^{-1}$, which is proportional to the rate of reaction. What is the effect of temperature on the rate?

Oxidation of iodides

Hydrogen peroxide oxidizes acidified potassium iodide:

$$H_2O_2(aq) + 2H^+(aq) + 2I^-(aq) \rightarrow I_2(aq) + 2H_2O(l)$$

If sodium thiosulphate (1 cm^3 of 0.01 M) and starch (1 cm^3 of 0.2 per cent) are present, the iodine reacts with the thiosulphate at first and then turns the starch blue after a time interval *t*.

Mix various volumes of hydrogen peroxide (0.1 M) and potassium iodide (0.1 M), sulphuric acid (0.5 M) and water in test-tubes, each containing sodium thiosulphate and starch. Specimen results of seven reactions are below. From them deduce how the rate of oxidation varies with the concentration of (*a*) the hydrogen peroxide (from 1, 2 and 3), (*b*) the potassium iodide (from 3, 4 and 5), and (*c*) the acid (from 3, 6 and 7).

Volume (cm^3)	H_2O_2	KI	H_2SO_4	H_2O	Total	*t* (s)
1	1	3	3	5	12	91
2	2	3	3	4	12	44
3	4	3	3	2	12	23
4	4	2	3	3	12	46
5	4	1	3	4	12	89
6	4	3	2	3	12	22
7	4	3	1	5	12	24

Collision Theory of reaction

According to the kinetic theory, the particles (atoms, molecules or ions) of substances in solutions, liquids and gases are constantly moving from place to place. The movement of any particular particle constantly changes, in both speed and directions, owing to collisions with other particles. The speeds of the particles differ greatly but the average speed increases with rise of temperature.

The collision theory states that before two or more substances can react together, their particles must collide. Therefore, reactions between solids, whose particles vibrate but do not move from place to place, do not occur. Particles of solutions, liquids and gases collide and some collisions between two substances result in chemical change, i.e. chemical bonds in the reactant particles break and new bonds are made to produce the products. The colliding particles need a certain minimum energy, called *activation energy*, before their chemical bonds can break and new bonds form. The effective collisions which produce reactions are usually few compared with ineffective collisions (except in explosive reactions). The collision theory explains the factors affecting rate of reaction.

Concentration. An increase in concentration of a solution, or pressure of a gas, increases the number of particles per unit volume. The chance of collision therefore increases and reaction is faster.

Temperature. Rise of temperature increases the speed of the particles and therefore their energy. There are more collisions per second and more colliding particles have the necessary activation energy for reaction. Usually a rise of 10 °C doubles the rate of reaction.

Surface area. If one reactant is a solid an increase in its surface area increases the number of collisions per second, and the reaction is faster. Powders and other finely divided solids react more quickly than the same mass in large lumps.

Catalysts. A catalyst lowers the activation energy and therefore increases the number of effective collisions per second and rate of reaction. Most catalysts used in industry are solids (metals, oxides, and charcoal). These *surface catalysts* must be finely divided (e.g. as powders, pellets, fibres or gauze) in order to have a large surface area. Probably some particles of one reactant attach themselves weakly to the catalyst surface, a process called *adsorption*, e.g. iron adsorbs nitrogen in the Haber process. The particles of the other reactant can then react more readily with the adsorbed particles. In some reactions, two gases are adsorbed and their particles react on the surface of the catalyst.

Light and reactions

Mixtures of hydrogen with chlorine or methane do not react in ordinary light but explode in sunlight. Light is essential for photosynthesis in green plants by which they convert carbon dioxide and water into sugar and starch. Light darkens silver salts on photographic paper by forming tiny particles of black silver:

$$2AgBr(s) + light \rightarrow 2Ag(s) + Br_2$$

In the above changes, energy from light is absorbed by one or more of the reacting particles and therefore the activation energy is attained readily and effective collisions become numerous.

Questions

1 When dilute hydrochloric acid and magnesium ribbon reacted, the lengths of ribbon and volumes of hydrogen formed were:

Length (cm)	1.0	2.0	3.0	5.0	6.0
Volume (cm^3/min)	2.2	3.6	5.2	9.2	10.8

Plot these results on a suitable graph and draw any conclusion you can from the graph. Estimate the rate of formation of hydrogen from 4.0 cm of metal.

2 Equal volumes of dilute acid of various concentrations were placed in five beakers. 0.26 g of the same zinc were added to each beaker. The times taken for reaction to be completed were noted.

Acid concentration	1.0 M	1.4 M	2.0 M	2.6 M	3.0 M
Time (s)	500	250	100	40	30
$Time^{-1}$ (s^{-1})	0.002	0.004	0.010	0.025	0.033

Draw concentration/time and concentration/$time^{-1}$ graphs. What conclusion can you reach from the graphs? The experiment was repeated with the same mass of zinc but in larger lumps; how would the times change and why? Show that the volume of hydrogen formed in each reaction is 90 cm^3 at s.t.p.

3 0.05 mole of a metal was placed in each of six flasks and various volumes of M hydrochloric acid were added. The volumes of hydrogen, at room temperature and pressure were recorded:

Acid (cm^3)	20	60	90	120	130	140
H_2 (cm^3)	242	720	1080	1200	1196	1200

Plot a suitable graph. Estimate from your graph the minimum volume of acid that will react completely with 0.05 mole of the metal. If the metal is iron show that this volume would be 100 cm^3 (from the equation).

4 2.0 g of calcium carbonate and 25 cm^3 (excess) of 2.0 M nitric acid were mixed and the loss in mass recorded at various time intervals:

Time (min)	2	4	6	8	10	12
Loss (g)	0.11	0.34	0.52	0.66	0.75	0.82

The maximum loss was 0.87 g. Plot a suitable graph. Show clearly that the rate of reaction was quickest during the 2–4 minute interval. Calculate from the equation what mass of carbon dioxide is formed.

5 0.192 g of magnesium was added to excess acid and the volume of hydrogen recorded at intervals:

Time (s)	30	60	90	120	150	180	210
H_2 (cm^3)	60	96	125	146	162	176	184

The maximum volume of hydrogen was 190 cm^3. Plot a suitable graph. At which of the stated times was the rate of reaction fastest? Calculate from an equation (hydrochloric acid) the volume of hydrogen formed at s.t.p.

6 0.01 mole of a solid metallic element X which forms an ion X^{2+}, was added to 40 cm^3 of 0.5 M sulphuric acid and the time taken for all of X to react was noted. This was repeated with the same mass of X and 80 cm^3 of 0.25 M sulphuric acid. Similar experiments used X in powder form. Hydrogen was evolved in all experiments. The results were:

Amount of X (mole)	Form of element	Sulphuric acid used (cm^3)	Time for all of X to react (s)
0.01	lump	40 (0.5 M)	280
0.01	lump	80 (0.25 M)	1485
0.01	powder	40 (0.5 M)	78
0.01	powder	80 (0.25 M)	135

(*a*) Write an equation for the reaction. (*b*) Show clearly that 0.2 mole is present in 40 cm^3 of 0.5 M sulphuric acid. (*c*) Calculate whether, in the reaction between 0.01 mole of *X* and 40 cm^3 of 0.5 M sulphuric acid, there is excess metal, excess acid, or the metal and acid just react exactly. (*d*) What information do the results give about the conditions which increase the rate of reaction between the metal and the acid? What other conditions could increase the rate of reaction? (L.)

7 $5.0\,cm^3$ of dilute acid were added to $50\,cm^3$ portions of sodium thiosulphate solution. The time intervals before fairly rapid precipitation of sulphur with different concentrations of sodium thiosulphate were:

Conc (M)	0.05	0.10	0.15	0.20	0.25
Time (s)	200	100	40	20	10

Plot a graph of concentration against time^{-1} (which is proportional to rate of reaction). What can you deduce from the graph?

13 Reactivity Series. Action of Electricity on Matter

Reactivity series of metals

Some metals are more reactive than others. They react more readily with air or oxygen, water and dilute acids. A list of the metals with the most active at the top and the least active at the bottom is called the *metal reactivity series.*

1 Lithium	**5** Magnesium	**9** Lead
2 Potassium	**6** Aluminium	**10** Hydrogen
3 Sodium	**7** Zinc	**11** Copper
4 Calcium	**8** Iron	**12** Mercury

The list can be made from (*a*) the reactions of the metals with oxygen, water and acids, (*b*) the chemical properties of their compounds, (*c*) the replacement by metals, of other metals from solutions of their salts.

1 Reactions of the metals

a *Air or oxygen*. See p. 29.
b *Water*. See pp. 54 and 61.
c *Dilute acids*. See pp. 48 and 61.

2 Chemical properties of compounds of metals

Metals high in the series are very active chemically. Therefore, their compounds are stable and decompose less readily than those of metals low in the series, e.g. sodium compounds are more stable than copper compounds. However, the activity series is only a general guide and the properties of compounds are not always in accordance with it, e.g. aluminium is high in the series but does not react with water and does not form a carbonate, which we would expect to be a stable compound.
a *Oxides*. See p. 107.
b *Hydroxides*. Lithium, potassium and sodium hydroxides are soluble in water; calcium and magnesium hydroxides are slightly soluble; and the others are insoluble. Heat does not decompose potassium or sodium

hydroxide, but the others form oxide and water when heated:

$$Cu(OH)_2(s) \rightarrow CuO(s) + H_2O(g)$$

c *Carbonates*. See p. 185
d *Nitrates*. See p. 233.

Metal	Action on oxides of: Hydrogen	Action on oxides of: Water	Action on hydroxides of: Water	Action on hydroxides of: Heat	Heat on nitrates
Li				Decomposes	
K			Very soluble	No action	Form nitrite and oxygen
Na		Form hydroxide			
Ca	No action		Slightly soluble		
Mg					
Al				Decompose to oxide and water	Form oxide, nitrogen dioxide, and water
Zn					
Fe					
Sn					
Pb	Reduced to metal	No action	Insoluble		
Cu					
Hg				Forms metal	Forms metal

3 Replacement of metals

The copper in copper(II) sulphate solution and the lead in lead(II) nitrate solution can be replaced by zinc:

$$Cu^{2+}(aq) + Zn(s) \rightarrow Cu(s) + Zn^{2+}(aq)$$

The essential change is that the more active metal (zinc) supplies electrons to ions of the less active metal. One metal replaces another metal lower in the series from its salts and is displaced by metals above it. Replacement occurs most readily if there is a big gap between the two metals in the series, e.g. zinc replaces copper more easily than it replaces lead.

To find, by replacement, the order of chemical activities of various metals

Take 20 test-tubes. Place concentrated (about M) solutions of the following separately into four tubes each: copper(II) sulphate, lead(II) nitrate, iron(II) sulphate, zinc sulphate and magnesium sulphate.

Take four small strips of each of these metals: copper, lead, iron, zinc, magnesium. Clean them well.

Place one strip of each metal into a solution of a salt of the other four metals, e.g. add copper to all solutions except copper(II) sulphate, lead to all solutions except lead(II) nitrate, etc. Let the tubes stand for a day or so. Observe if metal from the salt solution has deposited on the strip of metal added (it may appear as shiny crystals, a dark fur, or a grey tarnish).

Metal ion in solution	Replaced by
Cu^{2+}	All other metals
Pb^{2+}	Mg, Zn and Fe
Fe^{2+}	Mg and Zn
Zn^{2+}	Mg
Mg^{2+}	None of the metals

The order of activities is therefore: magnesium, zinc, iron, lead and copper. Aluminium is not used in the above experiment because a film of oxide, Al_2O_3, on its surface reduces its reactivity. Aluminium displaces lead from lead(II) bromide, p. 136. It has no action on copper(II) sulphate solution but if chlorine ions, e.g. sodium chloride, are added, a vigorous reaction soon occurs and copper is displaced by the aluminium.

Electrolysis

The 'electrolysis of water' is on p. 61.

To examine the electrolysis of copper(II) sulphate solution

Copper electrodes. Fill a coulometer (Fig. 13.1) with copper(II) sulphate solution and connect the circuit as in Fig. 5.10. Pass 1–2 amperes for some time. No gas is formed. Remove the electrodes and look at them. Copper has been transferred from anode to cathode. Weigh the electrodes before and after the electrolysis; the increase in mass of the cathode equals the decrease of the anode. The copper(II) sulphate solution does not change. *Copper anode and platinum cathode.* Repeat the electrolysis. No gas is formed. Copper is transferred from the anode to the cathode, which is *copper plated.* The copper(II) sulphate solution does not change.

Reverse the current for a time. The copper on the platinum (now the anode) is deposited on the copper cathode.

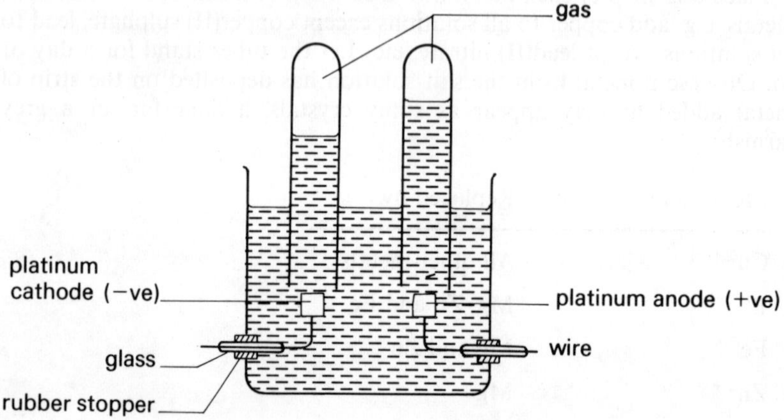

Fig. 13.1 Simple coulometer (platinum electrodes)

Platinum electrodes. Oxygen forms at the anode and copper on the cathode. The copper(II) sulphate solution becomes more dilute and its blue colour gradually disappears. Finally the electrolyte is sulphuric acid, which forms hydrogen and oxygen.

In class experiments, it is difficult to fill and invert ordinary test-tubes. Use rimless tubes (10 × 75 mm) which may usually be inverted whilst full of liquid without any loss, even without a finger over the end. Alternatively, press paper over the mouth of a filled tube, hold the paper in place whilst inverting the tube, carefully remove your finger, and air pressure keeps the paper and solution in place whilst the end is inserted into the electrolyte.

To obtain oxygen by electrolysis of copper(II) sulphate solution (with platinum anode)

Fig. 13.2 shows a coulometer used to collect oxygen evolved at the platinum anode. The glass tubing around the copper wire attached to the anode prevents oxygen forming on it and oxidizing the copper to its oxide.

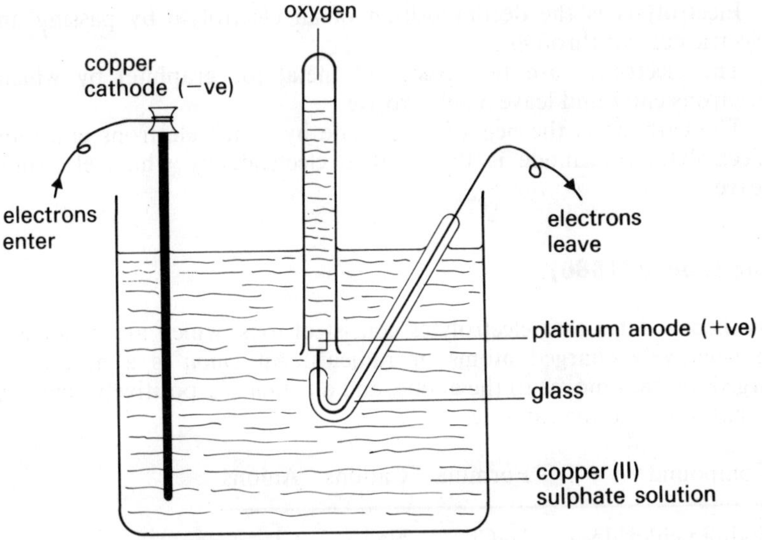

Fig. 13.2 Oxygen from copper(II) sulphate by electrolysis

To examine the electrolysis of copper(II) chloride solution

Use a coulometer with copper(II) chloride solution, a copper cathode and carbon anode. Connect the circuit as in Fig. 5.10. Pass a current and collect any gas. A green-yellow gas at the anode bleaches litmus paper; it is chlorine. Copper forms on the cathode.

Decomposing compounds by electricity

If sugar solution, ethanol, petrol or many other substances are used in the above experiments, no electric current passes. They are *non-electrolytes* (they are covalent). Electricity passes easily through dilute sulphuric acid, most other acids, sodium chloride solution, most other salt solutions, and through sodium hydroxide solution and other alkalis. These substances are *electrolytes* (they are ionic). Molten (fused) sodium chloride, sodium hydroxide, lead(II) bromide or iodide, and potassium iodide, etc., also conduct electricity and are electrolytes. Electricity does not pass readily through water, but a small current flows if a large voltage is used. Water is a very weak electrolyte.

An electrolyte is a compound which, when in solution or melted, conducts an electric current and is decomposed by it.

A non-electrolyte is a compound which, when in solution or melted, does not conduct an electric current.

Electrolysis is the decomposition of an electrolyte by passing an electric current through it.

The electrodes are two pieces of metal (or graphite) by which electrons enter and leave an electrolyte.

The cathode is the negative electrode by which electrons enter an electrolyte; the anode is the positive electrode by which electrons leave.

Ionic theory (1880)

This theory states that electrolytes consist of ions, which are positively and negatively charged atoms or radicals. An *anion* is a negatively charged ion that moves to the anode, and a *cation* is a positively charged ion that moves to the cathode.

Compound	Formula	Cations	Anions
Sodium chloride	$NaCl$	Na^+	Cl^-
Sodium hydroxide	$NaOH$	Na^+	OH^-
Copper(II) chloride	$CuCl_2$	Cu^{2+}	$2Cl^-$
Sulphuric acid	H_2SO_4	$2H^+$	SO_4^{2-}
Copper(II) sulphate	$CuSO_4$	Cu^{2+}	SO_4^{2-}

1 The properties of an ion differ from those of its element or radical. Ions are inert and stable because they have electronic configurations of noble gases.

2 Metals and hydrogen form positive ions and move to the cathode (− ve) during electrolysis; they are *electropositive*. Non-metals and acid radicals form negative ions and move to the anode (+ ve); they are *electronegative*.

3 The charge of an ion is the same as the valency of its atom or radical. Monovalent elements or radicals lose or gain 1 electron to form ions, e.g. Na^+ and OH^-; divalent elements and radicals lose or gain 2 electrons, e.g. Cu^{2+} and SO_4^{2-}.

4 A solution or molten compound is neutral, and the total charge of the positive ions equals that of the negative ions.

To find if ions move

Place a strip of filter paper along a watch glass or microscope slide. Clamp the ends of the paper to the glass with crocodile clips. Carefully add water, drop by drop, until the paper is wet as far as the clips. Drop a small crystal of potassium manganate(VII) or other coloured solute on the middle of the wet paper. Connect the clips to a 20 volts direct current supply and switch on. Observe what happens. Does the purple colour of the potassium manganate(VII) move towards one or both of the clips?

Movement of ions and electrons during electrolysis

During electrolysis, a battery or other direct current (d.c.) supply moves electrons through wire to the electrodes. This electron flow is the electric current outside the electrolyte. The electrons flow to the cathode (– ve) and cations receive these electrons. Cations move towards the cathode, and anions to the anode; this flow of ions is the electric current inside the electrolyte. The anions transfer electrons to the anode, and the electrons then move from the anode to the d.c. source (Fig. 13.3).

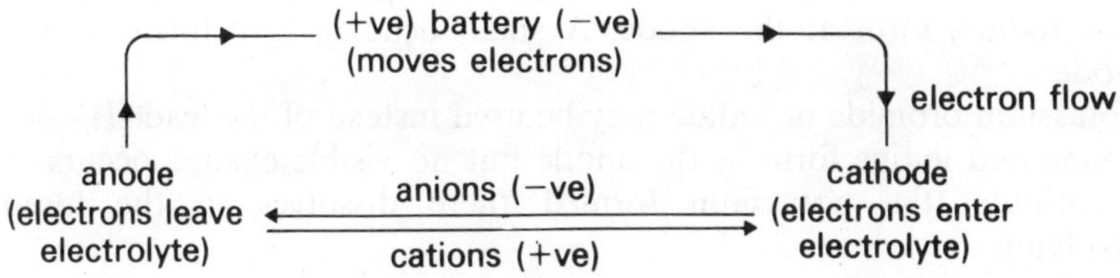

Fig. 13.3 Movement of electrons, anions and cations during electrolysis

Strong and weak electrolytes

Some electrolytes are very good conductors of electricity because they are completely ionized. They are *strong electrolytes*. Water, carbonic acid and acetic (ethanoic) acid are poor conductors because they form only a few ions. Only 1 out of every 600 million molecules of water is ionized into H^+ and OH^- ions, and only 3 out of 1000 molecules of ethanoic acid are ionized in dilute solution. They are *weak electrolytes.*

> A strong electrolyte is a compound which is completely ionized in dilute solution and in the molten state. A weak electrolyte is a compound which is only slightly ionized in dilute solution and in the molten state.

Strong electrolytes	Weak electrolytes	Non-electrolytes
Sulphuric acid	Water	Sugar
Hydrochloric acid	Carbonic acid	Alcohols
Nitric acid	Aqueous ammonia	Benzene
Sodium hydroxide	Ethanoic acid	Most organic compounds
Most salts		

To electrolyse lead(II) bromide solution

Make a saturated solution of lead(II) bromide (its solubility at room temperature is about 0.4 g in 100 g of water). Electrolyse the solution using carbon electrodes. A brown coloration caused by bromine appears around the anode and a grey powder forms on the cathode. Melt the grey powder in an ignition tube; it forms a bead of lead.

To electrolyse fused lead(II) bromide

Heat lead(II) bromide (or iodide) in a fume cupboard in a hard-glass test-tube until it melts. Electrolyse the molten salt, using carbon electrodes. The flame should just keep the salt molten in order to reduce poisonous vapours of lead bromide and bromine. Fumes of brown bromine (or purple iodine) form at the anode. A small bead of lead forms at the cathode.

Potassium bromide or iodide may be used instead of the lead(II) salts. Bromine and iodine form at the anode but no visible change occurs at the cathode (the potassium formed there dissolves in the fused electrolyte).

Electrode potentials

Metals and hydrogen form positive ions and are *electropositive*. When a metal rod is in a solution containing its ions the following equilibrium is established:

Metal(s) $\rightleftharpoons$ metal ions(aq) + electrons

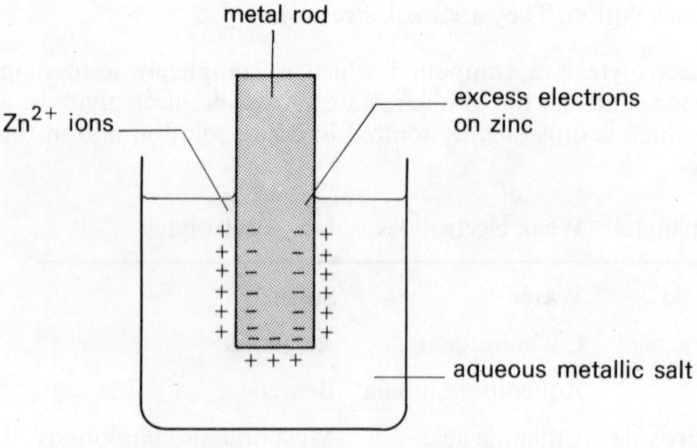

Fig. 13.4 Electrode potential of a metal, e.g. zinc

If a zinc rod is in zinc sulphate solution, some zinc passes into solution as Zn^{2+}(aq) and the rod becomes negatively charged (−0.8 volts):

$$Zn(s) \rightarrow Zn^{2+}(aq) + 2e$$

If a copper rod is in copper(II) sulphate solution, Cu^{2+} ions deposit on the metal from the solution and the rod becomes positively charged (+0.3 volts):

$$Cu^{2+}(aq) + 2e \rightarrow Cu(s)$$

The potential difference between an element and a solution of its ions is called its electrode potential. It is a measure of its tendency to form ions.

Daniell cell. When copper and zinc electrodes are immersed in solutions of their ions, copper is positive with respect to zinc, and the voltage (electromotive force, or e.m.f.) between them is 0.3 − (−0.8) volts = 1.1 V. *Electrochemical series.* A list of elements and radicals with the most electropositive at the top in the order of their electrode potentials is the *electrochemical series.* The metals occur in the same order as in the reactivity series (p. 61). The order of the only ions we study in electrolysis is:

Cations		Anions
K^+	Least easily discharged	SO_4^{2-}
Na^+		Cl^-
H^+		OH^-
Cu^{2+}	Most easily discharged	

To make a simple cell

A simple cell has two metals and one or more electrolytes. Pour aqueous zinc sulphate (about M) into a porous pot; place the pot in a beaker. Pour aqueous copper(II) sulphate (about M) in the beaker until the levels of the two solutions are about the same. Use emery paper or sandpaper to clean a strip of zinc and a strip of copper. Place the metals in their respective salt solutions. Measure the voltage of the cell. (Repeat using an iron nail and iron(II) sulphate instead of the zinc and zinc sulphate.)

A simple cell changes chemical energy into electrical energy. The chemical change is:

$$Zn(s) + Cu^{2+}(aq) \rightarrow Zn^{2+}(aq) + Cu(s) + 213\,kJ$$

This is a Daniell cell, Fig. 13.5, and its voltage is 1.1 volts. A Daniell cell is represented as follows:

$$Zn|Zn^{2+}(aq) \vdots Cu^{2+}(aq)|Cu \qquad E = +1.1\,V$$

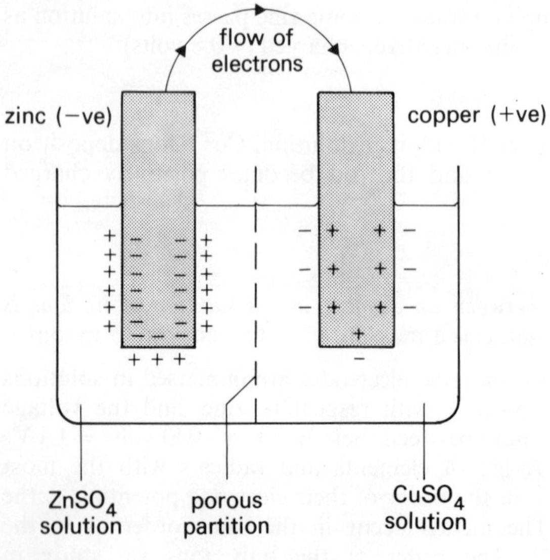

Fig. 13.5 Daniell cell (diagrammatic)

Factors affecting electrolysis

1 *Concentration of solution.* An ion is discharged more easily if its concentration is high. For example, OH^- ions are discharged in preference to Cl^- ions when dilute sodium chloride or dilute hydrochloric acid is electrolysed. However, concentrated sodium chloride and concentrated hydrochloric acid have a high concentration of Cl^- ions and they are discharged before the OH^- ions.

2 *The electrodes.* (*a*) In the electrolysis of copper(II) sulphate with copper electrodes, copper is transferred from anode to cathode. If a platinum anode is used, oxygen is formed there (p. 154).

(*b*) Usually hydrogen ions are discharged in preference to sodium ions when sodium chloride is electrolysed. However, if the cathode is mercury, sodium ions are discharged and sodium forms an amalgam (p. 280).

Electrolysis of dilute sulphuric acid ('electrolysis of water')

Ions are formed by the reactions:

$$H_2SO_4(aq) \rightarrow 2H^+(aq) + SO_4^{2-}(aq)$$

$$H_2O(l) \rightleftharpoons H^+(aq) + OH^-(aq)$$

At the cathode. H^+ ions move there, receive electrons (e) and become atoms, which combine to form molecules:

$$H^+(aq) + e \rightarrow H;\ 2H \rightarrow H_2(g)$$

SO_4^{2-} ions move away from the cathode and H^+ ions are discharged, therefore the concentration of acid decreases.
At the anode. SO_4^{2-} and OH^- ions both move there. OH^- ions are preferentially discharged. They transfer electrons to the anode and become hydroxyl radicals, which then form water and oxygen:

$$OH^-(aq) - e \rightarrow OH;\ 4OH \rightarrow 2H_2O(l) + O_2(g)$$

More water ionizes to replace the OH^- ions; the H^- ions also produced increase the concentration of acid. Note that 4 electrons transferred by the cathode produce $2H_2$ from $4H^+(aq)$, and 4 electrons transferred to the anode produce O_2 from $4OH^-(aq)$, i.e. the ratio of the gases by volume is 2:1.
Result. Two volumes of hydrogen form at the cathode for every volume of oxygen at the anode. The mass of acid is constant, but its concentration decreases around the cathode and increases around the anode. The final change is that only water is decomposed and therefore the process is called the 'electrolysis of water':

$$2H_2O(l) \rightarrow 2H_2(g) + O_2(g)$$

(The electrolysis seems to prove that water is a compound of hydrogen and oxygen in the proportions of 2:1 by volume.)

Electrolysis of copper(II) sulphate solution

Ions are formed by the reactions:

$$CuSO_4(aq) \rightarrow Cu^{2+}(aq) + SO_4^{2-}(aq)$$

$$H_2O(l) \rightleftharpoons H^+(aq) + OH^-(aq)$$

a *Copper electrodes*
At the cathode. Cu^{2+} and H^+ ions both move there. Cu^{2+} ions are lower in the series and are preferentially discharged receiving electrons and being deposited:

$$Cu^{2+}(aq) + 2e \rightarrow Cu(s)$$

At the anode. SO_4^{2-} and OH^- ions both move there, but neither is discharged. Instead, some copper anode forms ions and leaves electrons on the anode (*electrode ionization*):

$$Cu(s) - 2e \rightarrow Cu^{2+}(aq)$$

Result. The anode loses copper and the cathode gains an equal mass of copper. The concentration of the copper(II) sulphate does not change.

b *Platinum anode*

SO_4^{2-} and OH^- ions both move to the platinum anode. OH^- ions are preferentially discharged:

$$OH^-(aq) - e \rightarrow OH; 4OH \rightarrow 2H_2O(l) + O_2(g)$$

More water ionizes to replace the OH^- ions; the H^+ ions also produced form acid around the platinum.

Result. Copper is deposited on the cathode, oxygen is evolved at the anode, and the solution becomes acid. The concentration of copper(II) sulphate decreases, and its blue colour becomes paler. If electrolysis is long enough, the solution becomes colourless and sulphuric acid is the electrolyte, forming hydrogen and oxygen.

Electrolysis of copper(II) sulphate is used in industry.

1 *Extraction of copper*. Large boulders of impure copper are sometimes found. A cell is built around a boulder. Copper(II) sulphate is added as electrolyte to the cell; a strip of pure copper is made the cathode and the boulder is the anode. Copper is transferred from the boulder.

2 *Purification of copper*. The same arrangement is used to purify impure copper, which is made the anode in a copper(II) sulphate cell with pure copper as the cathode. Some impurities (iron, zinc, arsenic, etc.) pass into solution and others (silver, gold) drop from the anode as 'anode slime' from which they are sometimes extracted. Pure copper is deposited on the cathode.

3 *Copper plating*. The object is cleaned; if it is not a conductor of electricity, it is coated with graphite. It is made the cathode in copper(II) sulphate with a copper anode. Copper is deposited on the object, i.e. it is copper plated.

Other metals can be used instead of copper. The purpose of *electroplating* is to coat objects with a layer of another metal by electrolysis, e.g. knives and forks with silver, and iron with nickel or chromium. The plating prevents rusting and improves the appearance.

Summary of the results of electrolysis

The substance of the cathode has little effect, except for a mercury cathode in the electrolysis of sodium chloride.

Electrolyte	Anode	At anode	At cathode
1 Dilute sulphuric acid	Platinum	1 volume of oxygen; acidity increases (or alkalinity decreases)	2 volumes of hydrogen; acidity decreases (or alkalinity increases)
		Electrolyte does not change	
2 Copper(II) sulphate or chloride	Copper	Copper dissolved	Copper deposited
		Electrolyte does not change	
3 Copper(II) sulphate	Platinum	Oxygen and sulphuric acid	Copper deposited
		Electrolyte becomes more dilute	
4 Copper(II) chloride	Carbon	Chlorine	Copper deposited
		Electrolyte becomes more dilute	
5 Lead(II) bromide	Carbon	Bromine	Lead
6 Conc. sodium chloride (brine)	Carbon	1 volume of chlorine	1 volume of hydrogen: sodium hydroxide
7 Molten sodium chloride	Carbon	Chlorine	Sodium
8 Conc. hydrochloric acid	Carbon	Chlorine	Hydrogen

Faraday's Laws of Electrolysis (1830)

1. The mass of a substance liberated during electrolysis is directly proportional to the quantity of electricity passed (i.e. current × time).
2. One mole of various atoms is liberated by one or more moles of electrons.

Electric current is measured in amperes (A) and quantity of electricity in coulombs (C). One coulomb is the quantity of electricity passed when a current of 1 ampere flows for 1 second,

i.e. Quantity = current × time,

or Coulombs = amperes × seconds

Faraday Constant

The charge on 1 mole is the *Faraday constant F*. It is 96 500 coulombs per mole (more exactly, 96 487 C/mol or C mol^{-1}). The charge on 1 hydrogen ion, and on 1 electron, is

$$\frac{96\,500 \text{ coulombs}}{6 \times 10^{23}} = 1.6 \times 10^{-19} \text{ coulomb}$$

The charge on Cu^{2+} and Pb^{2+} is twice this value, and that on Fe^{3+} and Al^{3} is three times larger. Therefore, to liberate 1 mole of hydrogen, copper and aluminium atoms requires 1, 2 and 3 moles of electricity respectively, in accordance with Faraday's second law.

To find the quantity of electricity required to deposit 1 mole of copper during electrolysis

Connect the circuit as in Fig. 13.6. Adjust the rheostat (variable resistance) until a suitable current is flowing. Dry and clean the copper cathode and find its mass. Replace the cathode in the copper coulometer and pass the current for 30 minutes, measuring the exact number of seconds with a stop-watch. Wash the cathode with water, allow it to dry and find its mass again. The increase in its mass is the mass of copper deposited.

$$\begin{aligned} \text{Current} &= I \quad \text{(amperes)} \\ \text{Time} &= t \quad \text{(seconds)} \\ \text{Copper deposited} &= w \quad \text{(grams)} \end{aligned}$$

Mass w of copper is deposited by a quantity of electricity It.
$\therefore$ 63.5 g of copper are deposited by $63.5\,It/w$ coulombs.
(This quantity is about $2 \times 96\,500$ coulombs.)

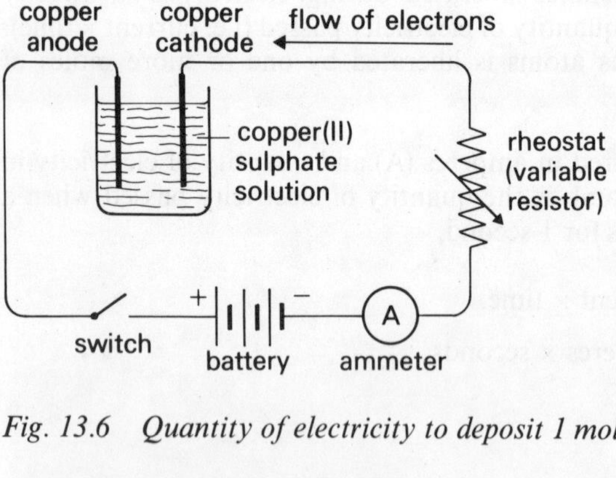

Fig. 13.6 Quantity of electricity to deposit 1 mole of copper atoms

To compare the quantities of electricity required to deposit 1 mole of copper and silver during electrolysis

Pass the same electric current through a silver nitrate coulometer and a copper(II) sulphate coulometer connected in series (Fig. 13.7). Find the masses of the platinum cathode and copper cathode at the beginning of the experiment and at the end. Silver and copper are deposited on them. The

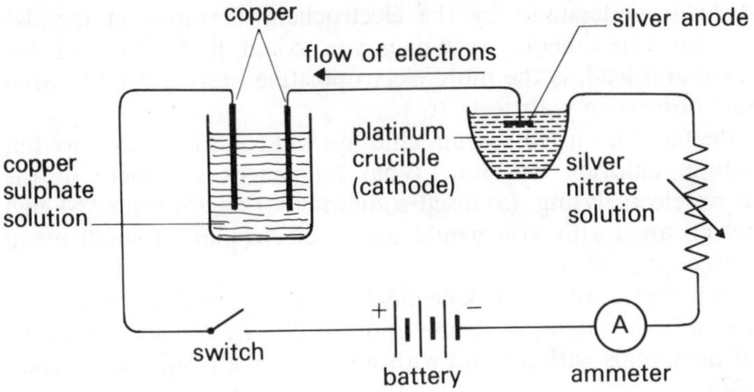

Fig. 13.7 Quantity of electricity to deposit 1 mole of copper or silver

increases in their masses are the masses of metals deposited by the same quantity of electricity.

$$\frac{\text{Moles of copper deposited}}{\text{Moles of silver deposited}} = \frac{\text{Mass of copper} \div 63.5}{\text{Mass of silver} \div 108}$$

The ratio is a simple whole number (1:2), and the experiment illustrates Faraday's second law of electrolysis.

To determine the quantity of electricity required to deposit 1 mole of lead during electrolysis

Fuse lead(II) bromide or iodide in a crystallizing dish. The depth of molten salt should be about 5 mm. Electrolyse the compound, using carbon electrodes, p. 158. Use a constant current I (about 3 amperes) for a known time t (about 900 seconds). Molten lead is deposited in the dish.

Pour away the molten electrolyte. Allow the lead to cool, rub off lead salt sticking to it, and find the mass w of the lead.
Mass w of lead is deposited by a quantity of electricity It.

$\therefore$ 207 g (1 mole) of lead are deposited by $\frac{207It}{w}$ C.

(This quantity should be about $2 \times 96\,500$ C.)

Questions

1 By comparing the reactions (if any) of (*a*) dilute hydrochloric acid, (*b*) water, (*c*) oxygen, on zinc, lead, copper and iron, arrange the metals in order of their activities. What would happen if zinc and iron plates were immersed in a beaker of dilute sulphuric acid and joined by a wire outside the beaker? (O.)

2 What do you understand by the electrochemical series of metals? Describe two experiments by which you could find which of the metals, zinc and lead, is the more electropositive, stating exactly what you would observe in your tests. (C.)

3 Explain the fact that fused sodium chloride will conduct electricity but solid sodium chloride will not. What differences are there in the products on electrolysing: (*a*) fused sodium chloride, (*b*) brine? Sketch and label an apparatus you would use to electroplate a small metal object with copper. (C.)

4 'Sodium is higher in the electrochemical or activity series than copper.' Explain what this statement means, and justify it by considering (i) the action of the metals with air and with water, (ii) the properties of their oxides. (L.)

5 Describe an experiment in which the products of the electrolysis of dilute sulphuric acid can be identified and their amounts measured. If the same current is passed through solutions of silver nitrate ($AgNO_3$) and copper sulphate ($CuSO_4$), how much silver will be liberated in the same time as 1.00 g of copper? (Cu = 63.5; Ag = 108.) (L.)

6 State Faraday's Laws of Electrolysis. The same quantity of electricity was passed through three coulometers, depositing copper in the first, silver in the second, and liberating 200 cm^3 of hydrogen (at s.t.p.) in the third. Calculate the masses of copper and silver deposited. 1000 cm^3 of hydrogen at s.t.p. has a mass of 0.09 g. (Cu = 63.6; Ag = 108.) (L.)

7 Describe and explain how you could prepare by electrolysis a specimen of pure copper from some impure metal. When using platinum electrodes in the electrolysis of copper(II) sulphate solution, what mass of copper is deposited if 56 cm^3 of oxygen, measured at s.t.p., are collected in the same experiment? (C.)

8 State what you understand by electrolytes and non-electrolytes, giving an example of each. Give the formulae (with charges) of the ions present in solutions of ammonium sulphate, aluminium(III) chloride, and copper(II) nitrate. What would you observe if a current were passed for a long time through dilute copper(II) sulphate, using platinum electrodes? What differences would be caused by using copper electrodes? (C.)

14
The Periodic Table

History

In 1817, a German scientist named Dobereiner realized there was a connection between relative atomic mass and chemical properties. In 1829 he arranged many elements into groups of three, called *Dobereiner's triads*, in which the relative atomic mass of the middle element is about the average of the masses of the other two:

Lithium	6.9	Sodium	23	Potassium	39
Chlorine	35.5	Bromine	80	Iodine	127

However, only a few elements form groups of three.

In 1864, a British chemist called Newlands arranged the elements in order of relative atomic mass and gave each one a number. Hydrogen, the lightest element, was number 1, lithium 2 (helium was not known at that time), and so on. He was the first scientist to list elements in numerical order, to leave spaces in his list for elements still undiscovered, and even to alter positions of elements when he believed the relative atomic mass was not correct. Newland's *Law of Octaves* stated that elements with similar chemical properties had numbers which differed by 7 (e.g. elements 1, 8 and 15 were similar, and so were 3, 10 and 17, and so on):

H	Li	Be	B	C	N	O
F	Na	Mg	Al	Si	P	S

However, Newland's law did not apply after element 17 (calcium).

The most successful of the early attempts at classification of the elements used relative atomic masses. In 1869 Mendeleef, a Russian scientist, stated that *the properties of the elements are a periodic function of their atomic masses*. This *periodic law* means that if the elements are arranged in order of increasing relative atomic mass, elements of similar properties appear at regular intervals.

Mendeleef's Periodic Table was incomplete because many elements (e.g. noble gases) were not known at that time, and it contained several errors which have since been corrected. A modern form of the table contains elements in order of their *proton numbers* or *atomic numbers*. The horizontal rows are *periods* and the vertical columns are *groups*.

THE PERIODIC TABLE

Period	1	2	Group number										3	4	5	6	7	8
1	1 H																1 H	2 He
2	3 Li	4 Be											5 B	6 C	7 N	8 O	9 F	10 Ne
3	11 Na	12 Mg	Transition elements										13 Al	14 Si	15 P	16 S	17 Cl	18 Ar
4	19 K	20 Ca	21 Sc	22 Ti	23 V	24 Cr	25 Mn	26 Fe	27 Co	28 Ni	29 Cu	30 Zn	31 Ga	32 Ge	33 As	34 Se	35 Br	36 Kr
5	37 Rb	38 Sr	39 Y	40 Zr	41 Nb	42 Mo	43 Tc	44 Ru	45 Rh	46 Pd	47 Ag	48 Cd	49 In	50 Sn	51 Sb	52 Te	53 I	54 Xe
6	55 Cs	56 Ba	57 — 71	72 Hf	73 Ta	74 W	75 Re	76 Os	77 Ir	78 Pt	79 Au	80 Hg	81 Tl	82 Pb	83 Bi	84 Po	85 At	86 Rn
7	87 Fr	88 Ra	89 — 103															
				57 La	58 Ce	59 Pr	60 Nd	61 Pm	62 Sm	63 Eu	64 Gd	65 Tb	66 Dy	67 Ho	68 Er	69 Tm	70 Yb	71 Lu
				89 Ac	90 Th	91 Pa	92 U	93 Np	94 Pu	95 Am	96 Cm	97 Bk	98 Cf	99 Es	100 Fm	101 Mv	102 No	103 Lw

Mendeleef's Table listed the elements by using relative atomic masses. It was not understood why this should fit elements (with some few exceptions) into groups with similar properties. In 1913, an English research student called Moseley investigated X-ray spectra of elements. He found that atomic number (proton number) is more important than relative atomic mass and that there were no exceptions in a Periodic Table based on this number. Two pairs of elements which are placed in the wrong order using relative atomic masses are:

Potassium	Argon	Iodine	Tellurium
39.1	39.95	126.9	127.6

Moseley's discovery that atomic number is more significant than relative atomic mass removed these and other anomalies in Mendeleef's table.

Characteristics of the Periodic Table

There are 8 groups and 7 periods.

Period 1 contains only hydrogen and helium. Hydrogen is placed in both groups 1 and 7 because its properties resemble those of the alkali metals and the halogens.

Periods 2 and 3 (*short periods*) contain 8 elements each.

Periods 4 and 5 (*long periods*) each contain 18 elements. Eight of these correspond to the 8 elements in the short periods. The other 10 are called *transition elements*, which show some properties similar to the elements before them and also some properties similar to those following them.

Periods 6 and 7 contain 32 and 17 elements.

Periodicity of properties of the elements

Physical properties of elements in the same group vary gradually and regularly. All group 1 alkali metals have low densities, low melting points and high conductivities. The melting points, boiling points and densities of the group 7 halogens rise regularly. (The first member of a group, e.g. lithium and fluorine, is usually slightly different from the rest of the group.)

Chemical properties vary gradually for the same group of elements. Of the alkali metals, potassium is more electropositive than sodium, which is more electropositive than lithium. Of the halogens, fluorine is most electronegative and iodine is least. Metals are on the left-hand side of the table and non-metals are on the right. In group 1, the metals are more reactive as their relative atomic masses increase; in group 7, the halogens are less reactive as their masses decrease.

Valencies of the short period elements vary gradually. The hydrogen valency increases from 1 to 4 and then decreases to 0; the maximum oxygen valency increases from 1 to 7.

Group	1	2	3	4	5	6	7	8
Hydride	NaH	CaH_2	BH_3	CH_4	NH_3	OH_2	ClH	none
Oxide	Na_2O	MgO	Al_2O_3	SiO_2	P_2O_5	SO_3	Cl_2O_7	
	←basic→		amphoteric	←	acidic		→	none

Note the gradual change in the nature of the oxides of period 3 elements.

The melting and boiling points (°C) of period 2 elements are:

Li	Be	B	C	N	O	F	Ne
181	1280	2027	3727	−210	−219	−220	−248
1431	2477	3927	—	−196	−183	−178	−250

Lithium, beryllium, boron and carbon consist of ions or atoms in a giant structure; nitrogen, oxygen and fluorine are diatomic elements and neon is monatomic.

The following table shows the variation in physical and chemical properties of period 3 elements:

	Na	Mg	Al	Si	P	S	Cl	Ar
Orbits	2,8,1	2,8,2	2,8,3	2,8,4	2,8,5	2,8,6	2,8,7	2,8,8
Atomic radius (nm)	0.186	0.160	0.143	0.117	0.110	0.104	0.100	
M.p. (°C)	98	650	659	1410	44	113	−101	−189
B.p. (°C)	890	1117	2447	2677	181	444	−34	−186
Density of solid (g/cm^3)	0.97	1.74	2.70	2.40	1.82	2.07	1.56	1.40
Hydride	NaH	MgH_2	AlH_3	SiH_4	PH_3	H_2S	HCl	
	ionic	←		covalent			→	
Chloride	NaCl	$MgCl_2$	$AlCl_3$	$SiCl_4$	PCl_3	S_2Cl_2		
	ionic	ionic	←	covalent		→		

The atomic radius decreases from sodium in group 1 to chlorine in group 7. In this period each atom has one more electron and one more proton than the preceding atom. The extra electron has little effect on the size of the atom because it is in the same outer orbit; however, the extra proton increases the charge on the nucleus and attracts all the electrons closer to the nucleus, decreasing the size of the atom.

The melting points depend on the strength of the forces holding the particles (ions, atom or molecules) together in the solid. Sodium, magnesium and aluminium consist of their ions (Na^+, Mg^{2+}, and Al^{3+}) surrounded by electrons (p. 103). The strength of the metallic bond between Mg^{2+} ions and the electrons is much greater than that between Na^+, with its single charge, and its electrons. Therefore the melting point of magnesium is much higher than that of sodium. The melting point of aluminium is a little higher than that of magnesium. Silicon has a three dimensional giant structure similar to that of diamond, p. 200. The covalent bonds are very strong and its melting point is high. The other four elements in the group consist of molecules: P_4, S_8, Cl_2 and Ar. The intermolecular attractions decrease from the largest molecules, sulphur, to the smallest, argon, and so do the melting points. Similar comments apply to the boiling points of the group 3 elements, which vary with the strength of the forces holding the particles in the liquids.

Families of elements

The Periodic Table is accounted for by the regular arrangement of electrons in atoms of the elements. The periodicity of electron configuration leads to periodicity of chemical properties, which depend on the configuration of the outermost orbit (or the two outermost orbits). The following examples make this clear:

Halogens	Noble gases	Alkali metals
— —	He 2	Li 2, 1
F 2, 7	Ne 2, 8	Na 2, 8, 1
Cl 2, 8, 7	Ar 2, 8, 8	K 2, 8, 8, 1
Br 2, 8, 18, 7	Kr 2, 8, 18, 8	Rb 2, 8, 18, 8, 1
I 2, 8, 18, 18, 7	Xe 2, 8, 18, 18, 8	Cs 2, 8, 18, 18, 8, 1

The noble gas configurations are very stable and the electrons are not used in chemical reactions. An alkali metal atom has one electron more than a noble gas structure. This electron is readily detached and the elements are therefore very electropositive (top of the electrochemical series). Halogens have one electron less than noble gas structures. Each atom tends to attract an electron to complete its outer octet and therefore halogens are very electronegative.

Alkaline earth metals (magnesium, calcium, etc.) have two electrons more than a noble gas. These can readily be detached and the metals are electropositive.

Transition metals

Iron and copper are two transition metals which follow calcium in period 4. Electron configurations of their atoms and ions (which need not be remembered) are:

Fe 2, 8, 14, 2	Fe^{2+} 2, 8, 14	Fe^{3+} 2, 8, 13
Cu 2, 8, 18, 1	Cu^{+} 2, 8, 18	Cu^{2+} 2, 8, 17

The ions do not have noble gas configurations. *Transition metals* are elements which can use electrons from *two* outer orbits for combination with other elements.

Characteristics of transition metals are:

1 Several electrons from each atom can be mobile (whereas only 1 electron from an alkali metal atom and 2 from a calcium or magnesium atom are mobile). The forces between transition metal ions in the metal crystals are strong and the ions are close-packed. The metals therefore have high densities, melting and boiling points.

2 Their valencies are variable, and their ions readily undergo oxidation or reduction:

$$Fe^{2+} - e \rightleftharpoons Fe^{3+}$$

This change makes them good catalysts. The metals readily adsorb gases on their surfaces and this also makes them catalysts in gaseous reactions.

3 They form coloured complex ions, e.g.

$Cu(H_2O)_4^{2+}$, blue; $Cu(NH_3)_4^{2+}$, deep blue;
$Fe(H_2O)_6^{3+}$, yellow

Questions

1 The number of outer electrons of an atom of an element determines the position of the element in a group of the Periodic Table. Explain this statement by referring to the following elements and their atomic numbers: hydrogen 1, helium 2, fluorine 9, neon 10, sodium 11, chlorine 17, potassium 19, and calcium 20.

2 Some elements (denoted by letters A to F, which are not chemical symbols) and their atomic numbers are: A 3, B 8, C 12, D 16, E 18, and F 20. State, with your reason or reasons, which, if any, of these elements: (*a*) is a noble gas, (*b*) is a halogen, (*c*) is an alkali metal, (*d*) are in the same group of the Periodic Table, (*e*) reacts readily with cold water, (*f*) has a valency of 3 or 4, (g) forms no common compounds.

3 The relative atomic masses of potassium and argon are 39.9 and 39.1 respectively, but their atomic numbers are 19 and 18 respectively and potassium comes after argon in the Periodic Table. Give an explanation of these facts.

4 The atomic numbers of sodium, magnesium and chlorine are 11, 12 and 17 respectively. How do the electron configurations of atoms of these elements account for (*a*) some of their chemical properties, and (*b*) their position in the Periodic Table in relation to elements next to them in the Table?

5 There are 54 elements in the first five periods of the Periodic Table. Periods 1 to 5 contain 2, 8, 8, 18 and 18 elements respectively. Some elements (denoted by letters G to N, which are not chemical symbols) and their atomic numbers are: G 6, H 7, I 13, J 34, K 35, L 36, M 37 and N 54. State, with your reason or reasons, which if any of these elements: (*a*) are noble gases, (*b*) is a halogen, (*c*) is an alkali metal, (*d*) are in the same group of the Periodic Table, (*e*) exists in polymorphic (allotropic) forms, (*f*) has a valency of 3, (g) combines with hydrogen to form a compound with a formula similar to that of water?

15
Heats of Reaction

Energy changes in chemical reactions

Heat is evolved or absorbed in many chemical reactions. Energy is neither created nor destroyed but is merely transformed. Chemical energy is transformed into heat energy or vice versa. Chemical energy is transformed into electrical energy in accumulators and other cells. Electrical energy is transformed into chemical energy during electrolysis.

The heat content of a chemical system is denoted by H. Changes in heat content are usually more important and are denoted by ΔH (delta H).

$$\Delta H = H\,(\text{products}) - H\,(\text{reactants})$$

The initial and final temperatures are 25 °C or 298 K and gases are at standard pressure of 101 325 Pa or 760 mmHg. To emphasize this, the symbol for heat change is sometimes $\Delta H(298)$.

The *heat of reaction* is the heat change when the number of moles of the reagents indicated by the chemical equation have reacted completely.

$$\text{C (graphite)} + O_2(g) \rightarrow CO_2(g)$$

$$\Delta H = -390\,\text{kJ g-equation}^{-1} \text{ or kJ/mol or kJ mol}^{-1}$$

This equation means that 390 kilojoules are *evolved* when 12 g of carbon combine with 32 g of oxygen.

$$\text{C (graphite)} + 2S \rightarrow CS_2(l)$$

$$\Delta H = +106\,\text{kJ/mol or kJ mol}^{-1}$$

This means that 106 kilojoules are *absorbed* when 12 g of carbon combine with 64 g of sulphur. ΔH is negative in an exothermic reaction (in which heat is evolved) and positive in an endothermic one (in which heat is absorbed).

The *heat of combustion* of a substance is the heat change when 1 mole of it is burnt completely in oxygen. The heat of combustion, ΔH, of carbon is therefore −390 kJ/mol. Other values in kJ/mol are

Hydrogen	−286	Methane	−890
Sulphur	−297	Ethane	−1560
Ethanol	−1367	Propane	−2220

To measure the heat of combustion of ethanol

Measure 250 cm^3 (i.e. 250 g) of water in a measuring cylinder and add it to a thin metal can. Add ethanol to a small bottle fitted with cork and wick, and find the mass of the simple lamp so formed.

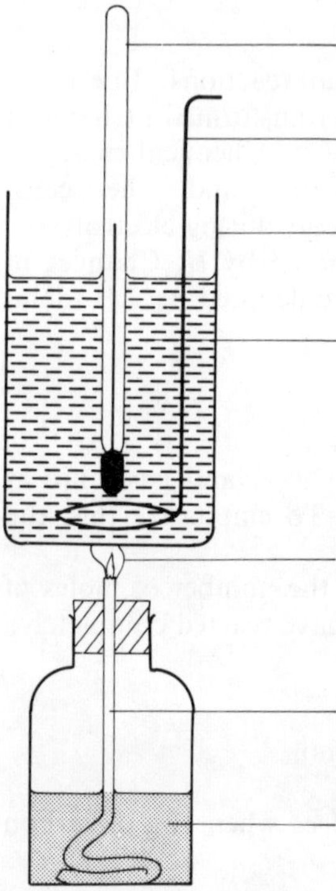

Fig. 15.1 Measuring the heat of combustion

Note the temperature of the water. Light the lamp and let it heat the water directly (use no gauze) until the temperature rises about 30 °C. Extinguish the flame. Note the final temperature of the water. Find the mass of the lamp when it is cold.

1 Temperature of cold water $= t_1$ °C
2 Temperature of warm water $= t_2$ °C
3 Mass of lamp at beginning $= W_1$ g
4 Mass of lamp at end $= W_2$ g

Specific heat capacity of water = 4.2 J/g °C

The heat gained by the water

= specific heat capacity × mass × rise in temperature

$= 4.2 \times 250(t_2 - t_1)$ joules $= (t_2 - t_1)$ kilojoules approximately

The mass of ethanol used $= (W_1 - W_2)$
The relative molecular mass of ethanol (C_2H_5OH) is 46.

$$\therefore \frac{(W_1 - W_2)}{46} \text{ mole of ethanol produce } (t_2 - t_1) \text{ kilojoules,}$$

$$\text{i.e. 1 mole of ethanol produces } (t_2 - t_1) \times \frac{46}{(W_1 - W_2)} \text{ kilojoules.}$$

This is the heat of combustion of ethanol.

The results are much lower than accurate values because some of the heat produced warms the can and the air and does not pass into the water.

Heats of solution

Heat is sometimes evolved or absorbed when substances are dissolved in water. The *heat of solution* of a solute is the heat change when 1 mole of the solute dissolves in a large volume of water. The words 'a large volume of' are important because the heat change depends on the quantity of water used. The quantity is large enough so that further dilution causes no more heat change.

Heat of solution of sulphuric acid. Add 53.5 cm^3 of concentrated sulphuric acid (i.e. 98 g or 1 mole) carefully to 900 cm^3 of water in a large, thin beaker. Stir well and record the rise in temperature. (The final solution is about M concentration, its mass is about 1000 g and its heat capacity is about 4.2 J/g °C.)

$$\begin{aligned} \text{Heat of solution} &= \text{specific heat capacity} \times \text{mass} \times \text{temperature rise} \\ &= 4.2 \times 1000 \times \text{temperature rise (J/mol)} \end{aligned}$$

(The temperature rise is about 17 °C, and the heat of solution is -70 kJ/mol.)

$$H_2SO_4(l) + aq \rightarrow M\ H_2SO_4(aq) \qquad \Delta H = -70\ \text{kJ/mol}$$

Heat of solution of ammonium nitrate. Add 80 g (1 mole) of the finely powdered nitrate to 920 cm^3 of water. Stir well until it dissolves. Record the fall in temperature. The concentration of the final solution is M, its mass is 1000 g, and its heat capacity is about 4.2 J/g °C. (The temperature fall is about 5 °C, and the heat of solution is about $+25$ kJ/mol.)

$$NH_4NO_3(s) + aq \rightarrow M\ NH_4NO_3(aq) \qquad \Delta H = +25\ \text{kJ/mol}$$

Energy level diagrams make it easier to visualize changes of energy.

They can be drawn to scale, e.g. 1 cm = 10 kilojoules. These two examples make the method clear.

$H_2SO_4(l) + aq$	
	$M\ NH_4NO_3$
7 cm ↓	↑ 2.5 cm
$M\ H_2SO_4$	$NH_4NO_3(s) + aq$
$\Delta H = -70$ kJ/mol	$\Delta H = +25$ kJ/mol

The diagrams show that the diluted acid has less energy (at the same temperature) than the pure acid and water; ammonium nitrate solution has more energy than the crystals and water.

More endothermic reactions

Dissolve citric acid (10.5 g) in water (50 cm^3) in a plastic beaker. Let the solution come to room temperature and record this. Add carefully but quickly sodium hydrogencarbonate (12.6 g) and stir rapidly. Carbon dioxide is evolved and may form a thick froth on the surface; blow on the froth to break it up and stop it overflowing. Record the temperature change (usually about 20 °C) and also feel the cold product with your hand.

The neutralization of potassium hydrogencarbonate with hydrochloric acid is also an endothermic reaction. Mix equal volumes of 1 M solutions (or more concentrated solutions) to demonstrate this.

Heats of neutralization

The *heat of neutralization* is the heat change when alkali which provides one mole of $OH^-(aq)$ reacts with acid which provides one mole of $H^+(aq)$. Some values are:

Acid	Base	ΔH (kJ)	Acid	Base	ΔH (kJ)
HCl	NaOH	−57.4	HNO_3	NaOH	−57.3
HCl	KOH	−57.3	HF	NaOH	−68.6
$\frac{1}{2}H_2SO_4$	NaOH	−61.3	HCN	KOH	−11.6

The heat of neutralization of a strong acid by a strong base is usually about 57 kilojoules (evolved). The only reaction that occurs is the formation of 18 g of water from hydrogen and hydroxide ions (refer to pp. 120–1):

$$H^+(aq) + OH^-(aq) \rightarrow H_2O(l) \quad \Delta H = -57\ \text{kJ/mol}$$

The heat of neutralization of a weak acid (e.g. ethanoic (acetic) acid and hydrogen cyanide) by a strong base is not constant; it can be more or less than −57 kJ/mol. The molecules of the acid have to ionize before neutralization can occur and the *heat of ionization* affects the total heat change.

Measuring heats of neutralization. Add 500 cm^3 of 2 M sodium hydroxide solution to 500 cm^3 of 2 M hydrochloric or nitric acid in a polythene beaker surrounded by lagging to prevent heat losses. Read the rise in temperature accurate to 0.1 °C.

The quantities of alkali and acid used are 1 mole. The final volume is 1000 cm^3 (i.e. 1 kg approximately) and a temperature rise of 1 °C therefore means that about 4.2 kilojoules have been evolved.

Heat of neutralization
= specific heat capacity × mass × temperature rise
= 4.2 × 1 × temperature rise (kJ/mol)

(The temperature rise is about 13 °C, and the heat of neutralization is therefore about 4.2 × 13 = about −55 kJ/mol.)

To measure the heat of precipitation of silver chloride

Use a measuring cylinder to add 25 cm^3 of 0.5 M silver nitrate solution to a plastic bottle or cup, of about 70 cm^3 capacity. Rinse the measuring cylinder with water and then add 25 cm^3 of 0.5 M sodium chloride (or potassium chloride or ammonium chloride) to it. Both solutions should be at room temperature. Measure the temperature of the chloride solution, preferably using a thermometer graduated to 0.1 °C. Add the chloride solution to the silver nitrate, shake well, and then measure the highest temperature produced. Silver chloride is precipitated. Let the rise in temperature be t °C (it is only a few degrees).

If 500 cm^3 of each solution had been used, the temperature rise would still be t °C, because the heat change is twenty times greater than with only 25 cm^3 but there is 20 times more product to heat. (However, heat losses to the plastic container and the air are not so important when larger volumes are used, and the results are more accurate.) If the concentrations of the solutions had been 2.0 M instead of 0.5 M, clearly the temperature rise would be $4t$ °C.

$Ag^+(aq)$	+ $Cl^-(aq)$	→ $AgCl(s)$	Rise
25 cm^3 0.5 M	25 cm^3 0.5 M	0.125 mole	t °C
500 cm^3 0.5 M	500 cm^3 0.5 M	0.25 mole	t °C
500 cm^3 2.0 M	500 cm^3 2.0 M	1.00 mole	$4t$ °C

When 1 mole of silver chloride is precipitated, the total volume of the product is about 1000 cm^3 and its mass is about 1000 g.

The heat of precipitation

= specific heat capacity × mass × temperature change

= 4.2 J/g °C × 1000 g × 4t °C

= 16 800t J/mol or 16.8t kJ/mol

ΔH for the reaction is −65.7 kJ/mol.

Heat of displacement of copper

Zinc or iron displace copper from copper(II) sulphate solution; the heat of displacement is measured by a method similar to the previous experiment. Add 50 cm^3 of 0.25 M copper(II) sulphate to a plastic bottle. Record the temperature of the solution, accurate to 0.1 °C. Add excess zinc or iron filings (about 1.0 g), shake well, and measure the highest temperature produced. Let the temperature rise be t °C.

$Cu^{2+}(aq)$	+ Zn(s) →	Cu(s)	+ $Zn^{2+}(aq)$	Rise
50 cm^3 0.25 M	excess →	0.125 mole		t °C
1000 cm^3 0.25 M	excess →	0.25 mole		t °C
1000 cm^3 1.0 M	excess →	1.0 mole		4t °C

If we assume that the mass of products is about 1 kg, then the heat of displacement

= specific heat capacity × mass × temperature rise

= 4.2 kJ/kg °C × 1 kg × 4t °C

= 16.8t kJ/mol or 16 800t J/mol.

The correct values are:

$Cu^{2+}(aq) + Zn(s) \rightarrow Cu(s) + Zn^{2+}(aq)$ $\Delta H = -218$ kJ/mol

$Cu^{2+}(aq) + Fe(s) \rightarrow Cu(s) + Fe^{2+}(aq)$ $\Delta H = -151$ kJ/mol

Bond energies and heats of reaction

Bond energies are important because all chemical reactions involve the breaking and making of bonds. Energy is required to break bonds and is evolved when bonds are formed; the stronger the bond the greater is this energy.

The *bond energy* (or *bond energy of formation*) is the energy evolved when 1 mole of covalent bonds is formed from free gaseous atoms, e.g.

$$H(g) + H(g) \rightarrow H{-}H \quad \Delta H = -433\,kJ/mol$$

Other values, in kJ/mol or kJ mol^{-1}, are:

O—O	−145	N—N	−163	Cl—Cl	−242
O—H	−461	C—H	−414	Br—Br	−193
H—Cl	−430	H—Br	−366	I—I	−152

The bond energies of single, double and triple bonds between carbon atoms are:

C—C −346 C=C −610 C≡C −810

Note that the values for the double and triple bonds are not two and three times that for the single bond.

The *bond dissociation energy* is the energy *absorbed* when 1 mole of covalent bonds breaks to form free gaseous atoms. Its value for a bond is the same as given above except it has a + sign, showing that energy is absorbed.

The energy of a substance is largely the energy of its bonds, which is greater than the kinetic energy of molecules, e.g.

Energy of hydrogen
= bond energy of H—H (large)
+ kinetic energy of molecules (small)

The reaction between hydrogen and chlorine is:

$$H{-}H + Cl{-}Cl \rightarrow 2H{-}Cl \quad \Delta H = -185\,kJ/mol$$

The energy required to break the hydrogen and the chlorine bonds is $433 + 242 = 675$ kilojoules. The energy evolved when the two hydrogen–chlorine bonds form is $2 \times 430 = 860$ kilojoules. The total heat evolved is $860 - 675 = 185$ kilojoules, which agrees with the experimental figure. In other words, the heat change in a chemical reaction is largely the difference between the heat evolved when bonds are formed and the heat absorbed when bonds are broken.

Nitrogen is inert because of the enormous energy (945 kJ/mol) required to break its bonds, and it does not burn because N—O bonds are weak. Hydrocarbon fuels are highly exothermic because of the strong H—O (461 kJ/mol) bonds in water and C=O (803 kJ/mol) bonds in carbon dioxide formed when they burn.

Questions

1 The heat of formation of water is −286 kilojoules per mole (kJ/mol or $kJ\,mol^{-1}$). Explain the meaning of this statement and write a suitable equation. When 1 mole of solid ammonium nitrate was dissolved in water (contained in a thin plastic vessel of negligible heat capacity) to form 1 kg of solution the temperature fall was 6 K. Show that the heat of solution of the nitrate is about +25 kJ/mol.

2 The heat of solution of concentrated sulphuric acid is −71 kJ/mol ($kJ\,mol^{-1}$). Show that the expected temperature change when 1 mole of the acid is added to water to form 1 kg of solution is about 17 °C.

3 Account for the fact that the heat of neutralization of any strong acid with any strong alkali is about −57 kJ/mol. 100 cm^3 of aqueous sodium hydroxide, containing 8 g of the solid alkali, was added to various volumes of aqueous nitric acid, and the heats evolved were calculated:

Volume of acid (cm^3)	60	80	90	100	120	140
Heat evolved (kJ)	6.6	8.9	9.9	11.0	11.1	10.9

(*a*) Show clearly that the alkali solution is of concentration 2.00 M and equals that of the acid solution. (*b*) Show that if 70 cm^3 and then 110 cm^3 of the acid solution were used in the experiment the heats evolved would be 7.7 kJ and 11.0 kJ respectively and explain your reasoning. (*c*) Calculate the heat evolved when 1 mole of the sodium hydroxide dissolved in 500 cm^3 of aqueous solution reacts completely with the acid. (*d*) Estimate the heat evolved when 1 mole of calcium hydroxide in saturated aqueous solution reacts completely with aqueous nitric acid, and give your reasons clearly. (*e*) The experiment was repeated with 2.00 M ethanoic acid, and the heats evolved were less than the figures in the above results. Account for this result with ethanoic acid.

4 The heats of combustion of three alcohols were measured by the method described in this chapter. 200 cm^3 of water was in the metal can, which was heated until the temperature of the water rose by 20 °C. Results were:

	Propan-1-ol	Butan-1-ol	Pentan-1-ol
Mass of alcohol used (g)	1.80	1.48	1.20
Molar mass of alcohol (g)	60	74	88
Heat of combustion ($kJ\,mol^{-1}$) (from experiment)	−560	−840	
Heat of combustion ($kJ\,mol^{-1}$) (from data book)	−2020	−2680	−3320

($C = 12$, $H = 1$, $O = 16$; specific heat capacity of water is 4.2 kJ/kg °C.) (*a*) Calculate the experimental value for the heat of combustion of pentan-1-ol. (*b*) Give reasons why all the experimental values are much less than the correct values taken from a data book. (*c*) Each alcohol differs from the next by one $—CH_2—$ group per molecule. Does this group make a consistent contribution to the energy contents of the alcohols (i) using the experimental results, and (ii) using the data values? (*d*) Explain why the correct heat of combustion of hexan-1-ol is likely to be about $-3980\,kJ\,mol^{-1}$. (*e*) What is the significance of the minus signs in front of the figures for heats of combustion?

5 A distillation apparatus was used to determine the heat of vaporization of propanone, C_3H_6O, at its boiling point, 329 K. The propanone was in the distillation flask which was heated by an immersion heater that produced 2.8 joules per second (J/s). The propanone began to boil steadily a few minutes after the heater had been switched on. The propanone then distilled over into an empty flask at a steady rate, and 22.0 g was collected in 10 minutes. (*a*) Sketch and label the apparatus as it looked while the propanone was distilling, and show clearly how you would reduce heat losses from the distillation flask. (*b*) What changes occurred to the propanone molecules as the propanone warmed from room temperature to its boiling point? (*c*) What further changes occurred to the molecules at the boiling point? (*d*) Show that the energy required to evaporate 1 molar mass of propanone at 329 K is about 44 kJ. (*e*) The heat of vaporization of propanone, given in a book of data, is 30.5 kJ/mol at its b.p. Explain why the experimental result differs from this value. (*f*) Why is the value for propanone similar to that of trichloromethane (30 kJ/mol) and very much less than that of sodium chloride (172 kJ/mol)?

6 The energies required to warm 1 kg of certain elements by 1 K are:

Element	Relative atomic mass	Energy (J/kg K)
Aluminium	27	900
Copper	64	353
Lead	207	130
Magnesium	24	104
Tin	119	230

(*a*) Calculate the moles present in 1 kg of each of the five elements. (*b*) Plot a graph of moles present in 1 kg against the energy in joules required to warm 1 kg by 1 K. (*c*) 450 J warm 1 kg of nickel by 1 K. Use your graph to show that the relative atomic mass of nickel is about 59.

16
Carbonates and Carbon Dioxide

Many rocks in the earth's crust are carbonates. Three examples are *chalk*, *limestone* and *marble*. The shells of sea-animals consist of calcium carbonate. When the animals die, the shells sink to the bottom of the sea. After thousands of years the shells form a layer of chalk. If other rocks cover the chalk, great pressure changes it to limestone. More pressure and heat change limestone to marble. *Coral*, *pearls* and many *shells* (e.g. egg-shells) contain calcium carbonate. The carbonates of zinc, iron, lead and copper occur naturally.

To study the action of dilute acids on carbonates

Place sodium carbonate in a test-tube and add dilute hydrochloric acid. Effervescence occurs and a colourless gas comes off. Test it with calcium hydroxide solution (limewater) by one of the methods shown in Fig. 16.1. Repeat the test using dilute sulphuric acid and then dilute nitric acid. Repeat the whole test using carbonates of potassium, calcium, magnesium, zinc, lead and copper.

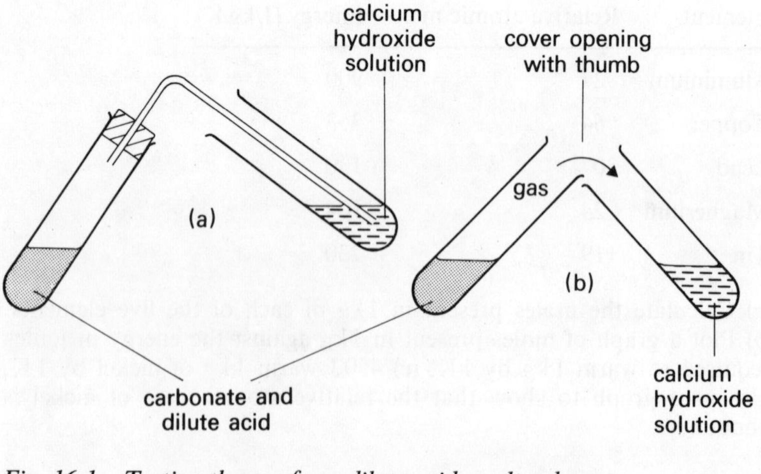

Fig. 16.1 Testing the gas from dilute acids and carbonates

To study the action of heat on carbonates

Heat solid copper(II) carbonate (green) in a dry, hard-glass test-tube. Note the colour of the solid residue. Repeat the test with carbonates of magnesium, zinc and lead (all white), but not calcium carbonate, which cannot be heated strongly enough in a test-tube.

To study the action of heat on limestone (or chalk or marble)

Wrap limestone (calcium carbonate) in nichrome wire (which does not change on heating) and arrange it as in Fig. 16.2. The crucible catches pieces that fall during the experiment. Heat the carbonate gently at first and then strongly until it glows white-hot for at least 10 minutes. Allow the residue to cool.

1 Note its appearance. It is a white powdery substance.

2 Place a piece on damp neutral or red litmus paper; the litmus turns blue (limestone has no action on litmus).

3 Add dilute hydrochloric acid to the product. There is no effervescence (limestone forms carbon dioxide).

The residue is calcium oxide (lime or quicklime), CaO. (Add 5 drops of water, one at a time, to the oxide and note what happens; see Fig. 22.3.)

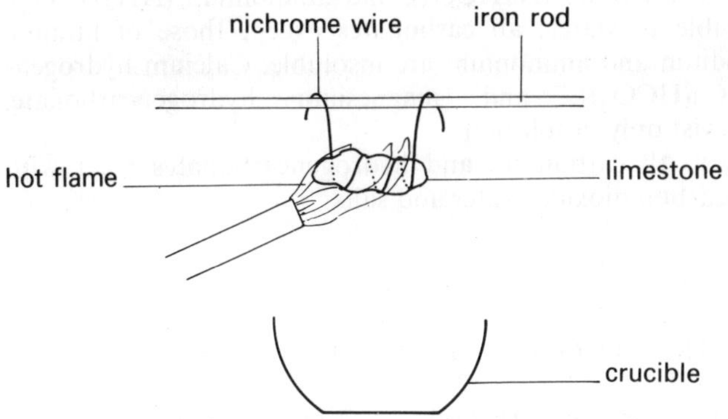

Fig. 16.2 Action of heat on calcium carbonate (limestone)

Fig. 16.3 shows a crucible furnace. The calcium carbonate can be heated in this. The furnace is iron lined with fireclay. A large burner is used and its flame is much hotter than that of an ordinary burner. The fireclay protects the iron from the heat and prevents loss of heat by conduction.

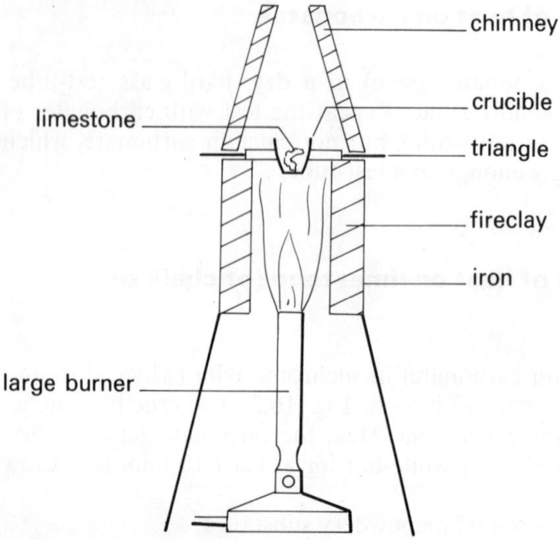

Fig. 16.3 Crucible furnace

Properties of carbonates and hydrogencarbonates

1 *Solubility*. There are three solid hydrogencarbonates; those of potassium ($KHCO_3$), sodium ($NaHCO_3$), and ammonium (NH_4HCO_3). They are soluble in water; all carbonates except those of lithium, potassium, sodium and ammonium are insoluble. Calcium hydrogencarbonate, $Ca(HCO_3)_2$, and magnesium hydrogencarbonate, $Mg(HCO_3)_2$, exist only in solution.

2 *Action of acids*. All carbonates and hydrogencarbonates react with acids to form carbon dioxide, water and salts:

$$\text{Carbonate} + \text{Acid} \rightarrow \begin{matrix}\text{Carbon}\\ \text{Dioxide}\end{matrix} + \text{Water} + \text{Salt}$$

$$CaCO_3 \quad + 2HCl \rightarrow CO_2(g) \quad + H_2O \quad + CaCl_2$$

ionically,

$$CO_3^{2-}(\text{s or aq}) + 2H^+(aq) \rightarrow CO_2(g) + H_2O(l)$$

$$HCO_3^-(\text{s or aq}) + H^+(aq) \rightarrow CO_2(g) + H_2O(l)$$

Dilute sulphuric acid reacts very little with calcium carbonate, and both dilute sulphuric and hydrochloric acids react little with lead(II) carbonate because the products [calcium sulphate, lead(II) sulphate and lead(II) chloride] are insoluble; they form a layer on the outside of the carbonate and stop further reaction. Since all nitrates are soluble, nitric acid reacts readily with all carbonates.

Tests for a carbonate or hydrogencarbonate. (i) Add dilute nitric acid. A carbonate or hydrogencarbonate forms carbon dioxide, which turns calcium hydroxide solution milky. (ii) Add magnesium sulphate solution to a solution of the substance. Carbonates form a white precipitate; hydrogencarbonates do not:

$$Mg^{2+}(aq) + CO_3^{2-}(aq) \rightarrow MgCO_3(s)$$

3 *Action of heat.* Carbonates of lithium, potassium and sodium do not decompose when heated; other carbonates decompose to form an oxide and carbon dioxide:

$$\text{(white) } PbCO_3(s) \rightarrow CO_2(g) + PbO(s) \text{ (yellow)}$$

$$\text{(green) } CuCO_3(s) \rightarrow CO_2(g) + CuO(s) \text{ (black)}$$

Zinc oxide is yellow when hot and white when cold; lead(II) oxide is reddish-brown when hot and yellow when cold.

The reactivity or electrochemical series helps to explain the properties of carbonates and hydrogencarbonates (aluminium carbonate does not exist):

	Carbonates		Hydrogencarbonates	
Metal	Solubility	Heat	State	Heat
Lithium				
Potassium	Soluble	No action	Solid	
Sodium				
Calcium				Form carbonate, carbon dioxide and water
Magnesium			Solution only	
Zinc	Insoluble in water	Form oxide and carbon dioxide		
Iron			Do not exist	Do not exist
Lead				
Copper				

Carbon dioxide, CO_2

To prepare carbon dioxide

Slide (do not drop) marble or limestone chips into a flask. Arrange the apparatus as in Fig. 16.4, collecting the gas either by downward delivery or over water. Pour water down the funnel to cover the carbonate and the end of the thistle funnel. Add concentrated hydrochloric acid until carbon dioxide forms at a suitable rate. A dropping funnel can be used

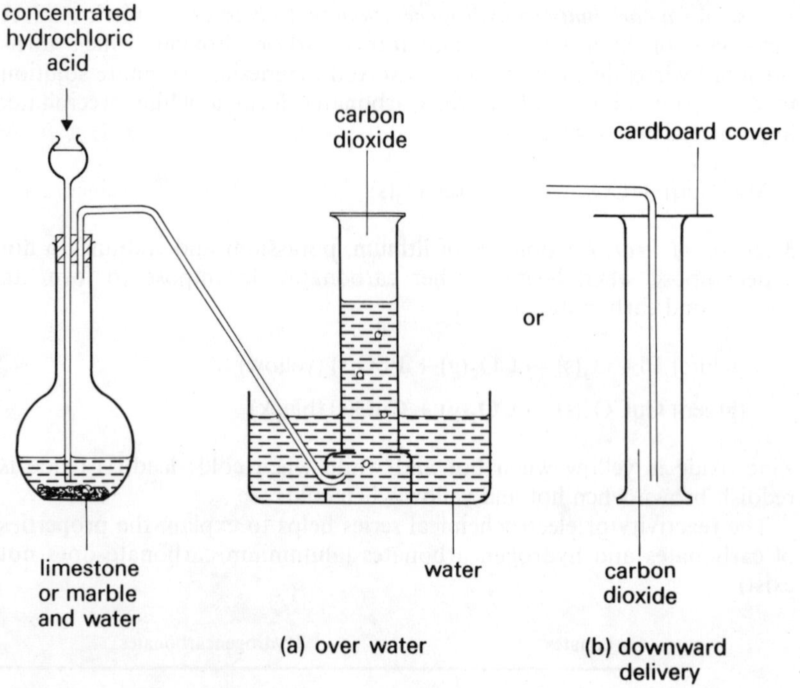

Fig. 16.4 Preparation of carbon dioxide

instead of a thistle funnel; add acid drop by drop to form the gas steadily.

$$CaCO_3(s) + 2HCl(aq) \rightarrow CO_2(g) + H_2O + CaCl_2(aq)$$

or $$CO_3^{2-}(s) + 2H^+(aq) \rightarrow CO_2(g) + H_2O$$

The gas can be dried by concentrated sulphuric acid or anhydrous calcium chloride.

Kipp's apparatus. A continuous supply of carbon dioxide can be obtained from a Kipp's apparatus (Fig. 5.3) using marble chips and dilute hydrochloric acid.

Properties of carbon dioxide

It is a colourless gas, with a very faint smell and a sharp pleasant taste. It is slightly soluble in water, which dissolves its own volume at room temperatures, and forms carbonic acid. This is a weak acid, and turns litmus pink:

$$H_2O(l) + CO_2(g) \rightleftharpoons H_2CO_3(aq) \rightleftharpoons 2H^+(aq) + CO_3^{2-}(aq)$$

Carbon dioxide does not burn. It extinguishes a burning splint.
Density. It is about $1\frac{1}{2}$ times denser than air. It can be poured downwards:
a. Lower a burning candle on a gas-jar spoon into a jar containing air. 'Pour' carbon dioxide on to the candle, which is quickly extinguished, Fig. 16.5.

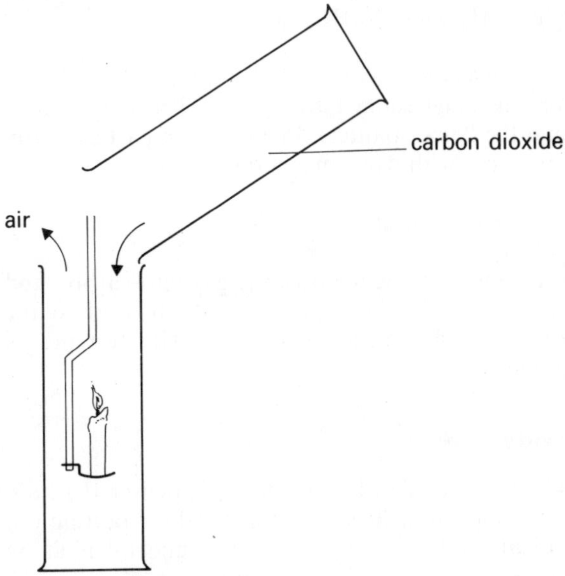

Fig. 16.5 Pouring carbon dioxide on to a burning candle

b. Hold one jar of carbon dioxide mouth upwards and a second jar mouth downwards. Remove the covers at the same time, wait about 15 seconds, and then push burning splints into the jars. The gas in the first jar extinguishes the splint, but the gas in the second jar does not.
Calcium hydroxide solution. This first turns milky, due to precipitation of calcium carbonate, which settles if the mixture is allowed to stand. The mixture turns clear again if more carbon dioxide is passed through it, because the insoluble carbonate forms soluble calcium hydrogencarbonate:

$$Ca(OH)_2(aq) + CO_2(g) \rightarrow CaCO_3(s) + H_2O$$
$$CaCO_3(s) + CO_2(g) + H_2O \rightarrow Ca(HCO_3)_2(aq)$$

Test for carbon dioxide. Carbon dioxide turns calcium hydroxide solution (limewater) milky.

Other alkalis. Invert a tube of carbon dioxide in sodium or potassium hydroxide solution. The gas is quickly absorbed:

$$2NaOH(aq) + CO_2(g) \rightarrow Na_2CO_3(aq) + H_2O(l)$$

If excess gas is bubbled through the alkali, sodium hydrogencarbonate is finally formed:

$$Na_2CO_3(aq) + CO_2(g) + H_2O \rightarrow 2NaHCO_3(aq)$$

These reactions are the same as those with calcium hydroxide.
Magnesium. Lower burning magnesium into the gas. The metal burns less easily than in air and the flame splutters. Black carbon particles form on the sides of the jar, together with white magnesium oxide:

$$2Mg(s) + CO_2(g) \rightarrow 2MgO(s) + C(s)$$

(Probably the burning magnesium decomposes the gas into carbon and oxygen, and the metal burns in the oxygen.) Add dilute acid to the products; it reacts with the oxide and leaves carbon. (This test proves that carbon dioxide contains carbon.)

Uses of carbon dioxide

1 *Fire extinguishers.* Carbon dioxide does not burn, is denser than air, and does not support combustion. It is therefore used for putting out fires, especially petrol and oil fires. Burning petrol and oil float on water and still burn.

a A *soda-acid extinguisher* contains sodium hydrogencarbonate solution. Above the solution is a bottle of concentrated sulphuric acid. When mixed, the two solutions form carbon dioxide which forces the water out through a nozzle of the metal container. The water cools the burning material, and the steam produced reduces the oxygen around the fire. One type of extinguisher has a plunger on top which breaks the acid bottle when pushed down. A second type operates when turned upside down; a stopper drops out of the acid bottle and the two solutions mix.

b A *foam extinguisher* also contains sodium hydrogencarbonate solution plus saponin, and the second solution is aluminium sulphate, which is acidic. When mixed, by moving a lever on top and inverting and shaking the metal container, the two solutions form a foam which is forced out of a nozzle by carbon dioxide. The foam consists of bubbles of carbon dioxide, and the saponin makes the foam last much longer. The foam smothers the flames by reducing the oxygen content near the burning material and it also cools the material. Foam must not be used on electrical fires because it is a conductor. It is most useful for fires of burning liquid when the liquid is in a vessel such as a pan, dish or oven, etc. Foam is only useful for liquids that do not mix with water, e.g. oil, petrol, cooking fat, waxes, paints, etc.

c A *water-carbon dioxide* extinguisher contains carbon dioxide in a small cylinder on top of water. Pushing a plunger releases the carbon dioxide, which forces a jet of water out of the container. It is similar to a soda–acid extinguisher. Its great advantage is that it can be used many times on the same fire if carbon dioxide cylinders are available, whereas the soda–acid type is difficult to re-fill and use quickly.

d A *carbon dioxide extinguisher* contains carbon dioxide under pressure. The gas comes out of a nozzle after removing the safety pin and squeezing a trigger. It is useful for electrical fires and for burning oil, petrol, etc. The gas displaces oxygen near the flames and smothers the fire. However, it does not cool the material and burning may start again if there is a draught or strong breeze. Since carbon dioxide does not support life, these extinguishers should not be used in an enclosed space.

2 *Aerated drinks*. Carbon dioxide dissolves slightly in water; the gas is much more soluble if the pressure is increased. It is used to give a pleasant taste to some drinks, e.g. lemonade, orangeade, and other *aerated drinks* or *mineral waters*. *Soda water* is a solution in water of carbon dioxide under pressure. *Health salts* contain tartaric or citric acid and sodium hydrogencarbonate, which effervesce when added to water.

3 *Refrigeration*. Carbon dioxide changes on cooling to a solid called *dry ice*. This does not melt like ice; it changes directly from solid to gas, i.e. it sublimes. Dry ice therefore does not leave a residue. It is used to 'deep freeze' food and to keep ice-cream cold.

4 *Ammonia-soda or Solvay process*. It is used to make sodium hydrogencarbonate and sodium carbonate (Fig. 16.6).

5 *Making rain*. Pieces of solid carbon dioxide are sometimes dropped into clouds to cool them enough to form rain.

6 *Cooking*. Yeast is added to flour, sugar and water (dough) when making bread, and baking powder (sodium hydrogencarbonate and an acid) is added to cake mixture. The yeast causes sugar in the dough to ferment and form carbon dioxide; baking powder forms carbon dioxide when heated in an oven. The gas forms bubbles inside the dough and cakes, which 'rise' and so are very light.

To prepare sodium hydrogencarbonate and sodium carbonate

Sodium hydrogencarbonate. Bubble carbon dioxide (free from acid spray) through concentrated sodium hydroxide solution. The hydrogencarbonate is precipitated as a white powder because it is only slightly soluble:

$$NaOH(aq) + CO_2(g) \rightarrow NaHCO_3(s)$$

Filter off the precipitate and wash it with a little distilled water. Dry it between filter papers or in sunshine.

Sodium carbonate. Heat sodium hydrogencarbonate in a hard-glass test-tube until no more steam and carbon dioxide come off. Sodium carbonate is left as a white powder (it does not change on heating):

$$2\,NaHCO_3(s) \rightarrow Na_2CO_3(s) + CO_2(g) + H_2O(g)$$

Dissolve the powder in the *minimum amount* of hot water and crystallize to obtain clear crystals, $Na_2CO_3{\cdot}10H_2O$.

The crystals lose water in air and become covered with a white powder.

Reactions of sodium hydrogencarbonate and sodium carbonate

1 *Dilute acids.* Both form carbon dioxide.

2 *Heat.* The anhydrous carbonate does not change (ordinary sodium carbonate contains impurities which may cause wrong results in this test); the hydrated carbonate loses all of its water. The hydrogencarbonate gives off both steam and carbon dioxide, and leaves white sodium carbonate:

$$2NaHCO_3(s) \rightarrow Na_2CO_3(s) + H_2O(g) + CO_2(g)$$

3 *Magnesium sulphate solution.* The carbonate forms a white precipitate but the hydrogencarbonate does not:

$$Mg^{2+}(aq) + CO_3^{2-}(aq) \rightarrow MgCO_3(s)$$

Ammonia-soda or Solvay Process

Sodium carbonate is manufactured by dropping brine (concentrated sodium chloride solution) slowly down an absorber tower up which ammonia passes. The ammonia dissolves. The ammonia brine flows slowly down a Solvay tower (Fig. 16.6) up which carbon dioxide passes. Ammonium hydrogencarbonate is formed:

$$NH_3(aq) + CO_2(g) + H_2O(l) \rightarrow NH_4HCO_3(aq)$$

and it at once reacts with sodium chloride to form the slightly soluble sodium hydrogencarbonate (and ammonium chloride):

$$Na^+(aq) + HCO_3^-(aq) \rightarrow NaHCO_3(s)$$

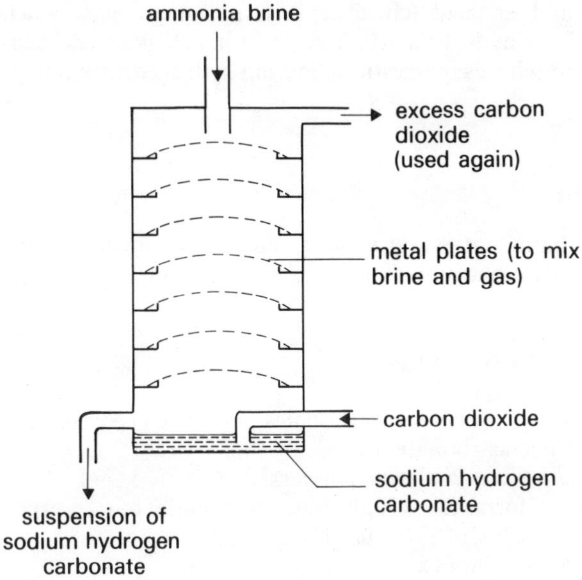

Fig. 16.6 Ammonia-soda or Solvay process

The hydrogencarbonate is filtered off and heated to form the carbonate; any ammonium chloride impurity sublimes off:

$$2NaHCO_3(s) \rightarrow Na_2CO_3(s) + CO_2(g) + H_2O(g)$$

The anhydrous carbonate, called *soda-ash*, is used in the manufacture of glass. It is also crystallized from water to form washing soda, the 10-water hydrate.

Formation of carbon dioxide. This is obtained by heating calcium carbonate and sodium hydrogencarbonate:

$$CaCO_3(s) \rightarrow CO_2(g) + CaO(s)$$

Regeneration of ammonia. Calcium hydroxide is made by adding water to the calcium oxide; it is mixed with ammonium chloride obtained as a by-product and heated by steam. The only waste product is calcium chloride.

Uses of sodium carbonate and sodium hydrogencarbonate

Sodium carbonate is used in making glass, soap, and sodium hydroxide and for softening water. The hydrogencarbonate is used in fire extinguishers and baking powder. 'Health salts' are mixtures of sodium hydrogencarbonate and an acid (citric or tartaric) which react when added to water. Sodium hydrogencarbonate in 'stomach powders' neutralizes excess acid and relieves indigestion. Sodium hydrogencarbonate is *baking soda*.

Other carbonates

Only carbonates of lithium, potassium, sodium and ammonium are soluble in water. The other carbonates are insoluble and therefore are usually prepared by precipitation:

$$Cu^{2+}(aq) + CO_3^{2-}(aq) \rightarrow CuCO_3(s)$$

Sodium carbonate precipitates basic carbonates, e.g. $ZnCO_3 \cdot Zn(OH)_2$, therefore sodium hydrogencarbonate is used.

Zinc and lead(II) carbonates are white powders.

Copper(II) carbonate forms as a light-blue precipitate but is green when dry. It is the basic salt $CuCO_3 \cdot Cu(OH)_2$.

Aluminium carbonate does not exist.

Ammonium carbonate is used in smelling salts because it slowly forms ammonia, which stimulates breathing:

$$(NH_4)_2CO_3(s) \rightarrow 2NH_3(g) + H_2O(g) + CO_2(g)$$

Hard water

Some kinds of water do not form a lather readily with soap. Instead, a scum forms and rises to the surface, and the water looks milky. Finally, when enough soap is added, a lather forms. *Soft water readily forms a lather with soap. Hard water does not readily form a lather with soap.*

How water becomes hard

Rain dissolves carbon dioxide as it falls. Rain-water is therefore very dilute carbonic acid:

$$H_2O(l) + CO_2(g) \rightleftharpoons H_2CO_3(aq)$$

If this water passes through rocks containing calcium carbonate or magnesium carbonate, some dissolves to form hydrogencarbonate:

$$CaCO_3(s) + H_2CO_3(aq) \rightleftharpoons Ca(HCO_3)_2(aq)$$
$$MgCO_3(s) + H_2CO_3(aq) \rightleftharpoons Mg(HCO_3)_2(aq)$$

Calcium sulphate-2-water occurs naturally as *gypsum*, $CaSO_4 \cdot 2H_2O$. If rain-water passes through the rocks containing calcium or magnesium sulphates, some dissolves. The water is hard because the *calcium and magnesium ions* in solution react with soap and stop it forming a lather readily.

To prepare soap

Mix sodium hydroxide (about $10\,cm^3$ of 5 M) with castor oil (about $2\,cm^3$) or lard, or other oil or fat in a beaker. Warm to boiling, and stir with a glass rod while it boils gently for 5–10 minutes. The soap remains in solution. Add saturated sodium chloride solution, boil gently and stir for a further 2 minutes, and allow to cool. Soap is insoluble in sodium chloride. Filter off the solid soap.

$$\text{Fat} + \text{Alkali} \rightarrow \text{Soap} + \begin{matrix}\text{Propanetriol}\\ \text{(glycerine)}\end{matrix}$$

$$\text{i.e. } \begin{matrix}\text{Glyceryl}\\ \text{stearate}\end{matrix} + \begin{matrix}\text{Sodium}\\ \text{hydroxide}\end{matrix} \rightarrow \begin{matrix}\text{Sodium}\\ \text{stearate}\end{matrix} + \text{Propanetriol}$$

Manufacture of soap. Oils and fats (coconut oil, palm oil, mutton fat, fats made by hydrogenation of oils, etc.) are heated by steam with sodium or potassium hydroxide. Sodium chloride is added to separate the soap as an upper layer (the ‘salting out’ of soap). (Potassium hydroxide forms ‘soft soaps’.) The propanetriol (glycerine or glycerol) is obtained by distillation.

Action of soap on water

Soap consists of the soluble sodium (or potassium) salts of a few organic acids, e.g. stearic acid, palmitic acid and oleic acid (now called octadecanoic, hexadecanoic and octadecenoic acid respectively). Ordinary soap is a mixture of sodium stearate, sodium palmitate and sodium oleate; ‘soft soap’ consists of the potassium salts. The formulae are complex, e.g. $C_{17}H_{35}COONa$ is sodium stearate. We can use a simple formula, NaSt, writing St for the stearate (palmitate or oleate) radical. If water is hard, soap first reacts with dissolved calcium and magnesium ions and forms a scum on the water

$$Ca^{2+} \text{ or } Mg^{2+}(aq) + 2St^-(aq) \rightarrow CaSt_2(s) \text{ or } MgSt_2(s), \text{ scum}$$

Calcium and magnesium hydrogencarbonates decompose on boiling, and then no longer make the water hard. Hardness due to sulphates is called *permanent hardness*.

Temporarily hard water is water which becomes soft on boiling. Permanently hard water is water which does not become soft on boiling.

How hard water is made soft

Distillation of water removes all hardness. Addition of sodium carbonate (washing soda) or passing water through permutit (sodium aluminium silicate, Na_2X) removes all hardness by removing Ca^{2+} (or Mg^{2+}) as insoluble compounds:

$$Ca^{2+}(aq) + CO_3^{2-}(aq) \rightarrow CaCO_3(s)$$

$$Ca^{2+}(aq) + X^{2-}(aq) \rightarrow CaX(s)$$

Boiling, calcium hydroxide (sometimes added to water in reservoirs) and aqueous ammonia remove only temporary hardness. They convert the soluble hydrogencarbonate to insoluble carbonate:

$$Ca(HCO_3)_2(aq) \rightarrow CaCO_3(s) + H_2O + CO_2(g)$$

$$Ca(HCO_3)_2(aq) + Ca(OH)_2(aq) \rightarrow 2CaCO_3(s) + 2H_2O$$

Disadvantages of hard water

1 *Waste of soap.* Hard water needs much soap to form a lather.
2 *Marks on clothes.* Soap and hard water form a scum, calcium stearate, which makes dirty marks on clothes and can also damage silk and nylon. Hard water causes wrong colours in dyeing processes and poor finish to leather during tanning (making leather from skins).
3 *'Fur' in kettles and pans.* Calcium and magnesium carbonates form as a 'fur' inside kettles and pans in which hard water is boiled. The 'fur' is a bad conductor of heat and therefore wastes fuel.
4 *Boiler scale.* Calcium and magnesium carbonates and sulphates form inside boilers. The solid is 'boiler scale', which wastes fuel because it is a bad conductor of heat. The scale may block narrow boiler tubes, causing steam pressure to rise and possibly damage or burst the pipes and boiler.

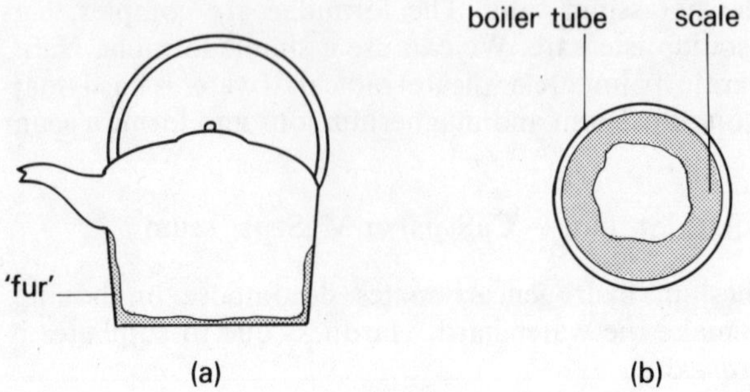

Fig. 16.7 (a) 'Fur' in a kettle
(b) Scale in a boiler tube

Advantages of hard water

1 *Teeth and bones*. These contain calcium compounds, usually calcium phosphate. The calcium compounds in hard water may help to form healthy teeth and bones.
2 *Water pipes*. Lead pipes cannot be used with soft water because soft water dissolves some lead, which is a *poison*. Hard water soon forms a coat of lead(II) carbonate and sulphate on the pipes, and this stops further reaction.
3 *Shells of animals*. The shells and eggs of many animals contain calcium carbonate, and some comes from hard water.

Stalactites and stalagmites

Rain-water dissolves carbon dioxide from the air. It dissolves more as it passes through soil containing living organisms, all breathing out the gas. In certain regions this water reacts with limestone and magnesium carbonate rocks and forms calcium and magnesium hydrogencarbonates.

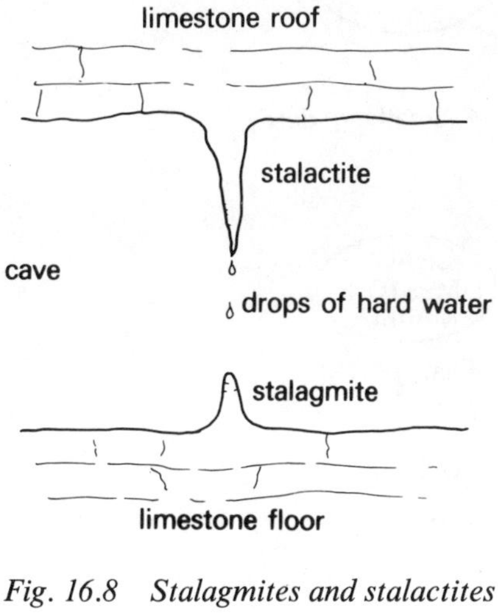

Fig. 16.8 Stalagmites and stalactites

As this solution drops from the roof of a cave, a little solid calcium and magnesium carbonate may be left on the roof and floor of the cave. The carbonate grows down from the roof and after hundreds of years forms a column, called a *stalactite*. The solid also grows up from the floor and forms a column, called a *stalagmite*. If the columns grow long enough they join.

The carbon cycle in nature

Carbon dioxide is added to the atmosphere by:

1 *Combustion*. The burning in air of fuels containing carbon (coal, coke, wood, petrol, oils, natural gas and wax).

2 *Respiration*. Animals and plants breathe air, and the oxygen oxidizes sugar in their bodies to form energy:

Sugar + Oxygen → Carbon dioxide + Water + Energy

$$C_6H_{12}O_6 + 6O_2 \rightarrow 6CO_2 + 6H_2O + 2800\,kJ$$

3 *Making lime*. See p. 282.

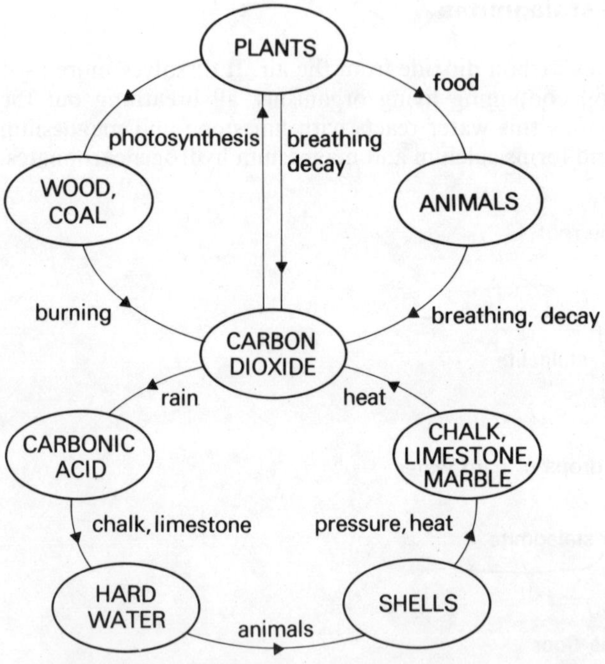

Fig. 16.9 Carbon cycle

4 *Making beer and wines*. Beer, whisky, wines, etc., are made when yeast changes sugar or starch to ethanol and carbon dioxide. The change is called *fermentation* (p. 305):

Sugar → Ethanol + Carbon dioxide

$$C_6H_{12}O_6(aq) \rightarrow 2C_2H_5OH(aq) + 2CO_2(g)$$

Carbon dioxide is removed from the atmosphere by:

1 *Solution in water*. Rain dissolves carbon dioxide, and rivers, lakes, seas and oceans contain much of it. The concentration in sea-water is 20 times that in air.

2 *Photosynthesis*. Green plants absorb carbon dioxide to make sugar (glucose):

$$6CO_2 + 6H_2O + 2800 \text{ kilojoules} \rightarrow C_6H_{12}O_6 + 6O_2$$

The green chlorophyll is a catalyst and sunlight is also necessary. The process is called *photosynthesis* which means 'building up by light'. The reaction is the opposite of that during respiration.

3 *Hardening of mortar*. Mortar and whitewash contain calcium hydroxide. This slowly reacts with carbon dioxide to form calcium carbonate:

$$Ca(OH)_2(s) + CO_2(g) \rightarrow CaCO_3(s) + H_2O(g)$$

The oxygen cycle in nature

Processes which remove oxygen from the atmosphere are (i) combustion of fuels, (ii) respiration, (iii) rusting of iron. Oxygen is added by photosynthesis.

Questions

1 Name three different naturally occurring forms of calcium carbonate. Starting with one of them, how would you prepare in the laboratory (*a*) calcium hydroxide, (*b*) calcium sulphate, (*c*) a solution of calcium hydrogencarbonate? Give four differences in properties between distilled water and calcium chloride solution. (L.)

2 Describe how to prepare some gas-jars of carbon dioxide. Explain the operation of a fire extinguisher which produces carbon dioxide. Explain the part played by carbon dioxide in the erosion of limestone. (O.)

3 Describe how, starting from calcium carbonate, you would prepare some temporarily hard water. How would you (*a*) show that this water is hard, and (*b*) remove the hardness? What are the uses of limestone and calcium sulphate-2-water? (C.)

4 How is sodium carbonate manufactured by the Solvay process? How does sodium carbonate solution react with (*a*) carbon dioxide, (*b*) copper(II) sulphate solution, (*c*) nitric acid? Give two uses of sodium carbonate. (C.)

5 What is the difference between temporary and permanent hardness of water, and what causes each kind of hardness? Explain how hardness can be removed from water. Describe how you would find whether a sample of water contained temporary, permanent, or both kinds of hardness. (N.)

6 Draw and label Kipp's apparatus for the preparation of carbon dioxide. What is the action of this gas on water, calcium hydroxide solution, sodium hydroxide solution, and heated charcoal? Mention three important uses of the gas. (L.)

7 State and explain two disadvantages of hard water. Explain two different methods by which all hardness can be removed chemically. What advantages can be claimed for some hardness in water? (O.)

8 Describe one method for the large scale production of sodium carbonate-10-water from common salt. Describe laboratory experiments by which the carbonate can be converted to (*a*) sodium hydroxide solution, (*b*) solid sodium hydrogencarbonate. (L.)

9 What is soap? Indicate briefly how it is made. Describe how you would find the ratio of permanent hardness to temporary hardness in a sample of water. (C.)

10 Explain briefly the following observations about a sample of hard water: (*a*) when boiled it formed some white precipitate; (*b*) even after boiling the water was still quite hard when tested with soap; (*c*) the water could be made completely soft by adding sodium carbonate. Explain the action on this water of permutit. (C.)

17
Carbon and Carbon Monoxide. Fuels. Silicon

Forms of carbon

Carbon exists as *diamond*, *graphite* and *'amorphous' carbon* (charcoal, lampblack, soot, coke). Diamond and graphite are crystalline and 'amorphous' carbon is non-crystalline, although some forms consist of minute crystals of graphite.

> Allotropy is the existence of an element in more than one form (without change of state). The various forms are allotropes. Carbon is allotropic.
>
> Polymorphism is the existence of a substance which can crystallize in more than one form. The various forms are polymorphs. Carbon is polymorphic.

(Polymorphism applies only to solids; allotropy also applies to different liquid and gaseous forms of an element, e.g. sulphur.)

Graphite. A crystal consists of layers of carbon atoms (Fig. 17.1). Each layer is a giant molecule or macromolecule in two dimensions only. Each carbon atom is at the corner of a regular hexagon and is equidistant from three similar atoms. The atoms in a layer are joined by strong covalent bonds, and their distance apart is 0.14 nanometre. The distance between layers is 0.34 nm, which is more than twice the distance between atoms in a layer. Layers are joined by weak intermolecular forces, and layers slide over each other easily. Graphite is therefore a soft substance. Some electrons in a layer are mobile, like those in metals. Graphite is therefore a good conductor along its crystals; it is a poor conductor across the crystals.

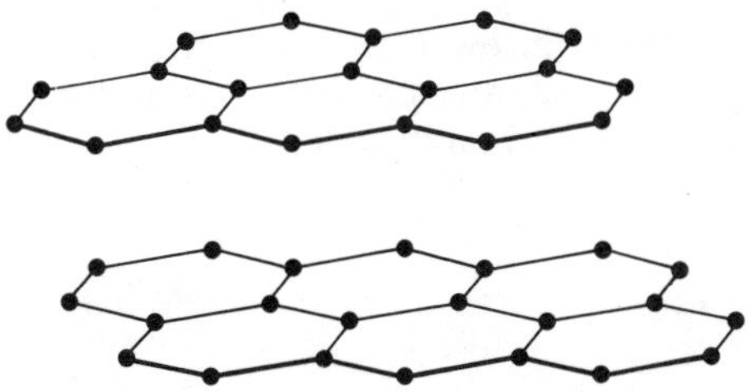

Fig. 17.1 Hexagonal rings in graphite

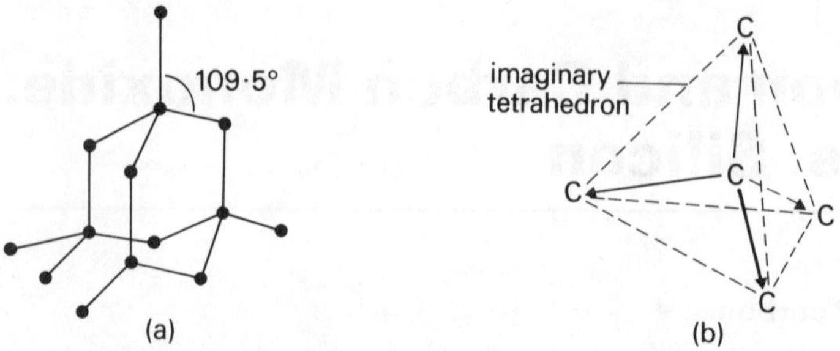

Fig. 17.2 Tetrahedral structure of diamond

Diamond. Each carbon atom is joined by covalent bonds to four others, and the four atoms are arranged tetrahedrally, Fig. 17.2. The distance between neighbouring atoms is 0.15 nm. A diamond crystal is a giant molecule in three dimensions. Diamond is denser than graphite because its atoms are closer. Diamond has no mobile electrons and it is an insulator.

Properties of carbon

	Diamond	Graphite	Amorphous carbon
Appearance	Colourless, transparent, sparkling	Grey-black, opaque, shiny	Black, opaque, dull
Density (g/cm^3)	Highest—3.5	2.3	Lowest—1.5 when air-free
Hardness	Hardest substance known	Soft; greasy or soapy	Soft
Burning in air	Least readily—at about 900 °C	At about 700 °C	Most readily—at about 500 °C
Conductivity (heat and electricity)	Poor conductor	Good conductor	Fair conductor

Carbon burns in oxygen to form carbon dioxide and heat. It readily removes oxygen from compounds, therefore it is a *reducing agent*. It reduces oxides of zinc and other metals below it in the activity series. Lead(II) oxide forms silvery beads of lead, and copper(II) oxide forms reddish copper; the carbon is oxidized to carbon dioxide:

$$2PbO(s) + C(s) \rightarrow 2Pb(s) + CO_2(g);$$

$$2CuO(s) + C(s) \rightarrow 2Cu(s) + CO_2(g)$$

Iron, zinc and lead are manufactured by reducing their oxides with carbon. Carbon reduces nitric acid to nitrogen dioxide and sulphuric acid to sulphur dioxide. Carbon does not dissolve in any common solvent; a deposit of carbon inside an engine can be removed only by scraping it off. Wood charcoal is porous and can absorb gases, e.g. chlorine, bromine, ammonia, etc. Animal charcoal absorbs coloured substances from solutions.

To examine some properties of charcoal

Density. Drop wood charcoal into water; it floats. Wrap wire gauze around the charcoal and drop it into boiling water. This drives out any air in it. Cool, remove the gauze, and drop the charcoal into cold water; it sinks.

Decolorizing action. Boil animal charcoal with litmus solution for 5 minutes, and then filter. The filtrate is colourless.

Copper(II) oxide. Heat black copper(II) oxide with powdered charcoal in a hard-glass test-tube fitted with a delivery tube. Test any gas evolved with calcium hydroxide solution, which turns milky. Red-brown copper can sometimes be seen in the mixture in the test-tube.

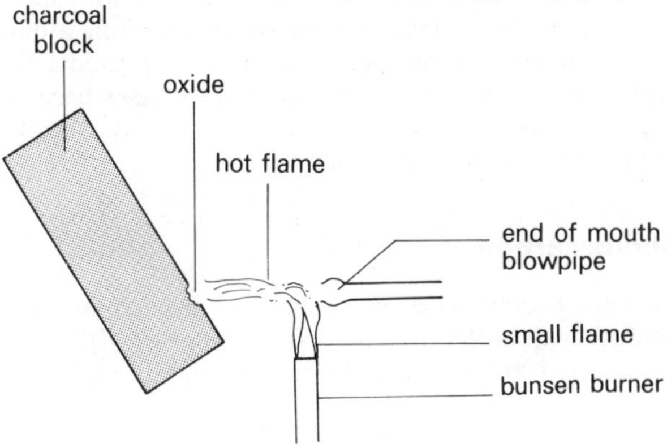

Fig. 17.3 Charcoal block test

Charcoal block test. Place lead(II) oxide in a small hole in a charcoal block, and wet it with one drop of water. Heat it with a mouth blowpipe, using a luminous bunsen flame (Fig. 17.4). A silver ball of lead forms.

Absorption of gases. (*a*) Invert a tube of ammonia gas over mercury in an evaporating basin. Push a lump of wood charcoal into the gas. The mercury rises, showing that the ammonia is absorbed. (*b*) Alternatively, add one drop of liquid bromine to a tube. Wait until bromine vapour fills the tube, add wood charcoal, and close the tube. The reddish colour of the bromine quickly disappears.

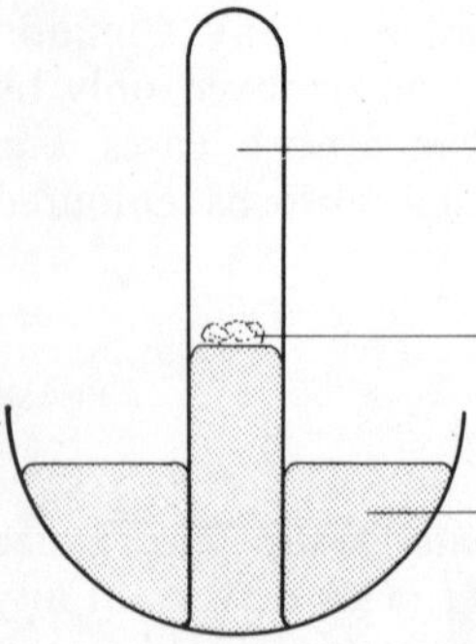

Fig. 17.4 Charcoal absorbs gases

Uses of carbon

Diamonds are valuable gems. They are also used for cutting and drilling glass, pottery and rock because they are so hard. The 'lead' of pencils is graphite mixed with clay. Graphite is used as a lubricant for dynamos, electric motors, and fast moving parts of machinery. Graphite is used as electrodes because it conducts electricity and does not react with most substances. Graphite is used in atomic piles in which uranium atoms split up to form energy; it absorbs neutrons evolved and prevents the action becoming explosive. Wood charcoal is used in gas-masks because it absorbs poison gas. Animal charcoal is used to remove the brown substances from crude sugar and make it white.

Forms of amorphous carbon

Wood charcoal is the black porous solid left when wood or coconut shells are heated out of contact with air (*destructive distillation of wood*). Wood charcoal can absorb about 100 times its volume of ammonia and other gases.

Animal charcoal is formed when bones are heated out of contact with air (*destructive distillation of bones*). It contains calcium phosphate. It absorbs the colour from solutions, e.g. litmus from water and brown substances from crude sugar.

Sugar charcoal is pure carbon made by dehydrating cane-sugar or glucose with concentrated sulphuric acid (p. 254) or by heating sugar in the absence of air to drive off water:

(Glucose) $C_6H_{12}O_6(s) \rightarrow 6C(s) + 6H_2O(g)$

(Cane sugar) $C_{12}H_{22}O_{11}(s) \rightarrow 12C(s) + 11H_2O(g)$

Lampblack, soot or carbon black is formed when petroleum, kerosine, turpentine, natural gas and other hydrocarbons burn in a limited supply of air. It is used to make Indian ink, black shoe polish, carbon paper, and printer's ink. About one-third of a rubber tyre is lampblack; it makes the tyre last much longer.

Coke is the solid left in the retorts when coal is heated out of contact with air (*destructive distillation of coal*). Coke is used as a fuel in furnaces, boilers and ovens.

To study what happens when coal and wood are heated out of contact with air

Coal. Fill a hard-glass tube with powdered coal and arrange the apparatus as in Fig. 17.5 but without the gas-jar. Slope the tube downwards slightly. Heat the coal strongly. When all the air is out of the apparatus, place the gas-jar on the shelf. A brown smoke comes off the coal. The distillate in the boiling-tube is a watery liquid on black coal tar.

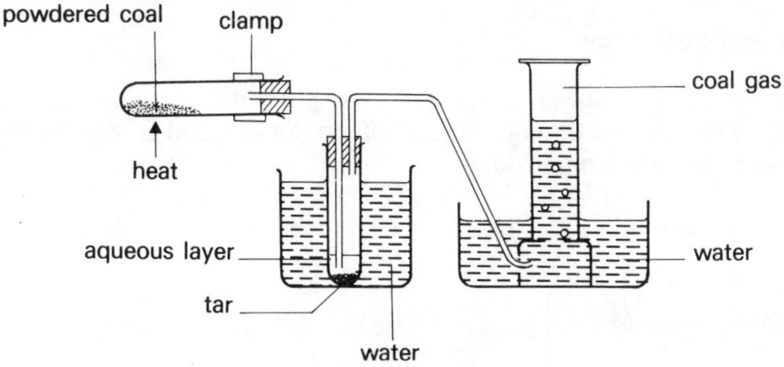

Fig. 17.5 Action of heat on coal (or wood, etc.)

The watery part turns litmus blue—it contains ammonia. The tar turns litmus red. The residue is coke. The gas is coal gas.

Coal → Coke + Ammonia liquor + Coal tar + Coal gas

Wood. Repeat the experiment using sawdust or broken wooden splints or wood wool. Similar changes occur; the residue is charcoal and the watery distillate turns litmus red, it contains ethanoic (acetic) acid.

Origins of coal

Coal is a mixture of compounds of carbon, hydrogen and oxygen, together with small amounts of nitrogen, sulphur and phosphorus compounds. It was formed millions of years ago. Plants of great forests died and were covered with sand and mud. Bacteria caused the vegetation to decay, and then heat and pressure changed the decayed material to coal.

Town gas and natural gas

Much town gas consists of coal gas mixed with natural gas, or is just natural gas. This gas occurs in the earth's crust either by itself or above petroleum deposits. It contains between 80 and 99 per cent methane, CH_4, and between 20 and 1 per cent of other alkanes (chapter 23).

Liquefied petroleum gas (LPG), sometimes called Calor gas and bottled gas, is a mixture of propane, butane and other alkanes. Usually these are gases, but they are liquids when under pressure in steel cylinders. LPG is obtained from natural gas and from distillation of petroleum. Town gas and LPG contain little or no sulphur compounds and therefore do not form corrosive sulphur dioxide when they burn.

Coke and coal fires

Air enters at the bottom of the fire. The hot coke burns to carbon dioxide, which passes through the rest of the hot fuel and is reduced by the carbon to carbon monoxide:

$$C(s) + O_2(g) \rightarrow CO_2(g); CO_2(g) + C(s) \rightarrow 2CO(g)$$

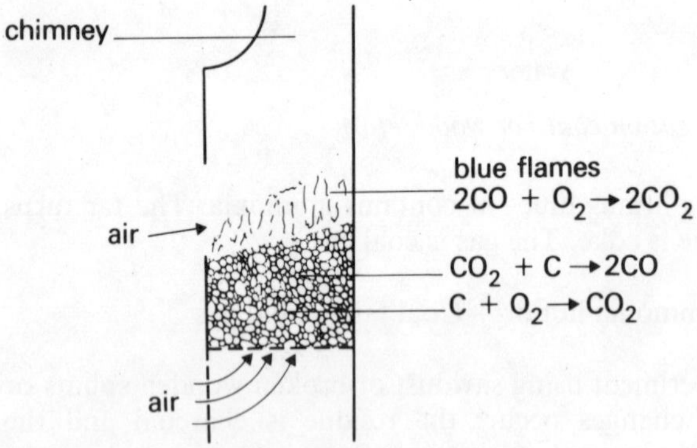

Fig. 17.6 Coke fire

Carbon monoxide passes out of the top of the fuel, where it burns in the air with a blue flame:

$$2CO(g) + O_2(g) \rightarrow 2CO_2(g)$$

Coke fires form poisonous carbon monoxide if the air supply is low. Coal burns with a smoky, luminous flame because of the volatile compounds it forms when hot.

Exothermic and endothermic reactions

An exothermic reaction is one in which heat is evolved.

Examples:

$$2SO_2 + O_2 \rightleftharpoons 2SO_3 + \text{heat}; N_2 + 3H_2 \rightleftharpoons 2NH_3 + \text{heat}$$

The combustion of coal, wood, petrol, oils, gases, etc., are all exothermic reactions.

An endothermic reaction is one in which heat is absorbed.

Examples:

$$C + H_2O \rightarrow CO + H_2 - \text{heat}; N_2 + O_2 \rightleftharpoons 2NO - \text{heat}$$

Carbon monoxide, CO

To prepare carbon monoxide from carbon dioxide

Fill a silica combustion tube with charcoal. Heat it in a furnace until it is red-hot. Pass carbon dioxide over the charcoal. Dissolve any excess

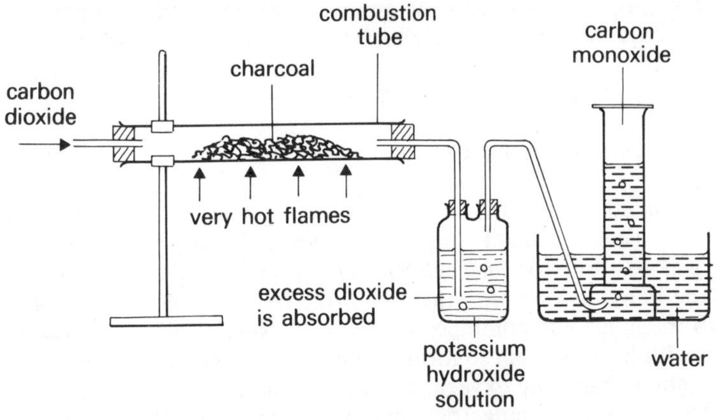

Fig. 17.7 Carbon monoxide from carbon dioxide

carbon dioxide by passing the gas through bottles of concentrated potassium hydroxide:

$$C(s) + CO_2(g) \rightarrow 2CO(g)$$

$$2KOH(aq) + CO_2(g) \rightarrow K_2CO_3(aq) + H_2O$$

Alternative method. This uses silica tubing connected by rubber tubing to two syringes (p. 30). First place the charcoal between two loosely packed plugs of glass wool in the silica tube. Heat the tube strongly while passing carbon dioxide through it; this removes moisture and dries the charcoal. Now connect the silica to two syringes, one of which contains about 50 cm^3 of carbon dioxide and the other is empty. Heat the silica and charcoal and pass the carbon dioxide *slowly* over it and back again. The glass wool prevents fine charcoal particles passing into the syringes.

From methanoic (formic) acid. Use the apparatus of Fig. 4.1. Add warm concentrated sulphuric acid to the flask and then add methanoic acid, drop by drop, from the dropping funnel. Collect the carbon monoxide over water. The reaction is a dehydration, p. 254):

$$HCOOH(l) \rightarrow CO(g) + H_2O(l)$$

Methanoic acid

Properties of carbon monoxide

Carbon monoxide is a colourless, tasteless, odourless gas. It is neutral to litmus, and only slightly soluble in water. It dissolves in ammoniacal copper(I) salts. Its density is slightly less than that of air. *Carbon monoxide burns in air with a blue flame*, forming carbon dioxide (this is a *test for the gas*). Since it readily removes oxygen from compounds, carbon monoxide is a *reducing agent*. It reduces oxides of copper, lead, iron and zinc to the metals (reddish-brown copper, silvery lead) and is itself oxidized to carbon dioxide (Fig. 17.8).

$$PbO(s) + CO(g) \rightarrow Pb(s) + CO_2(g)$$

The reduction of iron(III) oxide occurs in the blast furnace. *Carbon monoxide is poisonous.* Blood contains red haemoglobin, which combines with oxygen to form *oxyhaemoglobin.* This moves in the blood to all parts of the body and supplies them with the oxygen. The haemoglobin returns to the lungs and combines with more oxygen. Carbon monoxide combines with haemoglobin to form bright red *carboxyhaemoglobin.* This stops the blood absorbing oxygen. The person therefore soon becomes ill or dies. The gas is more dangerous than other poisonous gases because it has no colour or smell.

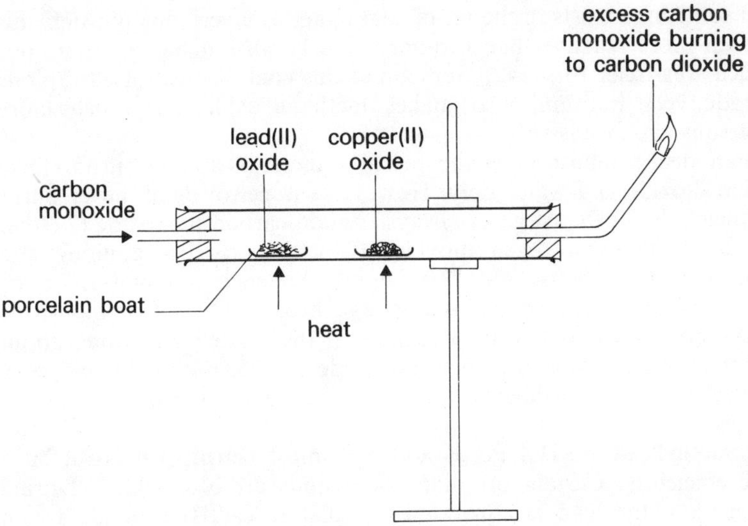

Fig. 17.8 Reducing action of carbon monoxide

Both gases are colourless and odourless, and do not support combustion.

The gas methane, CH_4, occurs in some mines and can cause explosions. Usually, an explosion itself may not kill many miners. However, it forms carbon monoxide which may poison miners and their rescuers:

$$2CH_4(g) + 3O_2(g) \rightarrow 2CO(g) + 4H_2O(g)$$

Carbon dioxide	Carbon monoxide
Not poisonous	Poisonous
Soluble in water and alkalis	Insoluble in water and alkalis
Turns litmus pale red	No action on litmus
Denser than air	Less dense than air
Does not burn	Burns with a blue flame
Turns calcium hydroxide solution milky	No action on calcium hydroxide solution
No action on oxides	Reduces some metallic oxides
Reacts with heated charcoal	No action on charcoal

Coal sometimes exists in the air of coal mines as a very fine powder; this is much more reactive than ordinary coal because it has an enormous surface area (refer to p. 147). Sometimes this coal dust can itself explode if made very hot and also makes methane explosions much more dangerous and extensive.

In an ideal combustion engine, petrol or diesel oil and air burn to form carbon dioxide and water only. However, the petrol or oil never burns completely and exhaust gases always contain carbon monoxide (2–9 per cent by volume), nitrogen dioxide (10–4000 parts per million), and unburnt hydrocarbons (300–12 000 ppm). An engine should never be run in a closed space, e.g. a closed garage, because the carbon monoxide is very poisonous. It is estimated that in the United Kingdom, about 7000 million kilograms of carbon monoxide and 250 million kilograms of nitrogen dioxide are added to the atmosphere each year by combustion engines.

Tetraethyllead, $(C_2H_5)_4Pb$, is added to most petrol to make it burn more efficiently. Certain bromine compounds are also added. During combustion, the lead is converted to volatile lead(II) bromide which passes through the exhaust into the atmosphere. About 1000 million kilograms of lead per year enter the atmosphere from petrol engines, and this increases the lead concentration in the atmosphere, seas and rivers. Lead is the most dangerous airborne pollutant; it can cause depression, irritability, and damage to the central nervous system and the brain.

Coal and coke fires form carbon monoxide if the air supply is limited. Badly ventilated fires are therefore dangerous.

Producer gas

Air is blown through hot coke. Carbon dioxide is first formed, and is reduced to the monoxide in the middle of the coke where there is no oxygen. The reaction is *exothermic*, and the coke becomes very hot:

$$C + O_2 \rightarrow CO_2 + \text{heat}; \; CO_2 + C \rightarrow 2CO$$

Representing air as $O_2 + 4N_2$, the equation is:

$$\underset{}{2C + O_2 + 4N_2} \rightarrow \underset{\text{2 volumes}}{2CO(g)} + \underset{\text{4 volumes}}{4N_2(g)} + \text{heat}$$

Producer gas is therefore one-third carbon monoxide and two-thirds nitrogen by volume, i.e. only one-third of the gas can burn. It also contains a little carbon dioxide.

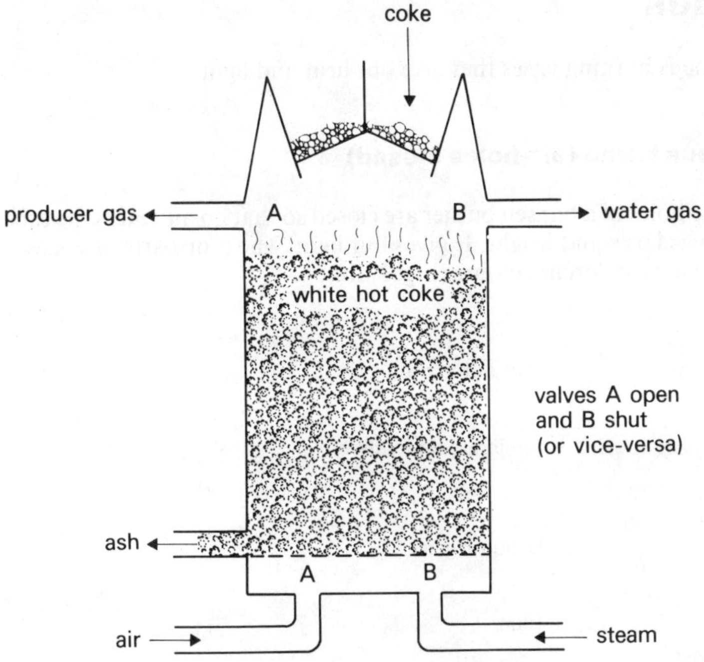

Fig. 17.9 Manufacture of producer gas or water gas

Water gas

Steam is blown through white hot coke:

$$H_2O(g) + C(s) \rightarrow \underset{1\ \text{volume}}{H_2(g)} + \underset{1\ \text{volume}}{CO(g)} - \text{heat}$$

Water gas consists of equal volumes of hydrogen and carbon monoxide, i.e. all the gas can burn. The reaction is *endothermic*, and the coke quickly cools to a temperature too low for reaction. Usually producer gas and water gas are made alternately; the coke becomes hot in the air stream and the steam cools it again.

Uses of these gases

Producer gas is used to heat the retorts during the manufacture of zinc, to heat lime-kilns, steel furnaces and glass furnaces. It is a source of nitrogen in the Haber process for the manufacture of ammonia. Water gas is used to manufacture hydrogen, p. 63.

Flames

A flame is burning gases that give out heat and light.

Luminous flame (air-holes closed)

When the holes of a bunsen burner are closed so that no air enters the tube, the flame is large and bright. It gives out light. The four parts or zones of the flame have different colours (Fig. 17.10):

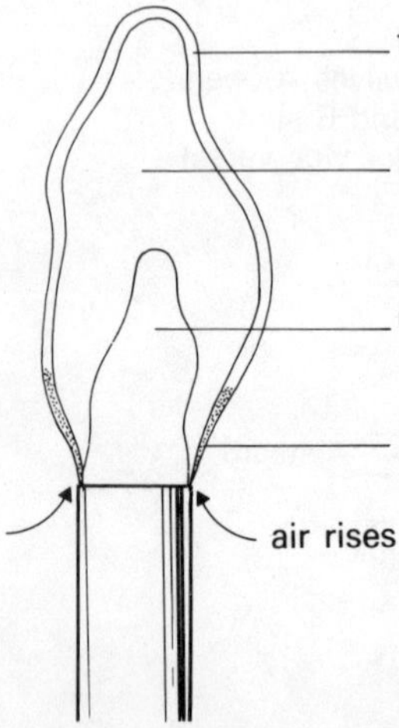

Fig. 17.10 Luminous flame

1 A dark inner zone of cool, unburnt gas.
2 A luminous yellow zone. The gas burns in this zone, but not completely as there is not enough air. Tiny particles of solid carbon form; they become white-hot and give out light. The flame blackens cold glass or porcelain.

$$2H_2 + O_2 \rightarrow 2H_2O;\ 2CH_4 + 3O_2 \rightarrow 4H_2O + 2CO$$
$$CH_4 + O_2 \rightarrow 2H_2O + C \text{ (soot)}$$

3 A thin outer zone, in which the *gas burns completely* as there is plenty of air. No carbon is present and therefore this zone does not give out light. It is difficult to see this zone.

$$CH_4 + 2O_2 \rightarrow CO_2 + 2H_2O;\quad 2CO + O_2 \rightarrow 2CO_2$$

4 A blue zone at the bottom of the flame. This part receives plenty of air because of rising convection currents. Burning is more complete than in the yellow zone.

Non-luminous flame (air-holes open)

When the holes are open, air enters the tube and mixes with the gas, which therefore burns quickly and completely. The flame becomes smaller and hotter. It gives out only a little light because it contains no white-hot carbon. The flames of gas-cookers and gas-fires are examples in everyday life. There are three zones (Fig. 17.11):

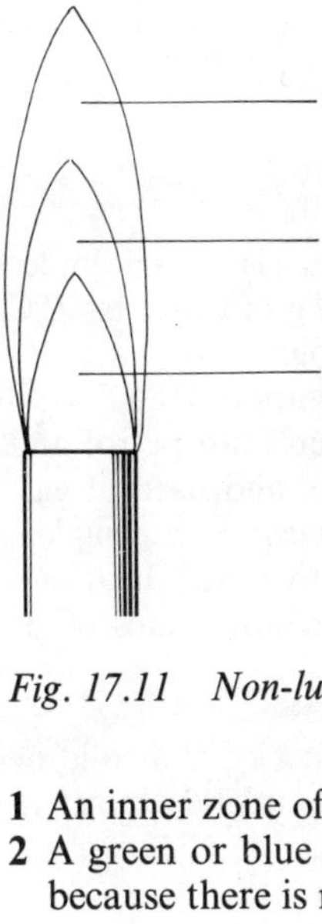

Fig. 17.11 Non-luminous flame

1 An inner zone of cool, unburnt gas.
2 A green or blue middle zone. Some gas burns in this zone, but not all because there is not enough air. No carbon is formed:

$$CH_4 + 2O_2 \rightarrow CO_2 + 2H_2O; \quad 2CH_4 + 3O_2 \rightarrow 2CO + 4H_2O$$

3 A pale blue or purple outer zone. In this zone *the burning is complete*, as before.

The candle flame

Candle wax is a mixture of hydrocarbons, which are compounds of hydrogen and carbon. In a candle flame, the wax melts, rises up the wick, and turns to vapour, which burns in air. The flame has the same four zones as a luminous bunsen flame (Fig. 17.12):

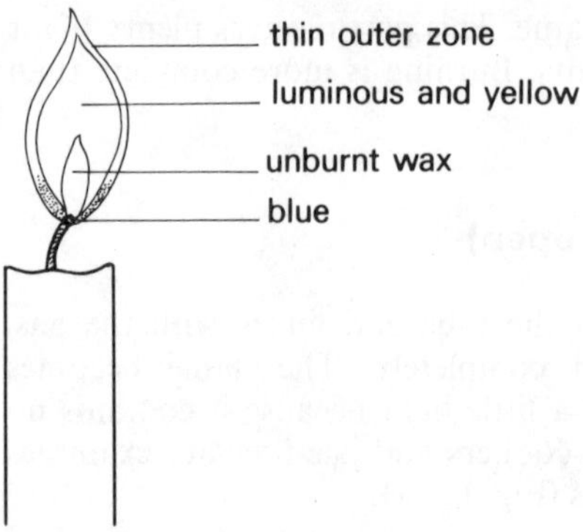

Fig. 17.12 The candle flame

Energy content of fuels

The heat change in a reaction is measured in joules (J) or kilojoules (kJ or 1000 J). The quantity of heat required to warm 1 g of water by 1 °C is about 4.2 joules, and that required to warm 1 kilogram of water by 1 °C is about 4200 joules or 4.2 kilojoules. The exact figure is 4185.5.

Solid fuels are coal, wood, coke, peat, etc.; liquid fuels are petrol and oil; gaseous fuels are coal gas, water gas, producer gas and natural gas. Under perfect conditions and with plentiful air, *combustion is complete* and they burn to form carbon dioxide and water together with heat and light. Normally, *combustion is incomplete* and some carbon comes off as soot or burns to carbon monoxide.

The energy content of a fuel is the heat evolved when 1 kg of a solid or liquid fuel (or 1 cubic metre of a gaseous fuel) is completely burnt in oxygen.

Energy content of foods

One purpose of food is to supply us with energy. The food or the products of the digestion of food are oxidized slowly and completely by oxygen in the blood to carbon dioxide and water, and energy is set free either as heat or muscular movement. A food produces the same quantity of energy whether it burns rapidly in oxygen or burns slowly in the body.

The energy in kilojoules we need in 24 hours depends on our body size, the climate, and our work or play. Some approximate figures are: person lying down, 7500 kJ; person doing clerical work 10 500 kJ; person doing manual work 15 000 kJ. Water, salts and vitamins supply no energy; the energy foods are carbohydrates (starches and sugars), fats and proteins. One way of determining the value of a food is to find its energy content. The energy in kilojoules per gram (kJ/g or $kJ\,g^{-1}$) produced is: carbohydrate, 17; fat, 37; protein, 17.

Silicon

The electron structure of a carbon atom is 2,4 and of silicon is 2,8,4. Carbon and silicon are therefore in group 4 of the Periodic Table, carbon in period 2 and silicon below it in period 3.

Almost one-quarter of the earth's crust is silicon, which is the second most abundant element in it. Sand, quartz and flint are impure silicon(IV) oxide, SiO_2, and rocks and clays contain silicates.

Silicon and carbon are typical non-metals. They do not form positive ions, their compounds are covalent, and their oxides are acidic. Silicon is a hard, brittle element with a high melting point (1410 °C). Like carbon, silicon is chemically unreactive but it does react with aqueous sodium hydroxide and with halogens, unlike carbon.

Silicon(IV) oxide, SiO_2. is not a dioxide because its crystals consist of giant molecules in three dimensions in which each silicon atom is bonded tetrahedrally to four oxygen atoms as shown in Fig. 17.13.

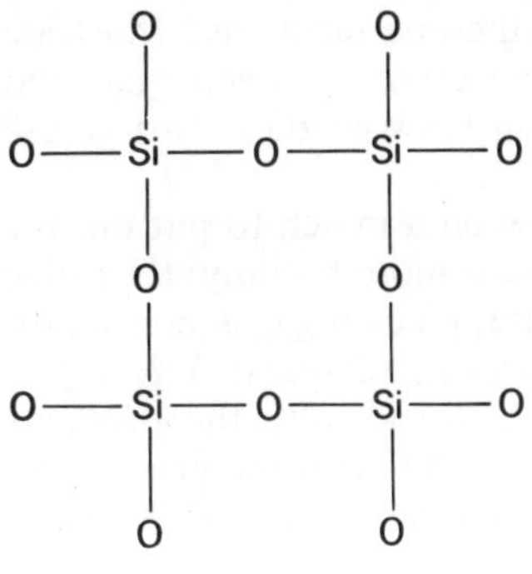

Fig. 17.13 Tetrahedral structure of silicon(IV) oxide, SiO_2

Its melting point is over 1600 °C. It softens only at about 1500 °C and replaces glass in apparatus that resists both heat and chemical reagents. Silicic acid, H_2SiO_3, is a weak acid that exists only in solution, like carbonic acid.

The silanes SiH_4, Si_2H_6, etc. correspond to the alkanes CH_4, C_2H_6, etc., p. 297. However, there are only about ten silanes but hundreds of alkanes; alkanes are very stable compounds but silanes are much less stable. Silicon does not form compounds similar to alkenes, e.g. Si_2H_4 does not exist.

Silicon tetrachloride, $SiCl_4$, is a colourless liquid like carbon tetrachloride. However, it is hydrolysed by water, unlike the carbon compound:

$$SiCl_4(l) + 2H_2O(l) \rightarrow 4HCl(g) + SiO_2(s)$$

Questions

1 Describe the manufacture of coal gas. Name three important gases present in it and give equations representing reactions taking place when they burn in bunsen flames. Mention three principal by-products during coal gas manufacture, and explain how they are obtained. (O.)

2 Describe carefully how you would prepare and collect carbon monoxide free from carbon dioxide. Give and explain three ways in which this gas differs from carbon dioxide. State one use for each of these gases. Where may each be found in dangerous proportions? (C.)

3 Describe with a diagram how you would demonstrate the reducing action of (*a*) carbon, (*b*) carbon monoxide on copper(II) oxide? Explain briefly how water gas and producer gas are obtained. (N.)

4 Name the chief constituents of coal gas, water gas and producer gas. Indicate the reactions by which water gas and producer gas are made, stating the conditions necessary for the reactions to take place. How is hydrogen manufactured from water gas? (L.)

5 What is meant by endothermic and exothermic reactions? Illustrate your answer by reference to the manufacture of water gas and producer gas. How would you distinguish between these two gases? (O.)

6 Explain each of the following: (*a*) we blow on a match to put out the flame, but we blow on a fire to make it burn more brightly; (*b*) a blue flame is often seen at the top of a coke fire; (*c*) coal gas is poisonous. What is meant by the energy content of sugar as a food? (C.)

7 Describe, with diagrams, how you would (*a*) identify the products formed when a candle burns, and (*b*) demonstrate that the products of the combustion of a candle weigh more than the loss in weight of the candle. To what do you attribute the gain in weight? (L.)

18
Nitrogen and Ammonia

To prepare ammonia

Obtaining ammonia readily. Concentrated aqueous ammonia is so readily available that usually it is unnecessary to prepare ammonia by chemical reaction. To obtain the gas, add solid sodium hydroxide to a filter flask fitted with a rubber stopper and tap funnel. Drop concentrated aqueous ammonia into the flask. The solid alkali displaces ammonia gas from the solution because its hydroxide ions move the following equilibrium to the right:

$$NH_4^+(aq) + OH^-(aq) \rightleftharpoons NH_3(g) + H_2O(l)$$

Chemical method. Ammonia is formed when calcium oxide or hydroxide (or any alkali) reacts with an ammonium salt, usually the chloride or sulphate. The equation is as above. Ammonia is very soluble in water but half as dense as air, so collect by upward delivery. Ammonia cannot be dried with concentrated sulphuric acid, which reacts to form ammonium sulphate or with calcium chloride, which forms the compound $CaCl_2 \cdot 8NH_3$. Dry the ammonia with lumps of calcium oxide, Fig. 18.1.

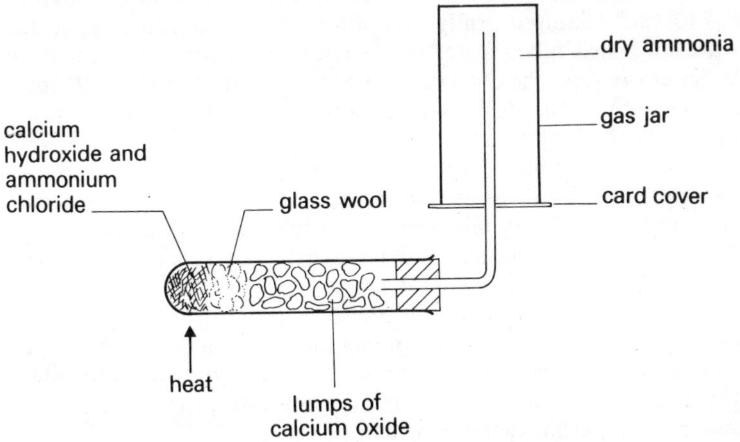

Fig. 18.1 Preparation of dry ammonia

Properties of ammonia

Ammonia is a colourless poisonous gas, with a characteristic choking smell. It liquefies at −33 °C. It extinguishes a burning splint and is less dense than air. It does not burn in air; it burns in oxygen with a greenish-yellow flame:

$$4NH_3(g) + 3O_2(g) \rightarrow 2N_2(g) + 6H_2O(g)$$

Ammonia is the most soluble of all gases (1 cm^3 of water dissolves about 800 cm^3 of ammonia at room temperature). The solution is about 15 M and 1 dm^3 contains about 250 g of ammonia. It contains ammonium and hydroxide ions, which turn red litmus blue. Ammonia is the only common alkaline gas and it is a *basic anhydride*. The density of the solution is 0.880 g/cm^3 (eight-eighty ammonia). In warm climates it is better to use a less concentrated aqueous ammonia, of density 0.910 g/cm^3 and about 13 M. Always cool large bottles of concentrated aqueous ammonia in ice or a refrigerator before opening the screw stopper. Turn the stopper slowly so that the high pressure of the ammonia gas is reduced gradually. Opening a warm bottle quickly may case ammonia gas to come off almost explosively and splash drops of the dangerous solution on the face and eyes.

Fountain experiment for solubility

Fill a large, dry, round-bottomed flask with dry ammonia (a thin-walled, flat-bottomed flask would probably collapse inwards if used). Place the mouth of the flask under water, coloured with red litmus, in a trough or gas-jar, Fig. 18.2. Clamp it firmly in position. Open the spring clip at the end of the long glass tube. Water slowly rises up the tube until one drop is at the jet at the top. The drop dissolves so much ammonia that there is a partial vacuum in the flask. Air pressure forces water rapidly up the tube and enters the flask as a fountain. The litmus turns blue.
Simple method. The fountain experiment takes a fairly long time and uses complex apparatus. To demonstrate the great solubility in a simple way, fill a dry test-tube with dry ammonia, close the tube with a cork, invert the tube in a beaker of water, and remove the cork. The water rises rapidly and fills or almost fills the tube.
Hydrogen chloride. Either hold the moist stopper of a bottle of concentrated hydrochloric acid in ammonia or invert a jar of hydrogen chloride over a jar of ammonia and press the vaselined surfaces together. Note the dense white fumes that form. It is not easy to separate the jars because there is a partial vacuum inside.

$$NH_3(g) + HCl(g) \rightarrow NH_4Cl(s), \text{ white}$$

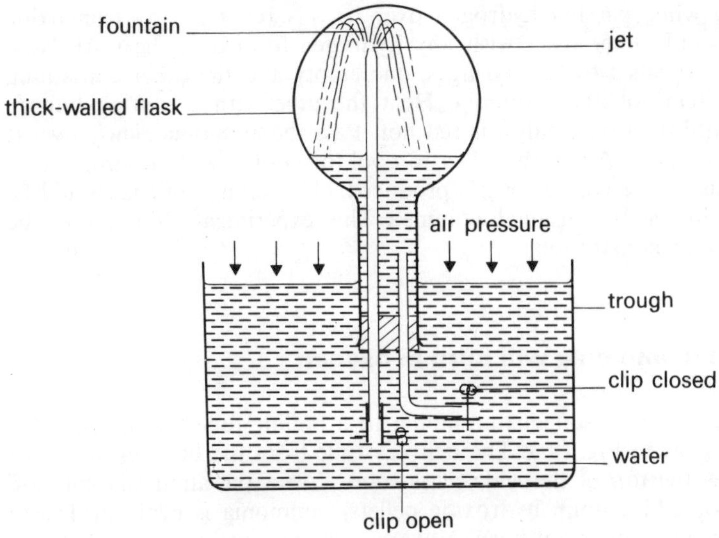

Fig. 18.2 Fountain experiment for solubility

Nitric acid and *sulphuric acid* form white, solid ammonium salts:

$$2NH_3(g) + H_2SO_4(aq) \rightarrow (NH_4)_2SO_4(s)$$

Test for ammonia. The gas has a characteristic choking smell. It turns wet litmus blue, and forms white fumes with hydrochloric acid or hydrogen chloride.

Reducing agents. Ammonia reduces oxygen (p. 218) and oxides of copper and lead (p. 220) and is itself oxidized to nitrogen. Ammonia burns spontaneously in chlorine, p. 263, forming white fumes of ammonium chloride.

Decomposition of ammonia. Heat or sparks decompose the gas:

$$2NH_3(g) \rightarrow N_2(g) + 3H_2(g)$$

Liquid ammonia is a source of hydrogen. It is transported more easily than cylinders of hydrogen and is readily decomposed into nitrogen and hydrogen by heated catalysts.

To decompose ammonia

The apparatus is silica tubing connected by rubber tubing to two syringes, p. 30. First place iron wool in the silica tube and keep it in position by two loosely packed plugs of glass wool. Heat the tube strongly while passing hydrogen over it; this removes any iron oxide (which would later react with any hydrogen formed in the test). Now connect the silica to two syringes, one empty and the other containing about 40 cm^3 of dry ammonia. Heat the tube with a roaring bunsen flame until the iron catalyst is red hot. Pass the ammonia *slowly* over it and back again. Allow the silica to cool (or cool it with a damp cloth) and measure the volume of gas produced. (The volume of gas should be almost double the original volume.) This experiment should only be done as a demonstration.

To find if ammonia will burn in oxygen

Add concentrated aqueous ammonia to a boiling-tube and arrange the apparatus as in Fig. 18.3. The delivery tube from the boiling-tube must be below the top of the wide glass tube. Warm the ammonia solution gently (or add sodium hydroxide pellets); ammonia is evolved. Try to light the gas; it does not burn. Now pass oxygen into the wide tube and again try to light the gas. The ammonia burns with a greenish-yellow flame:

$$4NH_3(g) + 3O_2(g) \rightarrow 2N_2(g) + 6H_2O(g)$$

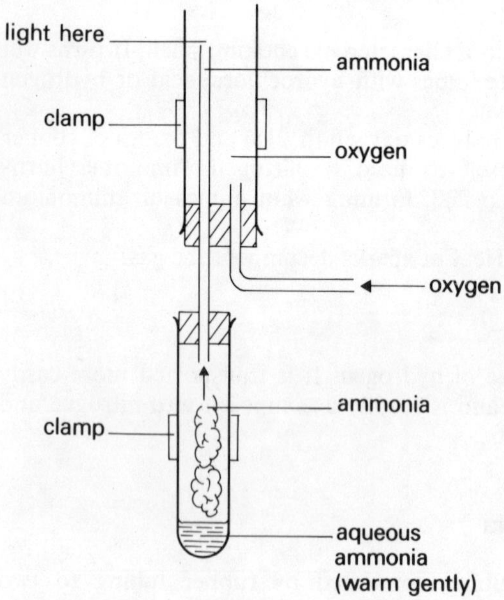

Fig. 18.3 Burning ammonia in oxygen

To show the catalytic oxidation of ammonia

Add concentrated aqueous ammonia to a beaker on white paper, so that any coloured fumes that form can easily be seen. Use platinum wire or copper wire as a catalyst in the following way. Wrap platinum wire (copper wire of at least 0.054 mm thickness can replace platinum) in a spiral around a rod. Leave three turns on the rod and bend the rest so that the spiral can hang just above the ammonia solution (Fig. 18.4). Heat the spiral in a

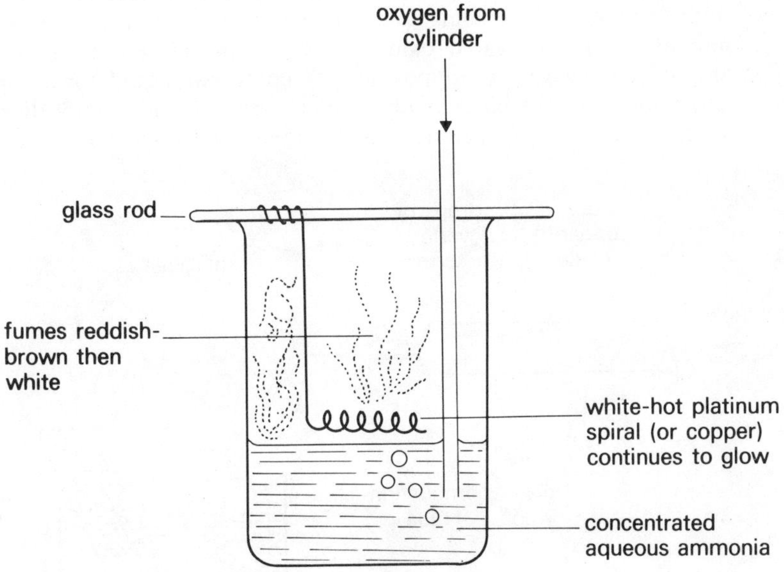

Fig. 18.4 Catalytic oxidation of ammonia

bunsen flame until it is white-hot. Pass oxygen from a cylinder (or prepared from hydrogen peroxide) or pass air through the ammonia. Place the hot platinum or copper catalyst in the beaker. Reddish-brown fumes of nitrogen dioxide should form. If not, reduce the proportion of ammonia by raising the tube delivering the oxygen so that it is not so far in the aqueous ammonia or is just above it. The metal catalyst stays red hot because the reaction is exothermic. (Sometimes slight but safe 'explosions' occur if the oxygen passes in very fast; they are caused by the oxygen and ammonia burning 'explosively'.)

$$4NH_3(g) + 5O_2(g) \rightarrow 4NO(g) + 6H_2O;$$

$$2NO(g) + O_2(g) \rightleftharpoons 2NO_2(g), \text{ reddish-brown}$$

Later the gases turn white because ammonium nitrate forms.

$$4NO_2(g) + O_2(g) + 2H_2O \rightarrow 4HNO_3(g)$$

$$NH_3(g) + HNO_3(g) \rightarrow NH_4NO_3(s), \text{ white}$$

This reaction is used in the manufacture of nitric acid.

To study the action of ammonia on copper(II) oxide

Arrange the apparatus as in Fig. 18.5 but without the test-tube. The glass wool stops copper(II) oxide being spread over the combustion tube. Pass dry ammonia over the heated oxide. When all the air is out of the apparatus, place the gas-jar in position. A colourless liquid forms in the combustion tube, the black oxide turns red-brown, and a colourless gas collects in the jar. Sometimes the liquid is pale blue due to the

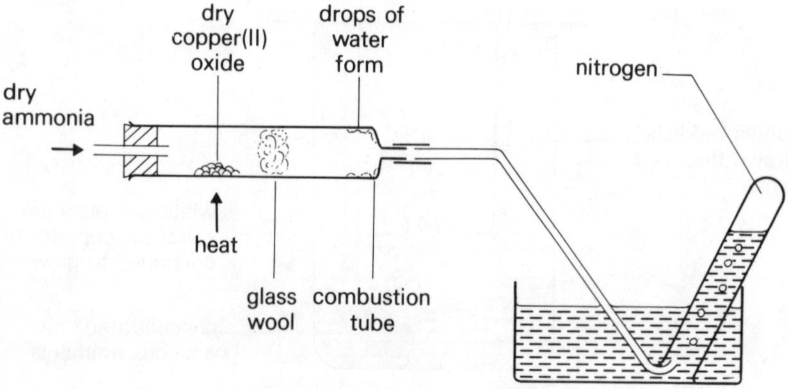

Fig. 18.5 Action of ammonia on copper(II) oxide or lead(II) oxide

formation of a little copper compound in it. Test the liquid with anhydrous copper(II) sulphate, which turns blue. Test the gas with a burning splint, with litmus, and with calcium hydroxide solution. There is no reaction; the gas is nitrogen. The ammonia reduces the copper(II) oxide to copper and is itself oxidized to nitrogen. Lead(II) oxide can be used instead of copper(II) oxide.

$$2NH_3(g) + 3CuO(s) \rightarrow N_2(g) + 3Cu(s) + 3H_2O$$

$$2NH_3(g) + 3PbO(s) \rightarrow N_2(g) + 3Pb(s) + 3H_2O$$

This experiment proves that *ammonia contains nitrogen and hydrogen and is nitrogen hydride* (the hydrogen in the water formed must come from ammonia because dry copper(II) oxide contains no hydrogen).

Aqueous ammonia and metallic ions

Aqueous ammonia reacts like sodium hydroxide when added to solutions of metallic salts—it forms precipitates of the metallic hydroxides, e.g.

$$Cu^{2+}(aq) + 2OH^-(aq) \rightarrow Cu(OH)_2(s)\text{, blue}$$

$$Fe^{3+}(aq) + 3OH^-(aq) \rightarrow Fe(OH)_3(s)\text{, red-brown}$$

$$Fe^{2+}(aq) + 2OH^-(aq) \rightarrow Fe(OH)_2(s)\text{, green}$$

There are differences between the actions of the two alkalis:

1 Copper(II) hydroxide does not dissolve in sodium hydroxide, but it dissolves in excess aqueous ammonia, forming a deep blue solution which contains the ion $Cu(NH_3)_4^{2+}$:

$$Cu(OH)_2(s) + 4NH_3(aq) \rightarrow Cu(NH_3)_4^{2+}(aq) + 2OH^-(aq)$$
Tetraamminecopper(II) ion

2 The amphoteric aluminium(III) and lead(II) hydroxides dissolve in sodium hydroxide but not in aqueous ammonia.

3 Zinc hydroxide dissolves both in sodium hydroxide and in aqueous ammonia, but the reactions are different:

$$Zn(OH)_2(s) + 2OH^-(aq) \rightarrow Zn(OH)_4^{2-}(aq)\text{, zincate ion}$$

$$Zn(OH)_2(s) + 4NH_3(aq) \rightarrow Zn(NH_3)_4^{2+} + 2OH^-(aq)$$
Tetraamminezinc ion

Refer to pp. 340–1.

To synthesise ammonia

Use the apparatus described on p. 30, with iron wool in silica tubing and two syringes. Place a three-way stopcock between the silica tube and one of the syringes. Carefully pass 20 cm^3 of nitrogen and 60 cm^3 of hydrogen (from cylinders) into this syringe via the stopcock. Now turn the stopcock to connect the syringe to the silica tube and other syringe. Heat the silica and iron wool strongly and pass the mixture of gases *slowly* through the iron catalyst two or three times. Turn off the flame, open the stopcock, and push some of the product on to damp red litmus paper. (It should turn blue, showing that some ammonia has formed.)

Manufacture of ammonia

Haber process. Nitrogen (from air, p. 41) and hydrogen (p. 63), are mixed in the ratio of 1:3 by volume. The mixture is passed over a catalyst of iron at a temperature of about 500 °C and a pressure of 200–1000

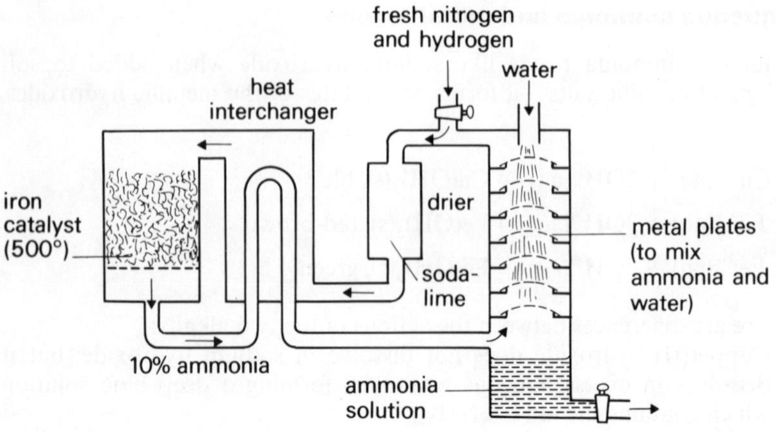

Fig. 18.6 Manufacture of ammonia by Haber process

atmospheres. About 10 per cent of the gases combine. The ammonia is either dissolved in water or liquefied. The unchanged gases are again passed over the catalyst until they react. The reaction between nitrogen and hydrogen is reversible and exothermic:

$$\begin{array}{lll} N_2(g) + & 3H_2(g) \rightleftharpoons & 2NH_3(g) + \text{heat} \\ 1\text{ vol.} & 3\text{ vol.} & 2\text{ vol.} \end{array}$$

The approximate percentages of ammonia at equilibrium and the time to reach equilibrium at various temperatures and pressures are:

Temp. (°C)	Pressure in atmospheres 10	200	1000	Time to reach equilibrium
250	30	75	96 per cent NH_3	hours
500	1	18	60 per cent NH_3	minutes
1000	0	0.1	1 per cent NH_3	seconds

(Refer to pp. 142–147 for the general effects of pressure, temperature and catalysts on reactions and for the collision theory of reactions.)

Effect of pressure. The equations show that 4 molecules combine to form 2 molecules. Therefore, by Avogadro's Principle, 4 volumes of reactants form 2 volumes of ammonia. High pressures cause a better *yield* of ammonia because they favour the formation of the smaller product. They also increase the *speed* of reaction because the reacting molecules are closer and collide more often.

Effect of temperature. At low temperatures the yield at equilibrium of ammonia is high, but the reaction is slow. At high temperatures the yield of ammonia is low but the reaction is fast. In practice the best temperature to use is 500 °C. The yield is good but the reaction is still too slow. A catalyst is therefore necessary to speed the reaction.
Effect of catalysts. A catalyst speeds the reaction but does not affect the equilibrium yield of ammonia. The catalyst should be finely divided because reaction occurs only at the surface.

Uses of ammonia

Ammonia is used to manufacture nitric acid which is converted into *explosives* and *fertilizers* (e.g. ammonium nitrate). Ammonium sulphate, a common fertilizer, is made from ammonia. In laundries and homes, ammonia solution is used to *soften water* and for removing grease stains from clothes. Ammonia from *smelling salts* (ammonium carbonate) acts on the heart and prevents fainting and dizziness. Liquid ammonia is a convenient source of *hydrogen* (p. 217).

Ammonium salts

All common ammonium salts are white solids, soluble in water. They are ionic and contain the ammonium ion, NH_4^+. The chloride, nitrate and sulphate can be prepared by neutralizing the appropriate acid with aqueous ammonia, using methyl orange as indicator (p. 127).
Test for ammonium salts. Heat with an alkali. All ammonium salts form ammonia, recognized by its smell and reaction with litmus.

To study the action of heat on ammonium chloride

1 Heat solid ammonium chloride in a test-tube, Fig. 18.7. Slope the tube so that only the bottom becomes hot. The solid *sublimes*, i.e. it changes directly into gas which on cooling changes back to the solid without condensing to a liquid. A white *sublimate* forms on the cool part of the tube. The cause of this sublimation is that ammonium chloride dissociates on heating into ammonia and hydrogen chloride, which recombine on cooling:

$$NH_4Cl(s) \rightleftharpoons NH_3(g) + HCl(g)$$

2 Place solid ammonium chloride at the bottom of a test-tube. Clamp the tube horizontally. Place damp neutral litmus paper near the chloride and glass wool or asbestos wool half-way down (Fig. 18.7).

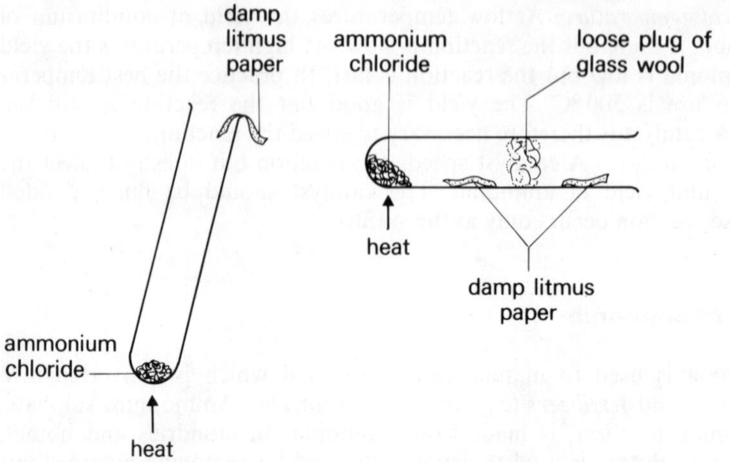

Fig. 18.7 Action of heat on ammonium chloride

Place damp litmus paper near the mouth of the tube. Heat the ammonium chloride and the wool. The litmus near the mouth turns blue and the other litmus turns red because the denser hydrogen chloride diffuses more slowly than the ammonia.

Iodine, carbon dioxide, sulphur, iron(III) chloride and naphthalene also sublime. Sublimation of ammonium chloride is explained by thermal dissociation, but this is not the cause of other sublimations.

Thermal dissociation is the decomposition of a compound by heat into simpler substances which recombine on cooling to form the original compound.

Examples are:

$$N_2O_4 \rightleftharpoons 2NO_2 \rightleftharpoons 2NO + O_2; \quad CaCO_3 \rightleftharpoons CaO + CO_2$$

Thermal decomposition is the decomposition of a compound by heat into simpler substances which do not recombine on cooling.

Ammonium sulphate decomposes at its melting point (235 °C) forming ammonia and either the hydrogensulphate, a colourless liquid which solidifies on cooling, or sulphuric acid.

$$(NH_4)_2SO_4(l) \rightarrow NH_3(g) + NH_4HSO_4(l)$$

$$NH_4HSO_4(l) \rightarrow NH_3(g) + H_2SO_4(l)$$

It is manufactured by saturating ammonia solution with carbon dioxide, and then adding powdered calcium sulphate:

$$(NH_4)_2CO_3(aq) + CaSO_4(s) \rightarrow (NH_4)_2SO_4(aq) + CaCO_3(s)$$

The insoluble calcium carbonate is filtered off, and the filtrate is crystallized.

To separate sodium chloride and ammonium chloride by sublimation

Place the mixture of ammonium chloride and sodium chloride in a Pyrex beaker and put it on a tripod. Half-fill a flask with cold water and place it on the beaker. Heat the beaker, Fig. 18.8. Ammonium chloride forms a white sublimate on the bottom of the flask. Heat strongly to drive off the last traces of ammonium chloride. The residue is sodium chloride.

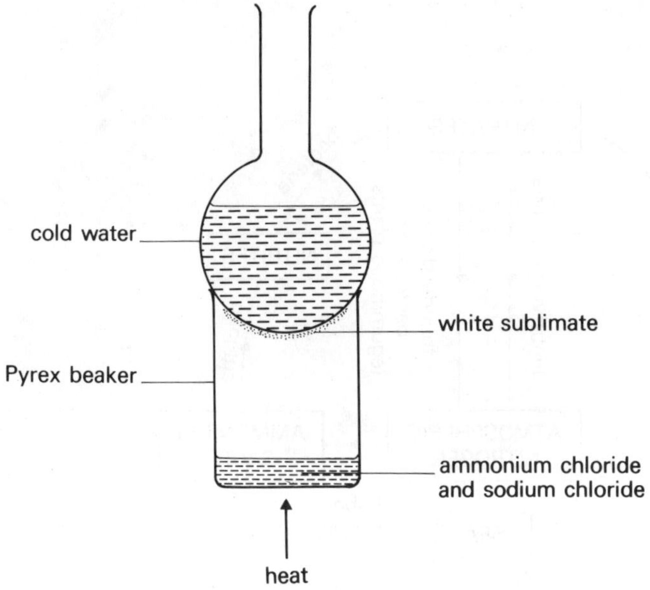

Fig. 18.8 Separating sodium and ammonium chlorides

The nitrogen cycle

The bodies of animals consist of proteins, which contain nitrogen. Animals cannot make proteins: they eat those made by plants. Plants obtain nitrogen by absorbing through their roots soluble nitrates from the soil. *Denitrifying bacteria* in soil decompose nitrates and set free nitrogen which passes into the atmosphere; they remove nitrogen compounds from soil.

Several natural processes add nitrates to soil:

Thunderstorms. Lightning causes nitrogen and oxygen to form nitrogen oxide, which then forms the dioxide. This is washed down as nitric acid by rain and forms nitrates in soil:

$$N_2(g) + O_2(g) \rightleftharpoons 2NO(g); \quad 2NO(g) + O_2(g) \rightleftharpoons 2NO_2(g)$$

$$4NO_2(g) + O_2(g) + 2H_2O(l) \rightarrow 4HNO_3(aq)$$

Decay. Animal excreta and the dead bodies of animals and plants contain nitrogen compounds. Bacteria change these to ammonia, then nitrites, and finally to nitrates. Gardeners and farmers add animal manure to soil; they also let waste plant material decay and form compost, a good manure. Much human excreta enters the sea as sewage and its nitrogen is wasted; part of the nitrogen is used when fish and other sea animals are eaten as food.

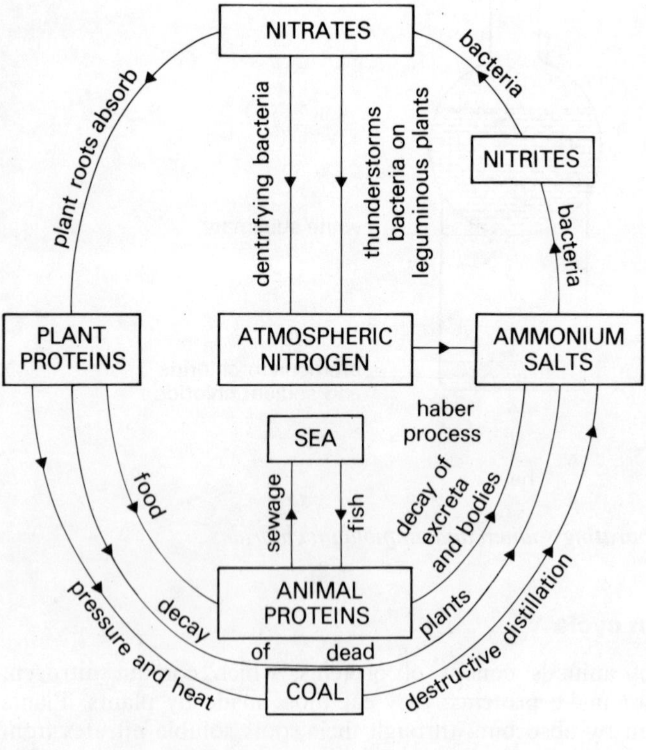

Fig. 18.9 Nitrogen cycle

Bacteria. Leguminous plants (peas, beans, clover) have on their roots bacteria which convert atmospheric nitrogen into compounds. If these plants are grown and ploughed into soil, it becomes richer in nitrogen compounds.

These processes do not maintain sufficient nitrogen in soil. Artificial fertilizers must be added. Sodium nitrate (Chile saltpetre) and ammonium sulphate, obtained during coal gas manufacture, were once the main fertilizers. Nowadays fertilizers are made from atmospheric nitrogen, and the process is *fixation of nitrogen.* Ammonia is made by the Haber process and converted either to ammonium sulphate or to nitric acid and then to nitrates. The circulation of nitrogen in nature is called *the nitrogen cycle.*

Plants are removed from cultivated soil and the elements in them are not returned to the soil. Cultivated soil usually needs nitrogen, phosphorus and potassium. Addition of fertilizers, e.g. *ammonium sulphate, potassium nitrate and superphosphates* (p. 250), supplies them.

To test some foodstuffs for nitrogen

Place about half a spatula measure of a protein foodstuff (e.g. meat, fish, cheese) in a test-tube and mix it with about twice its volume of sodalime. Heat the mixture and test any gases evolved with moist red litmus. Repeat the test with a piece of nylon if you wish.

(The gases evolved are a mixture and have an unpleasant smell. Do the above experiment either in a fume cupboard of near an open window.)

The test shows that an alkaline gas is evolved. Actually the gas is ammonia (although the above test by itself does not prove that this is so). Since sodalime contains no nitrogen, the test indicates that protein, and nylon, contain nitrogen.

Questions

1 Describe in detail the laboratory preparation and collection of dry ammonia. How is ammonia converted into (*a*) nitric acid, (*b*) ammonium sulphate? What is the reaction of ammonia with (i) chlorine, (ii) iron(III) chloride solution? (L.)

2 Describe briefly how ammonia is obtained (*a*) from ammonium salts in the laboratory, (*b*) from its elements industrially. What reactions occur between a solution of ammonia and (*a*) copper(II) sulphate solution, (*b*) hydrochloric acid, (*c*) iron(II) sulphate solution? (C.)

3 Draw and label the apparatus you would use to prepare and collect ammonia, starting from ammonium nitrate. What is the action of heat on (*a*) ammonia, (*b*) zinc nitrate crystals? (N.)

4 What tests would you make to distinguish between gas jars containing (*a*) nitrogen, (*b*) oxygen, (*c*) carbon dioxide? (N.)

5 Describe the reaction that takes place between ammonia gas and (*a*) copper(II) oxide, (*b*) chlorine gas, (*c*) iron(III) chloride solution. How would you show that ammonia is a very soluble alkaline gas? (C.)

6 Write the equation for the formation of ammonia by the Haber process. What is the effect of (*a*) temperature, (*b*) a catalyst, (*c*) pressure on (i) the rate of this reaction, (ii) the equilibrium yield of ammonia? (O.)

7 Sparks are passed through a mixture of 1 volume of nitrogen and 3 volumes of hydrogen in a tube inverted in a trough of dilute acid. After some time, none of the gas remains. Explain this observation. When an iron wire spiral is heated in a given volume of nitrogen oxide, the remaining nitrogen occupies half the volume of the original oxide (pressure and temperature remaining constant). What conclusion can you draw from this experiment about the formula of the oxide? (O.)

19
Nitric Acid. Oxides of Nitrogen

Nitric acid is prepared by the action of concentrated sulphuric acid on any nitrate, usually potassium nitrate (*saltpetre*) or sodium nitrate (*Chile saltpetre*):

$$H_2SO_4(conc.) + KNO_3(s) \rightleftharpoons HNO_3(g) + KHSO_4(l)$$
$$H^+(aq) + NO_3^-(s) \rightleftharpoons HNO_3(g\ then\ l)$$

This reaction is reversible. The nitric acid is the most volatile compound in the mixture and heating converts it to a gas. As the gas escapes, the reaction moves to the right. Potassium nitrate is better to use in this reaction than sodium nitrate, which is hygroscopic. The salt formed is the *acid salt, hydrogensulphate*. The normal salts (potassium and sodium sulphates) are formed only at high temperatures, which cannot be reached in glass apparatus.

To prepare nitric acid

Slide powdered potassium nitrate (or sodium nitrate) into a retort. Arrange as in Fig. 19.1. Use a small funnel to pour concentrated sulphuric acid on the nitrate. No reaction occurs in the cold. Place a glass

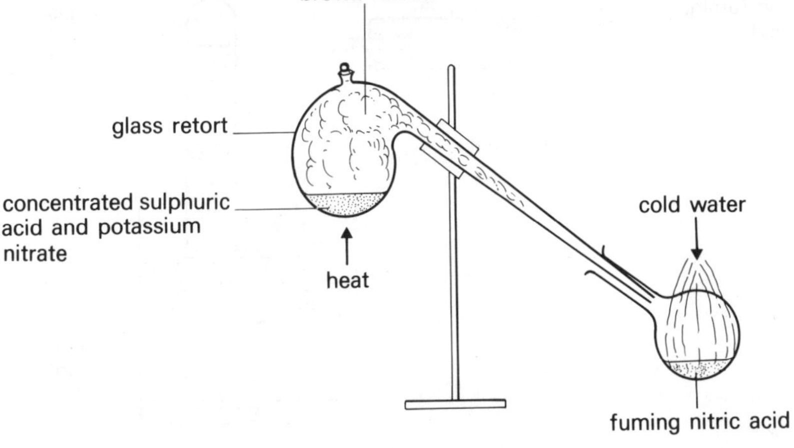

Fig. 19.1 Preparation of nitric acid

stopper in the retort. Note that there is no cork or rubber in the apparatus because nitric acid vapour readily attacks them. Run cold water on the flask; use a cloth to spread the water over the whole flask. Heat the retort on a sand bath. The solid dissolves and effervescence occurs. Reddish-brown fumes are evolved. The distillate (fuming nitric acid) is yellow because it contains dissolved nitrogen dioxide formed by the reaction:

$$4HNO_3(g) \rightarrow 4NO_2(g) + O_2(g) + 2H_2O(g)$$

Continue heating until no more acid distils over.

Properties of nitric acid

Fuming nitric acid is almost pure acid (b.p. 83 °C) but ordinary concentrated acid (b.p. 120 °C) is 68 per cent acid and 32 per cent water. Pure nitric acid is a colourless liquid. The fuming and concentrated acids are yellow because they contain dissolved nitrogen dioxide. This is the reddish-brown gas above the liquid in a bottle of the acid, which decomposes slightly even at room temperatures. The acid is very corrosive, e.g. it rapidly destroys skin, rubber, cork and other organic matter. It reacts as (*a*) an acid, and (*b*) an oxidizing agent.

Acid properties. Dilute nitric acid is a strong monobasic acid and is completely ionized:

$$HNO_3(aq) + H_2O(l) \rightarrow H_3O^+ + NO_3^-(aq)$$

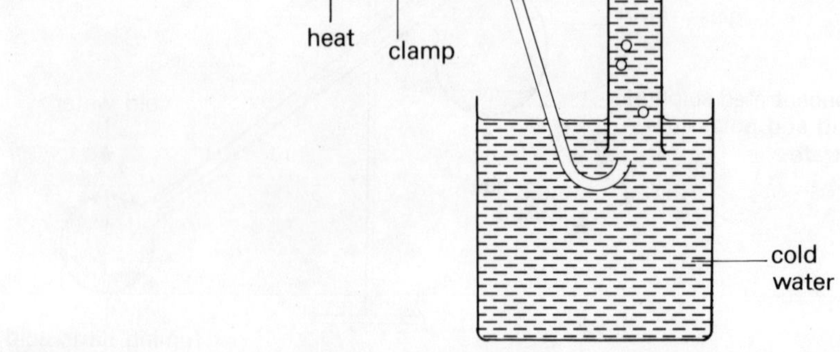

Fig. 19.2 Action of heat on nitric acid

It has a sour taste, turns litmus red, forms carbon dioxide with carbonates and hydrogencarbonates and forms salts with bases. It does not form hydrogen with metals (except magnesium and calcium); most metals reduce it to nitrogen dioxide or oxide.
Heat. Pour fuming nitric acid into a hard-glass test-tube. Add glass wool to soak up all the acid. Fill the rest of the tube with broken pot or porcelain, and then clamp it horizontally (Fig. 19.2). Heat the pot or porcelain. Do not warm the acid directly; it becomes hot enough by conduction. The acid decomposes to form a reddish-brown mixture of nitrogen dioxide and oxygen. The dioxide dissolves in the water, and oxygen collects in the test-tube:

$$4HNO_3(g) \rightarrow 4NO_2(g) + O_2(g) + 2H_2O(g)$$

Oxidizing reactions of nitric acid

Copper. Add copper turnings to concentrated nitric acid. A vigorous reaction occurs. Reddish-brown poisonous nitrogen dioxide is evolved, and green copper(II) nitrate forms. The essential change is that copper loses electrons to the acid and forms copper ions:

$$Cu(s) - 2e + \text{water} \rightarrow Cu^{2+}(aq)$$

$$2HNO_3(68\%) + e \rightarrow NO_2(g) + NO_3^-(aq) + H_2O$$

Concentrated nitric acid mixed with an equal volume of water (i.e. about 34 per cent acid) reacts less vigorously with copper. It forms colourless nitrogen oxide, which turns to reddish-brown nitrogen dioxide in air:

$$4HNO_3(34\%) + 3e \rightarrow NO(g) + 3NO_3^-(aq) + 2H_2O$$

$$2NO(g) + O_2(g) \rightarrow 2NO_2(g)$$

Other metals. Hydrogen is formed when *very dilute* (about 1 per cent) nitric acid reacts with magnesium or calcium:

$$Mg(s) + 2HNO_3(1\%) \rightarrow Mg(NO_3)_2(aq) + H_2(g)$$

All other metals form either nitrogen oxide or dioxide, and never hydrogen. Lead reacts like copper, but the reaction is slow with concentrated nitric acid. Aluminium and iron do not react with the concentrated acid because a coating of oxide forms and stops further action.
Sulphur. Warm sulphur in a basin with concentrated or fuming nitric acid. (A few drops of bromine act as a catalyst.) Reddish-brown nitrogen dioxide is evolved and the sulphur is oxidized to sulphuric acid:

$$S + 6HNO_3(\text{conc.}) \rightarrow H_2SO_4(aq) + 6NO_2(g) + 2H_2O$$

Dilute the product with water and filter or decant. Test the filtrate for a sulphate by adding aqueous barium nitrate. A white precipitate forms:

$$Ba^{2+}(aq) + SO_4^{2-}(aq) \rightarrow BaSO_4(s)$$

Carbon. Add fuming nitric acid to a watch-glass standing on white paper. Hold 4 wooden splints together, light them, and let them burn until their ends are charred to carbon. Put out the flames and push the red-hot carbon into the acid. The carbon burns and is oxidized to carbon dioxide and the nitric acid is reduced to reddish-brown nitrogen dioxide. (If the acid is warmed with charcoal, the same gases are formed; the carbon dioxide can be collected over water, which dissolves the nitrogen dioxide.)

$$C(s) + 4HNO_3(99\%) \rightarrow CO_2(g) + 4NO_2(g) + 2H_2O$$

Sawdust. Add a few drops of fuming nitric acid to hot sawdust in a basin. The sawdust burns and reddish-brown fumes are formed. Sawdust is mainly cellulose, $C_6H_{10}O_5$; it is oxidized to carbon dioxide and steam by the acid, which is reduced to nitrogen dioxide.

Iron(II) sulphate. Mix dilute sulphuric acid and iron(II) sulphate solution. Add concentrated nitric acid to the pale-green mixture. It turns dark-brown. Warm the solution; the dark-brown compound decomposes and the solution becomes yellow or light-brown (see p. 235).

Hydrogen sulphide and sulphur dioxide. See p. 247.

Manufacture of nitric acid

From ammonia. Nitric acid is manufactured by oxidizing ammonia with air in the presence of platinum as a catalyst (Fig. 19.3).

1 Ammonia (from the Haber process) is mixed with excess air and passed over platinum–rhodium gauze at about 700 °C and 9 atmospheres pressure. It is oxidized to nitrogen oxide:

$$4NH_3(g) + 5O_2(g) \rightarrow 4NO(g) + 6H_2O(g) + \text{heat}$$

No external heat is required once the reaction starts. Pressure increases the rate of reaction and the yield of acid, p. 147.

2 The gases are cooled, and nitrogen oxide combines with oxygen to form nitrogen dioxide:

$$2NO(g) + O_2(g) \rightleftharpoons 2NO_2(g)$$

3 The nitrogen dioxide and excess air are passed, still under pressure, up towers filled with broken bricks through which water flows slowly.

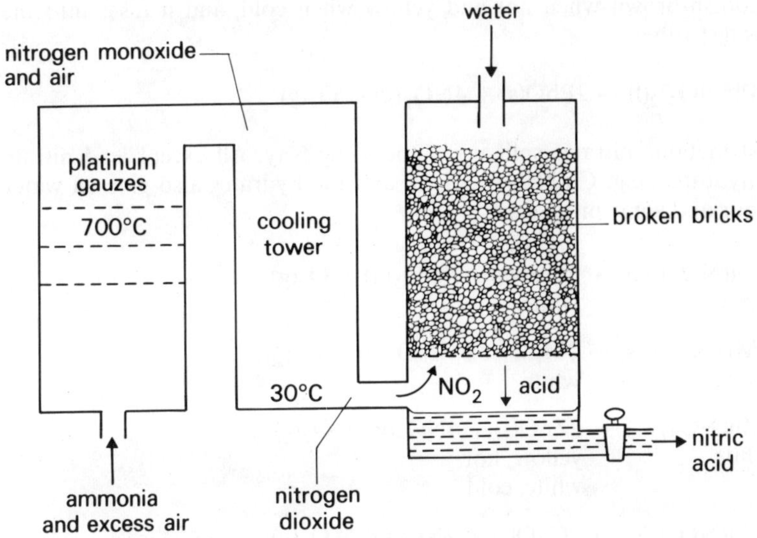

Fig. 19.3 Manufacture of nitric acid (diagrammatic)

They form nitric acid:

$$2NO_2(g) + H_2O \rightleftharpoons HNO_3(aq) + HNO_2(aq) \text{ (nitrous acid)}$$

$$2HNO_2(aq) + O_2(g) \rightarrow 2HNO_3(aq)$$

The rate of these reactions is increased by pressure, and smaller and cheaper towers can be used. The concentration of the acid is about 75 per cent. More concentrated acid is made by mixing the 75 per cent acid with concentrated sulphuric acid. The heat evolved during mixing vaporizes the nitric acid, which condenses to the fuming acid.

Nitrates

Action of heat on nitrates

Sodium and potassium nitrates melt to colourless liquids. They slowly decompose, forming oxygen and a pale-yellow nitrite:

$$2NaNO_3(l) \rightarrow O_2(g) + 2NaNO_2(l)$$

Lead(II) nitrate crackles because gas forms inside its crystals and splits them. It then melts at 470 °C and effervesces, forming a reddish-brown mixture of oxygen and nitrogen dioxide. The solid lead(II) oxide is reddish-brown when hot and yellow when cold, and it fuses into the glass test-tube:

$$2Pb(NO_3)_2(l) \rightarrow 2PbO(s) + 4NO_2(g) + O_2(g)$$

Most metallic nitrates split up in the same way. All except lead nitrate are hydrated, e.g. $Cu(NO_3)_2 \cdot 3H_2O$, and the hydrates also give off water vapour and some nitric acid.

$2Ca(NO_3)_2(s) \rightarrow 2CaO(s) + 4NO_2(g) + O_2(g)$
white — white

$2Mg(NO_3)_2(s) \rightarrow 2MgO(s) + 4NO_2(g) + O_2(g)$
white — white

$2Zn(NO_3)_2(s) \rightarrow 2ZnO(s) + 4NO_2(g) + O_2(g)$
white — yellow, hot; white, cold

$2Cu(NO_3)_2(s) \rightarrow 2CuO(s) + 4NO_2(g) + O_2(g)$
green — black

To carry out the tests for nitrates

1 *Brown ring test for soluble nitrates.* To a solution of a nitrate add an equal volume of fresh iron(II) sulphate solution. Slope the tube. Carefully pour concentrated sulphuric acid down its side. The dense acid sinks to the bottom. A brown ring, $FeSO_4 \cdot NO$, forms where the two layers meet (Fig. 19.4).

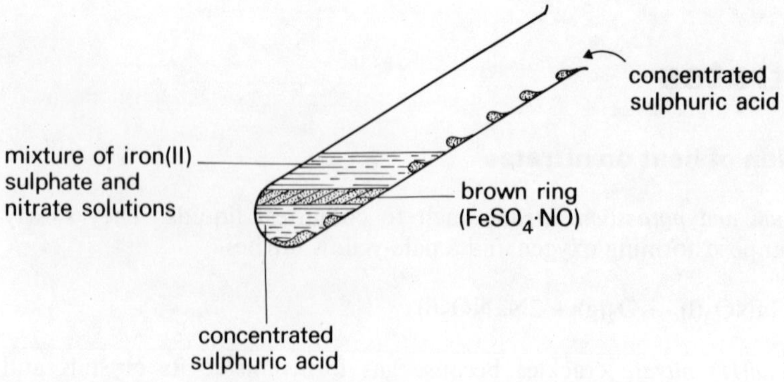

Fig. 19.4 Brown ring test for soluble nitrates

The reactions which occur are:

a Concentrated sulphuric acid and the nitrate form nitric acid:

$$H^+(aq) + NO_3^-(aq) \rightarrow HNO_3(aq)$$

b Some iron(II) sulphate reduces nitric acid to nitrogen oxide.

c The nitrogen oxide combines with iron(II) sulphate:

$$FeSO_4(aq) + NO(g) \rightleftharpoons FeSO_4 \cdot NO(aq)\text{, brown compound}$$

The concentrated sulphuric acid and water become hot if the mixture is shaken; the heat decomposes the brown compound. The solution then becomes pale yellow, due to iron(III) sulphate.

Small scale brown ring test. To one cavity of a porcelain tile, add one drop of solution or about 1 mg of solid to be tested for nitrate. Add two drops of concentrated sulphuric acid (or phosphoric acid). Now add a tiny crystal of iron(II) sulphate to the centre of the mixture; press it down with a glass rod if it floats. A brown ring forms around the crystal in about 1 minute if the substance being tested contains nitrate.

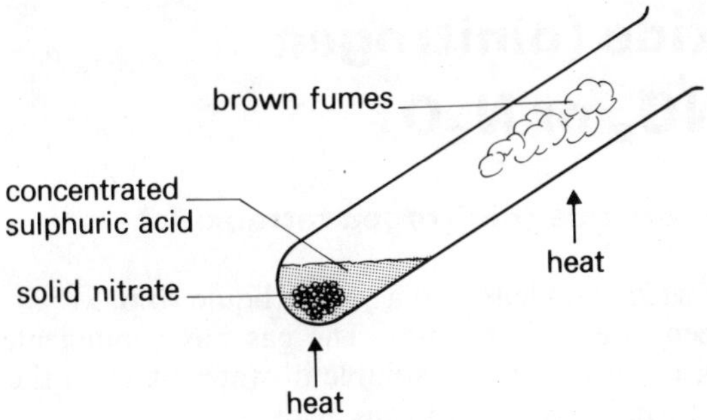

Fig. 19.5 Action of sulphuric acid on nitrates

2 *Hot concentrated sulphuric acid.* Heat a solid nitrate gently with concentrated sulphuric acid in a test-tube so that nitric acid is formed. Heat the top part of the tube to decompose the nitric acid. Reddish-brown nitrogen dioxide forms.

3 *Copper and concentrated sulphuric acid.* Mix a solid nitrate with copper. Heat gently with concentrated sulphuric acid, which forms nitric acid with the nitrate. Reddish-brown nitrogen dioxide is evolved:

$$Cu(s) + 4HNO_3(l) \rightarrow 2NO_2(g) + Cu(NO_3)_2(aq) + 2H_2O$$

Note. All nitrates are soluble in water, therefore no precipitation reactions can be used.

Uses of nitrates and nitric acid

Potassium nitrate, calcium nitrate, ammonium nitrate and nitro-chalk (a mixture of ammonium nitrate and limestone) are fertilizers. Trinitroglycerine (from nitric acid and glycerine), trinitrocellulose or gun-cotton (from cotton and nitric acid), and T.N.T. or trinitrotoluene (from toluene and nitric acid) are explosives; they are used in war and for mining and clearing rocks. All these nitro-compounds are not true nitrates, but they are much the same.

Gunpowder is a mixture of charcoal, sulphur, and potassium nitrate (not sodium nitrate, which is deliquescent). The mixture burns rapidly but quietly in an open space; the nitrate supplies the oxygen which oxidizes the sulphur and carbon to sulphur dioxide and carbon dioxide. If it burns in a closed space, the gases cause an explosion. (*Caution:* never try to make gunpowder.)

Oxides of nitrogen

Nitrogen dioxide (dinitrogen tetraoxide), NO_2 or N_2O_4

Properties of nitrogen dioxide (dinitrogen tetraoxide)

It is a reddish-brown gas which condenses to a yellow liquid (b.p. 21 °C). The liquid is usually green due to impurities. The gas has a pungent, irritating smell and is poisonous. It is very soluble in water (it gives the fountain experiment) and forms nitric and nitrous acids:

$$2NO_2(g) + H_2O(l) \rightarrow HNO_3(aq) + HNO_2(aq)$$

It is a *mixed acid anhydride*, behaving like N_2O_3 and N_2O_5. Alkalis form a mixture of nitrate and nitrite:

$$2NaOH(aq) + 2NO_2(g) \rightarrow NaNO_3(aq) + NaNO_2(aq) + H_2O$$

The gas is much denser than air and can be 'poured' downwards.
Heat. Take two corked boiling-tubes of the gas. Slightly loosen the cork of one, and heat this tube. The colour of the gas becomes much darker. The cold gas is pale-yellow and its vapour density is 46; it is dinitrogen tetraoxide, N_2O_4. On warming the gas dissociates into dark-brown nitrogen dioxide, NO_2 (vapour density = 23). The thermal dissociation is complete at 140 °C. On warming above 140 °C, the gas becomes colourless and the vapour density falls to about 15.3. This is caused by further

dissociation into nitrogen oxide and oxygen, which is complete at 620 °C:

$$N_2O_4(g \text{ or } l) \rightleftharpoons 2NO_2(g) \rightleftharpoons 2NO(g) + O_2(g) - \text{heat}$$
pale-yellow dark-brown colourless

Effect of pressure on the dissociation. Fill a 2 cm^3 syringe with the freshly prepared brown nitrogen dioxide. Press the nozzle firmly on to a rubber bung, to keep the gas in. Push in the plunger hard. The colour becomes yellow, because NO_2 molecules combine and therefore occupy less volume. Release the pressure. The brown colour returns. Repeat several times. (N_2O_4 is a polymer of NO_2.)

Nitrogen oxide (monoxide), NO

Properties of nitrogen monoxide

It is a colourless gas. Its smell and taste cannot be observed because it combines at once with oxygen of the air to form reddish-brown nitrogen dioxide. It is almost insoluble in water and neutral to litmus. It is slightly denser than air.
Oxygen and water. Take a jar half-full of nitrogen oxide and half-full of water. Invert it on a shelf in a trough. Pass oxygen into the jar. Reddish-brown nitrogen dioxide at once forms and it then reacts with the water to form a mixture of acids:

$$2NO(g) + O_2(g) \rightarrow 2NO_2(g)$$

$$2NO_2(g) + H_2O(l) \rightarrow HNO_3(aq) + HNO_2(aq), \text{ (nitrous acid)}$$

The level of the water rises.
Test for nitrogen oxide. The gas turns reddish-brown in air. It turns iron(II) sulphate solution dark brown.

Dinitrogen oxide, N_2O

To prepare dinitrogen oxide

The gas is obtained by cautiously heating ammonium nitrate and collecting over water. Since the nitrate is explosive, a mixture of an ammonium salt and sodium nitrate is safer:

$$NH_4NO_3(s) \rightarrow N_2O(g) + 2H_2O$$

Properties of dinitrogen oxide

It is a colourless gas with a faint sweet smell. A mixture of the gas and oxygen is used as an anaesthetic in minor operations, e.g. by dentists, because it produces insensibility for short periods. It is only slightly soluble and is neutral to litmus. It is $1\frac{1}{2}$ times denser than air. It does not burn.

Test for dinitrogen oxide. The gas re-lights a glowing splint.

Comparison of oxides of nitrogen

Nitrogen dioxide, N_2O_4 or NO_2	Nitrogen oxide, NO	Dinitrogen oxide, N_2O
Reddish-brown gas, pungent smell	Colourless gas; turns brown in air	Colourless gas; faint sweet smell
Very soluble in water	Almost insoluble	Fairly soluble
Turns litmus red	Neutral to litmus	Neutral to litmus
Denser than air ($2\frac{1}{2}$ times)	Very slightly denser than air	Denser than air ($1\frac{1}{2}$ times)
Extinguishes a burning splint and candle	Extinguishes a burning splint and candle	Re-lights a glowing splint

Heated copper and iron reduce all three gases to nitrogen:

$$4Cu(s) + 2NO_2(g) \rightarrow 4CuO(s) + N_2(g)$$

$$2Cu(s) + 2NO(g) \rightarrow 2CuO(s) + N_2(g)$$

$$3Fe(s) + 4N_2O(g) \rightarrow Fe_3O_4(s) + 4N_2(g)$$

Questions

1 How is nitric acid manufactured from ammonia? Describe experiments by which you could obtain from nitric acid (*a*) oxygen, (*b*) copper(II) nitrate crystals. (L.)

2 What is the action of nitric acid on (*a*) sulphur, (*b*) potassium iodide, (*c*) iron(II) chloride in the presence of dilute hydrochloric acid? State the conditions necessary for these reactions. How would you obtain hydrogen from nitric acid? (O.)

3 How would you (*a*) distinguish nitrogen oxide from dinitrogen oxide, (*b*) remove some nitrogen oxide present as an impurity in dinitrogen oxide, (*c*) obtain nitrogen from nitrogen oxide? (N.)

4 Describe and explain the results of (*a*) dropping concentrated nitric acid down a heated, sloping silica tube, (*b*) adding nitric acid to red lead oxide, Pb_3O_4, (*c*) warming dilute nitric acid with copper, (*d*) dropping fuming nitric acid on heated sawdust. State two large-scale uses of nitric acid. (C.)

5 Give one reaction in each case, mentioning the reaction conditions, of nitric acid on the following: (*a*) sawdust, (*b*) iron, (*c*) calcium hydroxide, (*d*) magnesium, (*e*) red lead oxide, Pb_3O_4, (*f*) hydrogen sulphide. (C.)

6 Mention (*a*) three differences between a mixture of 3 volumes of hydrogen with 1 volume of nitrogen and the compound ammonia; (*b*) two differences between a mixture of equal volumes of oxygen and nitrogen and the compound nitrogen monoxide. Indicate very briefly how the two mixtures mentioned may be made to combine to form the corresponding compounds. (O.)

7 Given lead(II) nitrate crystals, describe how you could obtain from them: (*a*) oxygen, (*b*) dinitrogen tetraoxide, N_2O_4, (*c*) lead(II) sulphate, (*d*) metallic lead. Describe the reactions that take place between nitrogen dioxide and (i) water, (ii) moist sulphur dioxide. (L.)

8 Nitric acid may be prepared in the laboratory by the action of concentrated sulphuric acid on a suitable nitrate and distilling off the nitric acid. Describe in detail such a preparation and answer the following questions concerning this preparation. (*a*) Why is an apparatus consisting of glass only desirable for the preparation? (*b*) Nitric acid and sulphuric acid are both liquids. Why does nitric acid only distil off and not sulphuric acid? (*c*) Pure nitric acid is colourless but the product in this preparation is usually yellow. Why is this? What precaution would you take in the preparation to reduce this colouration to a minimum? (*d*) If your product was yellow how would you obtain a colourless sample of nitric acid from it? (L.)

20
Sulphur and its Compounds

Extraction of sulphur

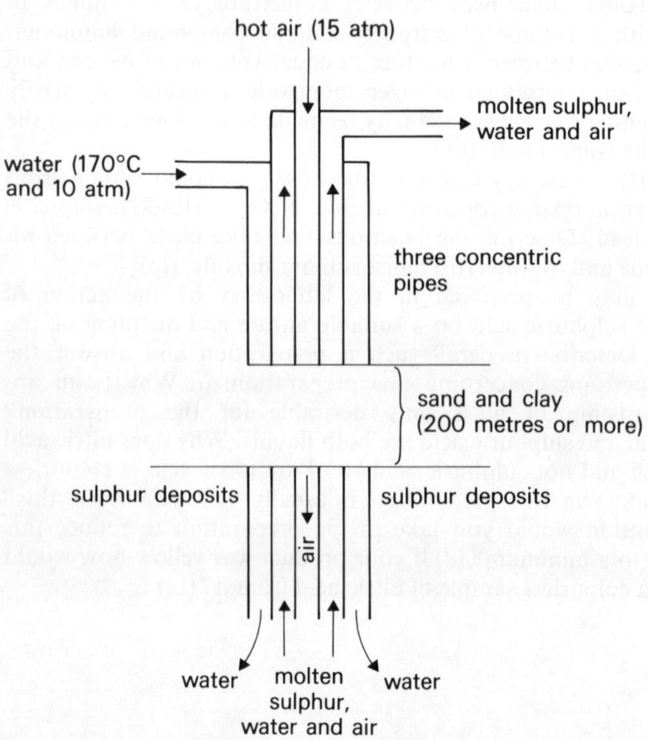

Fig. 20.1 Extraction of sulphur; Frasch process

From natural gas and petroleum. Natural gas and hydrocarbon gases obtained during the refining of petroleum contain hydrogen sulphide, which is absorbed in special solvents. The gas is removed from the solvents and about one-third is burned in air to form sulphur dioxide:

$$2H_2S(g) + 3O_2(g) \rightarrow 2H_2O(g) + 2SO_2(g)$$

The dioxide oxidizes the other two-thirds of the gas:

$$2H_2S(g) + SO_2(g) \rightarrow 2H_2O(g) + 3S(s)$$

This method is the largest source of sulphur.

Frasch process. In America, sulphur occurs 200 metres or more below the ground, under sand which makes mining impossible. It is melted (m.p. 113 °C) and is then forced to the surface. A hole is made to the sulphur. Three pipes (diameters about 2, 8, and 15 cm) are put down the hole. The pipes are arranged one inside the other. Water heated to about 170 °C at 10 atmospheres is forced down the outer pipe and hot compressed air is forced down the narrow pipe in the middle. A froth of molten sulphur, water and air is forced up the central (8 cm) pipe by the pressure. The mixture is run into large tanks and solidifies to yellow *roll sulphur*.

Sicily process. Sulphur, mixed with rocks, is mined in Sicily. Some is burned in a furnace (wood and coal are too scarce and cannot be used as fuels) and the hot gases formed are passed through a second furnace. The sulphur in this melts and flows out at the bottom of the furnace. Roll sulphur is formed when the liquid solidifies. Some vapour condenses in chimneys of the furnace as a sublimate called *flowers of sulphur*.

Uses of sulphur

Rubber is soft and sticky; it is made hard and strong by heating it with sulphur (*vulcanization of rubber*). Gunpowder, fireworks and matches contain sulphur. Sulphur ointment, tablets and drugs are used in medicine. Fruit trees are sprayed with sulphur, which kills insects and fungi which cause disease. Sulphuric acid is manufactured from sulphur in the Contact process. Sulphur is used to manufacture carbon disulphide, CS_2; sodium thiosulphate, $Na_2S_2O_3$, used in photography; and calcium hydrogensulphite, $Ca(HSO_3)_2$, used to dissolve lignin and to bleach other substances in wood pulp that cause paper made from the pulp to be yellowish brown.

To examine the action of heat on sulphur

Heat powdered sulphur very gently until it boils.

1 The lemon-yellow solid melts at 113 °C to a clear amber liquid which flows easily like water. Solid and liquid sulphur contain rings of 8 atoms, S_8. This liquid is not viscous because these rings flow readily over one another.

2 The colour darkens on further warming. At about 160 °C the sulphur becomes reddish-brown and viscous, i.e. it flows slowly. It remains like syrup in the tube even when inverted. The changes are caused by the breaking of rings of 8 atoms and formation of long chains—some with 100 000 atoms or more. The liquid is viscous because the chains twist together and do not flow readily over one another.

3 On further warming, the liquid becomes black and mobile again. The chains break and become shorter and therefore can flow more readily.

4 The sulphur boils at 444 °C and forms a brownish vapour. At 1000 °C the vapour is S_2 molecules, and at higher temperatures the molecules are monatomic, S. S_8, S_2, and S are gaseous allotropes. On cold surfaces the vapour condenses directly to a yellow sublimate, *flowers of sulphur*. This consists of S_8 and chain molecules.

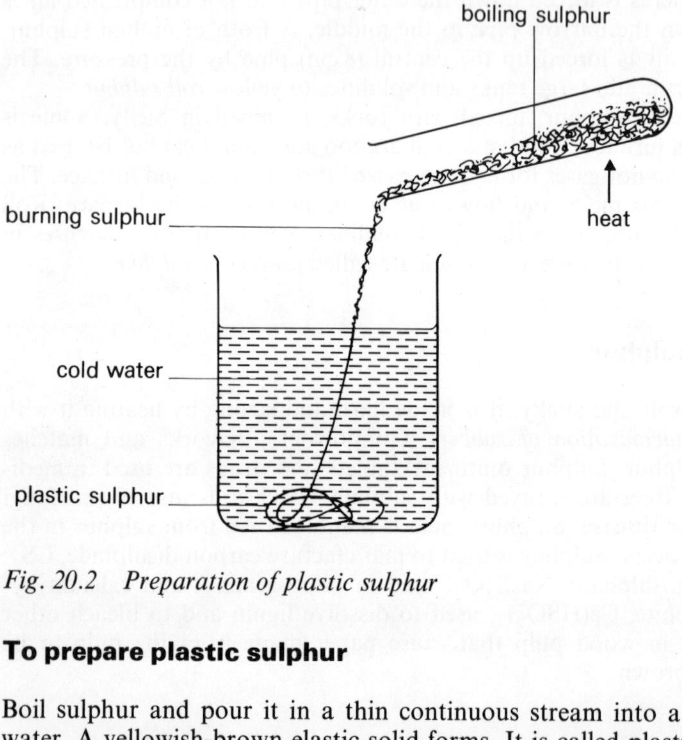

Fig. 20.2 Preparation of plastic sulphur

To prepare plastic sulphur

Boil sulphur and pour it in a thin continuous stream into a beaker of water. A yellowish-brown elastic solid forms. It is called plastic sulphur, a supercooled liquid, i.e. its molecules are arranged in chains at random as in the liquid, and there are no rings of eight atoms, S_8. It is insoluble in carbon disulphide. On standing for a few days it changes to hard, yellow, opaque rhombic sulphur, S_8.

To prepare the two crystalline allotropes of sulphur

Rhombic or alpha-sulphur (*α-sulphur*). Dissolve powdered roll sulphur (not flowers of sulphur) in methylbenzene. (This solvent is volatile and inflammable.) Filter the mixture through a *dry* filter paper and collect the filtrate in a beaker. Methylbenzene does not pass through wet paper. Cover the beaker with paper with a few holes in it so that the methylbenzene can evaporate slowly. Leave the solution in a fume cupboard. Bright yellow crystals form as the volatile solvent evaporates.

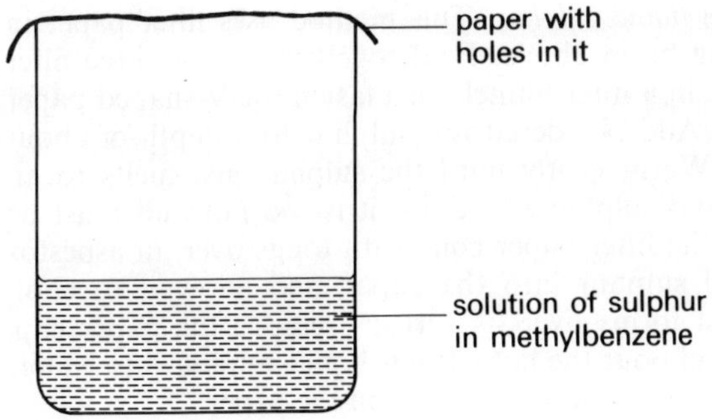

Fig. 20.3 Preparation of rhombic sulphur

Monoclinic or beta-sulphur (β-sulphur)
From liquid sulphur. **a** Warm an evaporating basin full of powdered roll sulphur with a small flame until it just melts. Add more powder and continue heating until the basin is almost full of molten sulphur. Allow the sulphur to cool. When a thin solid crust forms over its surface, make two holes in it. Pour liquid sulphur through one hole into a beaker of water. The second hole lets air in. Let the basin cool. Cut away the crust and lift it out. Look both under the crust and inside the basin. The pale-yellow crystals are like needles or thin prisms.

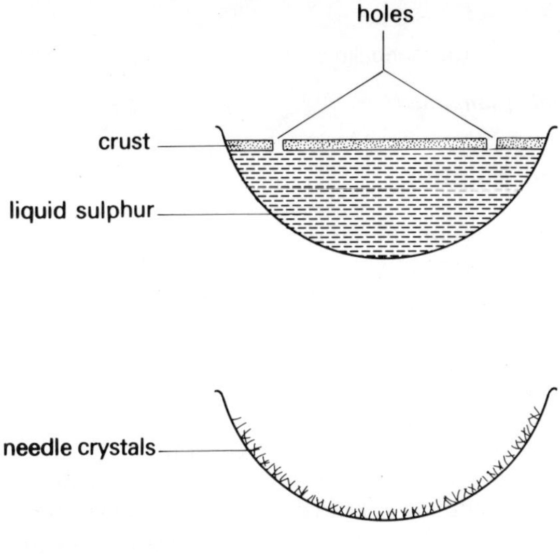

Fig. 20.4 Preparation of monoclinic sulphur

Alternative method from liquid sulphur. This method uses filter paper in place of the evaporating basin above. Fold together two or three filter papers as though to use in a filter funnel, then fasten the V-shaped paper cone with a paper clip. Add powdered roll sulphur to a depth of about 5–6 cm in a test-tube. Warm *gently* until the sulphur just melts to an amber liquid (if the liquid sulphur is reddish it is too hot and must be allowed to cool). Hold the filter paper cone with tongs over an asbestos square, pour the liquid sulphur into the paper, and allow it to cool. When a thin solid crust forms over its surface, remove the paper clip, open the filter papers, and pour the hot surplus liquid sulphur into water. Pale yellow crystals of monoclinic sulphur are on the paper.

b *From solution*. Add powdered roll sulphur to methylbenzene or dimethylbenzene about 3 cm deep in a test-tube and warm over a small flame to form a hot saturated solution, adding a little more sulphur if necessary. Do not boil. Wrap the tube in cotton wool to keep the temperature above 96 °C. Monoclinic crystals form as the solution slowly cools. (The liquids are inflammable but are safe with a low flame.)

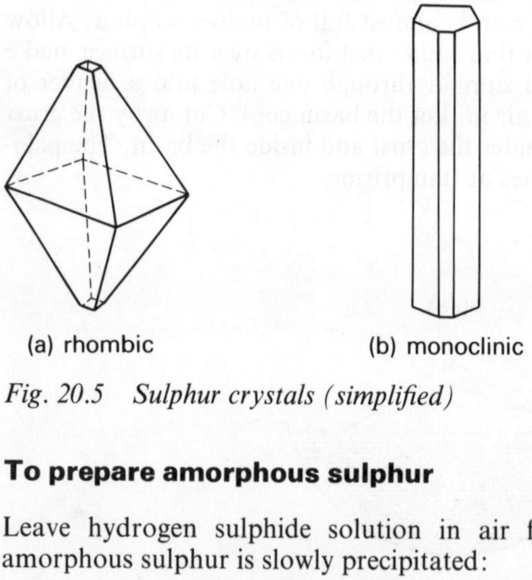

Fig. 20.5 Sulphur crystals (simplified)

To prepare amorphous sulphur

Leave hydrogen sulphide solution in air for a day or two. White amorphous sulphur is slowly precipitated:

$$2H_2S(aq) + O_2(g) \rightarrow 2S(s) + 2H_2O$$

The crystalline allotropes

Monoclinic sulphur changes when kept at room temperature. The clear crystals gradually become opaque, and then consist of tiny crystals of rhombic sulphur. If rhombic sulphur is heated at 96 °C for some time it changes to monoclinic sulphur; 96 °C is the *transition temperature* for the two forms.

The differences between these allotropes are:

Rhombic sulphur	Monoclinic sulphur
Stable below 96 °C	Stable above 96 °C
Octahedral crystals	Needle-shaped crystals
Bright yellow	Pale yellow
M.p. 113 °C	M.p. 120 °C
Density higher (2.06 g/cm^3)	Density lower (1.98 g/cm^3)

Two facts prove that the substances are allotropes:

1 One gram of monoclinic sulphur slowly changes at room temperature into one gram of rhombic sulphur.

2 One gram of either form will burn in oxygen to yield the same mass (2 g) of sulphur dioxide and nothing else.

More properties of sulphur

Sulphur is a yellow solid non-metal, insoluble in water but soluble in carbon disulphide, methylbenzene and dimethylbenzene.

Oxygen. Sulphur burns with a blue flame, p. 39.

Oxidizing agents. Sulphur is oxidized to sulphur dioxide by concentrated sulphuric acid (p. 253) and to sulphuric acid by concentrated nitric acid (p. 231).

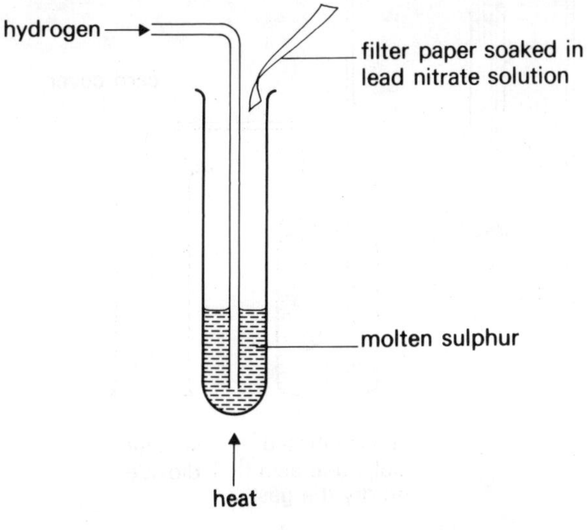

Fig. 20.6 Hydrogen and sulphur combine slightly

Metals. Sulphur combines with metals to form sulphides, p. 18.
Hydrogen. Bubble hydrogen through molten sulphur in a boiling-tube. Soak a filter paper in lead(II) ethanoate or lead(II) nitrate solution and hold it at the mouth of the tube. Brown-black lead(II) sulphide forms, proving that some hydrogen sulphide is formed:

$$H_2(g) + S(l) \rightleftharpoons H_2S(g)$$

Less than 1 per cent of hydrogen sulphide is formed. *This reaction is useless for preparing jars of the gas.*

Sulphur dioxide, SO_2

To prepare sulphur dioxide

Using sodium sulphite or sodium hydrogensulphite. Place sodium sulphite or hydrogensulphite crystals in a flask and arrange as in Fig. 20.7. Pour concentrated sulphuric or hydrochloric acid down the funnel. Some

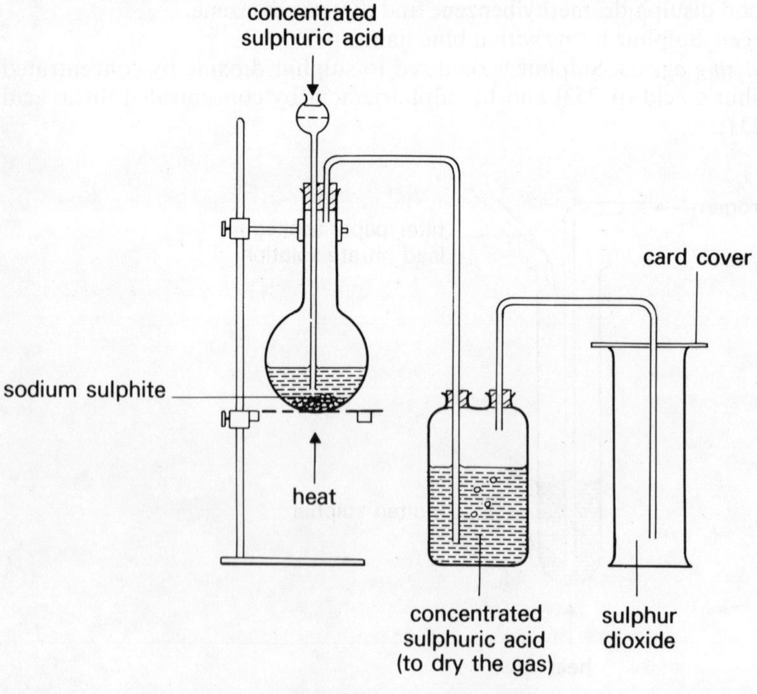

Fig. 20.7 Preparation of sulphur dioxide

reactions occurs in the cold. Heat the mixture gently and collect the gas:

$$SO_3^{2-}(s) + 2H^+(aq) \rightarrow SO_2(g) + H_2O$$

$$HSO_3^-(s) + H^+(aq) \rightarrow SO_2(g) + H_2O$$

Properties of sulphur dioxide

Sulphur dioxide is a colourless, poisonous gas with an irritating smell of burning sulphur. It is about $2\frac{1}{2}$ times denser than air. It liquefies at $-10\,°C$ and at ordinary temperatures under pressure; the liquid is available in glass siphons. It is very soluble in water ($1\,cm^3$ dissolves about $70\,cm^3$ of gas), forming sulphurous acid:

$$H_2O + SO_2 \rightleftharpoons H_2SO_3(aq) \rightleftharpoons 2H^+(aq) + SO_3^{2-}(aq)$$

It forms salts with alkalis. It does not burn, but combines with oxygen in the presence of a catalyst (p. 249).

Reducing reactions of sulphur dioxide

Sulphur dioxide, in the presence of water, reduces by supplying electrons to substances:

$$SO_3^{2-}(aq) + H_2O \rightarrow SO_4^{2-}(aq) + 2H^+(aq) + 2e$$

Carry out the tests on concentrated nitric acid, chlorine, bromine and iodine as described on p. 113. Test the products by adding dilute nitric acid and barium nitrate solution (test for a soluble sulphate); a white precipitate proves that sulphuric acid has been formed. Sulphur dioxide does not form sulphur when oxidized, as hydrogen sulphide does.
Air. A solution oxidizes slowly to sulphuric acid:

$$2H_2SO_3(aq) + O_2(g) \rightarrow 2H_2SO_4(aq)$$

Concentrated nitric acid. Reddish-brown nitrogen dioxide is evolved and the mixture becomes warm:

$$SO_2(g) + 2HNO_3(conc.) \rightarrow H_2SO_4(aq) + 2NO_2(g)$$

Chlorine, bromine and iodine. The coloured solutions (yellowish-green, reddish and brown respectively) are reduced to colourless solutions of their hydrogen compounds:

$$SO_2(g) + 2H_2O + Cl_2(aq) \rightarrow H_2SO_4(aq) + 2HCl(aq)$$

Potassium manganate(VII) and dichromate(VI). Purple acidified potassium manganate(VII) is turned colourless and yellow or orange acidified potassium dichromate(VI) is turned green by sulphur dioxide (and also by hydrogen sulphide), p. 113.
Bleaching. Add a blue or red flower to the moist gas. The colour is slowly bleached by reduction:

$$SO_2(g) + 2H_2O + \text{dye} \rightarrow H_2SO_4(aq) + (\text{dye}+2H), \text{colourless}$$

Atmospheric oxygen may slowly oxidize the bleached compound to a coloured substance, which explains why newspapers gradually turn yellowish.

Oxidizing reactions of sulphur dioxide

Hydrogen sulphide is oxidized to sulphur.
Magnesium. The burning metal continues to burn, forming white magnesium oxide and yellow sulphur (compare carbon dioxide):

$$2Mg(s) + SO_2(g) \rightarrow 2MgO(s) + S(g)$$

Uses of sulphur dioxide

Most sulphur dioxide is used in the *Contact Process* for the manufacture of sulphuric acid. It is used to *bleach* wool, silk, straw and sponges, all of which are damaged by chlorine. It is used to manufacture calcium hydrogensulphite, $Ca(HSO_3)_2$, used to make wood-pulp white in the manufacture of paper. The gas is poisonous and is used to kill germs in houses, clothing and grain (*fumigation*). It is used to destroy termites or white ants. It is added as a *preservative* to foodstuffs and fruit squashes, e.g. orange juice; it reacts with oxygen and prevents oxidation of the liquids.

Sulphur(VI) oxide (sulphur trioxide), SO_3

To examine the action of heat on iron(II) sulphate crystals

Half-fill a test-tube with the crystals. Arrange the apparatus as in Fig. 1.6. Heat the crystals gently at first, and then strongly. Identify the gases evolved by their colour and smell. Test the distillate for sulphuric acid.

The crystals at first lose their water of crystallization. The white anhydrous salt decomposes on stronger heating, forming reddish *iron(III)* oxide, sulphur dioxide and sulphur(VI) oxide.

The oxides of sulphur react with the water to form sulphurous and sulphuric acids:

$$FeSO_4 \cdot 7H_2O(s) \rightarrow FeSO_4(s) + 7H_2O(g)$$

$$2FeSO_4(s) \rightarrow Fe_2O_3(s) + SO_2(g) + SO_3(g)$$

To prepare sulphur(VI) oxide

Arrange the apparatus in a fume cupboard as in Fig. 20.8. Heat the combustion tube, wide tube and flask before use; if they are not dry the yield of sulphur(VI) oxide is small. Pass sulphur dioxide from a siphon and excess oxygen from a cylinder over the catalyst of platinized asbestos heated to about 500 °C:

$$2SO_2(g) + O_2(g) \rightleftharpoons 2SO_3(\text{g then s})$$

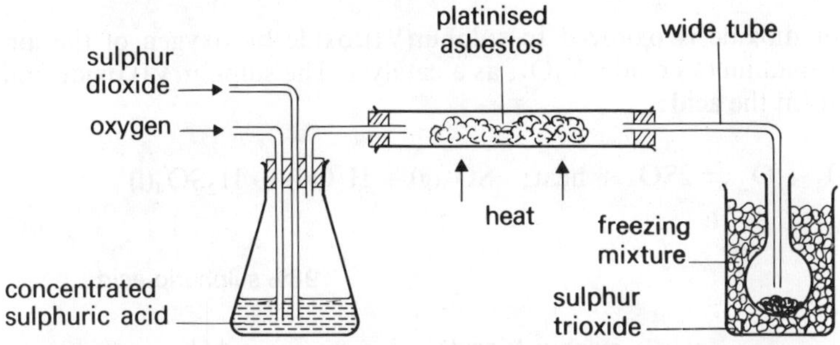

Fig. 20.8 Preparation of sulphur(VI) oxide

The platinum is spread out finely over the asbestos; therefore its area and catalytic action are greater than when it is in one lump. Dense white fumes form and condense to white silky needles in a freezing mixture of ice and salt.

Properties of sulphur(VI) oxide

It is a white solid (m.p. 17 °C, b.p. 45 °C). The solid (but not the gas) readily combines with water, making a hissing sound and giving out heat:

$$H_2O(l) + SO_3(s) \rightarrow H_2SO_4(aq) + \text{heat}$$

The vapour consists mainly of the trioxide but both vapour and solid contain polymers, $(SO_3)_x$.

Sulphuric acid, H_2SO_4

Millions of tonnes are used in the manufacture of chemicals, paints, dyes, plastics, detergents, explosives, and for obtaining petrol and oils from petroleum, from which it removes impurities. *Superphosphate fertilizer* is made from insoluble calcium phosphate rock, $Ca_3(PO_4)_2$, and sulphuric acid; it is a mixture of the more soluble calcium hydrogenphosphate $Ca(H_2PO_4)_2$ and calcium sulphate. Aqueous ammonia from gas-works is converted by the acid to ammonium sulphate fertilizer. Rayon (artificial silk) is made by squirting an alkaline solution of cellulose (from wood-pulp) into the acid. Iron is cleaned free from rust by the acid before it is coated with tin to make tinplate or with zinc to make galvanized iron. Lead–acid accumulators contain sulphuric acid.

Manufacture of sulphuric acid by contact process

Sulphur dioxide is oxidized to sulphur(VI) oxide by oxygen of the air, using vanadium(V) oxide, V_2O_5, as a catalyst. The sulphur(VI) oxide and water form the acid:

$$2SO_2 + O_2 \rightleftharpoons 2SO_3 + \text{heat}; \quad SO_3(g) + H_2O(l) \rightarrow H_2SO_4(l)$$

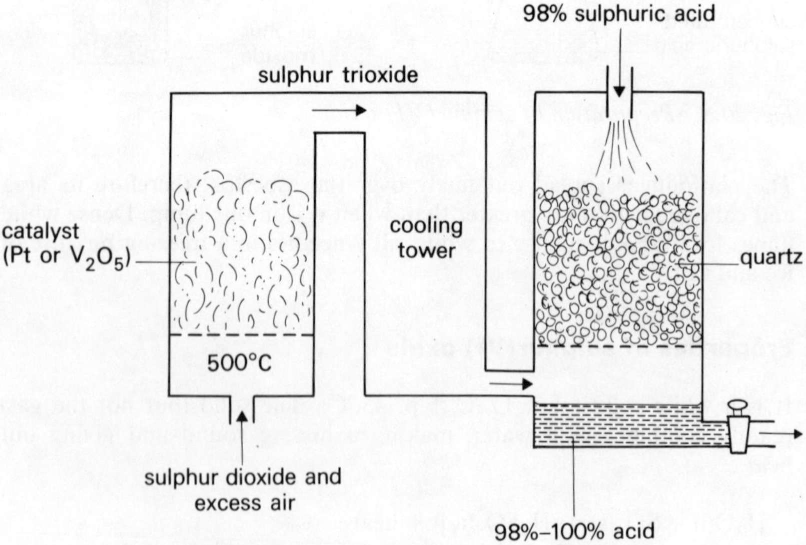

Fig. 20.9 Contact process (diagrammatic)

There are four stages in the process.

1 *Preparation of sulphur dioxide.* Sulphur dioxide is made by burning sulphur and sulphide ores (iron disulphide, FeS_2, or zinc sulphide) in air.

$$S(s) + O_2(g) \rightarrow SO_2(g)$$

$$2ZnS(s) + 3O_2(g) \rightarrow 2SO_2(g) + 2ZnO(s)$$

2 *Purification of gases.* The mixture of sulphur dioxide and excess air is purified to remove any dust, which would 'poison' the catalyst, i.e. make it useless.

3 *Conversion to sulphur(VI) oxide.* The gases are passed over a catalyst of finely-divided vanadium(V) oxide (which is cheaper and less easily 'poisoned' by impurities than platinum) at a temperature of 400–500 °C. No external heat is required once the exothermic reaction starts. Sulphur(VI) oxide is formed.

4 *Conversion of sulphur(VI) oxide to acid.* It cannot be dissolved directly in water because it forms a mist of acid. It is passed into concentrated sulphuric acid (98 per cent acid, 2 per cent water) and it reacts with this water. More water is added to keep the concentration of the acid about 98 per cent.

The reaction between sulphur dioxide and oxygen is reversible and exothermic. The effects of various factors on it are as follows (compare with the Haber process, p. 221 and also refer to pp. 142–7 and Figs. 20.10 and 20.11).

Effect of temperature. At low temperatures the equilibrium yield of sulphur(VI) oxide is high but the rate of reaction is slow. At high temperatures the reaction is fast but the yield is low. In practice a temperature of about 500 °C is used; the equilibrium yield is good at this temperature but the reaction is still too slow.

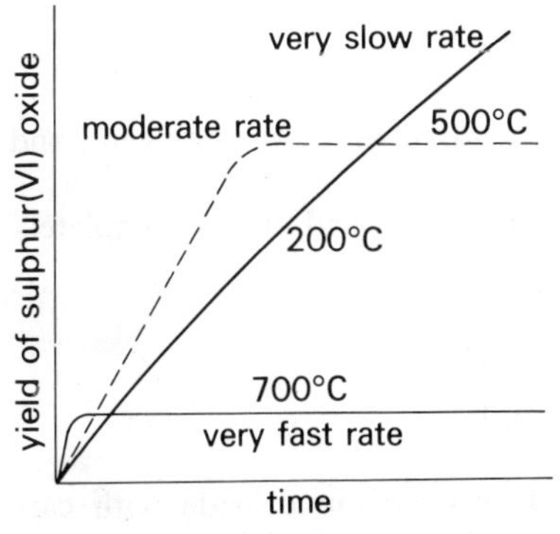

Fig. 20.10 The effect of temperature (contact process)

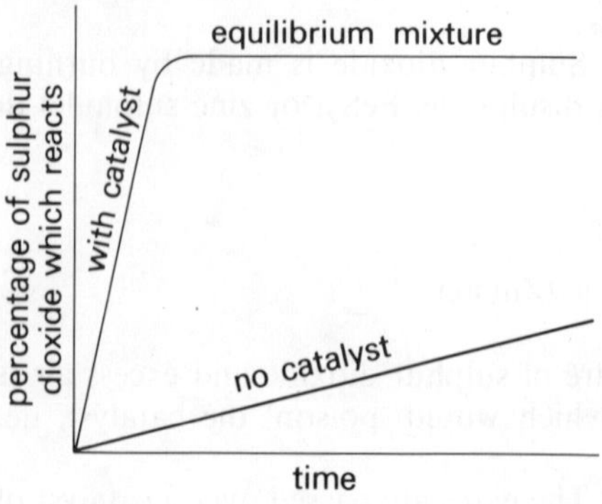

Fig. 20.11 The effect of a catalyst (contact process)

Effect of catalyst. A catalyst speeds the reaction but does not affect the equilibrium yield of sulphur trioxide. The catalyst is finely divided to increase its surface area.

Effect of pressure. From the equation we see that 3 molecules combine to form 2 molecules. Therefore by Avogadro's Principle, 3 volumes of reactants form 2 volumes of sulphur(VI) oxide. High pressures would cause a better yield of oxide as they favour the formation of the smaller product. In practice, they are too expensive to be worthwhile.

Excess air is used in the process to ensure that practically all of the expensive sulphur dioxide reacts.

Properties of sulphuric acid

Concentrated (98 per cent and about 36 M) sulphuric acid is a dense oily liquid (density 1.83 g/cm³). It decomposes at its boiling point (330 °C) forming white fumes:

$$H_2SO_4(l) \rightleftharpoons H_2O(g) + SO_3(g)$$

It reacts as (*a*) an acid, (*b*) a non-volatile acid, (*c*) an oxidizing agent, and (*d*) a dehydrating agent.

Acid properties. Dilute sulphuric acid is a dibasic acid and is completely ionized:

$$H_2SO_4(aq) + H_2O \rightarrow H_3O^+ + HSO_4^-(aq)$$
$$HSO_4^-(aq) + H_2O \rightarrow H_3O^+ + SO_4^{2-}(aq)$$

It has a sour taste, turns litmus red, forms carbon dioxide with carbonates and hydrogencarbonates, salts with bases, and hydrogen with many metals. One hundred per cent sulphuric acid is covalent and is not ionized; it does not affect litmus and does not form hydrogen with metals.

Non-volatile acid properties. Nitric acid and hydrogen chloride are much more volatile than concentrated sulphuric acid, which displaces them from their solid salts, e.g.

$$H^+(aq) + Cl^-(s) \rightarrow HCl(g)$$

$$H^+(aq) + NO_3^-(s) \rightarrow HNO_3(g)$$

Oxidizing reactions

The *hot concentrated* acid is an oxidizing agent as it accepts electrons from substances:

$$2H_2SO_4(l) + 2e \rightarrow SO_2(g) + 2H_2O + SO_4^{2-}(aq)$$

Metals. Hot concentrated sulphuric acid reacts with copper to form sulphur dioxide and white anhydrous copper(II) sulphate. Black copper(II) sulphide, CuS, is formed in a side reaction:

$$Cu(s) + 2H_2SO_4(conc.) \rightarrow SO_2(g) + CuSO_4(s) + 2H_2O$$

Non-metals. The hot acid slowly oxidizes *carbon* to carbon dioxide and *sulphur* to sulphur dioxide:

$$C(s) + 2H_2SO_4(conc.) \rightarrow CO_2(g) + 2SO_2(g) + 2H_2O$$

$$S(s) + 2H_2SO_4(conc.) \rightarrow 3SO_2(g) + 2H_2O$$

Hydrogen sulphide is oxidized to sulphur even in the cold.

Affinity for water

The acid has a great affinity for water. (*a*) Add concentrated acid carefully to cold water. The mixture becomes very hot. (*b*) Pour concentrated acid into a beaker and mark the level of the acid. Leave for a few days. The level slowly rises. The acid absorbs water vapour from the air, i.e. it is hygroscopic. For this reason it is used in desiccators and for drying most gases. It cannot be used to dry alkaline gases (ammonia) or reducing gases (hydrogen sulphide).

Never add water to the concentrated acid as the great heat formed may change some of the water explosively to steam which scatters the acid. Always add the acid to water; add it slowly and stir all the time to prevent the dense acid settling to the bottom.

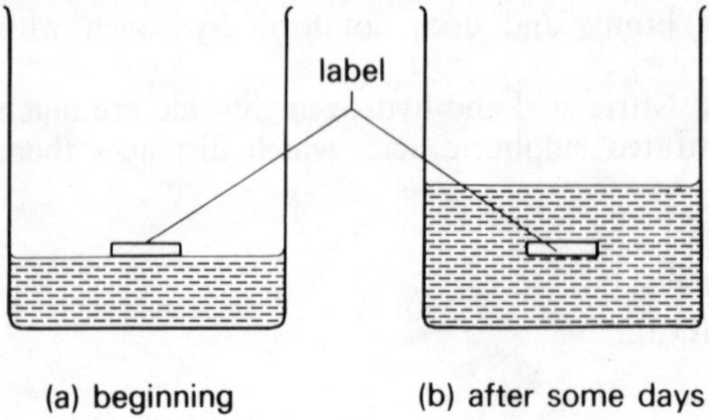

Fig. 20.12 Concentrated sulphuric acid in air

Dehydrating reactions of sulphuric acid

Concentrated sulphuric acid can *remove water or the elements of water* (hydrogen and oxygen) from many compounds. These are *dehydrating reactions* and the acid is a *dehydrating agent*.

Copper(II) sulphate crystals. **a**. Slide a crystal into the concentrated acid, so that part is in the acid and part outside. Leave for some time. **b**. Warm a second crystal gently with the acid. The blue crystals become white and change to a powder:

$$CuSO_4 \cdot 5H_2O(s) \rightarrow CuSO_4(s) + 5H_2O(l)$$

Sugar (glucose or sucrose). Do not smell the gases evolved in these tests because they usually contain some carbon monoxide. **a**. Add the acid to sugar in two test-tubes. Warm one only. The cold acid turns sugar brown; the hot acid turns it to a black solid foam of carbon.

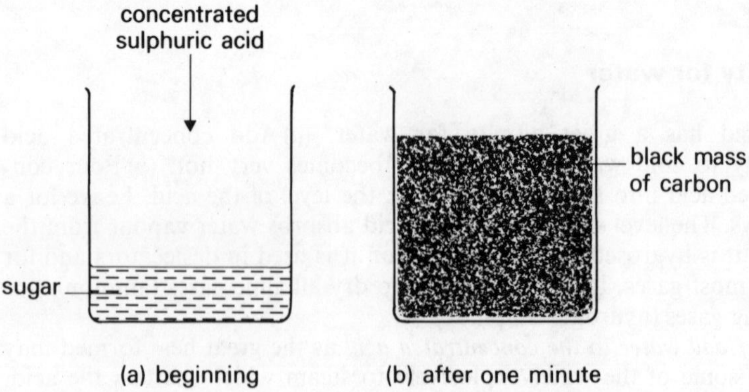

Fig. 20.13 Sulphuric acid dehydrates sugar

b. Place sugar in a beaker and just cover it with water. Add the acid slowly. The mixture becomes hot due to reaction between the acid and water. The black spongy carbon swells and may fill the beaker (Fig. 20.13):

$$\text{(Glucose) } C_6H_{12}O_6(s) \rightarrow 6C(s) + 6H_2O(\text{g or l})$$

$$\text{(Sucrose) } C_{12}H_{22}O_{11}(s) \rightarrow 12C(s) + 11H_2O(\text{g or l})$$

Most of the gas evolved is steam because the temperature rises to well over 100 °C. Much carbon monoxide is also evolved, together with a little carbon dioxide and sulphur dioxide (formed by reduction of the acid by carbon).

Paper, cloth and wood. These compounds contain cellulose $C_6H_{10}O_5$. Dip a glass rod in the acid and 'write' on filter paper, dry cloth, and damp cloth. Dip the end of a wooden splint in the acid. The acid makes holes in the paper and cloth (faster in damp cloth because heat is produced by the acid and water) and it chars wood:

$$\text{(Cellulose)} \quad C_6H_{10}O_5(s) \rightarrow 6C(s) + 5H_2O(l)$$

Flesh. The acid rapidly 'burns' the skin and flesh, causing painful wounds. The action is a dehydration.

Ethanol. Excess concentrated acid dehydrates the alcohol at 160 °C, forming ethene (p. 307):

$$C_2H_6O \quad \text{or} \quad C_2H_5OH(l) \rightarrow H_2O + C_2H_4(g), \text{ ethene}$$

Methanoic (*formic*) *acid*. This forms carbon monoxide, p. 206.

Test for sulphuric acid and soluble sulphates

To an aqueous solution of any sulphate add dilute nitric acid and barium nitrate solution. A white precipitate forms:

$$Ba^{2+}(aq) + SO_4^{2-}(aq) \rightarrow BaSO_4(s), \text{ white}$$

The nitric acid prevents the precipitation of other white barium compounds ($BaCO_3$, $BaSO_3$) because it decomposes them.

Questions

1 Describe the large-scale extraction of sulphur. Describe the preparation and collection of tubes of hydrogen sulphide, starting with powdered sulphur. Describe experiments to show the action of this gas (*a*) as a combustible substance, (*b*) as a reducing agent, (*c*) as an acid forming salts. (L.)

2 Describe experiments by which you could obtain (*a*) pure water from salt water, (*b*) rhombic sulphur crystals from a mixture of iron filings, sulphur and potassium nitrate. Describe how you would convert rhombic to monoclinic sulphur. (L.)

3 Starting from roll sulphur describe the preparation of (*a*) monoclinic sulphur, (*b*) sulphur dioxide, (*c*) hydrogen sulphide, (*d*) sodium sulphate. Outline the extraction of sulphur from natural deposits. (C.)

4 Describe fully the changes that take place when powdered sulphur is gradually heated to its boiling point. Mention briefly the proof that rhombic and monoclinic sulphur are allotropes. Calculate the mass of sulphur which, on complete combustion would yield 7 dm^3 of sulphur dioxide measured at 182 °C and 722 mmHg pressure. (N.)

5 What is the action of heat on iron(II) sulphate crystals? Give a diagram to show how to convert sulphur dioxide to sulphur trioxide. What is the action of sulphur dioxide on (*a*) nitric acid, (*b*) hydrogen sulphide, (*c*) chlorine? (O.)

6 Describe one method of manufacturing sulphuric acid. Name four important large-scale uses of this acid. Describe one experiment in each case to show how sulphuric acid can act as (*a*) an oxidizing agent, (*b*) a dehydrating agent. (C.)

7 Give a list of five chemical properties of concentrated sulphuric acid. Why is this acid said to be dibasic? How can sulphates and sulphides be identified in the laboratory? (N.)

8 Describe briefly the preparation of iron(II) sulphate crystals from iron. State and explain what happens when: (*a*) the crystals are heated alone, (*b*) a solution of the crystals is treated with ammonia and allowed to stand, (*c*) a solution of the crystals is boiled with a little nitric acid, (*d*) a solution is added to sodium nitrate in a test-tube and concentrated sulphuric acid is poured gently down the side of the tube. (L.)

9 Draw a labelled diagram of the apparatus you would use to prepare sulphur dioxide. How does this gas react with (*a*) chlorine water, (*b*) hydrogen sulphide, (*c*) sodium hydroxide solution? Indicate briefly how sulphur dioxide may be converted into sulphuric acid. (C.)

21 Chlorine and its Compounds. The Halogens

The halogens are the elements fluorine, chlorine, bromine, iodine and astatine. Astatine has been made artificially but probably does not occur naturally. Fluorine is so reactive that it is not prepared in schools. Chlorine is very reactive. Bromine and iodine resemble chlorine in many ways, and are less reactive. A halogen atom has 7 electrons in its outer orbit and readily accepts 1 electron to form an ion, X^-, which has a stable noble gas configuration, e.g. F^-(2.8) and Cl^-(2.8.8).

Uses of sodium chloride

Common salt is needed by all animals. It preserves meat and fish. Most sodium and chlorine compounds (e.g. washing soda, baking soda, sodium hydroxide, soap, hydrochloric acid, bleaching powder) are made from sodium chloride.

Properties of sodium chloride

Sodium chloride crystallizes in cubes, which contain no water of crystallization. 100 g of water dissolves about 36 g of salt at room temperature; the solubility increases slightly at higher temperatures. Ordinary common salt is hygroscopic but pure sodium chloride is not. The ordinary salt contains deliquescent magnesium and calcium chlorides.

Heat. Sodium chloride crystals break up with a loud crackling noise on heating. They melt to a clear liquid at 808 °C. No chemical change occurs. Potassium chloride behaves similarly. It melts at 772 °C.

Concentrated sulphuric acid. Add a few drops of the acid to sodium chloride in a test-tube. There is a vigorous effervescence and colourless hydrogen chloride is evolved; it forms misty fumes with damp air.

Hydrogen chloride, HCl

To prepare hydrogen chloride

Hydrogen chloride is prepared by the action of concentrated sulphuric acid on any chloride. It is a reversible reaction, but as the volatile hydrogen chloride escapes the equilibrium moves to the right:

$$H^+(aq) + Cl^-(s) \rightarrow HCl(g)$$

Sodium hydrogensulphate (*an acid salt*) is formed; the normal sulphate is formed only at temperatures above those possible in glass apparatus.

Slide lumps of rock salt (naturally occurring sodium chloride) into a flask or add powdered sodium chloride. Fit up the apparatus as in Fig. 20.7. The concentrated sulphuric acid in the wash-bottle is not necessary for drying the gas but it indicates the rate at which gas is evolved. Add concentrated sulphuric acid to cover the rock salt and gently heat the mixture. If powdered salt is used the reaction is very vigorous and much frothing occurs even in the cold, so use cold diluted acid (2 conc. acid : 1 water) which gives a steady stream of gas. Collect gas-jars and boiling-tubes of gas, and also fill a thick-walled, round-bottomed flask for the fountain experiment.

Properties of hydrogen chloride

Hydrogen chloride is a colourless gas. It forms misty fumes in damp air because it forms tiny drops of hydrochloric acid. It has a pungent choking smell and a sharp taste. It is very soluble in water, forming hydrochloric acid (1 cm^3 of water at room temperature dissolves about 450 cm^3 of gas), and in methylbenzene. Do the *fountain experiment* as described for ammonia, Fig. 18.2 (use blue litmus in the trough). The gas turns moist litmus red, but dry or liquid hydrogen chloride has no action on dry litmus paper. Hydrogen chloride does not burn, and it extinguishes a burning splint. It is about $1\frac{1}{4}$ times denser than air (vapour density = 18.25). It forms dense white fumes of ammonium chloride with ammonia:

$$NH_3(g) + HCl(g) \rightarrow NH_4Cl(s)$$

It forms a white precipitate of silver chloride with silver nitrate acidified with dilute nitric acid. (All soluble chlorides form this white precipitate with acidified silver nitrate.)

$$Ag^+(aq) + Cl^-(aq) \rightarrow AgCl(s), \text{ white}$$

Tests for hydrogen chloride. The gas forms misty fumes in moist air, turns litmus red, forms white fumes with ammonia, and forms a white precipitate with acidified silver nitrate solution.

To prepare a solution of hydrogen chloride in water (hydrochloric acid) and in methylbenzene

Arrange the apparatus as in Fig. 21.1. The rim of the funnel must be just below the surface of the water in the beaker. Gently warm the salt and acid. If a delivery tube was used instead of the funnel, water would 'suck back' into the preparation flask. Repeat, using methylbenzene instead of water.

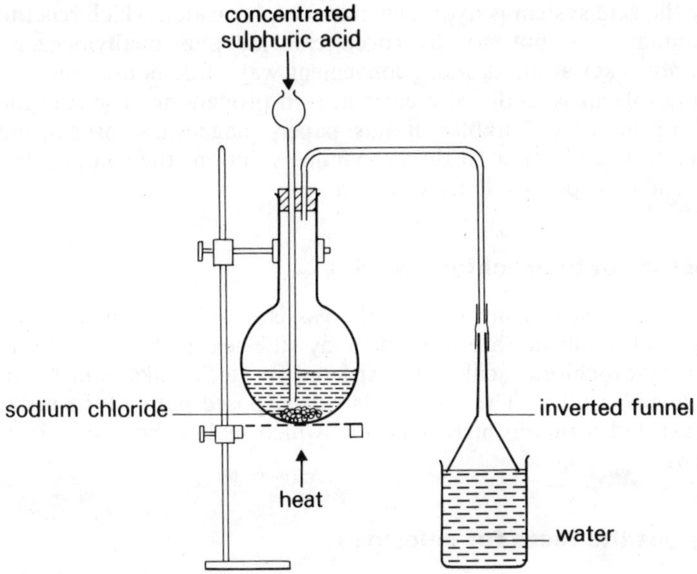

Fig. 21.1 Preparation of a solution of hydrogen chloride

Properties of hydrochloric acid

Dilute hydrochloric acid has typical acidic properties. It has a sour taste, turns litmus red, forms hydrogen with most metals, salts with bases, and carbon dioxide with carbonates.

When dilute hydrochloric acid is boiled, water comes off until the solution contains 20.2 per cent acid; this mixture boils at 110 °C without changing. Concentrated hydrochloric acid contains about 36 per cent of acid, and is about 12 M.

Oxidizing agents [manganese(IV) oxide and potassium manganate(VII)] oxidize the concentrated acid to chlorine:

$$2Cl^-(aq) - 2e \rightarrow Cl_2(g)$$

Properties of hydrogen chloride in methylbenzene. Hydrogen chloride does not ionize in dry methylbenzene, and is present as a covalent compound. The solution differs from the aqueous solution as follows:

1 It does not conduct electricity.
2 It does not react with litmus.
3 It does not form hydrogen with metals (magnesium, iron, zinc) because it contains no hydrogen ions.
4 It does not react with carbonates.
5 It forms a white precipitate when ammonia is passed into it (ammonium chloride is insoluble in methylbenzene).

Clearly the acid system is hydrogen chloride plus water, which react to form oxonium ions, but not hydrogen chloride plus methylbenzene, which do not react at all. A more convenient way of demonstrating the effect of the solvent is to dissolve citric acid in propanone. The solution has little or no effect on blue litmus paper, magnesium or calcium carbonate. Now add water to the propanone solution; the solution has the usual acidic properties. Refer to p. 118.

Manufacture of hydrochloric acid

Hydrogen is burned in chlorine, and the gas is dissolved in water. The hydrogen and chlorine are obtained by the electrolysis of brine (Fig. 22.1). Hydrochloric acid is transported in steel tanks, which are lined inside with rubber. The acid reacts with exposed parts of the metal or with rust and forms iron(III) chloride, which makes the commercial acid yellow.

To carry out the tests for chlorides

Test for a soluble chloride. Dissolve a chloride in *distilled* water, add dilute nitric acid and silver nitrate solution. A white precipitate forms:

$$Ag^+(aq) + Cl^-(aq) \rightarrow AgCl(s), \text{ white}$$

The nitric acid prevents the precipitation of other insoluble silver salts (e.g. silver carbonate); compare the action of nitric acid in the test for sulphate (p. 255).

Divide the silver chloride precipitate into two parts. To one add excess aqueous ammonia; the precipitate dissolves. Leave the other in light for a few minutes; its colour becomes violet.

Action of concentrated sulphuric acid. Add concentrated sulphuric acid to a solid chloride in a *dry* test-tube. Hydrogen chloride is evolved:

$$H^+(aq) + Cl^-(s) \rightarrow HCl(g)$$

Blow gently across the mouth of the tube; the gas forms misty fumes. Bring the moist stopper of an aqueous ammonia bottle near; white fumes form.

Manganese(IV) oxide and concentrated sulphuric acid. Mix a solid chloride with manganese(IV) oxide powder in a dry test-tube. Add concentrated sulphuric acid and warm gently. Chlorine is formed (mixed with much hydrogen chloride). Hold damp neutral litmus in the mouth of the tube; the litmus turns red and then is bleached:

$$H_2SO_4(conc.) + NaCl(s) \rightarrow HCl(aq) + NaHSO_4(aq)$$

$$4HCl(aq) + MnO_2(s) \rightarrow Cl_2(g) + MnCl_2 + 2H_2O$$

Chlorine, Cl_2

Chlorine is formed when hydrochloric acid is oxidized. Potassium manganate(VII) oxidizes concentrated hydrochloric acid even when cold, but manganese(IV) oxide reacts only with the hot acid.

To prepare chlorine and chlorine water

Using potassium manganate(VII) or bleaching powder. Place solid potassium manganate(VII) (or bleaching powder) in a flask and arrange the apparatus as in Fig. 21.2.

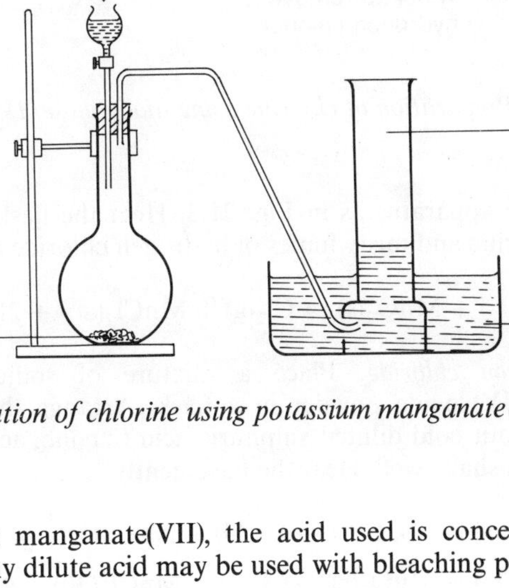

Fig. 21.2 Preparation of chlorine using potassium manganate(VII) or bleaching powder

With potassium manganate(VII), the acid used is concentrated hydrochloric acid; any dilute acid may be used with bleaching powder:

$$2Cl^-(aq) + 2e \text{ (from manganate)} \rightarrow Cl_2(g)$$

$$CaOCl_2(s) + 2H^+(aq) \rightarrow Cl_2(g) + Ca^{2+}(aq) + H_2O$$

Collect the gas over brine or hot water. If the gas is required dry, bubble it through two wash-bottles, one containing water (to remove hydrogen chloride) and the other containing concentrated sulphuric acid (Fig. 21.3), then collect by downward delivery. Also bubble the gas through water (preferably containing ice) to form yellowish *chlorine water*.

Using manganese (IV) oxide. Add concentrated hydrochloric acid to lumps of manganese(IV) oxide (powder is too reactive) in a flask.

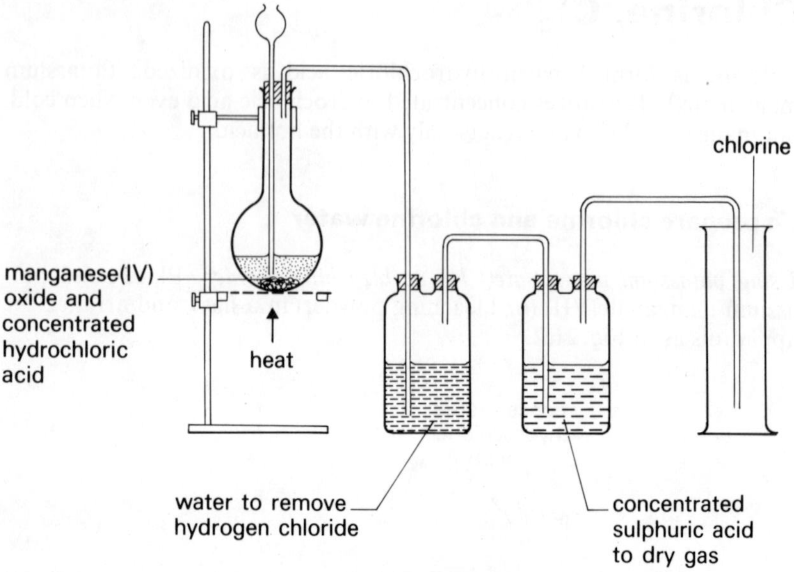

Fig. 21.3 Preparation of chlorine using manganese(IV) oxide

Arrange the apparatus as in Fig. 21.3. Heat the flask gently. Greenish-yellow chlorine and misty fumes of hydrogen chloride are evolved:

$$4HCl(conc.) + MnO_2(s) \rightarrow Cl_2(g) + MnCl_2(aq) + 2H_2O$$

Using sodium chloride. Place a mixture of sodium chloride with manganese(IV) oxide powder in a flask. Arrange the apparatus as in Fig. 21.3. Pour cold diluted sulphuric acid (2 conc. acid : 1 water) on the mixture and shake well. Heat the flask gently:

$$H_2SO_4(conc.) + NaCl(s) \rightarrow HCl(l) + NaHSO_4(aq)$$
$$4HCl(l) + MnO_2(s) \rightarrow Cl_2(g) + MnCl_2(aq) + 2H_2O$$

Using sodium chloride. Chlorine is conveniently prepared from a dry mixture of sodium chloride, sodium hydrogensulphate and potassium manganate(VII) in the ratio by mass of 3:6:1. Grind each reagent separately to a fine powder, and then mix well in a mortar. Gentle heating causes evolution of chlorine (in fact the mixture reacts slowly at room temperature). This method is most useful in a small-scale apparatus or test-tube for use by pupils because no corrosive acid is used.

By electrolysis. Electrolyse concentrated sodium chloride solution or concentrated hydrochloric acid. Chlorine is evolved at the anode, which must be of carbon, and hydrogen at the cathode.

Properties of chlorine

It is a greenish-yellow poisonous gas, which has a choking irritating smell and attacks the nose and lungs. It is fairly soluble in water (which dissolves about 3 times its volume of the gas) forming yellowish *chlorine water*, which contains hydrochloric acid and chloric(I) acid:

$$H_2O + Cl_2(g) \rightleftharpoons HCl(aq) + HClO(aq), \text{ chloric(I) acid}$$

It turns blue litmus red then bleaches it. The bleaching action is due to chloric(I) acid, and *dry chlorine does not bleach.* The gas does not burn and it extinguishes a burning splint. It is about $2\frac{1}{2}$ times denser than air (vapour density = 35.5). It is easily liquefied under pressure at ordinary temperatures and at −34 °C at 1 atmosphere.
Test for chlorine. It is a greenish-yellow gas which turns damp blue litmus paper red, then bleaches it.

Chlorine combining with the hydrogen of other compounds

Bleaching action. Add red and blue flowers and a piece of newspaper with ordinary ink on it to jars of moist chlorine. Also add them to a jar of chlorine dried with calcium chloride. Moist chlorine bleaches the colour of most dyes (but not of printers' ink, which is carbon). The bleaching is due to oxidation by chloric(I) acid, and therefore dry chlorine does not bleach:

$$HClO(aq) + \text{dye} \rightarrow HCl(aq) + (\text{dye} + O), \text{ colourless}$$

Chlorine water in sunlight. Place a long glass tube full of chlorine water in bright sunlight and leave for several hours. The yellowish chlorine water changes to colourless hydrochloric acid, and oxygen is formed by slow decomposition of chloric(I) acid:

$$Cl_2(aq) + H_2O \rightleftharpoons HCl(aq) + HClO(aq)$$

$$2HClO(aq) \rightarrow 2HCl(aq) + O_2(g)$$

Ammonia. Drop sodium hydroxide pellets into concentrated aqueous ammonia; pass ammonia gas which comes off through a delivery tube into chlorine. The ammonia burns spontaneously in the chlorine and is oxidized to nitrogen. The chlorine forms hydrogen chloride at first and this combines with excess ammonia to form white fumes of ammonium chloride. White fumes are also formed when concentrated aqueous ammonia is dropped into chlorine.

$$2NH_3(g) + 3Cl_2(g) \rightarrow N_2(g) + 6HCl(g)$$

$$NH_3(g) + HCl(g) \rightarrow NH_4Cl(s)$$

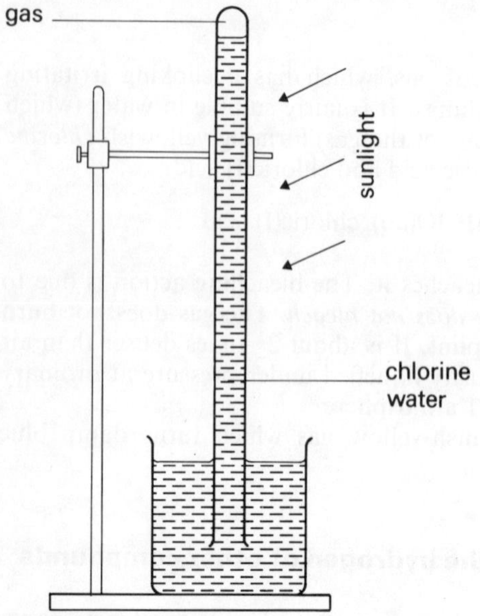

Fig. 21.4 Chlorine water in sunlight

Hydrogen sulphide. This is oxidized by chlorine gas or chlorine water to a yellowish precipitate of sulphur:

$$H_2S(g \text{ or } aq) + Cl_2(g \text{ or } aq) \rightarrow S(s) + 2HCl(g \text{ or } aq)$$

Action of metals and non-metals with chlorine

Fig. 21.5 shows two simple methods by which a metal or non-metal can be heated easily in chlorine and the product and reaction observed.
Fill the boiling-tube or syringe with chlorine in a fume cupboard and then heat the metal or non-metal until reaction starts.
Sodium, potassium, calcium and magnesium. The burning metals continue to burn, forming white fumes of the chlorides:

$$2Na(l) + Cl_2(g) \rightarrow 2NaCl(s); \quad Mg(s) + Cl_2(g) \rightarrow MgCl_2(s)$$

Iron. See p. 268.
Hydrogen. (Reactions between hydrogen and chlorine can be violent and must be demonstrated only.) Invert a boiling-tube of chlorine over a tube of hydrogen and mix the gases. Put a flame to one tube. The mixture explodes. It also explodes if placed in bright sunlight; it reacts slowly in

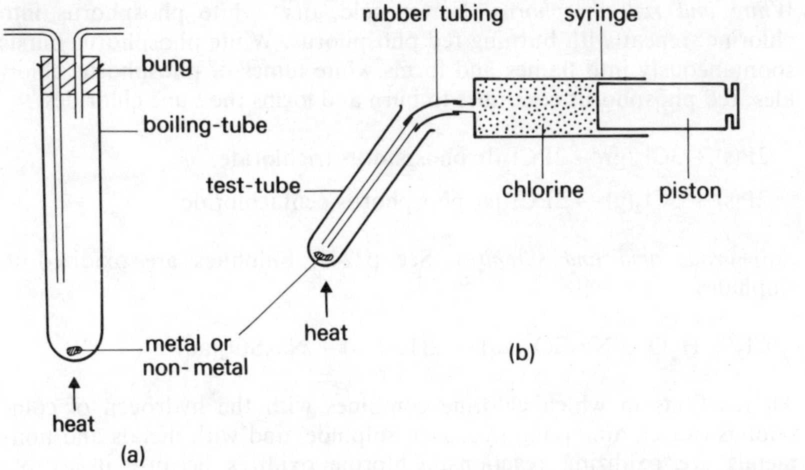

Fig. 21.5 Heating metals or non-metals in chlorine

diffused sunlight, and does not react in darkness. Burning hydrogen continues to burn quietly in chlorine, forming hydrogen chloride, Fig. 21.6:

$$H_2(g) + Cl_2(g) \rightarrow 2HCl(g)$$

These reactions show the great affinity of chlorine for hydrogen, and explain why it oxidizes many compounds.

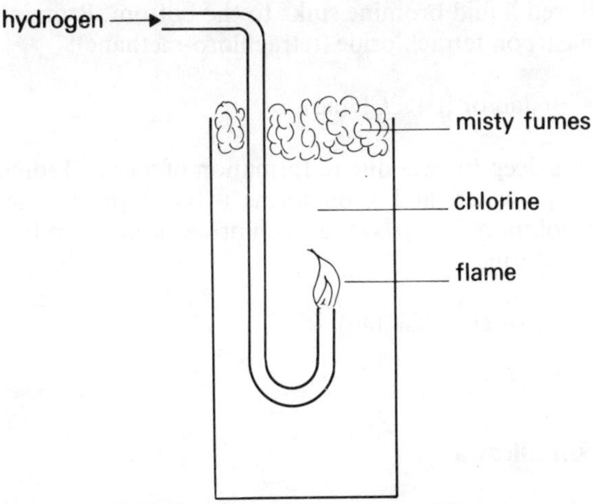

Fig. 21.6 Hydrogen burns in chlorine

White and red phosphorus. Lower cold, dry, white phosphorus into chlorine: repeat with burning red phosphorus. White phosphorus bursts spontaneously into flames and forms white fumes of phosphorus chlorides; red phosphorus continues to burn and forms the same chlorides:

$$2P(s) + 3Cl_2(g) \rightarrow 2PCl_3(l)\text{, phosphorus trichloride}$$

$$2P(s) + 5Cl_2(g) \rightarrow 2PCl_5(s)\text{, phosphorus pentachloride}$$

Sulphurous acid and sulphites. See p. 247. Sulphites are oxidized to sulphates:

$$Cl_2 + H_2O + Na_2SO_3(aq) \rightarrow 2HCl(aq) + Na_2SO_4(aq)$$

All reactions in which chlorine combines with the hydrogen of compounds (water, ammonia, hydrogen sulphide) and with metals and non-metals are oxidizing reactions. Chlorine oxidizes because it accepts electrons from substances:

$$Cl_2 + 2e \rightarrow 2Cl^-$$

Displacement reactions of chlorine

Potassium bromide and iodide. Bubble chlorine through saturated potassium bromide solution. Add carbon tetrachloride and shake. Repeat with potassium iodide solution. The bromide solution at first turns red, due to formation of bromine water; later the solution becomes saturated with bromine and dark-red liquid bromine sinks to the bottom. Bromine forms a red solution in carbon tetrachloride (tetrachloro-methane):

$$2Br^-(aq) + Cl_2(g) \rightarrow Br_2(aq\text{ or }l) + 2Cl^-(aq)$$

The iodide solution turns deep-brown, due to formation of iodine. Iodine is only slightly soluble in water, and soon forms a black precipitate. Iodine forms a violet solution in carbon tetrachloride. (Starch–iodide paper is turned blue by chlorine.)

$$2I^-(aq) + Cl_2(g) \rightarrow I_2(aq\text{ or }s) + 2Cl^-(aq)$$

Action of chlorine on alkalis

Cold dilute alkalis. Bubble chlorine slowly through cold dilute sodium hydroxide solution. The pale yellow solution smells of chlorine gas. It contains sodium chloride and *sodium chlorate(I)*:

$$2NaOH(aq) + Cl_2 \rightarrow NaCl(aq) + NaClO(aq) + H_2O$$

ionically, $$2OH^-(aq) + Cl_2 \rightarrow Cl^-(aq) + ClO^-(aq) + H_2O$$

Sodium chlorate(I) is used as a bleaching agent (it bleaches cloth, and removes ink stains from cloth and paper) and an antiseptic (it kills germs in the throat and mouth). Sodium chlorate(I) reacts with acids to form chlorine:

$$NaClO(aq) + 2HCl(aq) \rightarrow Cl_2(g) + NaCl(aq) + H_2O$$

Calcium hydroxide. Add it to a jar of chlorine. The colour and smell of the gas soon disappear, showing that it has been absorbed:

$$Ca(OH)_2(s) + Cl_2(g) \rightarrow H_2O + CaOCl_2(s), \text{ bleaching powder}$$

Since liquid chlorine is now readily available, bleaching powder is used less than it was some years ago. It smells of chlorine because the carbon dioxide in the air reacts with it:

$$CaOCl_2(s) + CO_2(g) \rightarrow Cl_2(g) + CaCO_3(s)$$

Uses of chlorine

Chlorine is a bleaching agent, a germicide, and a disinfectant. It is used to bleach cotton, linen and paper (but not wool, silk or straw, which it destroys). It kills cholera, typhoid and other germs in drinking water, so it is usually added to the water of reservoirs and to swimming baths. Hydrochloric acid is made by burning hydrogen in chlorine. Chlorine is used to manufacture the anaesthetic chloroform (trichloromethane), $CHCl_3$; the insecticides D.D.T. and Gammexane; antiseptics, e.g. T.C.P.; solvents, e.g. trichloroethene, C_2HCl_3, for removing grease from clothes. That is, chlorine or its compounds 'kills' colours, germs, pain, insect pests, and grease. It is also used in the manufacture of plastics.

To determine the formula of hydrogen chloride

The apparatus consists of two bulbs of equal volume. Fill bulb A with dry hydrogen and B with dry chlorine. Open the centre tap so that the gases mix. Leave the apparatus in diffused sunlight (the gases explode in direct sunlight) for two days. Place one end of the apparatus under mercury and open the tap; no gas escapes and no mercury enters. This

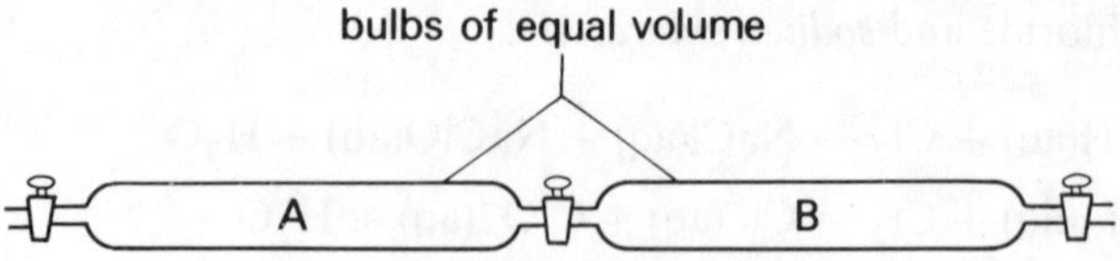

Fig. 21.7 Formula of hydrogen chloride

shows that the volume of residual gases is the same as that of the original gases. Close the tap. Now place one end of the apparatus under water containing potassium iodide and then open the tap. Water enters and fills both tubes completely, therefore all the hydrogen (insoluble) was used up. No brown colour due to iodine is seen, therefore all the chlorine was used up (chlorine liberates iodine from potassium iodide). The only product is the very soluble hydrogen chloride, which dissolves completely in the water.

1 volume of hydrogen + 1 volume of chlorine $\rightarrow$ 2 volumes of hydrogen chloride

Therefore, by Avogadro's Principle:

1 molecule of hydrogen + 1 molecule of chlorine $\rightarrow$ 2 molecules of hydrogen chloride

Hydrogen and chlorine are both diatomic, therefore

2 atoms of hydrogen + 2 atoms of chlorine $\rightarrow$ 2 molecules of hydrogen chloride

i.e. 1 atom of hydrogen + 1 atom of chlorine $\rightarrow$ 1 molecule of hydrogen chloride

The formula of hydrogen chloride is HCl.

To prepare iron(III) chloride by synthesis

Coil rust-free iron wire around a pencil. Place the coil in a combustion tube arranged as in Fig. 21.8. It should be in a fume cupboard or the excess chlorine should be dissolved in alkali. Pass dry chlorine to sweep air out of the apparatus. Heat the iron strongly and pass chlorine over it. Stop heating as soon as the iron starts to react; it glows red-hot. Warm the end of the combustion tube near the receiver; black crystals sublime into the bottle:

$$2Fe(s) + 3Cl_2(g) \rightarrow 2FeCl_3(s)$$

Some iron(III) chloride forms on the sides of the combustion tube. If warmed, it sublimes into the bottle.

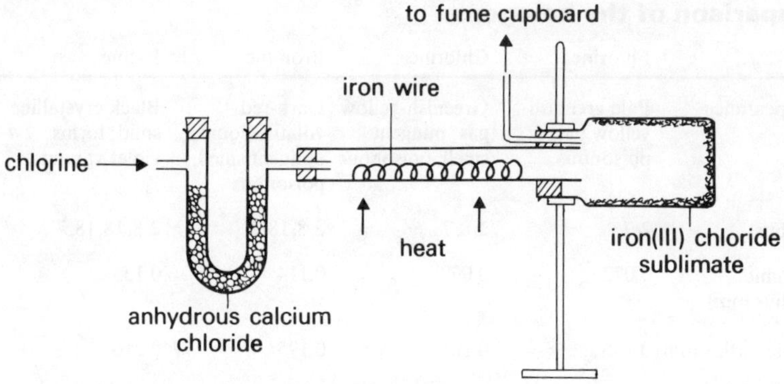

Fig. 21.8 Preparation of iron(III) chloride

Sodium chloride can be made in a similar way:

$2Na(l) + Cl_2(g) \rightarrow 2NaCl(s)$

Iron(II) chloride, a white solid, is made in the same way, using dry hydrogen chloride instead of chlorine:

$Fe(s) + 2HCl(g) \rightarrow FeCl_2(s) + H_2(g)$

Bromine and iodine, Br_2 and I_2

Occurrence and extraction

Bromides and iodides of sodium, potassium and magnesium are in sea-water. Bromine and iodine are also extracted from sea-water by acidifying with sulphuric acid and passing chlorine:

$2Br^-(aq) + Cl_2(g) \rightarrow Br_2(l) + 2Cl^-(aq)$

Some seaweeds contain iodides, from which the iodine is extracted by distillation with manganese(IV) oxide and concentrated sulphuric acid:

$NaI(s) + H_2SO_4(conc.) \rightarrow HI(aq) + NaHSO_4(aq)$

$4HI(aq) + MnO_2(s) \rightarrow I_2(g) + MnI_2 + 2H_2O$

Fluorine

Fluorine occurs as calcium fluoride (fluorspar), CaF_2, and sodium hexafluoraluminate (cryolite), Na_3AlF_6 (used in the extraction of aluminium). Bones and teeth contain fluorides.

Comparison of the halogens

	Fluorine	Chlorine	Bromine	Iodine
Appearance	Pale greenish-yellow gas; poisonous	Greenish-yellow gas; pungent smell, poisonous	Dark-red volatile liquid; pungent smell, poisonous	Black crystalline solid; forms violet vapour
Orbits	2,7	2,8,7	2,8,18,7	2,8,18,18,7
Atomic radius (nm)	0.072	0.099	0.114	0.133
Ionic radius (nm)	0.136	0.181	0.195	0.216
M.p. (°C)	−220	−101	−7	114 (but can sublime)
B.p. (°C)	−188	−34	58	183
Density (g/cm^3)	Gas	Gas	3.1	4.9
Water	Forms H_2O_2 and F_2O	Slightly soluble; forms acids, HCl and HClO; decomposes water in sunlight	Slightly soluble; forms acids, HBr and HBrO	Almost insoluble
Bleaching action	Very strong	Strong	Weak and slow	None
Hydrogen	Combines explosively	Combines explosively in sunlight	Combines only on heating; not explosive	Reacts slowly and reversibly
Oxidizing agent	Very strong	Strong	Fairly strong	Weak
Metals and non-metals	Combines vigorously (with even gold and platinum)	Reacts vigorously	Reacts moderately	Reacts least vigorously
Dilute alkalis	Forms fluorides and oxygen	Forms chlorides and chlorates(I)	Forms bromides and bromates(I)	Forms iodides and iodates(I)
Displacement reactions	Displaces other halogens from halides	Displaces bromine and iodine from bromides and iodides	Displaces iodine from iodides	None
Silver compound	White; soluble in water	White; insoluble; soluble in dilute aqueous ammonia	Pale-yellow; insoluble; slightly soluble in aqueous ammonia	Yellow; insoluble; insoluble in aqueous ammonia

Preparation. It can be obtained only by electrolysis. The electrolyte is potassium hydrogenfluoride, KHF_2, dissolved in hydrofluoric acid. The anodes must be carbon and the cell is a special alloy not attacked by fluorine.
Properties. Fluorine is a greenish-yellow, very poisonous gas (m.p. −220 °C; b.p. −188 °C). Many metals burn in it when heated gently. Hydrogen and fluorine combine explosively, and most other non-metals (except oxygen and nitrogen) combine to form fluorides, e.g. PF_5. Fluorine is the most electronegative element known. It displaces other halogens from aqueous solutions of their compounds:

$$2Cl^-(aq) + F_2(g) \rightarrow 2F^-(aq) + Cl_2(g)$$

It reacts with water:

$$2H_2O(l) + 2F_2(g) \rightarrow 4HF(aq) + O_2(g)$$

Fluorine compounds. Hydrogen fluoride is a liquid (b.p. 20 °C; m.p. −83 °C); other halogen halides are gases. Aqueous hydrofluoric acid is a weak acid, unlike the other halogen acids. Silver fluoride is soluble in water and calcium fluoride is insoluble.
Uses. Calcium fluoride is used in the iron industry (to make the slag more fluid and easier to remove from molten iron) and in glass melting (it lowers the melting temperature). Sodium fluoride is in wood preservatives because it kills fungi. Fluorides are added to some water supplies and toothpastes to reduce tooth decay. Hydrofluoric acid is used to etch glass. Some refrigerants and lubricants contain fluorine compounds.

Questions

1 Describe how you would prepare and collect some gas-jars of dry hydrogen chloride. How would you show experimentally that hydrogen chloride (*a*) contains hydrogen, (*b*) is very soluble in water? Describe one experiment in each case with hydrochloric acid to show (*c*) how it can act as a reducing agent, (*d*) how it may be identified. (L.)

2 Draw labelled diagrams of apparatus used to prepare from common salt (*a*) hydrogen chloride, (*b*) hydrochloric acid. What is the action of hydrochloric acid on (*c*) chalk, (*d*) manganese(IV) oxide, (*e*) silver nitrate solution? (L.)

3 How would you prepare from hydrochloric acid fairly pure specimens of (*a*) potassium chloride, (*b*) silver chloride? Describe and explain the action on chlorides of (*a*) concentrated sulphuric acid, (*b*) concentrated sulphuric acid in the presence of manganese(IV) oxide. (C.)

4 What is the action of hydrochloric acid on (*a*) manganese(IV) oxide, (*b*) iron(II) sulphide, (*c*) egg-shells, (*d*) red lead oxide, Pb_3O_4, and (*e*) bleaching powder? Describe all the visible changes, and give equations for all reactions. (C.)

5 Describe one method for the industrial production of chlorine. Describe the reaction of chlorine with (*a*) dry calcium hydroxide, (*b*) potassium iodide solution. Describe the changes which occur when chlorine is passed through water and the solution is left exposed to sunlight. How would you identify the final products? (O.)

6 Describe fully one good laboratory method of preparing and collecting chlorine. Give a different experiment in each case to show that chlorine (*a*) supports combustion, (*b*) can act as an oxidizing agent, (*c*) will react with a compound containing hydrogen. (N.)

7 Starting with common salt, how would you obtain in the laboratory (*a*) a few jars of hydrogen chloride, (*b*) a few jars of chlorine? Explain the bleaching action of chlorine and contrast it with the bleaching action of sulphur dioxide. (L.)

8 Draw labelled diagrams to show two separate methods of obtaining chlorine from sodium chloride. Give three uses of chlorine. Write equations for the action of chlorine on (*a*) sulphurous acid, (*b*) hydrogen sulphide, (*c*) iron(II) chloride. (O.)

9 Describe how you would prepare in the laboratory samples of (*a*) bleaching powder, (*b*) a solution containing sodium chlorate(I), in each case starting with chlorine. Mention the uses of each of these substances. (N.)

10 Bromine is a volatile, corrosive liquid which is liable to attack rubber and cork, and which has chemical properties similar to those of chlorine. Describe in detail how you would attempt to obtain a sample of bromine from potassium bromide, giving a careful account of the apparatus you would use. (L.)

22 Metals and Non-metals

Electronic nature of metals and non-metals

The essential difference between metals and non-metals is their affinity for electrons. *A metal is an element (except hydrogen) which forms positive ions by losing electrons; a non-metal is an element which forms negative ions by gaining electrons.*

Compare the electron configurations of metals and non-metals with those of noble gases:

Non-metals		Noble gases	Metals	
O 2.6	F 2.7	Ne 2.8	Na 2.8.1	Mg 2.8.2
S 2.8.6	Cl 2.8.7	Ar 2.8.8	K 2.8.8.1	Ca 2.8.8.2

Most metals have 1–3 electrons more than a noble gas; most non-metals have 1–4 electrons less than a noble gas. Metals therefore react by electron loss, forming ionic compounds; non-metals combine either by electron gain, forming ionic compounds, or by sharing electrons, forming covalent compounds.

Physical properties of metals and non-metals

Metals	Non-metals
Lustrous; can be polished	Not lustrous; cannot be polished
Strong and tough; high tensile strength	Low tensile strength
Malleable, i.e. can be made into sheets	Not malleable
Ductile, i.e. can be drawn into wire	Not ductile
Solids with high melting points (e.g. iron, 1539 °C or 1812 K)	About half are gases; the solids have low melting points (e.g. white phosphorus 44 °C, sulphur 120 °C) and low boiling points
High density (e.g. mercury 13.6 g/cm^3)	Low density (e.g. sulphur 2 g/cm^3; many are gases)
Good conductors of heat and electricity	Poor conductors
Sonorous, i.e. make a sound when hit	Not sonorous

Exceptional physical properties. Mercury is a liquid metal (m.p. −39 °C or 234 K). The metals sodium and potassium have low densities, 0.97 and 0.86 g/cm^3, and float on water; their melting points are low (Na 98 °C or 371 K, K 63 °C or 336 K); and they are soft enough to be cut by a knife. The non-metal carbon has a high melting point (about 3700 °C) and its allotrope graphite is a shiny solid and a good conductor of electricity.

It is easy to account for some of these physical properties. Many *non-metals* form diatomic molecules (H_2, O_2, Cl_2, N_2). Intermolecular forces between these molecules are relatively small and the elements are gases at normal temperatures. The exceptions are a liquid (Br_2) or a volatile solid (I_2). Non-metals which form larger molecules (S_8 and P_4) are less volatile. Carbon atoms in graphite form giant molecules of large area and in diamond giant molecules of large volume; in these non-metals, melting and boiling involve the breaking of chemical bonds and therefore melting and boiling points are high. Solid *metals* consist of closely packed ions (cations) held together by mobile electrons, p. 103. It is difficult to separate the ionic structure, which resembles that of ionic compounds such as sodium chloride, and melting and boiling points are usually high.

Many metals consist of layers of ions which can easily slip over one another. Therefore metals are malleable and ductile. The mobile electrons in metals can carry an electric current and also heat energy; metals are therefore good conductors.

Chemical properties of metals and non-metals

Metals	Non-metals
Oxides are basic	Oxides are usually acidic; some are neutral
Displace hydrogen from dilute acids	Do not react with dilute acids
Do not usually combine with hydrogen	Form stable hydrides with hydrogen
Chlorides are ionic (i.e. non-volatile, electrolytes, soluble in and not hydrolysed by water)	Chlorides are covalent (i.e. volatile, non-electrolytes, and hydrolysed by water)
Reducing agents	Oxidizing agents

Oxides. Metallic oxides are ionic and contain oxide ions O^{2-} formed by transfer of electrons from metal to oxygen. They are basic oxides and some (e.g. Na_2O, CaO, MgO) react with water to form alkalis:

$$O^{2-}(s) + H_2O(l) \rightarrow 2OH^-(aq)$$

Non-metallic oxides are covalent and do not contain oxide ions. Usually they are acid anhydrides:

$$CO_2(g) + H_2O(l) \rightleftharpoons H_2CO_3(aq) \rightleftharpoons 2H^+(aq) + CO_3^{2-}(aq)$$

A few non-metallic oxides (CO, N_2O, NO) are neutral.
Action on dilute acids. Acids contain hydrogen ions $H^+(aq)$. Metals can transfer electrons to these ions, forming hydrogen and metallic ions:

$$Zn(s) + 2H^+(aq) \rightarrow Zn^{2+}(aq) + H_2(g)$$

Metals below hydrogen in the reactivity series (e.g. Cu, Hg) cannot do this. Non-metals form ions by gaining electrons and cannot transfer electrons to hydrogen ions.
Combination with hydrogen. A hydrogen atom readily shares its single electron with another atom, forming a covalent bond. Non-metals can reach the noble gas configuration by sharing electrons; they do this with hydrogen and form stable hydrides, e.g. H_2S, NH_3.

Metal atoms tend to lose and not to share electrons and therefore rarely form hydrides. The very electropositive metals (K, Na, Ca) lose electrons so easily that they can transfer them to hydrogen and form hydrides (KH, NaH, CaH_2). In these, the hydrogen is a negative ion, H^-. Hydrogen forms at the anode when these molten hydrides are electrolysed.
Chlorides. The chlorine atom (2.8.7) needs 1 electron to complete its outer octet. Metal atoms transfer electrons to chlorine atoms and form ionic chlorides:

$$\underset{2.8.1}{Na} + \underset{2.8.7}{Cl} \rightarrow (\underset{2.8}{Na^+} + \underset{2.8.8}{Cl^-})$$

The chlorides are non-volatile and are electrolytes.

Non-metals share electrons with chlorine, forming covalent chlorides, which are hydrolysed by water:

$$PCl_3(l) + 3H_2O \rightarrow 3HCl(g) + H_3PO_3(aq), \text{ phosphorous acid}$$

Carbon tetrachloride (tetrachloromethane), CCl_4, is an exception because it is not hydrolysed by water.
Oxidizing and reducing agents. Metals supply electrons and therefore are reducing agents; non-metals accept electrons and therefore are oxidizing agents:

$$Na \rightarrow Na^+ + e; \quad Cl_2 + 2e \rightarrow 2Cl^-$$

Extraction of metals

The reactivity or electrochemical series is a valuable guide in the study of metals and their compounds. Only gold, silver, mercury and copper, unreactive metals near the bottom of the series, occur naturally. All other metals occur as compounds in mineral ores. The method of extraction depends on the stability of the ore. Mercury (near the bottom of the activity series) is obtained simply by heating its sulphide ore. Metals in the middle of the series (Pb, Sn, Fe, Zn) are obtained by reducing their oxides with coke or carbon monoxide. Coke is cheap but contaminates the metal. The sulphide or carbonate ores are first converted to oxides. Aluminium oxide is so stable that it has to be reduced electrolytically. Metals at the top of the series (Mg, Ca, and Na) are obtained by electrolysis of their chlorides.

The *extraction of metals is a reduction* process. The metals are in their ores as positive ions and are extracted by supplying the ions with electrons. Coke combines with oxide ions of oxides to release electrons; the cathode supplies electrons to the metallic ions during electrolysis:

$$(Zn^{2+} + O^{2-}) + C(s) \rightarrow Zn(g) + CO(g)$$

$$Na^{+}(l) + e \rightarrow Na(l) \text{ (at the cathode)}$$

Metal	Chief ores	Extraction
K	Chloride, $KCl \cdot MgCl_2 \cdot 6H_2O$	Electrolysis of fused chloride
Na	Rock salt, $NaCl$	
	Chile saltpetre, $NaNO_3$	
Ca	Chalk, limestone, marble, $CaCO_3$	Electrolysis of fused chlorides
	Gypsum, $CaSO_4 \cdot 2H_2O$	
	Anhydrite, $CaSO_4$	
	Carbonate, $CaCO_3 \cdot MgCO_3$	
Mg	Chloride, $KCl \cdot MgCl_2 \cdot 6H_2O$	
	Carbonate, $CaCO_3 \cdot MgCO_3$	
	Carbonate, $MgCO_3$	
Al	Bauxite, $Al_2O_3 \cdot 2H_2O$	Electrolysis of oxide
	Cryolite, Na_3AlF_6	
	Clays and rocks	
Zn	Zinc sulphide, ZnS	Reduction of oxide by carbon or carbon monoxide
	Zinc carbonate, $ZnCO_3$	
Fe	Oxide, Fe_2O_3	
	Oxide, Fe_3O_4	
	Iron(II) carbonate, $FeCO_3$	
	Iron disulphide (pyrites), FeS_2	
Sn	Tin(IV) oxide, SnO_2	
Pb	Lead(II) sulphide, PbS	
Cu	Copper pyrites, $CuFeS_2$	Roast in air
Hg	Mercury(II) sulphide, HgS	Heat ore

Alkali metals

These include lithium, sodium and potassium, with electron configurations 2,1, 2,8,1, and 2,8,8,1 respectively in group 1 of the Periodic Table. An alkali metal atom has 1 electron in its outer orbit, and it readily loses this electron to form an ion, X^+, which has a stable noble gas configuration, e.g. Li^+(2), Na^+(2.8) and K^+(2.8.8).

Lithium

Lithium is an alkali metal with the electron configuration 2,1. Its properties differ substantially from those of sodium and potassium; this is often true of the first member (period 2 of the Periodic Table) of a family of elements.

Air. Heat a tiny piece of lithium (about 1 mm^3) on a piece of broken porcelain held by tongs. The lithium burns with a dazzling flame (like magnesium), forming Li_2O.

Water. Add a tiny piece of lithium to water in a beaker. Reaction is slow. Hydrogen is evolved and the hydroxide, LiOH, forms.

Chlorine. Repeat the test as with sodium, p. 264. Lithium burns to form the chloride, LiCl.

The table below summarizes the similarities and differences between the three alkali metals. The lithium ion is much smaller than the other

	Lithium	Sodium	Potassium
M.p. (°C)	186	98	63
Density (g/cm^3)	0.53	0.97	0.86
Atomic radius (nm)	0.152	0.186	0.231
Ionic radius (nm)	0.06	0.095	0.133
Salts	Most are hydrated		Few are hydrated
Water	Reacts slowly	Vigorous reaction	Explosive reaction
Hydroxide	Fairly soluble (5 M) Moderate alkali	9.5 M Strong alkali	Most soluble (12 M) Strong alkali
	Decomposes above 650 °C	Very stable	Very stable
Carbonate	Anhydrous. Fairly soluble (0.2 M)	Hydrated. 0.8 M	Hydrated. Most soluble (5.3 M)
	Do not decompose in hot bunsen flame.		
Hydrogencarbonate	Only in solution	Solid	Solid
Nitrate	Decomposes below red heat	Decomposes at red heat	Decomposes at bright red heat
	All form nitrite and oxygen first; lithium nitrite decomposes readily forming brown fumes (NO_2).		
Fluoride	Slightly soluble	Soluble	Soluble

ions, and this accounts for several differences. For example, in lithium hydroxide the small Li^+ has a greater attractive force for OH^- than the larger Na^+ and K^+ ions; hence LiOH is not completely ionized and it is not a strong alkali. Similarly, lithium hydroxide and nitrate decompose more easily on heating than the sodium and potassium compounds; the small Li^+ ion attracts electrons of the OH^- and NO_3^- ions and tends to make these groups less stable. The M concentrations given are for saturated solutions at room temperature.

Potassium and sodium

Manufacture of sodium and chlorine

From molten sodium chloride. This compound is the natural source of sodium, is abundant, almost pure, and very cheap. Sodium is obtained by electrolysis of fused sodium chloride (m.p. 808 °C). At first there were four difficulties: (i) it was expensive to keep the electrolyte over 800 °C, (ii) the molten chloride was corrosive, (iii) sodium is fairly soluble in its molten chloride, and (iv) the vapour pressure of sodium at 800 °C is about 400 mmHg.

The difficulties were all overcome by adding calcium chloride to the sodium chloride to form a mixture that melts below 600 °C. It is cheaper to maintain this temperature, the mixture is non-corrosive, the sodium is almost insoluble and its vapour pressure is about 15 mmHg. Fig. 22.1 shows the cell. The iron gauze cylinder between anode and cathode

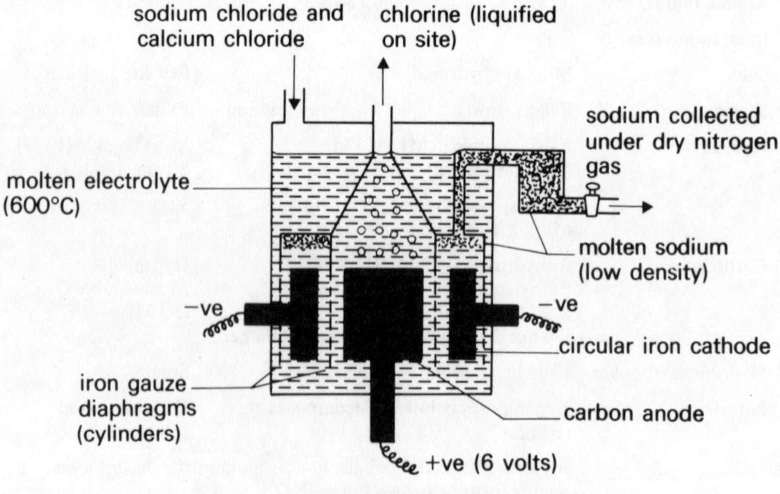

Fig. 22.1 Manufacture of sodium from sodium chloride

prevents the sodium and chlorine mixing. Liquid sodium leaves the cell in a riser pipe high enough for the low density metal but not high enough for the higher density chloride mixture to overflow continuously into a receiver. The process is continuous and a cell lasts about one year.

The reactions are:
$NaCl(l) \rightarrow Na^+(l) + Cl^-(l)$

At the cathode: $Na^+(l) + e \rightarrow Na(l)$

At the anode: $Cl^-(l) - e \rightarrow Cl; 2Cl \rightarrow Cl_2(g)$

Properties of potassium and sodium

They are soft metals with a silver lustre when freshly cut. Their tensile strengths, melting points and densities are low for metals. Potassium is the more active of the metals, which are at the top of the reactivity series.
Air. The metals tarnish rapidly because a film of oxide forms. Water vapour converts this to hydroxide, which slowly absorbs carbon dioxide. The final product is *solid* sodium carbonate or potassium carbonate *solution* (potassium carbonate is deliquescent):

$$4Na(s) + O_2(g) \rightarrow 2Na_2O(s)$$

$$Na_2O(s) + H_2O(l) \rightarrow 2NaOH(aq)$$

$$2NaOH(aq) + CO_2(g) \rightarrow Na_2CO_3(s) + H_2O(l)$$

The metals are stored under liquid paraffin or kerosine. Sodium burns in air or oxygen with a bright yellow flame, forming mainly the yellow peroxide Na_2O_2; the oxide Na_2O is formed in limited air or oxygen. Potassium burns with a lilac flame, forming a deep yellow oxide, KO_2.
Water. The metals react vigorously and displace hydrogen pp. 54–5.
Other reactions. The heated metals combine readily with chlorine and hydrogen:

$2Na(l) + H_2(g) \rightarrow 2NaH(s)$, sodium hydride

Sodium and potassium react with mercury to form amalgams, which react quietly with water to form hydrogen and sodium hydroxide.

Uses of potassium and sodium

The low melting point and high heat conductivity of sodium metal accounts for its use to 'cool' the fuel in nuclear energy reactors, e.g. to transfer heat from the reactor to a boiler in which steam is produced. A sodium–potassium alloy (m.p. $-11\,°C$) containing about 50 per cent of each metal is liquid at room temperature and is used as a 'coolant' in some reactors.

Electrolysis of concentrated sodium chloride (brine)

At the anode. Cl^- and OH^- ions both move there. The concentration of Cl^- ions is so great that they are preferentially discharged even though they are higher in the electrochemical series. They transfer electrons to the anode and become atoms, which combine to form molecules;

$$Cl^-(aq) - e \rightarrow Cl; 2Cl \rightarrow Cl_2(g)$$

Two electrons transferred by the cathode produce H_2 from $2H^+$, and 2 electrons transferred to the anode produce Cl_2 from Cl^-, i.e. the volumes of gases are equal.
Result. Hydrogen forms at the cathode and an equal volume of chlorine at the anode. Sodium hydroxide forms around the cathode. The final change is:

$$2NaCl(aq) + 2H_2O \rightarrow H_2(g) + Cl_2(g) + 2NaOH(aq)$$

Electrolysis of concentrated sodium chloride (mercury cathode)

The ions and action at the anode are as above.
At the mercury cathode. Na^+ and H^+ ions both move there. Na^+ ions are preferentially discharged even though they are higher in the electrochemical series. Sodium and mercury form sodium amalgam (which can react with water to form sodium hydroxide, hydrogen and mercury).

Manufacture of sodium hydroxide (chlorine and hydrogen)

Mercury cathode cell. The anode is carbon rods, which are not attacked by chlorine. The cathode is a stream of mercury which flows slowly across the bottom of the cell. The sodium amalgam formed drops into

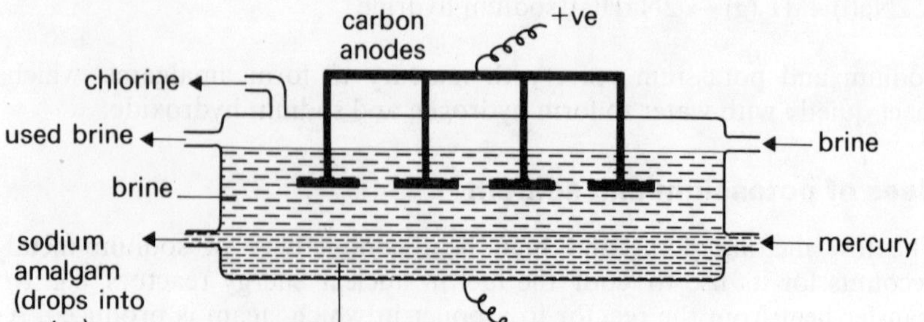

Fig. 22.2 Manufacture of sodium hydroxide (mercury cathode cell)

water and forms sodium hydroxide, hydrogen, and mercury, which is used again. The reaction between the amalgam and water is made very rapid by a carbon or metal strip touching the amalgam. The strip acts as a cathode and the amalgam as the anode of a 'cell', and since the electrodes are touching, the cell is short-circuited.

The sodium hydroxide solution is evaporated to dryness and the molten substance solidifies as sticks or pellets. The chlorine is dried, liquefied and stored. The hydrogen is collected or converted into synthetic hydrogen chloride by burning it with chlorine.

Calcium

Calcium and magnesium are in group 2 of the Periodic Table, with electron configurations 2.8.8.2 and 2.8.2 respectively. Each atom readily loses the two electrons in its outer orbit to form an ion X^{2+}, which has a stable noble gas configuration.

Properties of calcium

It is a soft, greyish metal. Its strength and density (1.55 g/cm^3) are low. Its melting point is 850 °C or 1123 K.
Air. The metal tarnishes rapidly. A white film of oxide forms first and reacts with water vapour to form hydroxide, $Ca(OH)_2$. Calcium burns with a red flame, forming oxide, CaO.
Water. It reacts quietly forming hydrogen, p. 56.
Other reactions. Heated calcium combines readily with chlorine and hydrogen, forming the chloride and hydride, CaH_2 (compare sodium and potassium).

Calcium sulphate occurs naturally as *anhydrite*, $CaSO_4$, and the 2-water hydrate (*gypsum*), $CaSO_4 \cdot 2H_2O$. On heating gypsum carefully it forms *plaster of Paris* $(CaSO_4)_2 \cdot H_2O$. This combines with water and sets to a hard mass of gypsum and expands slightly. It is therefore used for setting broken bones to ensure correct healing, and for making cements and plasters.

Calcium oxide (quicklime) and calcium hydroxide (slaked lime)

Lime (or quicklime) is a white solid (m.p. 2600 °C). It is hygroscopic, and in air it slowly forms calcium hydroxide:

$$CaO(s) + H_2O(g) \rightarrow Ca(OH)_2(s)$$

When water is added drop by drop to a lump of lime, heat is evolved, there is a hissing sound as the water touches the lime, and steam is formed. The lime swells and finally crumbles to a powder whose volume

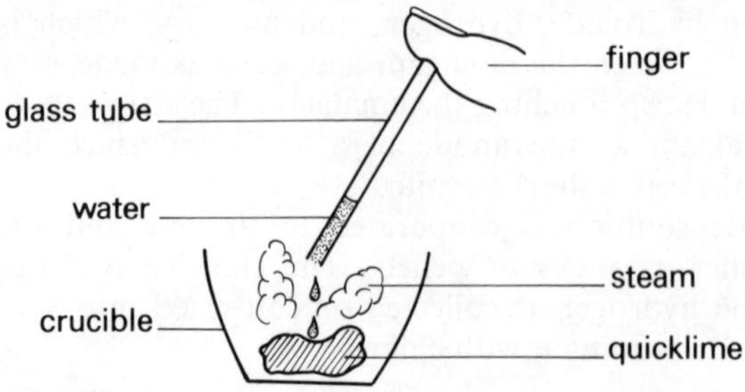

Fig. 22.3 Water on calcium oxide (quicklime or lime)

is much greater than that of the original lime. Slaked lime dissolves slightly and forms *limewater*. A milky suspension of limewater and solid slaked lime is *milk of lime*.

Manufacture of lime (quicklime)

Lime is made from limestone or chalk, which is mixed with coke and dropped into a lime-kiln. The coke burns and the heat decomposes the carbonate:

$$CaCO_3(s) \rightarrow CaO(s) + CO_2(g)$$

The lime sinks to the bottom of the kiln and is removed. The process is continuous and more carbonate and coke are added at the top as required. The lime is not pure because it contains ash left by the coke.

In a second method, coke is burnt separately in an oven at the side of the kiln, Fig. 22.4. Limestone or chalk is added to the kiln. The heat of

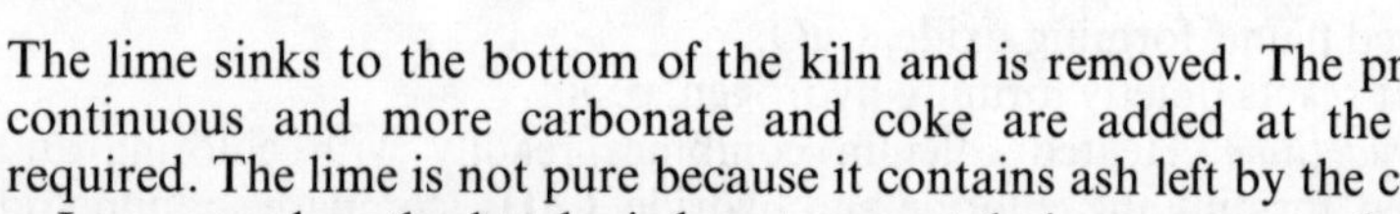

Fig. 22.4 Lime-kilns

the burning coke decomposes the carbonate. Lime made by this method contains no ash.

In a third method, producer gas is used as a fuel instead of coke. The gas burns and heats the carbonate. No ash is formed, and so the product is a pure lime.

Uses of calcium oxide and hydroxide (lime and slaked lime)

1 *Whitewash*. This is a suspension of slaked lime in water used to mark sports fields and brushed on walls of buildings. In a few days this absorbs carbon dioxide from the air and changes to calcium carbonate.

2 *Mortar*. This is a mixture of slaked lime, sand and water. It is used to stick bricks together and to form a smooth surface on walls of buildings. The water evaporates and leaves a hard, dry mixture of sand and calcium hydroxide. The sand makes the mixture porous, and air can slowly pass into it. Carbon dioxide of the air reacts slowly with the calcium hydroxide and forms calcium carbonate. The change may takes months or years. New mortar is calcium hydroxide and sand; old mortar is calcium carbonate and sand. Mortar dissolves in rain-water, and therefore that on outer walls of buildings gradually wears away.

3 *Cement and concrete*. Cement is a mixture of calcium silicates and aluminates made by heating lime or limestone and clay (hydrated aluminium silicate). Concrete is a mixture of cement, sand, stones, and water; it becomes very hard. Cement turns hard even under water.

4 *Soil treatment*. Lime is sometimes spread on soil to make plants or grass grow better. Most tropical soils need it because heavy rains soon dissolve the lime in them. Lime has a good effect on clay soils. Such soils do not let water pass easily through them because the tiny clay particles form a solid mass. Lime makes the particles form bigger ones, which are more porous. Show the action of lime on clay soils as follows. Shake dry powdered clay with water until it forms a cloudy liquid. Put the liquid into two glass bottles and add lime to one; the clay settles more quickly in this bottle.

5 *Softening water*. See p. 194.

6 *Drying agent*. It is used to dry ammonia and ethanol.

7 *Calcium dicarbide*. Made by strongly heating calcium oxide and coke in an electric furnace:

$$CaO(s) + 3C(s) \rightarrow CaC_2(s) + CO(g)$$

With water, it forms ethyne (acetylene), C_2H_2, which is used in the manufacture of organic compounds.

8 *Glass* is made by heating sand, sodium carbonate and lime or limestone. It is a mixture of sodium and calcium silicates.

Uses of calcium carbonate (chalk, limestone and marble)

1 *Lime*. Made from limestone or chalk.
2 *Buildings*. Marble can be polished until it has a smooth shining surface. It is used in buildings to make them attractive. In some countries, the walls of houses and other buildings are lumps of limestone.
3 *Roads*. Sometimes made from limestone. Small pieces are covered with tar, which sticks them together. They form a hard smooth surface which can last for several years.
4 *Putty*. Limestone mixed with linseed oil. It is used around windows to help retain them in position.

Magnesium

Extraction

It is made by electrolysis of fused anhydrous magnesium chloride mixed with chlorides of potassium, sodium and calcium. The temperature of the molten mixture is about 730 °C. A graphite anode and iron cathode are used. Chlorine forms at the anode and magnesium at the cathode. The molten metal (m.p. 650 °C or 923 K) rises to the surface, which is covered with inert gas to prevent oxidation (Fig. 22.5):

$Mg^{2+}(l) + 2e \rightarrow Mg(l)$ (at the cathode)

$2Cl^{-}(l) - 2e \rightarrow Cl_2(g)$ (at the graphite anode)

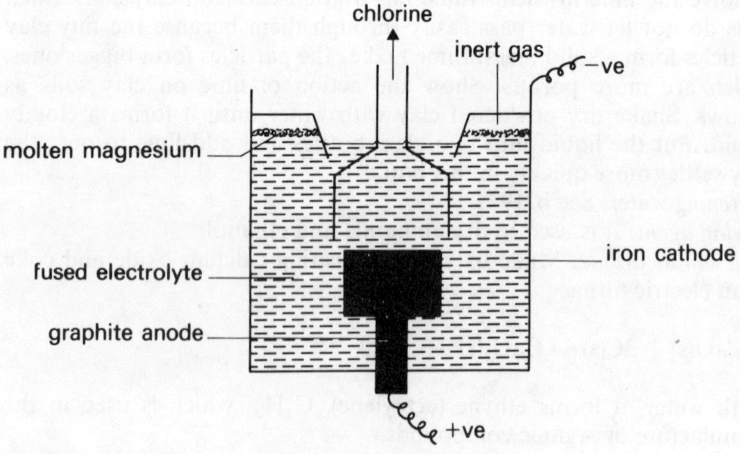

Fig. 22.5 Extraction of magnesium

Nowadays, much magnesium chloride for electrolysis is obtained from sea-water. The magnesium salts are precipitated as hydroxide or carbonate and then converted to chloride.

Properties of magnesium

Magnesium is a silvery lustrous metal. Its density (1.74 g/cm^3) is low, but its other physical properties are metallic.

Air. The metal tarnishes due to formation of an oxide film. This prevents further action, and therefore magnesium corrodes less than iron. The heated metal burns with a brilliant light, forming white oxide, p. 29.

Water. Magnesium reacts very slowly because a film of hydroxide stops further action. It reacts slowly with warm water, p. 56. The heated metal burns in steam and oxide is formed (the temperature is too high for the hydroxide to exist), p. 57.

Acids. Magnesium displaces hydrogen from dilute acids, and even from very dilute nitric acid, p. 48.

Other reactions. Magnesium burns in carbon dioxide, sulphur dioxide, chlorine and the oxides of nitrogen:

$$2Mg(s) + CO_2(g) \rightarrow 2MgO(s) + C(s);$$

$$Mg(s) + N_2O(g) \rightarrow MgO(s) + N_2(g)$$

Uses of magnesium

Photographic flash powders are mixtures of magnesium with oxidizing agents, e.g. potassium chlorate. Incendiary bombs contain the metal. Its low density makes it useful in light, tough alloys; unlike magnesium, the alloys do not burn easily.

Duralumin is mainly aluminium with some magnesium, copper, etc., and is used in aircraft and in moving parts of machinery.

Aluminium

Occurrence and extraction

Seven per cent of the earth's crust is aluminium; it is the third most plentiful element (after oxygen and silicon) and the second most important (after iron) in consumption. Most rocks and clays are aluminium silicates, but the metal cannot yet be extracted cheaply from these.

Aluminium is extracted by electrolysis of its oxide, Al_2O_3, which occurs as hydrated aluminium oxide (*bauxite*), $Al_2O_3 \cdot 2H_2O$. Aluminium chloride sublimes (m.p. 180 °C or 453 °C at 2.5 atm) and cannot be electrolysed (unlike chlorides of sodium, calcium and magnesium).

Bauxite is purified to remove impurities and then heated to remove water. The anhydrous oxide is dissolved in fused sodium hexafluoroaluminate (*cryolite*), Na_3AlF_6, in a steel tank lined with carbon, the cathode. Carbon anodes dip into the electrolyte. Aluminium forms at the cathode and the molten metal (m.p. 660 °C) collects at the bottom of the tank because it is denser than the electrolyte (2.3 and 2.1 g/cm^3 respectively at 1000 °C). Oxygen forms at the anode and burns away the carbon to carbon monoxide:

$Al^{3+}(l) + 3e \rightarrow Al(l)$ (at the cathode)

$2O^{2-}(l) - 4e \rightarrow O_2(g)$ (at the anode)

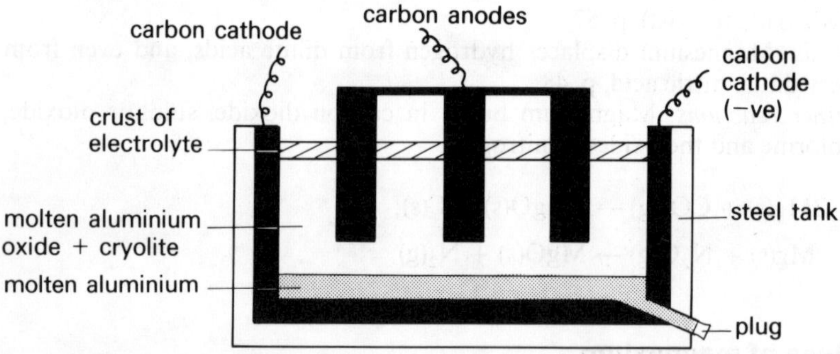

Fig. 22.6 Extraction of aluminium

Fig. 22.6 shows the electrolytic cell, and it is also a furnace. It is first filled with cryolite, and when the anodes are lowered on to this, a current (about 100 000 amperes) flows and melts the cryolite (m.p. 1000 °C). Then the anhydrous aluminium oxide is added, dissolves, and decomposes electrolytically.

Continuous process. The above cell must be stopped occasionally to replace the anodes. In a more modern cell, the anode is a block of carbon, and as it is oxidized at the bottom, a carbon paste is added to the top of the block and the process is continuous.

Properties of aluminium

Aluminium is a silvery white metal. Its tensile strength and density (2.7 g/cm^3) are fairly low.

Air. A thin film of oxide forms and prevents further action. The metal burns when heated strongly, forming oxide, Al_2O_3.

Water. Although high in the activity series, aluminium hardly reacts with water because the oxide film on its surface stops reaction. The film can be removed by rubbing with mercury; the aluminium then corrodes so rapidly in moist air that it becomes hot; aluminium hydroxide is formed. Aluminium also corrodes near the sea because sodium chloride in the atmosphere attacks the oxide film. See p. 153.
Acids. Aluminium displaces hydrogen slowly from dilute hydrochloric acid and quickly from the concentrated acid. The powder reacts similarly with warm dilute sulphuric acid. Dilute and concentrated nitric acid have no apparent action. Aluminium containers can therefore be used to transport and store nitric acid.
Alkalis. Aqueous sodium and potassium hydroxides react and form sodium or potassium aluminate and hydrogen:

$$2Al(s) + 2OH^-(aq) + 6H_2O \rightarrow 3H_2(g) + 2Al(OH)_4^-(aq), \text{ aluminate ion}$$

The formula of sodium aluminate is $NaAl(OH)_4$, sometimes written $NaAlO_2$, (by removing $2H_2O$).

Washing soda (sodium carbonate) is alkaline and must not be used to clean aluminium vessels.

Aluminium sulphate, $Al_2(SO_4)_3 \cdot 18H_2O$, forms the anhydrous salt when heated cautiously. It forms *alums*, e.g. aluminium potassium sulphate-12-water, $AlK(SO_4)_2 \cdot 12H_2O$. Other alums have sodium or ammonium in place of the potassium, and iron(III) or chromium(III) in place of the aluminium. Alums can form large crystals.

Uses of aluminium

Aluminium is used for making objects that must be as light as possible, e.g. parts of aeroplanes, railway trains and trucks, buses, lorries, tankers, furniture and cars, etc. Pure aluminium is not strong; its alloys are used. *Duralumin* is 95 per cent aluminium with magnesium and copper. Aluminium is used in moving parts of machinery, and in engines, e.g. pistons and cylinders. Space satellites contain much aluminium because it is so light.

Aluminium is used for making kitchen vessels such as pots, pans, etc., because its appearance is good (metallic lustre), it is light, a good conductor of heat, and not easily corroded by cooking solutions and liquids (except alkalis). Aluminium is used for overhead electricity cables, which have a core of steel to make them strong enough. Its silvery appearance accounts for its use as a paint, e.g. on petrol storage tanks; it reflects heat rays. It is deposited on glass to make mirrors which do not tarnish. It is so malleable that it can be made into thin sheets used (instead of tinfoil) to wrap chocolates, cigarettes, etc. Milk bottle caps are often of aluminium.

Thermite process

Aluminium is used as a reducing agent in the formation of iron (manganese and chromium). Thermite is a mixture of aluminium powder and iron(III) oxide. The powder is ignited with burning magnesium and the heat evolved melts the iron formed:

$$Fe_2O_3(s) + 2Al(s) \rightarrow 2Fe(l) + Al_2O_3(s) + heat$$

The molten iron is used to weld steel parts together.
Demonstration experiment. The reaction is so vigorous that it must be demonstrated only and a safety screen is essential. Dry iron(II) oxide (3–4 g) by heating in a dish. Mix the cold oxide with an equal volume of dry aluminium powder. Place the mixture in a silica crucible and stand in a tin filled with sand. Place a spatula of barium peroxide and magnesium powder, mixed together, on the iron oxide–aluminium mixture and stick a length of clean magnesium ribbon in the peroxide–magnesium mixture. Tie a taper to the end of a long glass tube and use this to light the magnesium ribbon. (The ribbon and peroxide–magnesium mixture are essential to ignite the thermite mixture, which is not always easy.) A vigorous reaction occurs in the thermite and light and smoke form. Observe a bead of iron at the end of the reaction.

Zinc

Properties of zinc

Zinc is a blue-grey metal, with all the usual metallic properties. Its density is 7.1 g/cm^3; its m.p. is 420 °C.
Air. Zinc slowly tarnishes and forms basic carbonate which prevents further action. It burns with a blue-green flame when strongly heated in air, forming white oxide, ZnO.
Water. Zinc does not react with water. Steam reacts with red-hot zinc, p. 61.
Acids. Zinc is high in the reactivity series and displaces hydrogen from dilute sulphuric and hydrochloric acids. Pure zinc reacts very slowly; impure zinc reacts more quickly. Copper sulphate speeds the reaction, p. 49.
Alkalis. Hot concentrated solutions of sodium and potassium hydroxides form hydrogen and a zincate (compare aluminium):

$$Zn(s) + 2OH^-(aq) + 2H_2O(l) \rightarrow H_2(g) + Zn(OH)_4^{2-}(aq)$$

The formula of sodium zincate is $Na_2Zn(OH)_4$, sometimes written Na_2ZnO_2, (by removing $2H_2O$).
Other reactions. Zinc combines with chlorine and sulphur.

Uses of zinc

Zinc does not corrode and is used to coat iron, forming *galvanized iron*, to stop it rusting. Galvanized iron is used to make buckets, dustbins, water tanks, bath tubs, wire fences, barbed wire, roofs and huts. Zinc is the negative electrode of Leclanché cells, e.g. the outer case of dry batteries. Brass is an alloy of copper with zinc (p. 295).

Iron

Extraction

Four per cent of the earth's crust is iron, which is the second most abundant metal (after aluminium). The chief ores are oxides, Fe_2O_3 and Fe_3O_4, and iron(II) carbonate, $FeCO_3$. They are roasted in air to drive off water; the carbonate loses carbon dioxide and forms iron(III) oxide:

$$FeCO_3(s) \rightarrow FeO(s) + CO_2(g);\ 4FeO(s) + O_2(g) \rightarrow 2Fe_2O_3(s)$$

Blast furnace. The roasted ore is mixed with coke and limestone and dropped into the furnace. Hot air at 800 °C is blown into the bottom of the furnace (Fig. 22.7). The reactions are:

1 The coke burns in the air, forming carbon dioxide and producing temperatures up to 1700 °C. Farther up the furnace the dioxide is reduced to monoxide:

$$C(s) + O_2(g) \rightarrow CO_2(g) + \text{heat};\ CO_2(g) + C(s) \rightarrow 2CO(g)$$

2 The carbon monoxide reduces the iron oxides to molten iron. The reactions are reversible and excess carbon monoxide is necessary to reduce the oxides completely:

$$Fe_2O_3(s) + 3CO(g) \rightleftharpoons 2Fe(l) + 3CO_2(g)$$

$$Fe_3O_4(s) + 4CO(g) \rightleftharpoons 3Fe(l) + 4CO_2(g)$$

The gases leaving the furnace contain about 25 per cent of carbon monoxide; they are burned to heat the air blast entering the furnace.

3 The limestone decomposes into calcium oxide. This combines with sand [silicon(IV) oxide, SiO_2] present as an impurity in the ore and forms a slag of calcium silicate:

$$CaCO_3(s) \rightarrow CaO(s) + CO_2(g);$$

$$CaO(s) + SiO_2(s) \rightarrow CaSiO_3(l)$$

The iron absorbs carbon as it moves down the furnace and this lowers its melting point. Both iron and slag are molten and drop to the bottom of the furnace. The less dense slag floats on top of the iron and prevents oxidation of the iron by the air blast. The iron and the slag are run out of separate holes from time to time. The process is continuous.

In modern furnaces, fuel oil mixed with the hot air replaces the coke. Since the oil cools the mixture, oxygen is added to the air blast to maintain the temperature at 1700 °C.

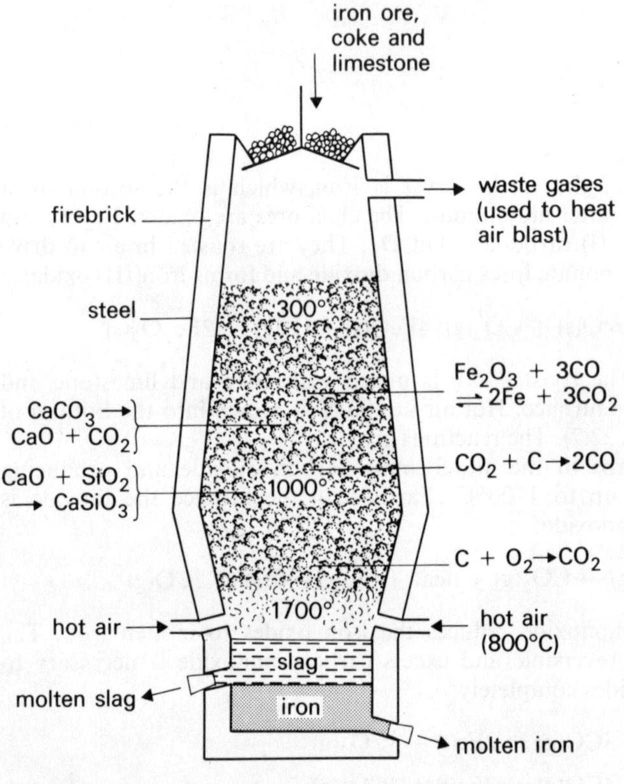

Fig. 22.7 Blast furnace

Pig-iron or cast iron

The molten iron is run into sand moulds and solidifies into lumps called 'pigs'. It is impure, containing 3–5 per cent of carbon (partly free and partly iron carbide, Fe_3C) and 2 per cent of phosphorus, sulphur, silicon and manganese. These impurities lower its melting point to about 1200 °C; pure iron melts at 1539 °C.

Pig-iron can be cast into various shapes by pouring the molten metal into moulds. It makes clear castings because it expands on solidification, and it is called *cast iron*. Cast iron is brittle, cannot be welded, and has a low strength. It is used to make cookers, stoves, hot-water radiators, railings, water pipes, posts, bases of bunsens, and other metal parts that need not be strong. It cannot be used for articles that require strength, e.g. girders, bridges, etc.

Wrought iron

This is the purest form of commercial iron. It is 99 per cent iron and contains less than 0.25 per cent of carbon.

Manufacture. Pig-iron is heated with haematite, Fe_2O_3, in a furnace. The oxide oxidizes most of the impurities to gaseous oxides (CO, SO_2, P_2O_5) and others to a slag, e.g. calcium silicate, which is removed by pressing the hot metal.

$$Fe_2O_3(s) + 3C(s) \rightarrow 2Fe(s) + 3CO(g)$$

Uses. Wrought iron is strong and malleable (not brittle, like cast iron). It can be shaped by hammering it at about 1000 °C, which is about 500 °C below its melting point. It is used for making nails, sheets, chains, horseshoes, gates, farm machines, and in cores of electromagnets because it cannot be permanently magnetized.

Steel

This is an alloy of iron with 0.15–1.7 per cent of carbon but in practice the percentage of carbon rarely exceeds 1 per cent and most structural steels contain less. Carbon is slightly soluble in iron and some is present as a carbon–iron solid solution. The rest is in the form of iron carbide, Fe_3C.

Steel is manufactured by oxidizing the impurities in molten pig-iron, using a jet of 'tonnage oxygen' (p. 42) directed vertically downwards on the metal. Formerly air was used, but the nitrogen made it difficult to reach the high temperatures necessary for fast steel making and nitrogen in the steel lowered its quality. After removal of impurities, the calculated mass of carbon (and nickel, cobalt, chromium and manganese if needed for special steels) is added.

The density ($7.9\ g/cm^3$) of steel is high and it rusts easily. Its mechanical properties depend on heat treatment processes of *hardening* and *tempering*. It is made hard but brittle by making it red-hot and then cooling it quickly in oil or water. By careful heating at about 300 °C (tempering) steel loses its brittleness but retains its hardness.

Mild steels (up to 0.5 per cent carbon) are used to make nails, screws, car bodies, railway lines, ships, bridges, girders, steel rods in concrete roads, pipes, etc. It is the commonest steel. *Hard steels* (0.6 per cent carbon or more) are used to make tools. *Stainless* and *rustless steels* contain chromium and nickel; they are made into knives, scissors, saws, etc. Steel with manganese is very hard and is used for rock-drills and railway points. Steel with tungsten is used for high-speed cutting-tools and drilling-tools; it remains hard even when hot. Cobalt steel is used for permanent magnets.

Properties of iron

Pure iron is a white, lustrous metal. Its physical properties are typical of those of metals.
Air. Iron rusts in damp air, forming hydrated iron(III) oxide or rust. Finely divided iron burns when heated strongly in air, forming blue-black iron(II) diiron(III) oxide or triiron tetraoxide.
Water. Water has no action on iron (if air is not present). Steam reacts with the heated metal, p. 58.
Acids. Iron displaces hydrogen readily from dilute hydrochloric and sulphuric acids, forming iron(II) salts. Dilute nitric acid forms iron(II) nitrate and oxides of nitrogen.
Other reactions. Iron reacts with sulphur (p. 18) and chlorine (p. 268).
Iron and copper are transition metals, p. 169.

Tin

Extraction

Tin occurs in Malaya and Indonesia as tin(IV) oxide, SnO_2. The ore is reduced by heating in a furnace with coal:

$$SnO_2(s) + 2C(s) \rightarrow Sn(l) + 2CO(g)$$

The tin runs from the furnace to a sloping surface. Impurities solidify but the tin flows on into moulds.

Properties of tin

Tin is a soft, silvery-white metal with a low melting point (232 °C). It can be pressed or rolled into 'tinfoil'.
Air. Air has no action at ordinary temperatures. Tin burns when heated strongly, forming tin(IV) oxide, SnO_2.
Water. Steam attacks tin only at very high temperatures:

$$Sn(s) + 2H_2O(g) \rightarrow 2H_2(g) + SnO_2(s)$$

Acids. Tin reacts only very slowly with dilute acids, forming tin(II) salts:

$$Sn(s) + 2HCl(aq) \rightarrow H_2(g) + SnCl_2(aq), \text{ tin(II) chloride}$$

Concentrated hydrochloric acid dissolves it readily, forming the tin(II) salt.

Alkalis. Hot concentrated alkalis form hydrogen and stannates:

$$Sn(s) + 2OH^-(aq) + 4H_2O \rightarrow H_2(g) + Sn(OH)_6^{2-}(aq)$$

The formula of sodium stannate(IV) is $Na_2Sn(OH)_6$, sometimes written as Na_2SnO_3 (by removing $3H_2O$).

Uses of tin

The chief use is to make tinplate, which resists corrosion. Sheets of iron are cleaned in acid (to remove rust) and dipped in molten tin. Tinplate is used as cans or 'tins' for food and other substances. Tin-foil is a wrapping paper, but aluminium foil is replacing it. *Solder* and *type metal* are alloys of tin and lead (p. 295).

Lead

Properties of lead

Lead is a greyish, lustrous metal when freshly cut. It is soft and malleable, has a low melting point (328 °C) and a high density (11.4 g/cm^3).
Air. Lead rapidly tarnishes, forming a film of lead hydroxide and carbonate, which stops further action. The film makes the metal dull. Molten lead gradually changes in air to lead(II) oxide, PbO, which is reddish-brown when hot and yellow when cold. It forms red lead oxide (trilead tetraoxide) at 450 °C:

$$2Pb(l) + O_2(g) \rightarrow 2PbO(s); \quad 6PbO(s) + O_2(g) \rightarrow 2Pb_3O_4(s)$$

Acids. Lead is low in the activity series. It has no action on dilute hydrochloric and sulphuric acid. Hot concentrated hydrochloric acid slowly forms hydrogen:

$$Pb(s) + 2HCl(aq) \rightarrow H_2(g) + PbCl_2(s), \text{ lead(II) chloride}$$

Hot concentrated sulphuric acid and dilute and concentrated nitric acid react the same as with copper (pp. 253 and 231).
Alkalis. No action occurs.

Uses of lead

Lead is used for some gas pipes because it does not corrode, is malleable, and bends easily. Cracks and breaks in the pipes are readily mended because the parts can be joined simply by melting them together. For similar reasons, lead is used for covering electricity and telephone cables and for putting under tile roofs to keep out rain and wind.

Accumulators and car batteries contain lead. Its low melting point accounts for its use in making lead shot and bullets. Weights and bobs of plumblines are made of lead because it does not corrode and has a high density. Thick lead sheets are used to absorb dangerous rays in atomic energy factories.

Type metal, used for printing, is an alloy of 76 per cent lead, 16 per cent antimony and 8 per cent tin; *plumber's solder* is an alloy of 70 per cent lead and 30 per cent tin, and *tinman's solder* is 40 per cent lead and 60 per cent tin. The low melting point of lead (and tin) accounts for their use in these alloys. Type-metal is readily melted after use, and can be used repeatedly. Type-metal has a low melting point and expands on cooling (like cast iron) so that it forms sharp, clear type. It is tough so that it does not wear easily when pressed on paper thousands of times. Plumber's solder is melted and used on pipe and lead cable joints. When this solder cools it becomes a paste and does not suddenly solidify, therefore the excess solder can be wiped off joints. Tinman's solder is used for electrical, radio and tin-can seams; it solidifies at 183 °C.

Copper

Extraction of copper

The copper iron sulphide (pyrites), $CuFeS_2$, is roasted in air to oxides, which are dissolved in dilute sulphuric acid. Electrolysis of the copper(II) sulphate solution causes deposition of almost pure copper on a copper cathode and iron is not deposited from the iron(II) sulphate also present in the electrolyte.

Properties of copper

Copper is a reddish metal which is very malleable and ductile. Its density is 8.94 g/cm^3; its m.p. is 1083 °C or 1356 K.

Air. Copper is low in the activity series. Dry air does not attack it, but damp air slowly forms a film of green basic carbonate, $CuCO_3 \cdot Cu(OH)_2$. Copper does not burn in air, but its surface changes to black copper(II) oxide.

Acids. Copper is below hydrogen in the activity series, and therefore never displaces the gas from acids. It reacts with oxidizing acids. Hot concentrated sulphuric acid is reduced to sulphur dioxide (p. 253). Concentrated nitric acid is reduced to nitrogen dioxide (p. 231), and diluted nitric acid to nitrogen oxide (p. 231).

Chlorine. Add Dutch metal (a Cu–Zn alloy with 80 per cent copper) to chlorine. It burns spontaneously. Hot copper powder catches fire when dropped into a jar of chlorine, forming yellow fumes of copper(II) chloride.

Copper(I) compounds, e.g. Cu_2O and Cu_2Cl_2, exist.

Uses of copper

Copper is very ductile and malleable, and can be shaped into wire, sheets, rods, etc. It is, apart from silver, the best conductor of heat and electricity, and therefore is used in boilers, kettles, electricity wires and cables, electric motors and dynamos.

Brass is an alloy of copper with 20–35 per cent of zinc. It is more malleable and stronger than copper and its colour is more golden; it is used for making screws, nuts, bolts, tubes, rods and ornaments.

Bronze is an alloy which contains about 90 per cent of copper and about 10 per cent of tin. Usually small amounts of other metals are added for various reasons. The bronze used to make armaments is called *gun-metal*; it contains zinc and lead so that it can be shaped accurately by machinery. *Bell-metal* contains about 20 per cent of tin. *Phosphor-bronze* contains about 10 per cent of phosphorus and is as hard as some steels. Aluminium replaces tin in *aluminium bronzes*, which are cheaper and much stronger than ordinary bronze.

Duralumin contains 95 per cent of aluminium with copper and magnesium.

Alloys

Pure metals are not used widely because their appearance, strength, resistance to corrosion, etc., can be improved by mixing with other elements. The mixtures are alloys. *An alloy is a uniform mixture of one metal with one or more other substances, usually metals or carbon.* Brass is an alloy of copper and zinc; it is stronger and more malleable than pure copper. Steel is an alloy of iron with carbon and chromium, manganese, cobalt, etc. The common alloys are:

Brass	Copper with 20–35 per cent zinc.
Duralumin	Aluminium (95 per cent) with magnesium and copper (p. 287).
Solder	Lead (70 per cent) and tin (30 per cent); lead (40 per cent) and tin (60 per cent); (p. 293).
Type metal	Lead (76 per cent), antimony (16 per cent) and tin (8 per cent) (p. 293).
Cast iron	Iron with carbon (3–5 per cent) and about 2 per cent of phosphorus, sulphur, silicon, manganese (p. 290).
Wrought iron	Iron with carbon (0.25 per cent) and other elements (p. 291).
Steel	Iron with carbon (0.15–1.7 per cent) and other elements (p. 291).

Questions

1 Give a list of the chemical properties which you regard as typical of a metal. Illustrate what you say by reference to sodium, nitrogen and iron. Name two physical properties each of sodium and carbon in which their behaviour is not as expected from their classification as metal and non-metal respectively. (L.)

2 State three physical properties and two chemical properties of a metal and of a non-metal, using as examples zinc and sulphur. Name two important alloys, and explain how their properties differ from those of the metals of which they are composed. (C.)

3 Briefly explain how (*a*) sodium and (*b*) aluminium are extracted from suitable chemical compounds. State the reactions (if any) of these metals with (*c*) air, (*d*) water. Explain how the uses of aluminium depend on its properties. (N.)

4 How does zinc react with (*a*) copper(II) sulphate, (*b*) sodium hydroxide, (*c*) dilute hydrochloric acid? How would you prepare zinc sulphate crystals from zinc? (L.)

5 Describe the manufacture of cast iron from iron ore, explaining the chemical reactions involved in the process. How would you prepare (*a*) iron(II) sulphate crystals, (*b*) iron(III) chloride, from iron? (C.)

6 Describe and explain how metallic copper can be purified. State three important uses of copper and three of lead. What is the action of concentrated hydrochloric acid on lead(IV) oxide, and of dilute nitric acid on lead(IV) oxide? (C.)

7 Describe and explain the conversion of pig-iron into steel. Describe two tests by which you could distinguish between iron(II) and iron(III) salts. Explain two ways of converting iron(II) sulphate to iron(III) sulphate. (N.)

8 Describe the action of (*a*) air, (*b*) water, (*c*) dilute hydrochloric acid on the following metals: magnesium, zinc, iron. Name three metals that react with sodium hydroxide and write equations for the reactions, naming the products formed. (O.)

23
Organic Chemistry

Meaning of organic chemistry

Organic chemistry means the chemistry of compounds of carbon except the oxides of carbon and the carbonates, hydrogencarbonates and carbides of metals, which are usually treated as part of inorganic chemistry.

Carbon differs from other elements in one unique way—its atoms can join together and form long chains. For example, octane (C_8H_{18}), one of the constituents of petrol, has a chain of 8 carbon atoms, and some organic molecules such as those of starch and cellulose contain chains of hundreds of atoms.

Alkanes

A hydrocarbon contains hydrogen and carbon only. Alkanes are hydrocarbons with the formula C_nH_{2n+2}, e.g.

Methane CH_4 Ethane C_2H_6 Propane C_3H_8

Structural formulae show the sequence and arrangement of the atoms in a molecule, e.g. ethane CH_3CH_3, and propane $CH_3CH_2CH_3$. *Displayed* or *graphic formulae* show the atoms and their bonds on a plane, e.g.

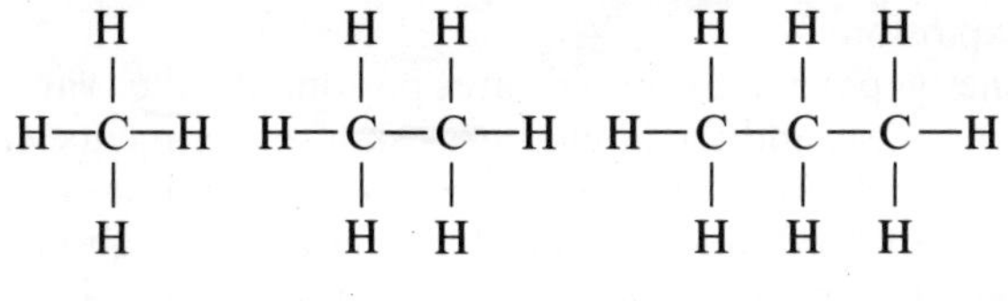

The displayed formulae represent three-dimensional molecules in only two dimensions. Therefore, make ball-and-spring and space-filling models of the above molecules. A carbon chain is zig-zag and not straight; the chain in butane, C_4H_{10}, is better as

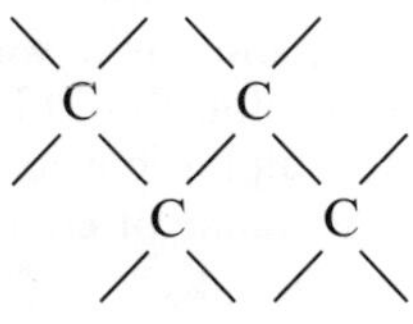

rather than

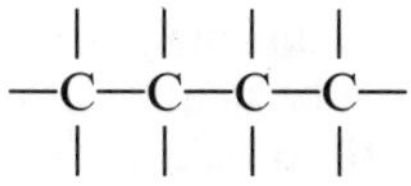

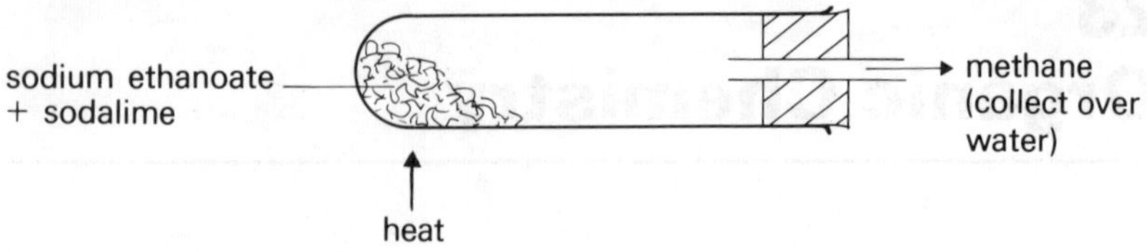

Fig. 23.1 To prepare methane, CH_4

To prepare methane

From sodium ethanoate (acetate). Methane is prepared by heating anhydrous sodium ethanoate with an alkali, usually sodalime:

$$CH_3COONa(s) + NaOH(s) \rightarrow CH_4(g) + Na_2CO_3(s)$$

Sodalime is a mixture of sodium and calcium hydroxides made by adding concentrated sodium hydroxide solution to quicklime. Unlike sodium hydroxide it is not deliquescent, does not melt so readily, and attacks glass less readily.

Tests on alkanes

Your teacher may demonstrate the following tests, using methane or ethane gas or pure hexane, C_6H_{14} (b.p. 69 °C), which is more convenient because it is a liquid.

1 *Combustion.* Ignite a jar of alkane gas or a few drops of hexane on a hard-glass clock glass. Observe if soot forms in the jar. Also, ignite in a boiling-tube (not a gas-jar) a mixture of alkane gas and air (be prepared for an explosion).

2 *Bromine.* (Bromine vapour and liquid are poisonous, the vapour irritates the eyes and nose, and the liquid burns skin. Experiments with liquid bromine must be done in a fume cupboard.) (*a*) Use a teat pipette to add 4 drops of bromine to a jar of alkane gas or to about 10 drops of hexane, and cover the jar. Note if the reddish-brown colour of bromine in the jar or hexane changes, and if any change is rapid or slow. Leave for 24 hours if necessary. (*b*) Add 3 drops of a solution of bromine in trichloromethane (chloroform) or tetrachloromethane (carbon tetrachloride) to a jar of alkane gas and shake well.

3 *Potassium manganate (VII).* Add about 2 cm^3 of the pink solution to a jar of the alkane gas or to about 10 drops of hexane, and shake well. Note if the potassium manganate(VII) solution is decolourized. (The solution used may be neutral of acidified with dilute sulphuric acid or made alkaline with sodium carbonate. Impurities in methane or ethane cause false changes, and it is better to use pure hexane.)

Properties of methane

Methane is a colourless, odourless gas. It is only slightly soluble in water and has no action on litmus. It is less dense than air. It is a stable compound and does not react with acids, alkalis, etc.

Combustion. It burns in air with a faintly luminous flame, forming carbon dioxide and water. A mixture of air and methane is explosive.

$$CH_4(g) + 2O_2(g) \rightarrow CO_2(g) + 2H_2O(g)$$

In *limited air* (e.g. in a luminous bunsen flame) carbon and carbon monoxide may be formed:

$$CH_4(g) + O_2(g) \rightarrow C(s) + 2H_2O(g);$$

$$2CH_4(g) + 3O_2(g) \rightarrow 2CO(g) + 4H_2O(g)$$

Chlorine. A mixture of methane and chlorine explodes when placed in bright sunlight or when sparked:

$$CH_4(g) + 2Cl_2(g) \rightarrow C(s) + 4HCl(g)$$

In diffused sunlight, substitution of hydrogen occurs:

$$CH_4(g) + Cl_2(g) \rightarrow HCl(g) + CH_3Cl(g), \text{ chloromethane}$$

$$CH_3Cl(g) + Cl_2(g) \rightarrow HCl(g) + CH_2Cl_2(l), \text{ dichloromethane}$$

$$CH_2Cl_2(l) + Cl_2(g) \rightarrow HCl(g) + CHCl_3(l), \text{ trichloromethane or chloroform}$$

$$CHCl_3(l) + Cl_2(g) \rightarrow HCl(g) + CCl_4(l), \text{ tetrachloromethane or carbon tetrachloride}$$

Liquid bromine reacts less vigorously than chlorine. Bromine and bromine solution are decolourized by alkanes, especially in bright sunlight. Reaction is very slow in the dark. Compounds CH_3Br, CH_2Br_2, $CHBr_3$ and CBr_4 are formed. Iodine does not react with alkanes.

Potassium manganate(VII) does not react with alkanes.

Occurrence of methane

Methane is formed in marshes and coal mines by the action of bacteria on cellulose and other organic matter. Coal gas contains about 30 per cent of methane, and natural gas, 80–99 per cent methane.

General properties of alkanes

The lower members (methane, ethane, propane and butane) are gases; the next twelve (C_5H_{12} to $C_{16}H_{34}$) are liquids; the rest are waxy solids, e.g. paraffin wax. All are practically insoluble in water and are less dense than water; their densities rise gradually with relative molecular mass. The lower members are soluble in ethanol, but their solubilities gradually decrease with rising relative molecular mass.

Name	Formula	M.p. (°C)	B.p. (°C)	Density (g/cm³)
Methane	CH_4	−182	−162	0.424
Ethane	C_2H_6	−183	−88	0.546
Propane	C_3H_8	−188	−42	0.582
Butane	C_4H_{10}	−138	0	0.579
Pentane	C_5H_{12}	−130	36	0.626
Hexane	C_6H_{14}	−95	69	0.659
Octane	C_8H_{18}	−57	126	0.703
Decane	$C_{10}H_{22}$	−30	174	0.730

Alkanes are inert and do not react with chemical reagents under ordinary conditions. They burn in air, forming carbon dioxide and water. Chlorine (and bromine) substitutes one or more of the hydrogen atoms.

Saturated compounds and substitution

In all alkanes, carbon exerts its normal valency of 4 and hydrogen has its normal valency of 1. No more atoms can be added, and the alkanes are called saturated compounds.

A saturated compound is one in which all its atoms exert their usual combining power with other atoms and whose molecules contain neither double nor triple bonds.

A new atom can enter the molecule of a saturated compound only if one or more existing atoms is replaced, i.e. by substitution. The reaction of alkanes with chlorine or bromine in diffused sunlight is a substitution reaction.

Substitution is the replacement of an atom or radical by other atoms or radicals.

Alkyl radicals

Removal of one hydrogen atom from an alkane molecule leaves a monovalent group called an alkyl radical. Examples are:

Methyl CH_3— Ethyl C_2H_5— Propyl C_3H_7—

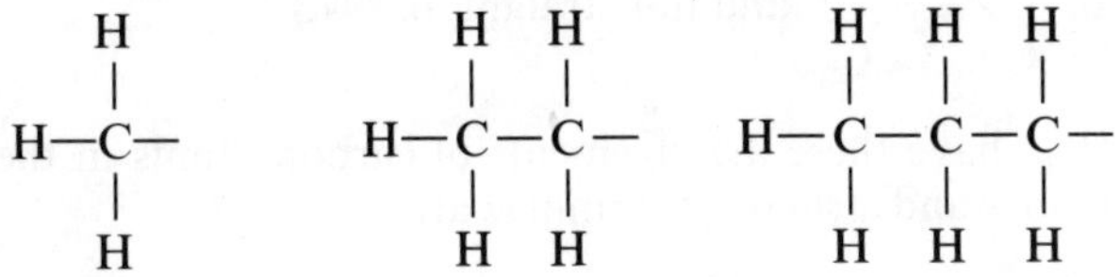

Examples of alkyl compounds are: methyl ethanoate, CH_3COOCH_3, and ethyl hydrogensulphate, $C_2H_5HSO_4$.

Uses of alkanes

Methane occurs in natural gas and coal gas, which are fuels. When heated up to 1000 °C, methane decomposes into hydrogen and carbon black (lampblack), which is used to make printers' ink, paints, carbon paper, etc. *Bottled gas* is propane and butane liquefied and stored under pressure in steel cylinders; it is used as a fuel and is replacing acetylene for welding. Petrol, paraffin (kerosine), diesel oil, lubricating oils, paraffin wax and asphalt are all mixtures of various alkanes.

Homologous series

A homologous series is a group of compounds of similar structure in which each member differs from the next by the presence of an additional —CH_2 group.

Usually all the compounds in any one homologous series, e.g. the alkanes,

a can be prepared by similar methods;
b can be represented by a general formula;
c have similar chemical properties; and
d show a gradual change of physical properties.

There are 75 alkanes with the formula $C_{10}H_{22}$, and 366 319 of formula $C_{20}H_{42}$. The advantages of studying series of organic compounds rather than individual compounds are obvious.

Isomerism of alkanes

Compounds which have the same molecular formula but different displayed (graphic) formulae are *isomers* and the phenomenon is *isomerism*. Four carbon atoms can be joined in two ways: an unbranched chain of four atoms or a branched chain having the fourth atom joined to the middle of three other atoms:

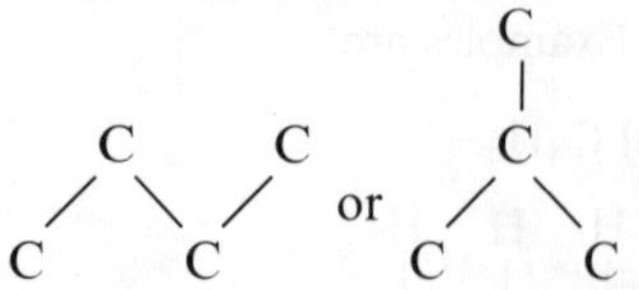

(The chain of C atoms is zig-zag and not straight, p. 297.)

Two alkanes, C_4H_{10}, have these arrangements of carbon atoms in their molecules. Their names and structural formulae are:

Butane
$CH_3CH_2CH_2CH_3$

Methylpropane
CH_3CHCH_3 (with CH_3 on the middle C) or $(CH_3)_2CHCH_3$

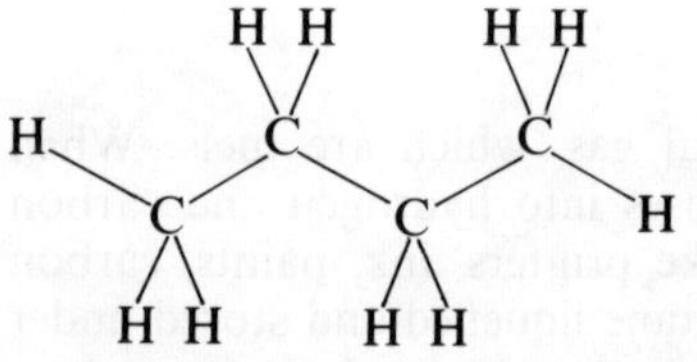

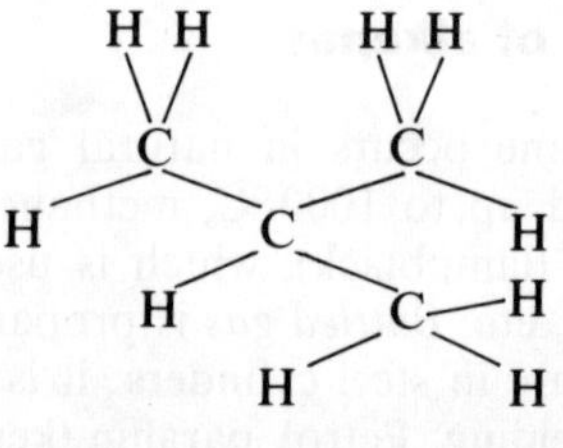

Three alkanes are isomers with the formula C_5H_{12}. Five carbon atoms can be joined in three ways and the longest chain can have either five carbon atoms (as in pentane) or four or three:

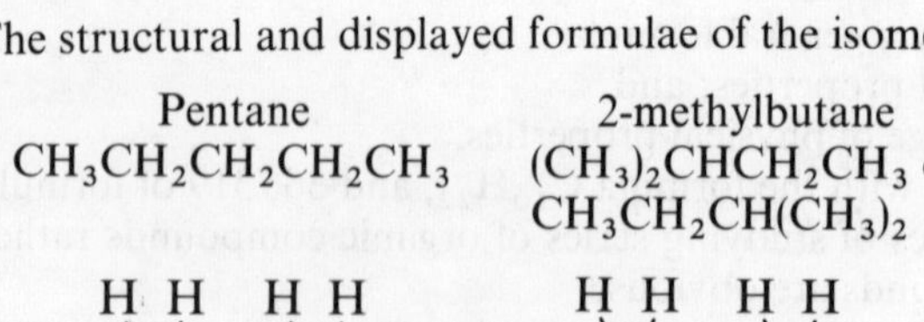

The structural and displayed formulae of the isomers are:

Pentane
$CH_3CH_2CH_2CH_2CH_3$

2-methylbutane
$(CH_3)_2CHCH_2CH_3$ or $CH_3CH_2CH(CH_3)_2$

2,2-dimethylpropane
$(CH_3)_4C$

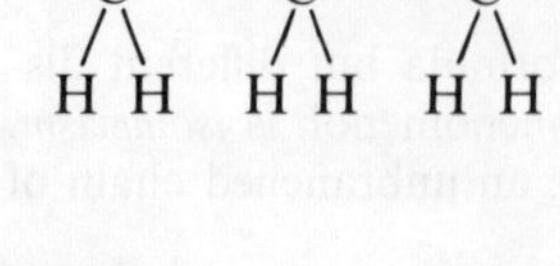

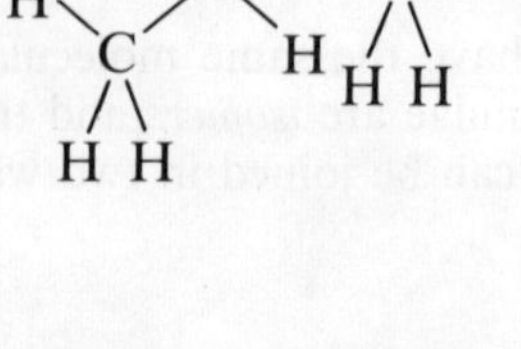

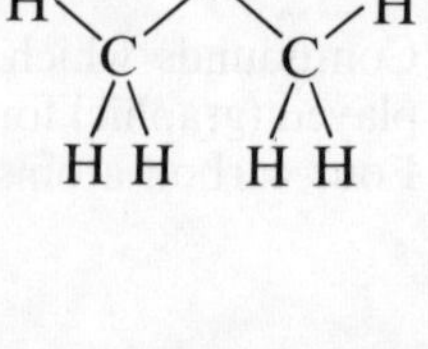

Petroleum

The name petroleum means 'rock oil'. It comes out of the ground as a thick, green or dark-brown liquid. Oil deposits are usually found with sand, salt and brine; oil was formed from the remains of microscopic plants and animals which lived in warm inland seas millions of years ago. Their dead bodies sank to the bottom of the seas and were soon covered with mud and sand. The chemical effects of pressure, heat and bacteria converted the remains into oil just as they converted forests into coal. Oil is usually found in a layer of porous rock, e.g. sandstone, between two layers of non-porous rock. *Natural gas* is above the oil. This is a mixture of many gases, but contains between 80 and 99 per cent of methane.

Fractionation of crude petroleum

Petroleum is a mixture of many alkanes, which are separated by fractional distillation. It is heated until most of it vapourizes. The vapour passes into the bottom of a tall fractionating tower. This is divided into several compartments, each cooler than the one below. Petrol, the most

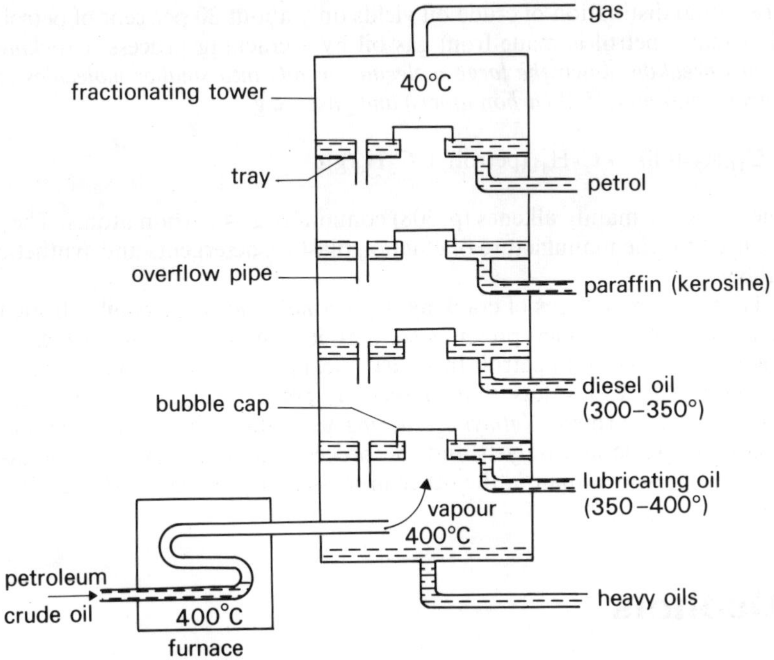

Fig. 23.2 Fractional distillation of petroleum

volatile fraction, condenses at the top, paraffin oil in the compartment below, then diesel and lubricating oils; the non-volatile heavy oils run out at the bottom of the column. Each fraction is re-distilled (refined).

Fraction	Distilling temperatures (°C)	Uses
Gas	Below 40	Bottled gas; fuel
Petrol (naphtha)	40–175	Motor and aviation fuel
Paraffin oil (kerosine)	175–250	Lighting; heating; diesel engines
Gas oil	250–300	To make petrol; heating buildings
Diesel oil	300–350	Diesel engines; furnaces
Lubricating oil	350–400	Lubrication
Waxes	Above 400	Vaseline, greases, candles
Bitumen	Above 400	On roads, runways

Cracking of oils

Fractional distillation of crude oil yields only about 20 per cent of petrol. Nowadays, petrol is made from gas oil by a cracking process. *Cracking means breaking down the large molecules of oils into smaller molecules of petrol* (*containing* 5–9 *carbon atoms*) *and gases*, e.g.

$$C_{10}H_{22}(oil) \rightarrow C_7H_{16}(petrol) + C_3H_6(g)$$

The gases are mainly alkenes (p. 308) containing 2–4 carbon atoms. They are used for the manufacture of ethanol, plastics, detergents and synthetic rubber.

There are three types of cracking. In *thermal cracking*, gas oil is heated at about 500 °C under pressure so that it remains a liquid, which is fractionated to obtain petrol. In *steam cracking*, oil and steam are heated to about 900 °C for less than a second; petrol, fuel oil, alkenes and hydrogen are formed. *Catalytic cracking* uses aluminium(III) oxide and silicon(IV) oxide as catalysts and the process occurs at lower temperatures and pressures than in the other processes; it produces better quality petrol.

Alcohols

Alcohols are organic compounds which contain a hydroxyl group (—OH) joined to a grouping of carbon and hydrogen atoms only. Their general formula is $C_nH_{2n+1}OH$; it can be written RCH_2OH where R is a hydrogen atom or an alkyl group (CH_3—, C_2H_5—, etc.).

Methanol
CH_4O or CH_3OH
or HCH_2OH

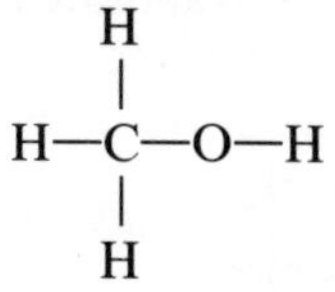

Ethanol
C_2H_6O or C_2H_5OH or CH_3CH_2OH

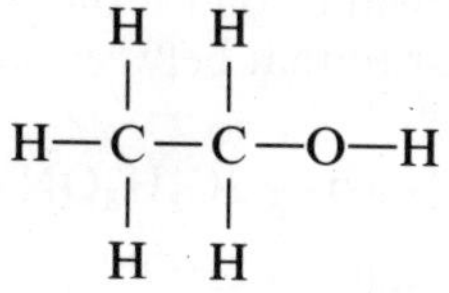

To prepare ethanol

It is prepared by fermentation of glucose in the presence of yeast. Yeast contains the enzyme zymase which catalyses the reaction:

$$C_6H_{12}O_6(aq) \rightarrow 2C_2H_5OH(aq) + 2CO_2(g)$$

Dissolve glucose in a little hot water and pour the solution into a large (2-litre) bottle containing cold water. Make brewers' yeast (ordinary yeast does not act so well) into a paste with water and add to the bottle. Add ammonium phosphate and potassium nitrate to provide food for the yeast cells. Leave at about 30 to 35 °C for two days. Bubbles of carbon dioxide are evolved. Pour the product into a distillation apparatus with fractionating column (Fig. 2.8) and distil, collecting the fraction below 95 °C. Re-distil this fraction, collecting the distillate between 78–82 °C (ethanol boils at 78 °C). If required, dry the alcohol with calcium oxide in a corked flask, pour off the liquid after a day or so, and re-distil.

Tests on alcohols

1 *Combustion.* Add a few drops of alcohols to separate watch-glasses and burn them. Note the flames.
2 *Sodium.* Add tiny pieces of freshly cut sodium to about 1 cm^3 of a pure dry alcohol. Ignite the gas produced. Evaporate the solution to dryness on a water bath.
3 *Phosphorus pentachloride.* Add small pieces of the pentachloride to about 2 cm^3 of a dry alcohol.
4 *Ethanoic (acetic) acid.* To 2 cm^3 of ethanol in a boiling tube add 1 cm^3 of pure ethanoic acid and 3 drops of concentrated sulphuric acid. Warm gently for 5 minutes. Allow to cool, carefully add sodium carbonate solution to neutralize the acids, and smell the product. Repeat with pentanol instead of ethanol (pentyl ethanoate is formed).

Properties of ethanol

Ethanol is a colourless, mobile, hygroscopic liquid. It has a pleasant smell and burning taste. Its density is 0.8 g/cm^3. It mixes with water in any proportions.

Sodium reacts quietly with ethanol to form hydrogen and sodium ethoxide, which remains as a white solid if the product is evaporated to dryness. The reaction is similar to that between sodium and water:

$$2C_2H_5OH(l) + 2Na(s) \rightarrow 2C_2H_5ONa(aq) + H_2(g)$$

compare: $$2HOH(l) + 2Na(s) \rightarrow 2HONa(aq) + H_2(g)$$

Phosphorus pentachloride reacts vigorously; hydrogen chloride fumes are evolved and phosphorus trichloride oxide and chloroethane are formed:

$$C_2H_5OH(l) + PCl_5(s) \rightarrow C_2H_5Cl(l) + POCl_3(l) + HCl(g)$$

Evolution of hydrogen chloride when phosphorus pentachloride is added shows the presence of a hydroxyl group (—OH) in an organic compound.

Phosphorus trichloride forms chloroethane and phosphorous acid:

$$3C_2H_5OH(l) + PCl_3(l) \rightarrow 3C_2H_5Cl(l) + H_3PO_3(l)$$

Concentrated sulphuric acid reacts at once to form ethyl hydrogensulphate with evolution of heat:

$$C_2H_5OH(l) + H_2SO_4(l) \rightleftharpoons C_2H_5HSO_4(l) + H_2O(l)$$

An acid reacts with an alcohol to form an *ester* and water only, and the process is called *esterification* (compare the action of an acid on an alkali and neutralization):

$$\text{Alcohol} + \text{Acid} \rightleftharpoons \text{Ester} + \text{Water}$$
$$C_2H_5OH + HX \rightleftharpoons C_2H_5X + H_2O$$

compare: $$NaOH + HX \rightarrow NaX + H_2O$$

Ethanoic (acetic) acid and other weak acids react slowly with alcohols, and the reaction is catalysed by hydrogen ions, e.g. from sulphuric acid. Esterification differs from neutralization:

a it is slower, because it is between molecules not ions;
b it is reversible; and
c esters are covalent compounds, salts are ionic.

Dehydration. Excess concentrated sulphuric acid at 160 °C dehydrates ethanol and forms ethene (ethylene):

$$C_2H_5OH(l) \rightarrow C_2H_4(g) + H_2O(l)$$

Oxidizing agents. Ethanol burns with a blue flame:

$$C_2H_5OH(l) + 3O_2(g) \rightarrow 2CO_2(g) + 3H_2O(g)$$

Potassium dichromate(VI) acidified with dilute sulphuric acid is a mild oxidizing agent and converts ethanol to ethanal:

$$CH_3CH_2OH(l) + O \rightarrow CH_3CHO(l) + H_2O(l)$$

Ethanal is also formed when air and ethanol vapour are passed over a catalyst of platinized asbestos or copper gauze:

$$2CH_3CH_2OH(l) + O_2(g) \rightarrow 2CH_3CHO(l) + 2H_2O(l)$$

Excess of acidified potassium dichromate(VI) or manganate(VII) oxidizes ethanol first to ethanal and then to ethanoic acid:

$$CH_3CHO(l) + O \rightarrow CH_3COOH(l)$$

Vinegar (dilute ethanoic acid) is formed when ethanol is oxidized by air in the presence of certain bacteria.

General properties of alcohols

The lower members are liquids, completely miscible with water; butanol is liquid but is not completely miscible; the higher alcohols are greasy solids and almost insoluble. Their physical properties show a regular change with rising relative molecular mass.

Commercial alcohol

Ethanol is manufactured from starch (potatoes, rice, bananas, barley), molasses (the residues left from the purification of cane sugar or beet sugar), and ethene, p. 309. It is the most important constituent of beers, wines and spirits. Methanol is a poison. Ethanol is used in the manufacture of perfumes, flavours, drugs, varnishes, etc. It is used in thermometers measuring low temperatures. Methanol and ethanol are added to some petrols. Countries like Brazil, which can make cheap ethanol from cane-sugar which they grow in abundance, already add about 20 per cent ethanol to petrol. In the future it is probable that petroleum will become more scarce and expensive, and the addition of ethanol to petrol will become more widespread.

Alkenes

Alkenes are hydrocarbons with the general formula C_nH_{2n} where n is 2 or more (CH_2 does not exist):

Ethene (ethylene), C_2H_4 Propene, C_3H_6

$$\begin{array}{lcl} CH_2 & & H{-}C{-}H \\ \| & \text{or} & \quad\| \\ CH_2 & & H{-}C{-}H \end{array} \qquad \begin{array}{l} CH_3{-}CH \\ \qquad\;\; \| \\ \qquad\; CH_2 \end{array}$$

All alkenes contain a *double bond* between two carbon atoms (C=C) and are unsaturated compounds.

An unsaturated compound is one in which some atom (or atoms) is not exerting all its combining power with other atoms. A double bond is weaker than a single bond. It makes the compound reactive because it is readily converted to a single bond by addition of other atoms.

To obtain ethene (ethylene) from ethanol

Ethene is obtained by dehydration of (removal of the elements of water from) ethanol. Ethanol vapour is passed over hot broken pot, pumice stone or aluminium(III) oxide at about 400 °C, Fig. 23.3:

$$CH_3CH_2OH(g) \rightarrow C_2H_4(g) + H_2O(l)$$

The ethanol is on the wool. Heat the broken pot strongly. The ethanol vapourizes and its vapour passes through the hot pot or over aluminium oxide. Collect the ethene over water in test-tubes.

Do the three tests as for methane, p. 298. It is more convenient to use cyclohexene (b.p. 83 °C), a liquid.

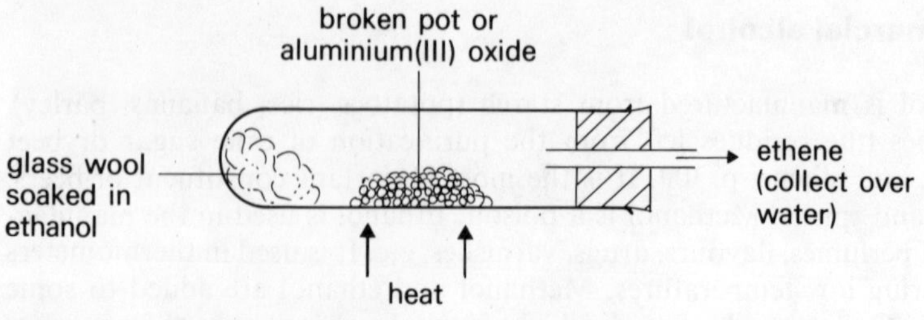

Fig. 23.3 To prepare ethene (ethylene), C_2H_4

Properties of ethene (ethylene)

Ethene is a colourless gas with a faint sweet smell. It is only slightly soluble in water and does not affect litmus. Its density is about the same as that of air.
Combustion. Ethene burns in air with a bright smoky flame:

$$C_2H_4(g) + 3O_2(g) \rightarrow 2CO_2(g) + 2H_2O(g)$$

It also burns in chlorine with a red flame, forming carbon:

$$C_2H_4(g) + 2Cl_2(g) \rightarrow 2C(s) + 4HCl(g)$$

Addition reactions of ethene
Hydrogen. Ethene and hydrogen combine when passed over a catalyst of heated nickel or platinum:

$$\begin{array}{ccccc} CH_2 & & H & & CH_3 \\ \| & + & | & \rightarrow & | \\ CH_2 & & H & & CH_3 \end{array} \quad \text{ethane}$$

This is a simple example of *catalytic hydrogenation*.
Chlorine and bromine. Chlorine adds on to ethene when the two gases are mixed and left in sunlight, forming a colourless oily liquid:

$$\begin{array}{ccccc} CH_2 & & Cl & & CH_2Cl \\ \| & + & | & \rightarrow & | \\ CH_2 & & Cl & & CH_2Cl \end{array} \quad \text{dichloroethane}$$

When ethene is passed through liquid bromine, a colourless oily liquid is formed:

$$\begin{array}{ccccc} CH_2 & & Br & & CH_2Br \\ \| & + & | & \rightarrow & | \\ CH_2 & & Br & & CH_2Br \end{array} \quad \text{dibromoethane}$$

Pink *acidified potassium manganate(VII)* is turned colourless; ethane is oxidized to ethanediol, CH_2OHCH_2OH.
Water. Ethene and steam combine at about 300 °C, 70 atm pressure and with phosphoric acid as a catalyst to form ethanol:

$$\begin{array}{ccccc} CH_2 & & H & & CH_3 \\ \| & + & | & \rightarrow & | \\ CH_2 & & OH & & CH_2OH \end{array} \quad \text{ethanol}$$

Hydrogen chloride. This adds slowly to ethene:

$$\begin{array}{lcl} CH_2 & H & CH_3 \\ \| \quad + & | \rightarrow & | \qquad \text{chloroethane} \\ CH_2 & Cl & CH_2Cl \end{array}$$

Sulphuric acid. The fuming or concentrated acid absorbs ethene, forming an oily liquid:

$$\begin{array}{lcl} CH_2 & H & CH_3 \\ \| \quad + & | \quad \rightarrow & | \qquad \text{ethyl hydrogensulphate} \\ CH_2 & HSO_4 & CH_2HSO_4 \end{array}$$

This reaction can be used to separate ethene from methane (which is not absorbed) or to separate any unsaturated hydrocarbons from saturated alkanes.

Test for unsaturation. **a**. Add 2 drops of a solution of bromine in trichloromethane or tetrachloromethane to a compound. If the bromine is decolourized, the compound is unsaturated.

b. Add a few drops of pink acidified potassium manganate(VII) to a compound. If the solution is decolourized, the compound is unsaturated.

General properties of alkenes

Ethene and propene are colourless gases, the next 14 members of the series are liquids, and the higher members are solids. All are practically insoluble in water, but soluble in benzene and other organic solvents. They burn with a more luminous and smoky flame than the corresponding alkanes, since they contain a greater percentage of carbon. Their double bond makes them chemically active and addition reactions are easy.

Uses of ethene

Poly(ethene) or *polythene* is a white wax-like solid obtained by heating ethene at a very high pressure. It is a good electrical insulator and is therefore used in making cables. It resists acids, alkalis and other chemicals and is therefore used in chemical factories. Bottles and parts of some apparatus are now made of polythene.

Alkene isomers

There are three alkenes of molecular formula C_4H_8. Two of them have a chain of four carbon atoms in their molecules, and the third has a chain of three carbon atoms plus a branched chain:

C—C—C=C C—C=C—C C—C(—C)=C

The names and structural formulae are:

But-1-ene	But-2-ene	Methylpropene
$CH_3CH_2CH{=}CH_2$	$CH_3CH{=}CHCH_3$	$CH_3C(CH_3){=}CH_2$

Five alkenes are isomers with the formula C_5H_{10}. Two of them (pentenes) have five carbon atoms in a chain, with the double bond in different places:

1 2 / C=C—C—C—C   1 2 3 / C—C=C—C—C

Three have four carbon atoms in a chain:

C=C(—C)—C—C (1 2 3 4)   C=C—C(—C)—C (1 2 3 4)   C—C(—C)=C—C (1 2 3 4)

Write displayed formulae showing the ten hydrogen atoms in each of the five isomers. Make ball and stick, and also space filling models of these isomers. These models help to make clear that the carbon arrangement C—C—C—C=C is merely the same as the first isomer, C—C—C=C—C the same as the second, and C—C(—C)=C is the same as the fifth.

Organic acids

The general formula for organic acids is $C_nH_{2n+2}O_2$, or *R* COOH, where *R* is hydrogen or an alkyl radical. The acids contain the carboxyl group —COOH or –C(=O)—O—H.

Methanoic (formic) acid	Ethanoic (acetic) acid
HCOOH	CH_3COOH or H—C(H)(H)—C(=O)—O—H
H—C(=O)—O—H	

Acid	Formula	M.p. (°C)	B.p. (°C)	Density (g/cm^3)
Methanoic (formic)	$HCOOH$	8	101	1.22
Ethanoic (acetic)	CH_3COOH	17	118	1.05
Propanoic	C_2H_5COOH	−21	141	0.99
Butanoic	C_3H_7COOH	−4	164	0.96

To prepare ethanoic acid from ethanol

Add concentrated sulphuric acid (9 cm^3) *carefully* to cold water (10 cm^3) in a small (about 50 cm^3) flask. Then add sodium dichromate(VI) (11 g) to the mixture. Fit a vertical condenser into the neck of the flask. This is called a *reflux condenser* because vapours from the flask condense and run back into the flask.

Add water (8 cm^3) to ethanol (4 cm^3) in a test-tube. Use a small pipette to add this aqueous ethanol, 1 cm^3 at a time, to the flask through the condenser. Allow about 1 minute for each portion of ethanol to be oxidized by the acidified dichromate:

$$CH_3CH_2OH + 2O \text{ (from dichromate)} \rightarrow CH_3COOH + H_2O$$

Heat the mixture gently under reflux for 15 minutes or so to ensure that oxidation is complete.

Allow the apparatus to cool. Arrange the condenser for ordinary distillation. Distil the mixture and collect about 15 cm^3 of distillate, which is aqueous ethanoic acid.

(You do not need to remember the volumes and masses. Larger quantities may be used if larger apparatus is used.)

Properties of ethanoic acid

It is a colourless liquid with a smell of vinegar. On cooling it freezes to colourless ice-like crystals (m.p. 17 °C) and hence the pure acid is called *glacial ethanoic acid*. It is hygroscopic and is miscible with water in all proportions. It burns and blisters the skin, and is sometimes used to remove warts. It is a weak acid:

$$CH_3COOH(l) + H_2O(l) \rightleftharpoons H_3O^+ + CH_3COO^-(aq)$$

It reacts with metals to form hydrogen, and forms salts called ethanoates with bases and carbonates:

$$CH_3COOH(l) + NaOH(aq) \rightarrow H_2O(l) + CH_3COONa(aq),$$
sodium ethanoate

$$2CH_3COOH(l) + Na_2CO_3(aq) \rightarrow H_2O(l) + CO_2(g) + 2CH_3COONa(aq)$$

Alcohols (*ester formation*). Refer to p. 306. Ethanoic acid and ethanol form ethyl ethanoate, $CH_3COOC_2H_5$.

Questions

1 Outline a laboratory method of preparing ethanol. Explain briefly how you would convert ethanol into ethyl ethanoate. State ways in which esterification differs from neutralization. (N.)

2 How is methane prepared in the laboratory? Describe two chemical reactions of this gas, giving equations. Outline two reactions which distinguish methane from hydrogen. (N.)

3 How would you prepare (*a*) methane, (*b*) ethene? Compare their properties and account for any differences. (L.)

4 Write a concise essay on 'petroleum', dealing especially with the various substances obtained from it and their uses.

5 What are hydrocarbons? What is the chief source of such compounds? Write about 'hydrogenation of oils'.

6 Chlorine reacts with methane to form substitution products. By reference to these reactions, explain the meaning of 'substitution'.

7 Name three homologous series. Name and write the full displayed (graphic) formulae of the first three members of each series. How do the melting points, boiling points, densities and solubilities in water change with increasing relative molecular mass for any one series (no figures are required)?

8 Describe briefly, with equations, the reactions of (*a*) sulphuric acid on ethanol and on ethene, (*b*) oxidizing agents on ethanol, and (*c*) chlorine on ethene.

9 Explain, with one example in each case, the meanings of the following terms: alkane, alkene, double bond, addition, substitution, and esterification.

24
More about Organic Compounds

Plastics are the most important products manufactured from petroleum, and they include polythene, polystyrene, Perspex, Terylene and nylon. Plastics are man-made materials composed of giant molecules (macromolecules) based on carbon atoms. In 1930 two chemists studying the effects of high temperatures and pressures on ethene obtained a solid waxy substance. This was the polymer now known as polythene; its commercial production started in 1940. Ethene is obtained from petroleum by cracking (p. 304) heavy oils.

To demonstrate the cracking of heavy oils

Use the apparatus shown in Fig. 19.2. Soak the glass wool in medicinal paraffin (a mixture of alkanes). Heat the porous pot strongly and let the vapours from the medicinal paraffin pass through it. Collect gases formed in the test-tube. Show that the gases burn and decolorize dilute bromine water or bromine solution in trichloromethane (chloroform). They are alkenes.

In this experiment the long molecules of medicinal paraffin are 'cracked' to form shorter molecules and also the alkane molecules lose some hydrogen (dehydrogenation) and become unsaturated alkenes, which are reactive and more useful for forming other substances.

$$—CH_2—CH_2— \rightarrow —CH{=}CH— + H_2\text{, dehydrogenation}$$

To study the action of heat on plastics

Hold a small piece of a plastic in tongs. Heat it gently above a flame and then, if no change occurs in about one minute, heat in the flame. Observe any effects.

Thermoplastics (e.g. polythene, polystyrene, Perspex, nylon) soften on warming and become rigid on cooling; softening and hardening are reversible. *Thermosetting plastics* (e.g. bakelite, rubber) decompose when heated.

Polymerization and polymers

Polymerization (or addition polymerization) is the formation of a single molecule by the combination of two or more molecules of the same kind with no loss or gain of matter.

Dinitrogen tetraoxide is a polymer of nitrogen dioxide, and both have the general formula $(NO_2)_n$. The general equation for addition polymerizations is: $nX = X_n$. X is the *monomer* ('one part') and X_n is the *polymer* ('many parts'). Several organic compounds polymerize to form *high polymers* in which n is a large number (several hundreds). Therefore polymerization can convert small molecules into giant molecules or *macromolecules*, containing hundreds of atoms. Polythene, polystyrene, Terylene, nylon and Perspex are high polymers.

Carbon's valency bonds in space

The valency bonds of carbon have been represented on a plane surface at right angles to each other. This is not correct because there should then be two dichloromethanes:

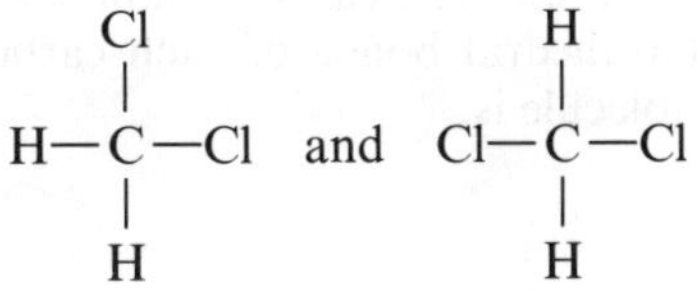

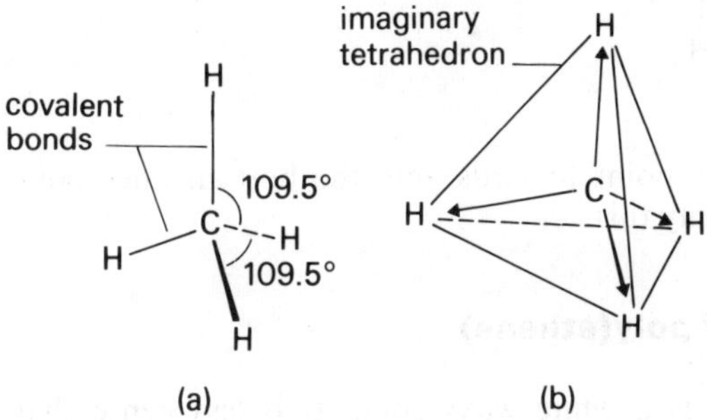

Fig. 24.1 Tetrahedral structure of methane

There is only one. We now know that all four covalent bonds of carbon are alike in every respect and symmetrical in three dimensions. The bonds are directed towards the corners of an imaginary tetrahedron, of which the carbon atom is the centre (*tetrahedral distribution of bonds*). The angle between two adjacent bonds is 109.5°. Make ball-and-spoke and/or space-filling models of methane and ethene molecules.

Manufacture of poly(ethene) (polythene or polyethylene)

High pressure process. Ethene is heated to 200 °C under 1500 atm pressure with a little oxygen as catalyst. The product is low density poly(ethene) or LDPE. Its density is 0.92 g/cm^3.

Ziegler process. This is a low temperature and low pressure process of polymerization. Ethene is dissolved in a hydrocarbon solvent containing various complex catalysts. The temperature is about 70 °C and the pressure about 5 atmospheres. The product is high density poly(ethene), HDPE, of density 0.96 g/cm^3.

Structure of poly(ethene) (polythene or polyethylene)

Poly(ethene) contains chains of about 1200 carbon atoms:

$$nC_2H_4 \rightarrow (C_2H_4)_n \quad n = \text{about } 600$$

$$\text{or } n(CH_2{=}CH_2) \rightarrow (-CH_2-CH_2-)_n$$

There is a CH_3 group at each end of a molecule. The carbon chain is zig-zag and not 'straight' because of the tetrahedral bonds of each carbon atom. A better formula for part of the molecule is:

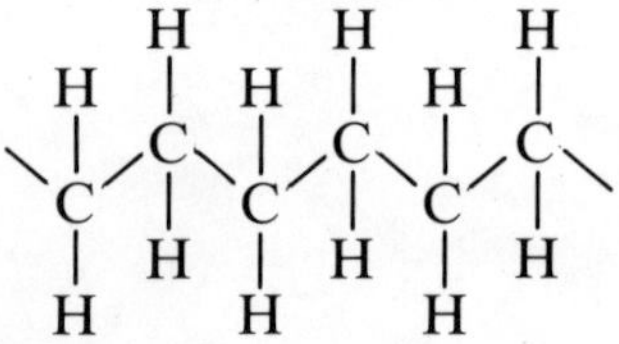

If the top hydrogen atoms point towards you, the bottom ones point away. Make a model to verify this.

Properties and uses of poly(ethene)

Poly(ethene) or polythene is a white waxy solid. It is less dense than water, tough, insoluble in all solvents at room temperature, and a good electrical insulator. It does not rot, corrode or react with common chemical reagents. Low density poly(ethene) softens at about 95 °C. All the carbon atoms in a molecule are not 'straight' and there are about 40 side chains, e.g.

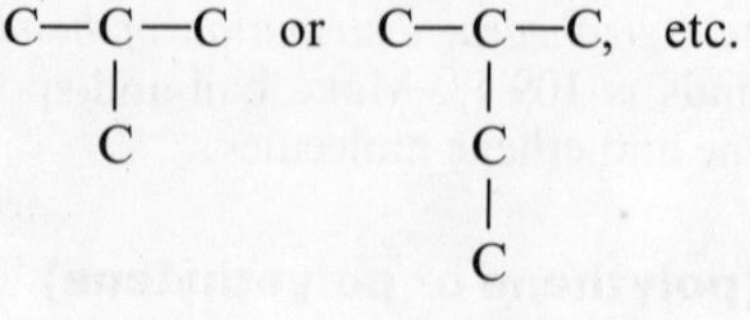

The side chains stop the molecules packing closely and account for the low density and lower softening temperature (the forces between the molecules are weaker because of their distance apart and therefore less energy is required to overcome the forces). Since its molecules are of various lengths, poly(ethene) softens like a mixture and does not melt at a definite temperature.

Molecules of high density poly(ethene) contain few side chains. They pack closely, and this accounts for its higher density and higher softening temperature of about 120 °C.

Uses of poly(ethene). A film of the plastic is used for carrier bags and containers for cans, bottles and cartons, sacks to hold fertilizers, chemicals, animal feedstuffs, solid fuel and agricultural products. It prevents contamination, damage and pilfering. A film used (instead of glass) to cover plants, protects them from bad weather and lengthens the growing season in many countries. Dustbins, toys, car carpets, ropes, cold and hot water pipes, and bottles for milk and fruit juices are made from the high density plastic. The low density plastic is used to cover underground and overhead telephone cables on land and under the sea, because it keeps out water and is a good insulator.

Phenylethene (styrene) and poly(phenylethene) (polystyrene)

Phenylethene is a substituted ethene, $CHY{=}CH_2$, in which Y is $C_6H_5—$, the phenyl group. It polymerizes to poly(phenylethene), commonly called polystyrene:

$$nC_8H_8 \rightarrow (C_8H_8)_n \quad n = \text{up to } 5000$$

$$\text{or } n(CHY{=}CH_2) \rightarrow (—CHY—CH_2—)_n$$

Since the carbon atoms in the chain are zig-zag a better formula is:

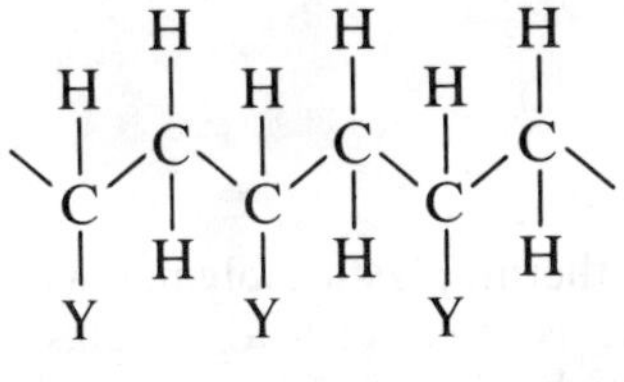

$Y = C_6H_5$

The large C_6H_5 groups prevent the large macromolecules vibrating, bending and rotating easily; they account for the relatively high softening and melting points of the plastic.

To polymerize phenylethene (styrene). Mix equal volumes (about 10 cm^3) of phenylethene and kerosine, a catalyst. Boil at about 150 °C for 1 hour, using a reflux air condenser. Allow the mixture to cool and pour it into five times its own volume of methanol. Poly(phenylethene) (polystyrene) separates as a white solid. Place the solid in fresh methanol and work it with a spatula until it forms a wax.

Properties and uses of poly(phenylethene) (polystyrene)

It is a hard transparent plastic with a melting point about 230 °C. Like poly(ethene) it does not rot or corrode, resists chemical reagents, and is a good insulator. It is used to make containers and tableware, and in the electrical industry.

To study the action of heat on Perspex

Place small pieces of Perspex (about 5 g) in a hard-glass test-tube and arrange the apparatus as in Fig. 1.6. Heat the Perspex with a moderate flame and collect the distillate in the cooled test-tube. Do the experiment in a fume cupboard or near an open window, because poisonous fumes are formed. The distillate contains the methyl ester of an unsaturated acid:

$$\begin{array}{l} \quad\quad\ CH_3 \\ \quad\quad\quad | \\ H_2C{=}C \\ \quad\quad\quad | \\ \quad\quad\ COOCH_3 \end{array} \qquad \text{(methyl methylpropenoate)}$$

This is the monomer of Perspex. It is a disubstituted ethene, with $-COOCH_3$ and $-CH_3$ groups in place of two hydrogen atoms of one carbon atom of each ethene molecule.

To prepare Perspex. Warm water in a beaker to about 50 °C and stand the test-tube containing the above distillate in the warm water. Add a few drops of catalyst (dodecanoyl peroxide) and leave for about 2 hours. Maintain the water temperature at about 50 °C during this time. A specimen of Perspex gradually forms.

Properties and uses of Perspex

Perspex is a hard, brilliantly transparent thermoplastic polymer with a softening temperature of about 95 °C. It is used instead of glass in aircraft, helicopters, and buildings in which glass windows would be dangerous. One disadvantage is that Perspex scratches easily.

Nylon

A fibre is a solid whose length can be thousands of times greater than its width and which is strong and flexible enough to make cloth, ropes, belting, etc. Silk is the most valued natural fibre. It consists of macromolecules with long chains of atoms. Nylon (and Terylene) contain similar molecules made by *condensation polymerization*, which is the formation of a single molecule by the combination of many molecules and the elimination of water. Each of the two molecules has two reactive groups (—OH, $—NH_2$ or —COOH), one at each end.

Nylon 66 is made from hexanedioic acid, $HOOC(CH_2)_4COOH$, and hexanediamine, $H_2N(CH_2)_6NH_2$. They are polymerized at high temperature and pressure. The product is called 66 because both molecules contain 6 carbon atoms. A simple equation for the reaction forming nylon 66 is:

$$H_2N—X—NH_2 + HO—CO—Y—CO—OH \rightarrow —HN—X—NH—CO—Y—CO— + 2H_2O$$

nylon (a polyamide)

$X = (CH_2)_6 \quad Y = (CH_2)_4$

Nylon 6 is made from aminohexanoic acid, $H_2N(CH_2)_5COOH$, which contains the reactive NH_2 and COOH groups in one molecule. A simple equation is:

$$2H_2N(CH_2)_5COOH \rightarrow H_2N(CH_2)_5CONH(CH_2)_5COOH$$

The full formulae (which need not be remembered) are:

$HO[OC(CH_2)_4CONH(CH_2)_6NH]_nH$
Nylon 66 $\quad n$ = about 75

$H_2N(CH_2)_5[CONH(CH_2)_5]_nCOOH$
Nylon 6

The relative molecular mass of each is about 15 000.

Nylon contains many amide groups (—CO—NH—) in each molecule and it is a *polyamide*. A block diagram makes its structure clear:

[X]—NH—CO—[Y]—CO—NH—[X] etc. Nylon

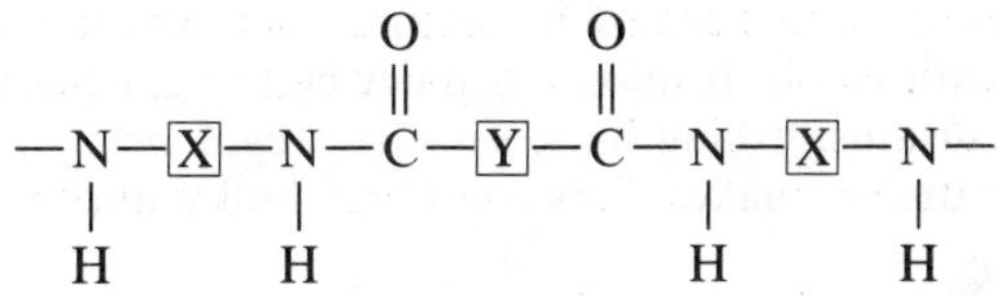

X and Y are the same, $(CH_2)_5$, in nylon 6. Nylon 6 melts at 210 °C and nylon 66 at 250 °C. Both are unreactive and insoluble in most solvents. They are light, elastic, do not absorb water, do not fade, keep their shape, are insect-proof, can be dyed, and keep permanent creases. They are used for clothing, carpets, curtains, parachutes, etc.

To prepare nylon

Make 2 cm^3 of a 5 per cent solution of hexanedioyl chloride in tetrachloromethane or cyclohexane. Add the solution to a crucible or 5 cm^3 beaker. Now add 2 cm^3 of a 5 per cent aqueous solution of hexanediamine. The two solutions must not mix. Use forceps to pull a fibre of nylon from the interface between the solutions. Wrap the fibre around a glass rod and keep turning the rod.

Terylene and rubber

Terylene is made from ethanediol, $HOCH_2CH_2OH$, and benzenedicarboxylic acid, $HOOCC_6H_4COOH$. The reactive OH and COOH groups combine and water is eliminated. The product is a *polyester*. A simple equation and a block diagram show the reaction:

$$\underset{\text{Ethanediol}}{H{-}O{-}X{-}O{-}H} + \underset{\text{Acid}}{HO{-}CO{-}Y{-}CO{-}OH} \rightarrow \underset{\text{Terylene (a polyester)}}{{-}O{-}X{-}O{-}CO{-}Y{-}CO{-}} + 2H_2O$$

$$\boxed{X}{-}O{-}CO{-}\boxed{Y}{-}CO{-}O{-}\boxed{X}\ \text{etc. Terylene}$$

$${-}O{-}\boxed{X}{-}O{-}\overset{\overset{\displaystyle O}{\|}}{C}{-}\boxed{Y}{-}\overset{\overset{\displaystyle O}{\|}}{C}{-}O{-}\boxed{X}{-}O$$

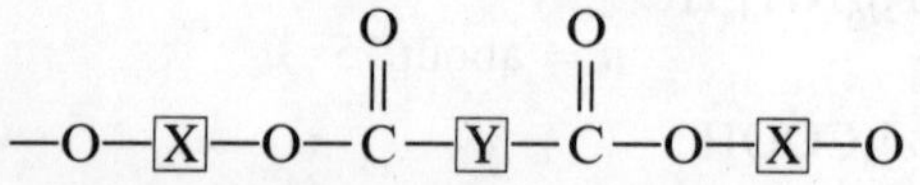

$$X = CH_2{-}CH_2 \quad Y = C_6H_4$$

The full formula (which need not be remembered) is:

$$HOCH_2{-}[CH_2OOC{-}C_6H_4{-}COOCH_2]_n{-}COOH$$

Its relative molecular mass is about 15 000 (the same as nylon).

Terylene is used for making suits because its texture resembles that of wool (usually it is mixed with wool). It makes drip-dry clothing, trousers with permanent creases, curtains, fishing lines, sails, conveyor belts, and similar articles. Steam treatment makes Terylene fibres bulky and produces Crimplene.

Natural rubber is a polymer with long carbon chains:

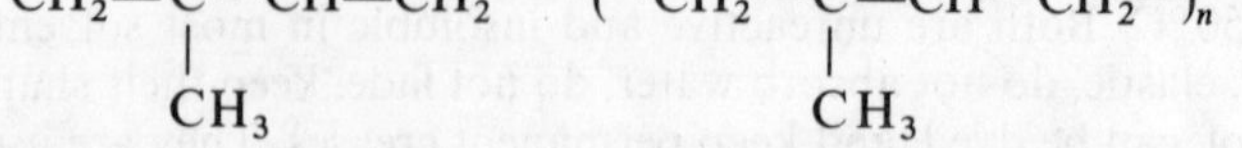

$$\underset{\text{2-methyl-1,3-diene}}{CH_2{=}\underset{\underset{\displaystyle CH_3}{|}}{C}{-}CH{=}CH_2} \qquad \underset{\text{Natural rubber } (n = 1000 \text{ to } 5000)}{({-}CH_2{-}\underset{\underset{\displaystyle CH_3}{|}}{C}{=}CH{-}CH_2{-})_n}$$

Hot rubber reacts with sulphur to form strong, elastic commercial rubber. The sulphur adds to a few double bonds (about 1 in 75). The carbon chains are now cross-linked by carbon–carbon and carbon–sulphur covalent bonds:

Commercial rubber

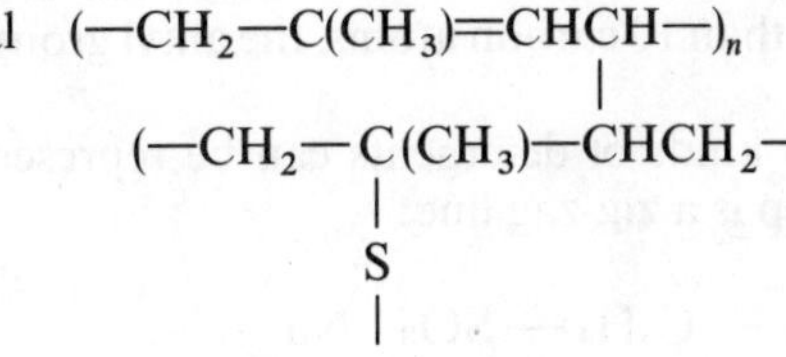

Molecules of poly(ethene), poly(phenylethene), and other polyalkenes, which have no cross-links, are held in place only by relatively weak intermolecular forces (p. 12). At high temperatures these forces are not strong enough; the polymers soften on heating but solidify on cooling. The change is physical and reversible. Commercial rubber (and bakelite) are called *thermosetting* plastics because each softens and decomposes on heating. Heat breaks the covalent cross-links in the rubber molecules. The change is chemical and irreversible.

Petroleum as a source of organic compounds

The cracking of heavy oils in petroleum yields alkenes which are raw materials for a large manufacturing industry.

Ethanol is obtained by addition of steam to ethene (ethylene) in the presence of a heated catalyst:

$$H_2C{=}CH_2(g) + HOH(g) \rightarrow CH_3CH_2OH(g \text{ then } l)$$

Water is added indirectly by absorbing ethene in concentrated sulphuric acid and diluting with water.

Ethanediol is made by addition of atmospheric oxygen to ethene in the presence of a heated catalyst, and then letting the ethene oxide react with water:

$$2H_2C{=}CH_2(g) + O_2(g) \rightarrow 2(CH_2)_2O(g), \text{ ethene oxide}$$

$$(CH_2)_2O(g) + H_2O(l) \rightarrow (CH_2OH)_2, \text{ ethanediol}$$

Ethanediol is used to manufacture Terylene.

Detergents

A *detergent* is any substance that facilitates the emulsification and removal of grease. Soap is a detergent, but the name is usually used for synthetic substitutes for soap.

Detergents are made by treating the higher alkanes with sulphuric acid to produce organic acids and then forming the sodium salts. The formula is $RC_6H_4SO_3Na$. R is an alkyl group with a chain of 10 to 18 carbon atoms and sometimes with side-chains or rings of carbon atoms. If it contains more than 18 carbon atoms, the sodium salt is not soluble in water; if it contains less than 10 carbon atoms, the alkyl group is not soluble enough in grease.

The formulae of two kinds of detergents can be represented as below, in which the alkyl group is a zig-zag line:

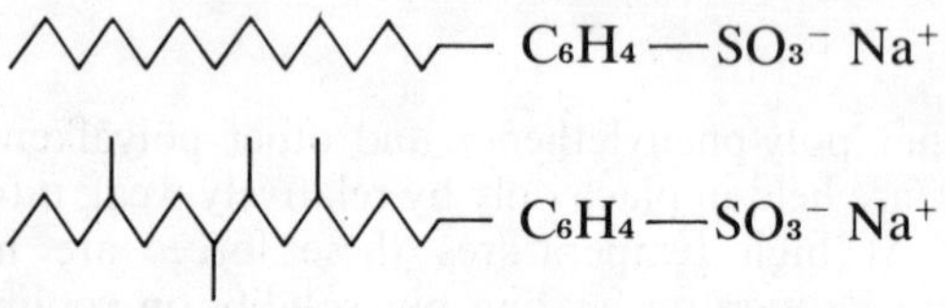

Note the side chains in the second formula. Detergent molecules with such chains cannot be broken down by bacteria and are called non-biodegradable. Foam from such detergents pollutes streams and rivers. Molecules with unbranched alkyl groups are biodegradable and are destroyed by bacteria.

How detergents clean

A detergent molecule is made up of two parts. One has a strong affinity for water, i.e. it is water-soluble; this part is SO_3Na. The RC_6H_4 group has a strong affinity for oils and fats, i.e. it is fat-soluble. The water-soluble group in ordinary soap ($C_{17}H_{35}COONa$) is COONa and the fat-soluble part is the chain of 17 carbon atoms, $C_{17}H_{35}$.

The fat-soluble part of detergent penetrates grease while the water-soluble group remains in the water. The grease splits up into tiny globules which are then carried away by the water.

To prepare a detergent from castor oil

Add about 1 cm^3 of castor oil (or coconut oil) to a test-tube and then use a teat pipette to add about 2 cm^3 of concentrated sulphuric acid, stirring the mixture with a glass rod. The mixture becomes hot, viscous and dark in colour (because of some charring). Add the product to about 10 cm^3 of distilled water and stir to remove excess acid. Decant the aqueous part and wash the solid detergent with distilled water. (Oil and alkali form soap, p. 193.)

Proteins and carbohydrates

These substances contain natural macromolecules. *Proteins* occur in meat, milk, hair, wool, silk, leather, etc. They are condensation polymers of which the monomers are amino acids (organic acids with —COOH and $-NH_2$ groups). Twenty six amino acids occur in proteins. Water is eliminated when amino acids polymerize:

$$2NH_2{-}X{-}COOH \rightarrow NH_2{-}X{-}CO{-}NH{-}X{-}COOH + H_2O$$

$$X{=}CH_2 \text{ or } CH_2{-}CH_2 \text{ or } C_6H_4 \text{ etc.}$$

The —NH—CO— group is a *peptide linkage* (compare the amide link in nylon). Hundreds of amino-acid molecules can link together, and some proteins contain 2000 or more amino-acid molecules and 20 or more different amino acids; they are the most complex substances known. Common proteins are albumen (white of egg), haemoglobin (in blood), gelatin (in bones) and casein (in milk). When proteins are boiled with acids or alkalis, water adds to the peptide linkage by hydrolysis and amino acids are produced. This change occurs during digestion as a result of the catalytic action of enzymes.

Carbohydrates are compounds of carbon, hydrogen and oxygen, and their general formula is $C_xH_{2y}O_y$. The formula $C_x(H_2O)_y$ is incorrect because they do not contain water. Glucose, $C_6H_{12}O_6$, is present in leaves of plants and many fruits; it is formed by photosynthesis. When glucose is warmed with Fehling's solution, it forms a red precipitate of copper(I) oxide, Cu_2O.

Starch and *dextrin* have the formula $(C_6H_{10}O_5)_n$ in which n can be 3000 and the relative molecular mass about 500 000. Starch is probably formed from glucose by condensation polymerization:

$$n(C_6H_{12}O_6) \rightarrow (C_6H_{10}O_5)_n + nH_2O$$

The reverse change, hydrolysis, occurs when starch is warmed with dilute acids and when the enzyme ptyalin, present in saliva, acts on cooked starch. Dextrin is formed when dry starch is heated to about 200 °C, e.g. when toasting bread. It is similar to starch but its relative molecular mass is not so high.

Prepare starch solution by mixing 1 g of starch with 10 cm^3 of water and pouring the paste into about 100 cm^3 of boiling water. Boil and stir for about 2 minutes.

To break down starch to glucose by hydrolysis

a Boil starch solution with dilute hydrochloric acid for 5 minutes, cool, neutralize with aqueous sodium hydroxide, and test the product with Fehling's solution.

b Add diastase (or saliva, which contains the enzyme ptyalin) to starch solution and warm to about 35 °C. Allow reaction to proceed for several minutes and then test the product with Fehling's solution.

(Fermentation breaks down glucose farther to ethanol, and heat breaks down ethanol to ethene.)

Structures of carbohydrates

Glucose (grape sugar) and fructose (fruit sugar) are isomers of empirical formula CH_2O and molecular formula $C_6H_{12}O_6$. They can be represented simply by a block diagram showing only one of their hydroxyl groups:

$\boxed{G}$—O—H $\boxed{F}$—O—H
Glucose Fructose

Sucrose (cane sugar, beet sugar) is formed when one molecule of each of these two simple sugars combine with loss of water:

$$C_6H_{12}O_6 + C_6H_{12}O_6 \rightarrow C_{12}H_{22}O_{11} + H_2O$$

A block formula is $\boxed{G}$—O—$\boxed{F}$ (sucrose). A molecule of starch is formed when up to 3000 molecules of glucose combine with loss of water. Its block formula is

—$\boxed{G}$—O—$\boxed{G}$—O—$\boxed{G}$—O—$\boxed{G}$— (starch).

Questions

1 Outline one method by which you would prepare and collect one gas-jar of ethene. What is meant by the polymerization of nitrogen dioxide and of ethene, and how do their polymerizations differ?

2 How is ethene used in the manufacture of poly(ethene), ethanol and ethanediol, $(CH_2OH)_2$. Write a displayed (graphic) formula of ethanediol.

3 Describe briefly how the following plastics are made: (*a*) a polyalkene polymer, (*b*) a polyamide or polyester polymer. Indicate briefly the structures of the polymers you choose.

4 Describe one experiment you have done to depolymerize Perspex to its monomer methyl methylpropenoate. Outline how you would break down naturally occurring macromolecules (e.g. starch or a protein).

5 What are the advantages of man-made fibres over natural ones such as silk and wool? Write block diagrams showing the structure of one kind of nylon and of Terylene (use X and Y to represent complex groups present). Explain why these plastics are called polyamide and polyester compounds.

6 Describe experiments you have done or seen (*a*) to make a specimen of plastic, (*b*) to break down a named plastic into its monomer, and (*c*) to make a specimen of detergent. Explain the changes that occur in each experiment.

25
Volumetric Analysis

The object of volumetric analysis is to determine the mass of a compound in a solid or solution. Two aqueous solutions are used; the concentration of one is known and the concentration of the other is unknown. The essential process (*titration*) consists of running one solution, from a burette, into a known volume (10 or 25 cm^3) of the other until the two solutions have just reacted completely. When this is so, the *neutral-* or *end-point* of the titration is reached, and the volume of the solution used from the burette is noted.

Standard and M solutions

A *standard* solution is one which contains a known mass of a solute in a given volume of solution.

The *concentration* (symbol *c*) of a solution is the amount of solute divided by the volume of solution.

$$\text{Concentration} = \frac{\text{Amount of solution (mol)}}{\text{Volume of solution (dm}^3\text{)}}$$

The unit of concentration is mol/dm^3. The unit for *mass concentration* is g/dm^3. A solution of concentration 1.00 mol/dm^3 is called a M solution. M solutions are often too concentrated and it is usual to use more dilute solutions. *A* 0.1 M *solution contains one-tenth of a mole of a solute in* 1000 *cm^3 of solution.*

If a solution of known concentration is diluted:

(Concentration × Volume) of original solution = (Concentration × Volume) of diluted solution

Calculations using M concentrations

Consider a reaction in which 1 mole of acid reacts with 1 mole of alkali or carbonate, e.g.

$HCl(aq)$	$+ NaOH(aq)$	$\rightarrow NaCl + H_2O$
36.5 g or	40 g or	
1000 cm^3 M acid	1000 cm^3 M alkali	

$$\therefore \frac{\text{(Concentration × Volume) of acid}}{\text{(Concentration × Volume) of alkali}} = \frac{1}{1} = \frac{\text{moles of acid}}{\text{moles of alkali}}$$

If 1 mole of acid reacts with 2 moles of alkali or carbonate (or vice versa), e.g.

$$2HCl(aq) + Na_2CO_3(aq) \rightarrow 2NaCl + CO_2 + H_2O$$

2000 cm^3 M acid; 1000 cm^3 M carbonate

$$\frac{(\text{Concentration} \times \text{Volume}) \text{ of acid}}{(\text{Concentration} \times \text{Volume}) \text{ of carbonate}} = \frac{2}{1} = \frac{\text{moles of acid}}{\text{moles of carbonate}}$$

Indicators

These are litmus, methyl orange, screened methyl orange, and phenolphthalein.

	Colour		
Indicator	Acid	Alkaline	Unsuitable for
Litmus	Red	Blue	Carbonate titrations, unless the solution is boiled to drive off the carbon dioxide.
Methyl orange	Red	Yellow	Titrations with weak acids,
Screened methyl orange	Violet	Green	e.g. ethanoic (acetic) acid, ethanedioic (oxalic) acid.
Phenolphthalein	Colourless	Red	Titrations with aqueous ammonia.

Standard solutions

Sodium carbonate absorbs water from the air, but the moisture can be removed by heating and the pure, dry carbonate can be weighed in air without change. Similarly, pure ethanedioic acid is readily obtainable and does not change during storage. It is easy to prepare standard solutions of these substances.

To prepare a standard solution of sodium carbonate, approximately 0.05 M

Principle. The molar mass of sodium carbonate is 106 g.

∴ 1000 cm^3 of 0.05 M sodium carbonate contains 5.3 g and 250 cm^3 of 0.05 M sodium carbonate contains 1.325 g. The 0.05 M solution is prepared by dissolving exactly 1.325 g of pure sodium carbonate in water to make 250 cm^3 of solution. Pure, dry sodium carbonate is obtained in two

ways:
a Sodium carbonate can be bought free from all impurities except water. It is dried by heating before use.
b Sodium hydrogencarbonate is heated until all the water and carbon dioxide have been driven off and the mass of the residual sodium carbonate is constant:

$$2NaHCO_3(s) \rightarrow Na_2CO_3(s) + CO_2(g) + H_2O(g)$$

Method

1 *Preparation of pure, dry sodium carbonate.* Prepare the carbonate in one of the following ways:
a Place sodium carbonate in a dish and heat gently to drive off moisture. Allow to cool in a desiccator and then find the mass of the dish and contents. Repeat until the mass is constant, i.e. until all the moisture has been driven off.
b Heat sodium hydrogencarbonate in a clean, dry evaporating dish. Carbon dioxide and steam are given off. Cool and find the mass as in the first method. Repeat until a constant mass is reached.

2 *Finding the mass of the sodium carbonate.*
a Find the mass of a clean dry watch-glass. Add about 1.32 g of sodium carbonate to the watch-glass and find the total mass.
b Put about 1.5 g of sodium carbonate, i.e. a little more than is required, into a weighing bottle or on to a watch-glass and find the total mass accurately. Transfer most of the carbonate into a beaker and find the total mass again. The difference between the masses is the mass of sodium carbonate used.

3 *Preparation of the solution.*
a Tip the sodium carbonate into a beaker containing warm distilled water. If the water is cold, the carbonate forms hard lumps which do not dissolve readily. Stir with a glass rod until the carbonate completely dissolves.
b Carefully pour the solution into a clean (but not necessarily dry) 250 cm^3 graduated flask. Place a filter funnel in the neck of the flask so that the solution can be added without spilling it. Use a wash bottle to wash the beaker and stirring rod with cold distilled water and pour the washings into the flask. Also wash the sides of the filter funnel. Every drop of solution must be transferred into the flask.
c Fill the flask up to the mark, using distilled water, adding the last few drops by means of a pipette. The bottom of the meniscus must be on the mark.
d Place the stopper in the flask and invert and shake until the solution is thoroughly mixed. Do not add any more water even if the meniscus is now below the mark.

Specimen result

1 Mass of watch-glass = 6.45 g
2 Mass of watch-glass + carbonate = 7.86 g

Mass of sodium carbonate = 1.41 g
This mass was dissolved to form $250\,cm^3$ of solution.
Hence $1000\,cm^3$ of solution contain $4 \times 1.41 = 5.64$ g.
106 g of sodium carbonate in $1\,dm^3$ of solution is a M solution.
$\therefore$ 5.64 g of sodium carbonate in $1\,dm^3$ of solution is

$$\frac{5.64}{106}\,M = 0.053\,M.$$

To prepare an approximately 0.1 M hydrochloric acid and to standardize it against standard sodium carbonate solution

Principle. The molar mass of the acid HCl is 36.5 g.

$\therefore$ $1\,dm^3$ of 0.1 M acid contains 3.65 g of acid.

i.e. $250\,cm^3$ of 0.1 M acid contain $\frac{3.65}{4}\,g = 0.9125$ g of acid.

It is impossible to measure accurately 0.9125 g of the acid. Pure, concentrated hydrochloric acid contains about 36 per cent by mass of hydrogen chloride and is about 11 M. If this is diluted 100 times the diluted acid is about 0.1 M.

Method

1 *Dilute the acid.* Add about $10\,cm^3$ of concentrated hydrochloric acid to a flask and add about $1\,dm^3$ of water. Mix thoroughly. You do not need to measure these volumes accurately.

2 *Filling the burette with the diluted acid.*

a Wash out the burette with water.

b Wash out the burette with a few cm^3 of the diluted acid. The whole of the inside of the burette should be wet with acid. Clamp it vertically in its stand.

c Fill the burette with the acid. Open the tap or clip and ensure that the jet is filled with acid and does not contain an air bubble. The level of the acid must be at or below the zero mark.

d Align your eye, level with the bottom of the meniscus. Hold a piece of white paper behind the burette and note the reading, accurate to at least $0.05\,cm^3$ (Fig. 25.1).

3 *Measuring $25\,cm^3$ (or $10\,cm^3$) of standard sodium carbonate.*

a Wash four conical flasks with water.

b *Using a pipette.* Suck the standard sodium carbonate solution into a 25- or $10\text{-}cm^3$ pipette until the level is above the mark. Allow the solution to run into the sink. The inside of the pipette is now wet only with the carbonate solution it is to measure.

c Suck sodium carbonate solution into the pipette until the level is above the mark and then close the end with the moistened tip of the

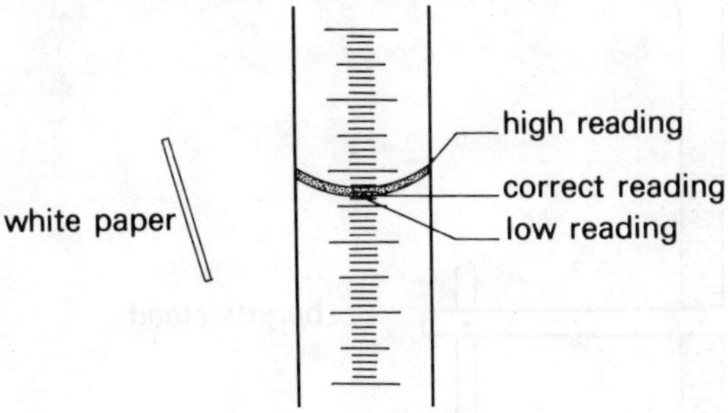

Fig. 25.1 Reading a burette

forefinger (not the thumb). Gently release the pressure until the level is exactly at the mark—your eye must be level with the meniscus and the bottom of the meniscus must be at the mark (Fig. 25.2).

d Allow the carbonate solution to run into one of the conical flasks. Let the pipette drain for 15 seconds and then touch the surface of the solution with the end of the pipette—do not blow or shake out the last drop of solution.

e Fill the three remaining conical flasks with 25 cm^3 (or 10 cm^3) of solution.

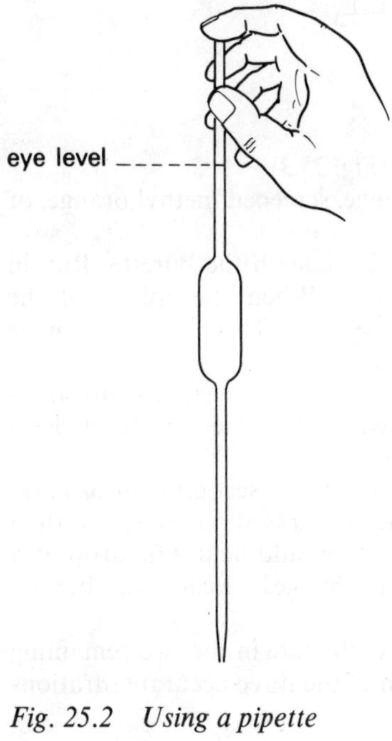

Fig. 25.2 Using a pipette

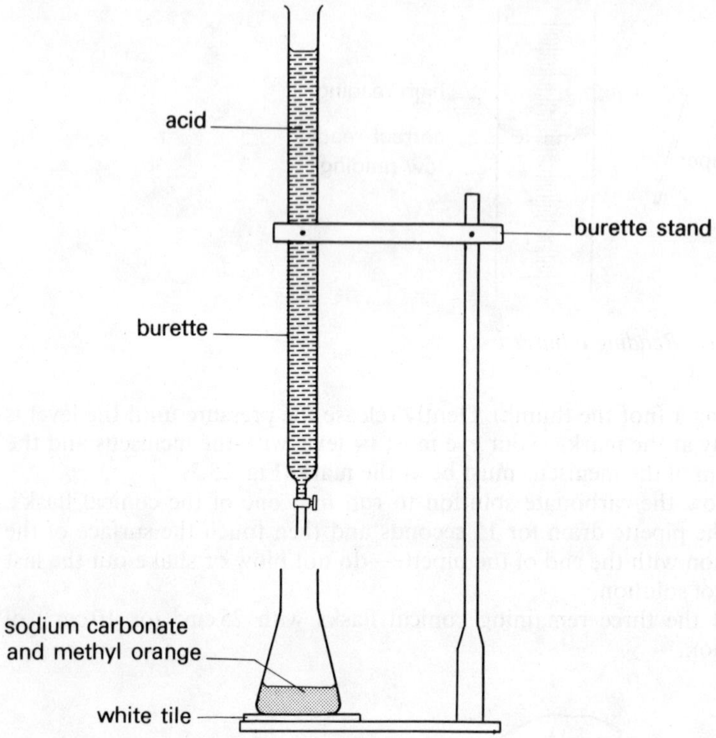

Fig. 25.3 Titration apparatus

4 *Titration of the carbonate with the acid* (*Fig. 25.3*).

a Add 2 drops of indicator (methyl orange, screened methyl orange, or methyl yellow) to each conical flask.

b Stand one of the flasks on a white tile beneath the burette. Run in the acid, adding about 1 cm^3 at a time. When the colour of the indicator changes, note the level of the acid. This first titration is approximate.

c Add more acid to the burette if necessary. However, two titrations can often be done before more acid needs to be added. Note the level of the acid.

d Repeat the titration with the carbonate in the second conical flask. In this accurate titration, run in a volume of acid of about 1 cm^3 less than that used in the approximate titration. Now add acid, one drop at a time, until the indicator colour just changes. Read the burette accurately.

e Repeat the titration with the sodium carbonate in the two remaining flasks. The volumes of acid used in each of the three accurate titrations should not differ by more than 0.1 cm^3.

From the titration 25 cm³ of 0.053 M carbonate solution neutralize 22.70 cm³ of hydrochloric acid solution.

$$\frac{(\text{Concentration} \times \text{Volume}) \text{ of acid}}{(\text{Concentration} \times \text{Volume}) \text{ of carbonate}} = \frac{2}{1} \text{ (see p. 326)}$$

$$\therefore \frac{\text{Concentration of acid} \times 22.70}{0.053 \times 25} = \frac{2}{1}$$

$$\text{i.e. Concentration of acid} = 0.117\,\text{M}$$

M acid contains 36.5 g of acid per 1000 cm³.

∴ 0.117 M acid contains 0.117 × 36.5 g of acid per 1000 cm³ = 4.27 g acid.

The hydrochloric acid contains 4.27 g of acid per 1000 cm³.

Titration	Volume of Na_2CO_3 (cm³)	Burette readings First	Burette readings Second	Volume of HCl used (cm³)
Trial	25	1.50	24.50	23 (*approx.*)
1st	25	24.50	47.15	22.65 (*accurate*)
2nd	25	0.15	22.85	22.70 ”
3rd	25	22.85	45.55	22.70 ”

Average 22.70

To prepare approximately 0.1 M sodium hydroxide and to standardize it against standard hydrochloric acid

Principle. The molar mass of sodium hydroxide is 40 g.

1000 cm³ of 0.1 M hydroxide solution contains 4 g of sodium hydroxide.

∴ 250 cm³ of 0.1 M hydroxide solution contain 1 g of sodium hydroxide.

It is not possible to measure accurately 1 g of sodium hydroxide because the solid rapidly absorbs water and carbon dioxide from the air. Approximately 1 g of the solid is dissolved in 250 cm³ of solution to make an approximately 0.1 M solution.

Method.

a Measure on a watch-glass about 1 g of sodium hydroxide. Transfer it to a beaker and dissolve in water. Make up the solution to about 250 cm³ and shake well.

b Place 25 cm³ (or 10 cm³) of the alkali in each of four flasks. Add 2 drops of indicator and titrate until three results have been obtained. Any indicator except phenolphthalein is suitable. Calculate the M concentration of the sodium hydroxide, p. 325.

To prepare approximately 0.05 M ethanedioic acid and to use it to standardize sodium hydroxide solution

Principle. The molar mass of the acid crystals, $(COOH)_2 \cdot 2H_2O$, is 126 g.
1000 cm^3 of 0.05 M acid contains 6.3 g of crystals.

$\therefore$ 250 cm^3 of 0.05 M acid contain 1.575 g of crystals.

Method.
a Find the mass of a watch-glass. Add about 1.60 g of hydrated acid and find the accurate mass again.
b Transfer the crystals to a beaker and dissolve in distilled water. Make up to 250 cm^3 in graduated flask.
c Fill the burette with the sodium hydroxide solution.
d Titrate 25 cm^3 (or 10 cm^3) of the acid solution with the alkali, using phenolphthalein as indicator, until three concordant results have been obtained.
Specimen result. The equation is:

$$(COOH)_2 \cdot 2H_2O + 2NaOH \rightarrow (COONa)_2 + 4H_2O$$

$$\therefore \frac{(\text{Concentration} \times \text{Volume}) \text{ of alkali}}{(\text{Concentration} \times \text{Volume}) \text{ of acid}} = \frac{2}{1}$$

The concentration of acid is known and the volumes are obtained by titration. Therefore the concentration of alkali can be calculated.

To determine the number of molecules of water of crystallization in sodium carbonate (washing soda) crystals

Principle. A standard solution of washing soda is prepared by dissolving a known mass a of crystals in a definite volume of solution. The mass of the anhydrous sodium carbonate b in these crystals is determined by titration against standard acid solution.
Mass a of crystals contains mass b of anhydrous salt,

$$\text{i.e.} \frac{\text{water}}{\text{anhydrous salt}} = \frac{(a-b)}{b}$$

The formula for the crystals may be written

$$\begin{array}{ll} Na_2CO_3 \cdot & yH_2O \\ 106 & 18y \end{array}$$

$$\therefore \frac{\text{water}}{\text{anhydrous salt}} = \frac{18y}{106} = \frac{(a-b)}{b}$$

and the value of y can be calculated.

Questions

1 What are the M concentrations of the following solutions?
a sulphuric acid containing 19.6 g per dm^3;
b sodium hydroxide containing 8 g per 100 cm^3 of solution;
c sodium hydrogencarbonate containing 8.4 g per 400 cm^3 of solution.

2 What mass of pure substance is contained in each of the following solutions?
a 5 dm^3 of 0.1 M hydrochloric acid;
b 250 cm^3 of 0.2 M sodium hydroxide solution;
c 25 cm^3 of 2 M potassium hydroxide solution.

3 1 g of pure calcium carbonate was added to 120 cm^3 of 0.5 M hydrochloric acid. What mass of acid remained unchanged?

4 What volume of 0.9 M acid can be made from 1 dm^3 of 1.2 M acid? What volume of M alkali would be neutralized by 50 cm^3 of the 0.9 M acid?

5 (*a*) What is a 0.1 M solution of (i) sulphuric acid, (ii) potassium hydroxide, and what mass per dm^3 of the reagent does each solution contain? (*b*) What is the M concentration of a solution of (i) 7 g of sulphuric acid per dm^3, (ii) 7 g of hydroxide per 1000 cm^3? Describe fully how you would prepare a 0.1 M solution of sodium carbonate. (O.)

6 Describe how to perform the following operations, stating with reasons the precautions necessary to ensure accuracy:
(*a*) To transfer exactly 20 cm^3 of a 1.0 M solution of sodium carbonate to a beaker, using a pipette; (*b*) To set up and fill a wet burette with a given volume of sulphuric acid; (*c*) to titrate this acid against the sodium carbonate solution. What was the M concentration of the acid solution if 30 cm^3 of it were used in (*c*)? (N.)

7 Calculate the molar mass of (*a*) nitric acid, (*b*) sulphuric acid. 25 cm^3 of a monobasic acid is neutralized by 24 cm^3 of a solution containing 5 g of sodium hydroxide per dm^3. Calculate the M value of the acid solution. If the acid solution contained 2.4 g per dm^3, what is the relative molecular mass of the acid? How many cm^3 of this would be needed to neutralize 25 cm^3 of 0.1 M alkali? Describe briefly how such a titration would be carried out. (N.)

8 Define the molar mass of (*a*) an acid, (*b*) a base. What is meant by (*c*) a standard solution, (*d*) a 0.1 M solution? 1.50 g of an acid HX was dissolved in water and its solution made up to 250 cm^3. If 30.2 cm^3 of this acid solution neutralized 25 cm^3 of 0.115 M potassium hydroxide solution, calculate the relative molecular mass of the acid. (L.)

9 Assuming you are provided with 0.05 M solution of sulphuric acid, describe how you would find the percentage of sodium carbonate in a powder known to be a mixture of sodium carbonate and sodium chloride only. Show how you would calculate the result. (C.)

26
Qualitative Analysis

Recognition of gases

Gases are often given off by the action of heat or of reagents on substances. Most can be identified by three tests (see p. 335):
1 Note the colour and smell of the gas.
2 Put a burning splint in the gas.
3 Put moist red and moist blue litmus paper in the gas.

Confirmatory tests can be done on some of the gases:
Hydrogen chloride. Aqueous ammonia or acidified silver nitrate tests (p. 258).
Hydrogen bromide. As for hydrogen chloride.
Hydrogen Iodide. As for hydrogen chloride.
Sulphur dioxide. Smell of burning sulphur.
Hydrogen sulphide. Smell of bad eggs. Blackens filter paper dipped in lead(II) nitrate or lead(II) ethanoate solution.
Ammonia. Concentrated hydrochloric acid test (p. 216).
Carbon dioxide. Turns calcium hydroxide solution milky.
Water vapour. Anhydrous copper(II) sulphate test on the liquid (p. 46).

Preliminary examination of substance

Test 1
Note its appearance, colour and smell. The inference below is not a definite proof.

Observation	Inference
Black colour	Oxide or sulphide
Green colour	Iron(II) or copper salt
Yellow colour	Lead(II) oxide or iron(III) salt
Blue colour	Copper salt
Smell of ammonia	Ammonium salt
Smell of hydrogen sulphide	Sulphide
Smell of sulphur dioxide	Sulphite
Deliquescent	Chloride or nitrate

Gas	Colour	Smell	Action with splint	Litmus
Chlorine	Greenish-yellow	Irritating, characteristic	Does not burn or support combustion	Turns red then is bleached
Hydrogen chloride (bromide or iodide)	Colourless, misty in damp air	Irritating	Does not burn or support combustion	Red
Nitrogen dioxide	Reddish-brown	Irritating, characteristic	Does not burn or support combustion	Red
Nitric acid vapour	Pale yellow fumes	Irritating	Splint burns	Red
Sulphur(VI) oxide	White fumes	Irritating	Does not burn or support combustion	Red
Sulphur dioxide	None	Burning sulphur	Does not burn or support combustion	Red
Hydrogen sulphide	None	Rotten eggs	Burns with blue flame, depositing yellow sulphur on cold surface	Faint red
Ammonia	None	Choking, characteristic	Does not burn or support combustion	Blue
Hydrogen	None	None (if pure)	Burns with blue flame; explodes if mixed with air	None
Oxygen	None	None	Relights glowing splint	None
Carbon dioxide	None	Faint (not easy to detect)	Does not burn or support combustion	Faint red
Water vapour	None	None	Does not burn or support combustion	None
Nitrogen	None	None	Does not burn or support combustion	None

Test 2. Action of heat

Heat a little of the substance in an ignition tube or in a small, dry test-tube until no further change occurs.

Observation	Inference
Water vapour	Water of crystallization; hydrogencarbonate; hydrogensulphate; hydroxide
White sublimate	Ammonium salt
Changes colour	
yellow hot, white cold	Zinc oxide
red-brown hot, yellow cold	Lead(II) oxide
Oxygen	Nitrate; peroxide or (IV) oxide
Nitrogen dioxide	Nitrate
Carbon dioxide	Carbonate; hydrogencarbonate
Ammonia	Ammonium salt
Sulphur dioxide	Sulphite; certain sulphates

Test 3. *Flame test*
Place a little of the substance on a watch-glass, moisten it with pure, concentrated hydrochloric acid, and heat a little on a clean platinum or nichrome wire (Fig. 26.1). Note the colour of the flame. If you think potassium is present, look at the flame through blue glass.

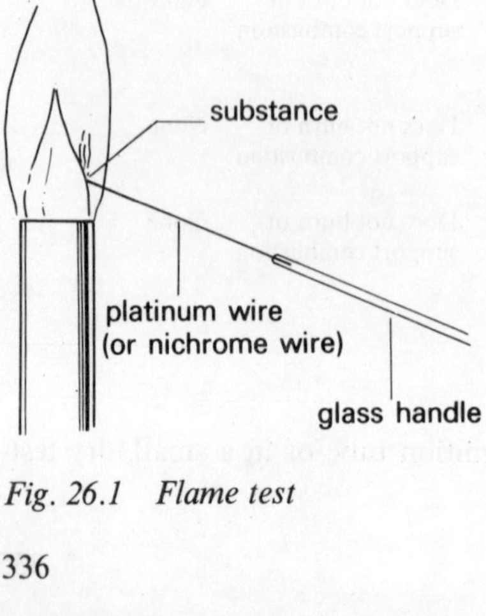

Fig. 26.1 Flame test

Observation	Inference
Brilliant yellow	Sodium
Red	Calcium
Blue	Lead
Blue-green	Copper
Lilac (crimson through blue glass)	Potassium

Detection of acid radicals

Test 4. Action of dilute hydrochloric acid
Add cold, dilute hydrochloric acid to the solid substance in a test-tube. If there is no reaction, warm gently.

Observation	Inference
Carbon dioxide	Carbonate; hydrogencarbonate
Sulphur dioxide	Sulphite
Hydrogen sulphide	Sulphide

$$CO_3^{2-}(s) + 2H^+(aq) \rightarrow CO_2(g) + H_2O$$
$$SO_3^{2-}(s) + 2H^+(aq) \rightarrow SO_2(g) + H_2O$$
$$S^{2-}(s) + 2H^+(aq) \rightarrow H_2S(g)$$

Test 5. Action of concentrated sulphuric acid
Add cold, concentrated sulphuric acid to the solid substance in a test-tube. If there is no reaction warm gently, but *do not boil*.

Observation	Inference
Carbon dioxide	Carbonate; hydrogencarbonate
Sulphur dioxide	Sulphite
Hydrogen sulphide	Sulphide
Hydrogen chloride	Chloride
Hydrogen bromide (with brown bromine)	Bromide
Hydrogen iodide (with violet iodine)	Iodide
Nitrogen dioxide or nitric acid vapour	Nitrate

$$Cl^-(s) + H^+(aq) \rightarrow HCl(g)$$
$$Br^-(s) + H^+(aq) \rightarrow HBr(g)$$
$$I^-(s) + H^+(aq) \rightarrow HI(g)$$
$$NO_3^-(s) + H^+(aq) \rightarrow HNO_3(g)$$
$$4HNO_3(g) \rightarrow 4NO_2(g) + O_2(g) + 2H_2O$$

Concentrated sulphuric acid oxidizes a little of the hydrogen bromide and hydrogen iodide to brown bromine and violet iodine respectively:

$$2HBr(g) + H_2SO_4(l) \rightarrow Br_2(g) + SO_2(g) + 2H_2O(l)$$

If this test indicates the presence of a chloride, bromide or iodide confirm at once by adding manganese(IV) oxide to the test-tube containing the substance and the concentrated sulphuric acid and warming the mixture. Evolution of chlorine gas (which bleaches litmus) confirms chloride, evolution of bromine confirms bromide, and evolution of iodine confirms iodide:

$$MnO_2(s) + 4HCl(aq) \rightarrow Cl_2(g) + MnCl_2(aq) + 2H_2O$$

If this test indicates the presence of nitrate confirm at once by adding copper turnings to the test-tube containing the substance and the concentrated sulphuric acid and warming the mixture. Evolution of red-brown nitrogen dioxide confirms nitrate.

$$Cu(s) + 4HNO_3(aq) \rightarrow 2NO_2(g) + Cu(NO_3)_2(aq) + 2H_2O$$

Tests in solution

The test for sulphate and the various confirmatory tests for the acid radicals require a solution of the original substance. Prepare the solution by dissolving a little of the substance in either (*a*) cold water, (*b*) hot water, (*c*) cold, dilute nitric acid or (*d*) hot, dilute nitric acid. In elementary work the use of other solvents, e.g. dilute or concentrated hydrochloric acid, is rarely necessary.

Test 6. Test for sulphate
To some of the solution add dilute nitric acid and then barium nitrate solution. A white precipitate indicates the presence of sulphate.

$$Ba^{2+}(aq) + SO_4^{2-}(aq) \rightarrow BaSO_4(s), \text{ white}$$

Test 7. Confirmatory tests
a *Nitrate—brown ring test.* To some of the solution add cold iron(II) sulphate solution. Carefully pour cold, concentrated sulphuric acid down the side of the test-tube so that the acid sinks to the bottom and forms a

separate layer there. Formation of a brown ring where the acid meets the other liquid confirms nitrate. A small-scale test is on p. 235.

b *Chloride, bromide and iodide*. To some of the solution add dilute nitric acid and then silver nitrate solution. A white precipitate, which turns violet when exposed to light and is soluble in aqueous ammonia, confirms chloride. A pale yellow precipitate slightly soluble in dilute aqueous ammonia confirms bromide; a yellow precipitate insoluble in aqueous ammonia confirms iodide.

$$Ag^+(aq) + Cl^-(aq) \rightarrow AgCl(s), \text{ white}$$

$$Ag^+(aq) + Br^-(aq) \rightarrow AgBr(s), \text{ pale yellow}$$

$$Ag^+(aq) + I^-(aq) \rightarrow AgI(s), \text{ yellow}$$

Tests for bromides and iodides

Test	Bromide	Iodide
1 Warm solid with conc. H_2SO_4	Misty fumes of HBr mixed with red Br_2	Misty fumes of HI mixed with violet I_2
2 Warm solid, MnO_2 and conc. H_2SO_4	Red gas and red liquid (Br_2)	Violet vapour and black solid (I_2)
3 Add $AgNO_3$ solution to aqueous solution	Pale yellow precipitate, slightly soluble in dilute aqueous ammonia	Yellow precipitate, insoluble in aqueous ammonia
4 Add chlorine water to aqueous solution	Red solution, then red liquid bromine	Brown solution, then black precipitate of iodine

c *Sulphite*. (i) To some of the solution add a few drops of iodine solution or of bromine water. These coloured solutions are decolourized by sulphite:

$$Na_2SO_3(aq) + Br_2(aq) + H_2O(l) \rightarrow Na_2SO_4(aq) + 2HBr(aq)$$

(ii) To some of the solution add barium nitrate solution. Formation of a white precipitate which is soluble in dilute nitric acid (contrast test 6) confirms sulphite:

$$Ba^{2+}(aq) + SO_3^{2-}(aq) \rightarrow BaSO_3(s), \text{ white}$$

$$BaSO_3(s) + 2H^+(aq) \rightarrow SO_2(g) + H_2O + Ba^{2+}(aq)$$

Detection of metallic ions

Test 8. *Action of sodium hydroxide solution*

To the solution add sodium hydroxide solution in small quantities at a time until it is present in excess. If there is no precipitate, warm gently and test for ammonia.

Observation	Inference
White precipitate, insoluble in excess	Calcium
White precipitate, soluble in excess	Lead(II), zinc or aluminium(III) salt
Blue precipitate, insoluble in excess	Copper(II) salt
Green precipitate, insoluble in excess	Iron(II) salt
Reddish-brown precipitate, insoluble in excess	Iron(III) salt
Ammonia given off on warming	Ammonium salt

$Ca^{2+}(aq) + 2OH^-(aq) \rightarrow Ca(OH)_2(s)$, white

$Pb^{2+}(aq) + 2OH^-(aq) \rightarrow Pb(OH)_2(s)$, white

$Zn^{2+}(aq) + 2OH^-(aq) \rightarrow Zn(OH)_2(s)$, white

$Al^{3+}(aq) + 3OH^-(aq) \rightarrow Al(OH)_3(s)$, white

$Cu^{2+}(aq) + 2OH^-(aq) \rightarrow Cu(OH)_2(s)$, blue

$Fe^{3+}(aq) + 3OH^-(aq) \rightarrow Fe(OH)_3(s)$, reddish-brown

$Fe^{2+}(aq) + 2OH^-(aq) \rightarrow Fe(OH)_2(s)$, green

$NH_4^+(aq) + OH^-(aq) \rightarrow NH_3(g) + H_2O$

Hydroxides of lead, zinc and aluminium are amphoteric and dissolve in excess sodium hydroxide solution:

$Pb(OH)_2(s) + 2OH^-(aq) \rightarrow Pb(OH)_4^{2-}(aq)$, plumbate ion

$Zn(OH)_2(s) + 2OH^-(aq) \rightarrow Zn(OH)_4^{2-}(aq)$, zincate ion

$Al(OH)_3(s) + OH^-(aq) \rightarrow Al(OH)_4^-(aq)$, aluminate ion

Test 9. Action of aqueous ammonia
To the solution add aqueous ammonia in small quantities at a time until it is present in excess.

Observation	Inference
White precipitate, soluble in excess	Zinc salt
White precipitate, insoluble in excess	Lead(II) or aluminium salt
Pale-blue precipitate, soluble in excess forming a deep blue solution	Copper(II) salt
Green precipitate, insoluble in excess	Iron(II) salt
Reddish-brown precipitate, insoluble in excess	Iron(III) salt

Copper(II) hydroxide and zinc hydroxide dissolve in excess aqueous ammonia to form complex compounds:

$$Cu(OH)_2(s) + 4NH_3(aq) \rightarrow Cu(NH_3)_4^{2+}(aq) + 2OH^-(aq)$$

$$Zn(OH)_2(s) + 4NH_3(aq) \rightarrow Zn(NH_3)_4^{2+}(aq) + 2OH^-(aq)$$

Tetraamminecopper(II) and tetraamminezinc ions.

Test 10. *Confirmatory tests for lead salts*
To separate portions of the original solution add
(i) dilute sulphuric acid; a white precipitate,
(ii) concentrated hydrochloric acid; a white precipitate soluble in hot water,
(iii) potassium iodide solution; a yellow precipitate,
(iv) potassium chromate(VI) solution; a yellow precipitate.

$$Pb^{2+}(aq) + SO_4^{2-}(aq) \rightarrow PbSO_4(s), \text{ white}$$

$$Pb^{2+}(aq) + 2Cl^-(aq) \rightarrow PbCl_2(s), \text{ white}$$

$$Pb^{2+}(aq) + 2I^-(aq) \rightarrow PbI_2(s), \text{ yellow}$$

$$Pb^{2+}(aq) + CrO_4^{2-}(aq) \rightarrow PbCrO_4(s), \text{ yellow}$$

Test 11. *Confirmatory tests for iron salts*
To separate portions of the original solution add
(i) potassium hexacyanoferrate(II) solution,
(ii) potassium hexacyanoferrate(III) solution, and
(iii) potassium thiocyanate solution.

Reagent	Iron(II) salt	Iron(III) salt
Potassium hexacyanoferrate(II)	Light blue or nearly white precipitate	Dark blue precipitate
Potassium hexacyanoferrate(III)	Dark blue precipitate	Dark solution; no precipitate
Potassium thiocyanate	No reaction (but traces of iron(III) salt give colour)	Deep red solution

Method of writing results

Experiment	Observation	Inference
1 The appearance was observed	Colourless and crystalline needles	Coloured salts, e.g. salts of copper, iron(II), iron(III), etc., probably absent
2 Solid was heated in a dry test-tube	Water vapour given off (turned white copper(II) sulphate blue); vapours turned blue litmus red. Residue was yellow when hot, white when cold	Salt contains water of crystallization. Residue probably zinc oxide
3 Flame test	No definite colour seen	Sodium, potassium, calcium, lead, copper probably absent
4 Solid was warmed with dilute hydrochloric acid	No gas evolved	Carbonate, sulphite, sulphide probably absent
5 Solid was warmed with concentrated sulphuric acid	No gas evolved	Chloride and nitrate probably absent
6 Solid was dissolved in water. Dilute nitric acid and barium nitrate solution were added	White precipitate	Sulphate present
7 Sodium hydroxide was added gradually to aqueous solution of solid	White precipitate dissolved in excess alkali	Confirms zinc present
8 Aqueous ammonia was added to aqueous solution	White precipitate dissolved in excess alkali	Confirms zinc present

The salt was hydrated zinc sulphate, $ZnSO_4 \cdot 7H_2O$.

Questions

1 You are provided with solutions of *(a)* a copper compound, *(b)* a lead compound, *(c)* a sulphate, *(d)* a nitrate, and *(e)* a chloride. Describe the reactions (one in each case) that you would use in qualitative analysis to identify the metallic element in *(a)* and *(b)* and the radical in *(c)*, *(d)* and *(e)*. (N.)

2 You are given three powders. The first is either sodium nitrate or ammonium nitrate; the second, either potassium sulphate or potassium chloride; the third, either manganese(IV) oxide or copper(II) oxide. Describe six experiments, two for each powder, showing how you would find out what the powders are. (L.)

3 You have five beakers, each containing a sample of a clear colourless liquid. Describe experiments you would do in order to identify the liquids if you knew they were distilled water, dilute sulphuric acid, dilute hydrochloric acid, calcium hydroxide solution, and aqueous potassium nitrate. (O.)

4 A white solid is known to be one of the following: powdered calcium chloride, or zinc sulphide, or lead(II) chloride. Describe briefly two tests for each substance that will enable you to distinguish it from the other two compounds. (C.)

5 Describe how you would distinguish between sodium carbonate and sodium hydrogencarbonate. An unknown salt is found on analysis to be lead(II) carbonate. Describe fully the tests you would carry out, and the results you would observe, in performing this analysis. (C.)

6 Describe simple chemical tests which would enable you to label correctly six test-tubes containing the following solids: common salt, calcium hydroxide, calcium carbonate, sodium sulphate, calcium nitrate and sodium nitrate. (L.)

7 How would you distinguish between the substances in the pairs listed below? A test for each substance in the pair is required, and describe your observations during each test. (*a*) Sodium carbonate and sodium nitrate. (*b*) Lead(II) carbonate and zinc carbonate. (*c*) Zinc sulphide and zinc sulphite. (C.)

Examination type Questions

1 (*a*) Sketch and label an apparatus you would use in order to prepare and collect a gas-jar of either oxygen or hydrogen. (*b*) State briefly why the method you use in (*a*) cannot be used to prepare the gas commercially. (*c*) Write equations for the reactions of hydrogen with nitrogen and ethene, and state the conditions under which the two reactions occur. (*d*) Calculate the mass of uranium that can be obtained by reducing 108 g of its oxide, UO_2. (U = 238; O = 16.)

2 Lithium is an element of atomic number 3, relative atomic mass 6.94, and with two isotopes of mass numbers 6 and 7. (*a*) How many electrons, protons and neutrons are there in one atom of isotopes ^{6}Li and ^{7}Li? (*b*) Explain clearly which of the two isotopes is more abundant in lithium. (*c*) Show by calculation that there are about 15 times more atoms of one lithium isotope than of the other. (*d*) Show by simple diagrams how lithium hydride, LiH, an ionic compound like sodium chloride, is formed from one atom of lithium and hydrogen (the diagrams must show the nuclei and electrons of the particles).

3 Concentrated nitric acid was added in excess to copper in the bottom of a tall gas-jar, which was then covered with cardboard. Red-brown gas formed at once and the colour moved slowly up the jar. At first the colour was darkest at the bottom but after some 20 minutes the colour was the same everywhere inside the jar. (*a*) Write either one molecular equation or two ionic equations for the reaction, and name the gas formed. (*b*) Why is the colour of the gas in the jar darkest at the bottom after about 60 seconds? (*c*) Explain why the colour of the gas becomes the same everywhere inside the jar after 20 minutes. (*d*) Explain how and why the observations would differ if the gas-jar were surrounded by hot water during the whole experiment. (*e*) Outline one experiment which demonstrates Brownian movement.

4 (*a*) Elements A, B and C have atomic numbers of 6, 9 and 19 respectively. Write down the electron configuration of their atoms. (*b*) Draw a simple diagram, showing all the electron orbits or shells, to make clear how atom B combines with atom C. Discuss the forces between the particles in the compound. (*c*) Carbon contains about 99 per cent of an isotope of mass number 12; the other isotope has a mass number of 13. Calculate the relative atomic mass of ordinary carbon.

5 P_4O_6 and P_4O_{10} are the molecular formulae of two oxides of phosphorus. (*a*) What are their empirical formulae? (*b*) With water, the oxides react to form the acids H_3PO_3 and H_3PO_4 respectively. Write equations (omitting state symbols) for the two reactions.

(*c*) Both oxides consist of molecules. Mention two probable physical properties of the oxides. (*d*) Magnesium oxide is an ionic compound ($Mg^{2+} + O^{2-}$). Its crystal structure resembles that of sodium chloride. Draw a diagram showing the type of particles and their arrangement in the crystal lattice of magnesium oxide. (*e*) Fluorine has only one kind of atom of mass number 19, but its relative atomic mass is about 18.998. Explain briefly why the two numbers differ.

6 (*a*) Write an equation for the combustion of tetraethyllead (TEL), $Pb(C_2H_5)_4$, in excess oxygen, if the lead forms lead(II) oxide. (*b*) What is the molar mass of tetraethyllead? (*c*) TEL is a liquid of density 1.62 g/cm^3. 500 litres of petrol contain 1 mole of TEL. How many litres of petrol contain 1 cm^3 of TEL? (*d*) Show clearly that about 8 litres of air (at room temperature and pressure) are required for the complete combustion of 1 cm^3 of TEL. (Assume air contains 20 per cent oxygen by volume, and molar volume of a gas is 24 dm^3 at room temperature and pressure. Pb = 207; C = 12; H = 1.)

7 (*a*) A current of 0.8 amperes was passed for 12 minutes through concentrated hydrochloric acid using carbon electrodes. What quantity of electricity was passed? (*b*) Calculate the volume of hydrogen measured at room temperature and pressure formed at the cathode. What would this volume be if the formula for a hydrogen ion was H^{2+}? (*c*) What gas other than hydrogen is formed? Write equations for the reactions which occur at the cathode and anode respectively. (*d*) Explain why the volume of the second gas formed is slightly less than that of the hydrogen. Mention one physical and one chemical test for this gas. (Molar volume of a gas at room temperature and pressure is 24 dm^3; Faraday constant = 96 000 C/mol.)

8 Molten lead(II) iodide was electrolysed using carbon electrodes. (*a*) Sketch and label a suitable apparatus, showing the coulometer and the electrical circuit. (*b*) What changes would you see at the cathode and anode, and write equations for the chemical changes at the electrodes? (*c*) If a current of 0.4 amperes and a quantity of 96 coulombs was passed, for how long in minutes did the current flow? (*d*) Calculate the mass of product formed at the cathode. (*e*) State and explain the mass of product formed at the cathode if lead(II) bromide is used instead of iodide in exactly the same experiment. (F = 96 000 C/mol; Pb = 207; Br = 80.)

9 A current of 0.5 amperes was passed for 2400 seconds through two coulometers in series. One contained dilute sodium hydroxide and the other molten potassium iodide. The electrodes were of carbon. (*a*) What quantity of electricity was used? (*b*) Write ionic equations for the reactions occurring at (i) the two anodes, and (ii) the two cathodes. (*c*) How many moles of electrons passed through (i) the sodium hydroxide, and (ii) the potassium iodide? (*d*) What mass of product is liberated at the cathode in the potassium iodide? (*e*) How many moles of product are liberated at the anode in the potassium iodide? (F = 96 000 C/mol; K = 39; I = 127; H = 1; O = 16.)

10 A test-tube containing a solid was heated uniformly in a beaker of water. A thermometer was used to record the temperature of the substance in the tube and to stir the substance carefully. Some readings were:

Temp. (°C)	20	56	50	79	79	83	98	99	99
Time (s)	0	20	40	80	140	160	200	240	300

Plot a graph of temperature (vertical axis) against time. From the graph (*a*) what was the melting point of the solid and the boiling point of the water? (*b*) Explain what happened to the molecules of solid during the period from 80 to 140 seconds. (*c*) What happened to these molecules during the time 20 to 40 seconds? (*d*) At the end of the above experiment, the test-tube, contents and thermometer were removed and allowed to cool for 5 minutes, during which the temperature of the contents fell to 40 °C. Make a rough sketch of the cooling curve you would expect to be obtained.

11 A compound contains 15.8 per cent of carbon and sulphur only. Its relative molecular mass is 76. Its boiling point is 46 °C. (*a*) Calculate its empirical and molecular formulae. (*b*) Give a reason why you think the bonding in this compound is covalent and not ionic. (*c*) Write an equation for the combustion in excess oxygen of this compound and also for its reaction with hydrogen to form methane, CH_4, and hydrogen sulphide, H_2S. (*d*) Calculate the volumes at s.t.p. of methane and hydrogen sulphide that should be formed by 38 g of the compound. (H = 1; C = 12; S = 32.)

12 One oxide of phosphorus, a reactive non-metal, contains 56.3 per cent of oxygen by mass. Strontium, Sr, is a reactive metal and is in group 2 of the Periodic Table. (*a*) Calculate the empirical formula of the phosphorus oxide. (*b*) Write equations for the reactions between water and this phosphorus oxide and strontium oxide. Mention a simple test to distinguish between the two solutions formed. (*c*) Write an equation for the reaction with excess water of strontium phosphide, Sr_3P_2, to form a gas of formula PH_3 and an aqueous strontium compound. (*d*) Calculate the volume at s.t.p. of the gas formed by one mole of strontium phosphide. (P = 31; O = 16.)

13 The total mass of a sealed flask containing 5 g of zinc and 5 g of sulphur and no air was 98 g. The flask and contents were heated strongly until reaction was complete. (*a*) State, with explanation, the mass of the flask and contents after heating. (*b*) Calculate the mass of zinc sulphide, ZnS, in the flask after heating. (*c*) Calculate the mass of sulphur dioxide (assumed to be the only product) formed when 5 g of sulphur are burnt in excess air. (*d*) What mass of sulphur dioxide is formed when the contents of the heated flask are burnt completely in air? (O = 16; S = 32; Zn = 65.)

14 A calibrated tube has a capacity of 100 cm^3. It contains a mixture of sulphur dioxide and air and is sealed at one end and stoppered at the other. (*a*) Describe clearly how you would determine the percentage by volume of sulphur dioxide in the mixture. (*b*) Draw a simple diagram to show the arrangement of electrons (outer orbits only) in one molecule of sulphur dioxide. (*c*) State and explain what particles are present in an aqueous solution of sulphur dioxide.

15 Substance X oxidizes potassium iodide to iodine. The rate of this reaction was studied as follows. To each of five test-tubes were added: 20 cm^3 (excess) aqueous potassium iodide, 3 cm^3 aqueous sodium thiosulphate, and 1 cm^3 of starch solution. 20 cm^3 of solution X was then added to one tube and the time t for the blue colour to appear was observed (the potassium iodide is oxidized to iodine, which then reacts with the sodium thiosulphate, when all of the thiosulphate has been used up the iodine then formed gives the usual blue colour with starch). The experiment was repeated with 20 cm^3 of solution X of various concentrations. The results were:

Concentration of X (M)	0.1	0.3	0.4	0.6	0.8
Time t for colour to appear (s)	120	40	30	20	15

(*a*) Calculate the five values of $1/t$ (t^{-1}). (*b*) Explain why the rate of reaction is proportional to $1/t$. (*c*) Plot $1/t$ (vertical axis) against concentration of X. (*d*) Deduce from your graph how the rate of reaction varies with the concentration of X. (*e*) What would be the effect on the above times if (i) the concentration of the sodium thiosulphate were doubled, and (ii) the concentration of the iodine were doubled?

16 (*a*) Write the ionic equation for the reactions between sodium and water and between zinc and dilute hydrochloric acid. Explain why these reactions are called oxidations of the metals. (*b*) Copper(II) sulphate solution speeds up the rate of reaction between pure zinc and dilute sulphuric acid. Give a brief explanation of this fact. (*c*) Explain why the reaction between calcium, a very reactive metal, and dilute sulphuric acid is very slow. (*d*) Account for the fact that sodium reacts quickly with water, at a slightly faster rate with dilute ethanoic acid, but almost explosively with dilute hydrochloric or sulphuric acid.

17 Below are the formulae, relative molecular masses M_r, and volumes V occupied by 1 g under ordinary conditions:

	Ne	CO	H_2S	N_2O	Cl_2
M_r	20	28	34	44	71
V/cm^3	1200	860	706	540	338

(*a*) Plot a graph of V (vertical axis) against M_r. (*b*) From the graph deduce the probable volume under ordinary conditions of 1 g of (i) N_2, (ii) O_2, (iii) Ar, (iv) CO_2. (*c*) Name two gases for which V is 800 and 380 respectively. (*d*) Sketch and label an apparatus you would use to find the mass of a known volume of either air or sulphur dioxide at room temperature and pressure. (Relative atomic masses are on pp. 352–3.)

18 (*a*) Name two gases in each case which (i) turn damp litmus paper red, (ii) burn in air, (iii) do not burn in air but can combine with oxygen, (iv) decolourize acidified potassium manganate(VII) solution. (*b*) Describe four different chemical tests (one in each case) which would distinguish between the pairs of gases named in your answers to section (*a*).

19 (*a*) Draw and label an apparatus used to pass carbon dioxide from a cylinder over heated carbon, remove any carbon dioxide that does not react, and collect a gas-jar of carbon monoxide. (*b*) Show clearly that 44 g of carbon dioxide can produce by this method a maximum of 48 dm^3 of carbon monoxide, measured at room temperature and pressure. (*c*) Name and write the graphic formulae of three organic compounds which contain the carbonyl group,

$$-\overset{|}{C}=O.$$

20 (*a*) Explain why an alkaline solution is formed when ammonia gas is passed into water; write an equation or equations in your answer. (*b*) Write ionic equations to show the reactions which occur when aqueous ammonia is added gradually to dilute sulphuric acid until it is neutralized. (*c*) Explain how to obtain good crystals from the neutral solution formed in (*b*). (*d*) Dilute aqueous ammonia is boiled gently. Explain why the solution gradually loses ammonia gas and becomes less and less alkaline.

21 Sulphur and selenium (Se) are immediately below oxygen in group 6 of the Periodic Table. (*a*) In what periods are sulphur and selenium? (*b*) Selenium forms a solid oxide which reacts with water. Write probable equations for the reactions. (*c*) Hydrogen selenide contains 2.47 per cent by mass of hydrogen and selenium only. Calculate its empirical formula (Se = 79). (*d*) Predict the probable molecular formula and relative molecular mass of hydrogen selenide. (*e*) Suggest what happens to hydrogen selenide when (i) it is heated strongly (without air) and (ii) it is bubbled into chlorine water.

22 (*a*) Draw and label a diagram showing a 100 cm^3 syringe containing 60 cm^3 of nitrogen oxide, NO, which is connected in turn to a 3-way tap, a silica tube containing nickel wire, and then a second syringe. (*b*) The nitrogen oxide is passed from one syringe, over the heated nickel, into the other syringe; and the process is repeated until only nitrogen gas remains. Calculate the volume of the nitrogen. (*c*) What volume of nitrogen would be formed by 60 cm^3 of gases of formulae (i) N_2O, and (ii) NO_2? (*d*) Write equations for the reactions with water of the gases (i) NO_2, and (ii) N_2O_3. (All volumes of gases are to be under the same conditions of temperature and pressure.)

23 Selenium exists as rhombic and monoclinic allotropes, and also as a third allotrope in which selenium atoms are joined in long chains. (*a*) Write the probable molecular formula of rhombic selenium. (*b*) State and explain which of the three allotropes has the highest melting point. (*c*) Explain why the boiling point of bromine is higher than that of chlorine. (*d*) Explain why the melting point of magnesium is higher than that of sodium.

24 The first member of the halogen family is fluorine, F, and the last member is astatine, At, the others being chlorine, bromine and iodine. (*a*) Name two halogens which are probably solid at room temperature. (*b*) Suggest a reason why fluorine is the most powerful oxidizing agent. (*c*) What visible changes occur when fluorine reacts with (i) moist litmus paper, (ii) aqueous sodium bromide, (iii) aqueous sodium iodide; write ionic equations where possible. (*d*) Name one halogen which is probably radioactive. State a reason for your answer. (*e*) Name two halogens which are obtained commercially only by electrolysis. Sketch and label one cell used in the electrolytic process.

25 Phosphorus pentachloride is a solid prepared by dropping liquid phosphorus trichloride drop by drop into a flask cooled in ice through which a steady stream of dry chlorine is passed. (*a*) Write an equation for the reaction. (*b*) Sketch and label an apparatus to prepare phosphorus pentachloride, including that used to prepare the dry chlorine. (*a*) Write equations for the reaction of one phosphorus chloride on (i) water, (ii) ethanoic acid, (iii) ethanol.

26 The angles between the four bonds in molecules of methane, CH_4, ammonia and water are $109\frac{1}{2}°$, 107°, and 105° respectively. (*a*) Explain the shapes of these three molecules, mentioning lone pair repulsion in your answer. (*b*) State the inter-bond angles you would expect in (i) ammonium ion NH_4^+, (ii) mercury(II) chloride, $HgCl_2$. (*c*) The angle between the bonds in hydrogen sulphide, H_2S, is only 92°. Suggest why this angle is so much less than that in water.

27 10 M sulphuric acid is both a *concentrated* acid and a *strong* acid; 10 M ethanoic acid is a concentrated acid and a *weak* acid. (*a*) Explain the meanings of the three terms in italics. (*b*) Explain why hydrogen chloride forms a strong acid in water but a weak acid in methylbenzene. (*c*) Concentrated sulphuric acid and solid ethanedioic acid, $(COOH)_2$, react when warmed to form a mixture of carbon dioxide and carbon monoxide in equal volumes. Draw and label an apparatus you would use to obtain a jar of reasonably pure carbon monoxide by this reaction.

28 The metal titanium is obtained from its oxide, TiO_2, by chlorination to the chloride, $TiCl_4$, and reduction of the chloride by magnesium.

Chlorination is done by passing chlorine over a heated mixture of the oxide and coke. Reduction is done by heating the chloride with magnesium in an inert atmosphere. (*a*) Write an equation for the chlorination reaction, assuming one product is carbon monoxide. (*b*) The melting and boiling points of titanium(IV) oxide are −23 °C and 136 °C respectively. Suggest methods of collecting and then purifying the chloride. (*c*) Write an equation for the reduction of the chloride by magnesium. (*d*) During the reduction, titanium is so reactive that it combines readily with carbon, oxygen, nitrogen, silicon, etc. Name two gases suitable to provide an inert atmosphere for the reduction. (*e*) Suggest an alternative method of obtaining titanium from its oxide ore. (*f*) What differences would you expect between the properties of covalent titanium(IV) chloride and sodium chloride?

29 Magnesium is obtained commercially by electrolysis of the fused anhydrous chloride, $MgCl_2$. The anode is carbon and the cathode is steel. The molten magnesium rises to the surface of the electrolyte. (*a*) Why is sodium chloride or potassium chloride added to the molten magnesium chloride? (*b*) Why is carbon and not a metal used for the anode? (*c*) When heated, hydrated magnesium chloride, $MgCl_2 \cdot 6H_2O$, first forms $MgCl_2 \cdot 2H_2O$, which then hydrolyses to form some oxide, MgO. What is meant by hydrolysis? (*d*) Aluminium cannot be prepared by electrolysis of aluminium chloride because this compound sublimes on heating. What is meant by sublimes? (*e*) Outline how aluminium is manufactured by electrolysis of its oxide.

30 Write equations and name the gases formed in the reactions which occur when sodium hydroxide is heated with (i) sodium ethanoate, (ii) sodium methanoate, (iii) sodium propanoate, (iv) sodium propenoate, $CH_2{=}CHCOONa$. Sketch and label a simple apparatus you would use to collect the gas formed in one of these reactions.

31 The fractionation of crude oil commercially produces hydrocarbon mixtures, which may be cracked; unsaturated hydrocarbons are produced. The unsaturated hydrocarbons may be either polymerized or hydrogenated. (*a*) Explain clearly the meanings of these words in the statement: fractionation, hydrocarbon, cracked, unsaturated, polymerized and hydrogenated. (*b*) Write equations which illustrate (i) cracking, (ii) polymerization, and (iii) hydrogenation. (*c*) Write displayed formulae for two isomers of molecular formula C_4H_8.

32 The formulae of five organic compounds are: $CH_3CH_2CH_3$, $CH_3CH{=}CH_2$, CH_3CH_2OH, CH_3COOCH_3, and HCOOH. Write down each formula in turn and after it write (i) the name of the compound, (ii) its graphic or displayed formula, (iii) the name of the homologous series to which it belongs, (iv) the equation for one chemical reaction of the compound. Complete combustion of 1 mole of one of these five compounds produced 44 g of carbon dioxide. State and explain which compound it is.

33 (*a*) Explain the difference between addition polymerization and condensation polymerization by reference to the formation of poly(ethene) and either nylon or Terylene. (*b*) Mention briefly how fats can be hydrolysed to soap. (*c*) Describe one way of converting starch to a simple sugar in the laboratory.

34 (*a*) How may aqueous sodium hydroxide be used to distinguish between soluble copper(II) and lead(II) compounds? (*b*) Calculate the number of coulombs required to liberate (i) 9 g of aluminium, and (ii) 36 g of silver. (*c*) Write an equation for the conversion of oxygen into its allotrope ozone, O_3. (*d*) 30 cm^3 of oxygen passed through an apparatus which converted 20 per cent of the gas into ozone. Calculate the total volume of gas produced (oxygen and ozone) if all volumes are measured at the same temperature and pressure. (Al = 27; Ag = 108; F = 96 000 C/mol.)

Relative Atomic Masses and Physical Properties

Element	Symbol	Relative atomic masses (standard, ^{12}C = 12.000 0) Exact	For calculations	Atomic number	Melting point (°C)	Density (g/cm^3)	Valency
Actinium	Ac	227	—	89	—	—	3
Aluminium	Al	26.98	27	13	660	2.7	3
Americium	Am	243	—	95	850	11.7	3
Antimony	Sb	121.75	—	51	630	6.7	3, 5
Argon	Ar	39.948	—	18	*−189*	(1.4)	—
Arsenic	As	74.92	—	33	(814)	5.7	3,5
Astatine	At	211	—	85	—	—	1
Barium	Ba	137.34	137	56	725	3.5	2
Berkelium	Bk	249	—	97	—	—	3
Beryllium	Be	9.012	—	4	1280	1.8	2
Bismuth	Bi	208.98	—	83	271	9.8	3, 5
Boron	B	10.81	—	5	2300	2.6	3
Bromine	Br	79.904	80	35	*−7*	3.1	1
Cadmium	Cd	112.40	—	48	321	8.6	2
Caesium	Cs	132.91	—	55	28	1.9	1
Calcium	Ca	40.08	40	20	850	1.5	2
Californium	Cf	249	—	98	—	—	3
Carbon	C	12.011	12	6	3727	3.5	4
Cerium	Ce	140.12	—	58	800	6.7	3, 4
Chlorine	Cl	35.453	35.5	17	*−101*	(1.9)	1
Chromium	Cr	52.00	52	24	1890	7.2	3, 6
Cobalt	Co	58.93	—	27	1495	8.9	2
Copper	Cu	63.55	63.5	29	1083	8.9	1, 2
Curium	Cm	245	—	96	—	—	3
Dysprosium	Dy	162.50	—	66	—	—	3
Einsteinium	E	254	—	99	—	—	3
Erbium	Er	167.26	—	68	—	—	3
Europium	Eu	152.0	—	63	1150	—	3
Fermium	Fm	255	—	100	—	—	3
Fluorine	F	19.00	—	9	*−220*	(1.1)	1
Francium	Fr	223	—	87	—	—	1
Gadolinium	Gd	157.25	—	64	—	—	3
Gallium	Ga	69.72	—	31	30	5.9	3
Germanium	Ge	72.59	—	32	960	5.3	4
Gold	Au	196.97	—	79	1063	19.3	1, 3
Hafnium	Hf	178.50	—	72	1700	13.3	4
Helium	He	4.002 6	—	2	*−272*	(0.2)	—
Holmium	Ho	164.93	—	67	—	—	3
Hydrogen	H	1.008 0	1	1	*−259*	(0.1)	1
Indium	In	114.82	—	49	156	7.3	3
Iodine	I	126.90	127	53	114	4.9	1
Iridium	Ir	192.2	—	77	2450	22.4	3
Iron	Fe	55.85	56	26	1539	7.9	2, 3
Krypton	Kr	83.80	—	36	*−157*	(2.2)	—
Lanthanum	La	138.91	—	57	826	6.2	3
Lead	Pb	207.20	207	82	328	11.3	2, 4

Relative atomic masses (standard, $^{12}C = 12.0000$)

Element	Symbol	Exact	For calculations	Atomic number	Melting point (°C)	Density (g/cm³)	Valency
Lithium	Li	6.941	—	3	186	0.5	1
Lutecium	Lu	174.97	—	71	—	9.7	3
Magnesium	Mg	24.305	24	12	651	1.7	2
Manganese	Mn	54.94	55	25	1260	7.4	2, 7
Mendelevium	Mv	256	—	101	—	—	3
Mercury	Hg	200.59	—	80	*−39*	13.5	1, 2
Molybdenum	Mo	95.94	—	42	2620	10.2	3, 6
Neodymium	Nd	144.24	—	60	840	6.9	3
Neon	Ne	20.18	—	10	*−249*	(1.2)	—
Neptunium	Np	237.05	—	93	640	20.5	4, 5
Nickel	Ni	58.71	—	28	1455	8.9	2
Niobium	Nb	92.91	—	41	2500	8.6	3,5
Nitrogen	N	14.007	14	7	*−210*	(0.8)	3
Nobelium	No	256	—	102	—	—	3
Osmium	Os	190.2	—	76	2700	22.5	4, 8
Oxygen	O	15.9994	16	8	*−218*	(1.1)	2
Palladium	Pd	106.4	—	46	1550	12.0	2, 4
Phosphorus	P	30.974	31	15	44	1.8	3, 5
Platinum	Pt	195.09	—	78	1773	21.5	2, 4
Plutonium	Pu	242	—	94	635	16.0	4
Polonium	Po	210	—	84	—	—	2
Potassium	K	39.098	39	19	63	0.9	1
Praseodymium	Pr	140.91	—	59	940	6.5	3
Prometheum	Pm	145	—	61	—	—	3
Protoactinium	Pa	231.04	—	91	—	—	5
Radium	Ra	226.03	—	88	700	5.0	2
Radon	Rn	222	—	86	*−71*	(4.4)	—
Rhenium	Re	186.2	—	75	3200	20.5	4, 7
Rhodium	Rh	102.91	—	45	1970	12.4	3
Rubidium	Rb	85.47	—	37	38	1.5	1
Ruthenium	Ru	101.1	—	44	1950	12.6	3, 8
Samarium	Sm	150.4	—	62	1300	7.7	3
Scandium	Sc	44.96	—	21	1200	2.5	3
Selenium	Se	78.96	—	34	220	4.8	2, 6
Silicon	Si	28.09	28	14	1420	2.4	4
Silver	Ag	107.868	108	47	960	10.5	1
Sodium	Na	22.999	23	11	98	0.9	1
Strontium	Sr	87.62	—	38	774	2.6	2
Sulphur	S	32.06	32	16	119	2.1	2, 6
Tantalum	Ta	180.95	—	73	3000	16.6	5
Technetium	Tc	98.91	—	43	—	—	4, 7
Tellurium	Te	127.60	—	52	450	6.2	2, 6
Terbium	Tb	158.93	—	65	330	—	3
Thallium	Tl	204.37	—	81	302	11.9	1, 3
Thorium	Th	232.04	—	90	1845	11.2	4
Thulium	Tm	168.93	—	69	—	—	3
Tin	Sn	118.69	—	50	232	7.3	2, 4
Titanium	Ti	47.90	—	22	1800	4.5	3, 4
Tungsten	W	183.85	—	74	3370	19.3	6
Uranium	U	238.03	—	92	1133	18.7	4, 6
Vanadium	V	50.94	—	23	1710	6.0	3, 5
Xenon	Xe	131.3	—	54	*−112*	(3.5)	—
Ytterbium	Yb	173.04	—	70	1800	—	3
Yttrium	Y	88.91	—	39	1490	5.5	3
Zinc	Zn	65.38	65	30	420	7.1	2
Zirconium	Zr	91.22	—	40	1860	6.4	4

Answers to Numerical Questions

Chapter 1 (p. 11). **3** 30.9 g. **5** 14.3 g.

Chapter 6 (p. 81). **2** (*a*) 5.0 g, (*b*) 4.55 g.
9 (*a*) 177.2 cm^3, (*b*) 311.6 cm^3, (*c*) 168 cm^3. **11** 32.9 g. **12** 8.39 g.

Chapter 7 (p. 90). **1** 11.65 g, 21.2%. **2** (*b*) 44.
3 24%. (*a*) 1.48 g, (*b*) 1.79 dm^3. **4** $CuSO_4 \cdot 5H_2O$. **5** 70.5 g, 11.25 g.
6 14 cm^3 CO_2, 16 cm^3 CO, 20 cm^3 N_2. **8** 3287.5 dm^3.

Chapter 11 (p. 139). **1** 32.5 g. **2** 56 g. **3** 48.2%. **4** 31.9 g.
5 12 g. **9** 5.1 g. **10** 28 g, 18.7 g, 2, 3; 56.

Chapter 12 (p. 148). **1** (*a*) 7.2 cm^3/min. **3** 120 cm^3. **4** 0.88 g.
5 189.5 cm^3.

Chapter 13 (p. 165). **5** 3.40 g. **6** 0.57 g, 1.94 g. **7** 0.16 g.

Chapter 15 (p. 180). **3** (*c*) 55 kJ, (*d*) 110 kJ. **4** (*a*) 1232 kJ/mol.
6 (*a*) 37, 15.6, 4.8, 41.7, 8.4.

Chapter 20 (p. 256). **4** 5.7 g.

Chapter 25 (p. 333). **1** (*a*) 0.2 M, (*b*) 2 M, (*c*) 0.25 M.
2 (*a*) 18.25 g, (*b*) 2.0 g, (*c*) 2.8 g. **3** 1.46 g. **4** 1333.3 cm^3, 45 cm^3.
5 (*a*) 9.8 g, 5.6 g, (*b*) (i) 0.07 M, (ii) 0.125 M. **6** 0.67 M.
7 (*a*) 63 g, (*b*) 98 g; 0.12 M, 20, 20.8 cm^3. **8** 63.

Examination type questions (p. 344). **1** (*d*) 95.2 g. **4** (*c*) 12.01. **6** (*b*) 323 g, (*c*) 2.5 litres. **7** (*a*) 576 C, (*b*) 72 cm^3, 36 cm^3. **8** (*c*) 4 min, (*d*) 0.1035 g, (*e*) 0.1035 g. **9** (*a*) 1200 C, (*c*) (i) 0.0125 (ii) 0.0125, (*d*) 0.486 g, (*e*) 0.0125. **10** (*a*) 79 °C, 99 °C. **11** (*a*) CS_2, CS_2, (*d*) 11.2 dm^3, 22.4 dm^3. **12** (*a*) P_2O_5, (*d*) 44.8 dm^3. **13** (*a*) 98 g, (*b*) 7.46 g, (*c*) 10 g, (*d*) 10 g. **15** (*a*) 0.0083, 0.025, 0.033, 0.05, 0.66. **17** (*b*) 860 cm^3, 760 cm^3, 600 cm^3, 540 cm^3. (*c*) nitrogen oxide, sulphur dioxide. **21** (*a*) 3, 4, (*c*) H_2Se, (*d*) H_2Se, 81. **22** (*b*) 30 cm^3, (*c*) 60 cm^3, 30 cm^3. **23** Se_8. **26** (*b*) $109\frac{1}{2}°$, 180°. **32** HCOOH. **34** (*b*) 96 000 C, 32 000 C, (*d*) 28 cm^3.

Index

(The more important references are given first.)